Library of
Davidson College

POLICYMAKING IN THE GERMAN DEMOCRATIC REPUBLIC

POLICYMAKING IN THE GERMAN DEMOCRATIC REPUBLIC

Edited by
Klaus von Beyme
and
Hartmut Zimmerman

St. Martin's Press   New York

© Klaus von Beyme and Hartmut Zimmermann 1984

All rights reserved. For information, write:
St Martin's Press, Inc., 175 Fifth Avenue, New York, NY 10010
Printed in Great Britain
First published in the United States of America in 1983

943.1
P766

Library of Congress Cataloging in Publication Data

Main entry under title:
Policymaking in the German Democratic Republic.

   Bibliography: p.
   1. Germany (East) – Politics and government – Addresses, essays, lectures.
   I. Beyme, Klaus von.   II. Zimmermann, Hartmut.
   JN3971.5.A3 1983 .P64   943.1087   82-5544

84-4462

ISBN 0-312-62032-2

Contents

List of contributors   vii

Introduction   ix
    Klaus von Beyme, University of Heidelberg,
    Hartmut Zimmermann, Free University, Berlin

1   Power distribution and opportunities for participation: aspects of the socio-political system of the GDR   1
    Hartmut Zimmermann

2   Economic system and economic policy: the challenge of the 1970s   109
    Jürgen Strassburger, Free University, Berlin

3   Foreign trade relations of the GDR   144
    Hanns-Dieter Jacobsen, Foundation for Science and Politics, Ebenhausen, Saarland

4   Military policy in the GDR   169
    Gero Neugebauer, Free University, Berlin

5	The education system and society Gert-Joachim Glaessner, Free University, Berlin	190
6	Continuity and change: cultural policy in the German Democratic Republic since the VIIIth SED Party Congress in 1971 Irma Hanke, Technical University, Munich	212
7	Social policy and the transformation of society Helga Michalsky, University of Heidelberg	242
8	Relations between the two German states Gerhard Wettig, Federal Institute for East European and International Studies, Cologne	272
9	Output policy in the GDR in comparative perspective Klaus von Beyme	301
10	Bibliography Walter Völkel, Free University, Berlin	315
Index		395

Contributors

Klaus von Beyme is Director of the Institute of Political Science at the University of Heidelberg, and serves 1982–1985 as President of the International Political Science Association. His books include: *Die Parlamentarischen Regierungssysteme in Europa* (1970), *Challenge to Power, Trade Unions and Industrial Relations in Capitalist Countries* (1980), *Economics and Politics within Socialist Systems. A Comparative and Developmental Approach* (1982), *The Political System of the German Federal Republic* (1983).

Gert-Joachim Glaessner is Professor of Political Science at the Free University of Berlin. He is the author of *Herrschaft durch Kader* (1977), *Sowjetische Systeme* (1982) and many articles in the field of conceptional problems of research on communist countries and educational policies.

Irma Hanke is Professor of Political Science at the Technical University of Munich. Her main field of research and publications are cultural policy, politics and literature in the GDR.

Hans-Dieter Jacobsen is Research Fellow at the Foundation 'Wissenschaft und Politik' at Ebenhausen/Bavaria. He is author of numerous publications on international interdependence, CMEA integration, East–West and transatlantic relations. His books include *Die wirtschaftlichen Beziehungen zwischen West und Ost* (1975) and *Die Ostwirtschaftspolitik der USA* (1980). *Asymmetrien und Interdependenzen in den transatlantischen Wirtschaftsbeziehungen* (1981).

Helga Michalsky is Lecturer of Political Science at the University of Heidelberg. She is the author of *Bildungspolitik und Bildungsreform in Preussen* (1978) and articles on the economic and social policies in the two German systems.

Gero Neugebauer is Research Fellow at the Institute for Social Science Research at the Free University of Berlin. His work is concentrated on institutions and military policy of the GDR including a book on *Partei und Staatsapparat in der DDR* (1978).

Jürgen Strassburger is teaching at the Free University of Berlin. Publications are mainly in the field of planning of the economy, labour market and incomes policy and industrial organisation in the GDR.

Walter Völkel is Research Fellow at the Institute for Social Science Research at the Free University of Berlin. At the moment he prepares a systematic bibliography on the Russian occupied zone, the GDR since 1945.

Gerhard Wettig, Director of the Department of Foreign Policy of the Federal Institute of East European and International Studies at Cologne. His books include *Postdam und die deutsche Frage* (1970), *Frieden und Sicherheit in Europa* (1975), *Community and Conflict in the Socialist Camp. The Soviet Union, East Germany and the German Problem 1965–1972* (1975), *Broadcasting and Détente. Eastern Policies and their Implications for East–West Relations* (1977), *Umstrittene Sicherheit* (1982).

Hartmut Zimmermann is Director of the GDR Section of the Institute of Social Science Research at the Free University of Berlin. He is an expert on politics, economics and society in the GDR. His numerous publications include 'The GDR in the 1970's' (*Problems of Communism*, 1978).

Introduction
*Klaus von Beyme, University of Heidelberg,
Hartmut Zimmerman, Free University, Berlin*

The different paradigms in the study of Socialist systems have for a long time strengthened the bias towards input studies. Both the model of a totalitarian society and the interest group approach were input oriented. The criteria which were seen as explaining the difference between democratic societies on the one hand and Communist systems on the other were the instruments of social control and the institutions of decision-making. The theories of convergence were the only ones which entailed a certain preference for the study of policy outcome. From Sorokin and Aron to Tinbergen and others nobody suggested that the institutions and decision-making bodies in the two social systems were growing more similar, though there seemed to be a rapprochement in certain fields (planning, for instance). But it was the impact of industrial society on the conditions of life in the two systems which brought certain tendencies to greater similarity.

The convergence theories were mostly concerned with global comparisons between East and West. Oddly enough, the two German states were hardly ever taken as proof of the general hypothesis and those similar features which were reminders of former national unity and the German 'national character' — or German 'political culture' — were given greater emphasis than the growing social similarity.

However, the propositions of the theories of convergence proved too global to be properly operationalised for empirical falsification. The policy-oriented approaches had two advantages: they abandoned the idea of comparing whole societies and limited their attention to sectoral comparisons; and they relinquished the exchange of ideological statements on the superiority of one side or the other and started from the basis of performance which could be measured by objective indicators.

In addition to these comparative approaches regional research, i.e. concentration on one society and its political system, has also acquired considerable importance. This enables more attention to be paid to the particular features of a system and a more detailed consideration of traditions which are still effective, as well as the social, economic and political processes and their interdependence. Studies of one sociopolitical system such as that of the German Democratic Republic also provide the essential basic material for comparative analyses. On the other hand regional research will have to deal with major questions and meet the requirements of comparative studies if it is to work with appropriate breadth and not become entangled in ultimately irrelevant detail.

Most of the contributions in this book point in this direction. They are examples of and show the limits of a concern with developments in the GDR from the viewpoint of political science in the Federal Republic of Germany. Not the least of the authors' hopes is that their publication will strengthen dialogue with colleagues in the English-speaking world who are working in the same or similar areas.

The authors of this volume aim to focus on the policy output of the German Democratic Republic without neglecting policy input and the decision-making process. Hartmut Zimmermann discusses the reception of the systems approach in East German ideology and gives a survey of the division of power and the possibilities for GDR citizens to participate in the decision-making process. Jürgen Strassburger analyses both the institutions of the economic system and the economic policies of the 1970s. Social policy is treated by Helga Michalsky in the broader interpretation of the German concept of 'Gesellschaftspolitik' (policy on society as a whole, ('socio-policy') which transcends the technicalities of social security and touches on the policies of the redistribution of social opportunities in the broader sense; the fields covered include housing, health care and family policies. The education system, in the analysis by Gert-Joachim Glaessner, is also seen in the context of a redistribution of opportunities in a society which in spite of its ideological hopes has not yet managed to overcome social stratification. Irma Hanke deals with continuity and change in the cultural policies of the GDR. She includes areas which normally lie beyond the narrower interests of political scientists but are necessary for an understanding of the system and its legitimation as a whole.

Three articles complete the picture by discussing those aspects of GDR policy which are directed outwards: Gero Neugebauer delineates the link between domestic and international aspects of military policy,

Hans-Dieter Jacobsen shows the growing importance of foreign economic relations and Gerhard Wettig describes the special problem of relations between the two German states. All the contributions aim to use quantifiable data; none of the authors, however, think that data are a substitute for qualitative analysis. Klaus von Beyme finally tries to sum up various aspects of the analysis of policy outcome in a comparative perspective, dealing with the neglected topic of the German Democratic Republic and her performance in the camp of Socialist countries. Most comparative studies in the Anglo-Saxon world also neglect the GDR as East European studies generally focus on the Slavic language area. Deviating from the custom followed in German Political Studies Volumes 1 to 4 of offering a comprehensive bibliography on the Federal Republic, Walter Völkel aims to give a comprehensive bibliography for the GDR, concentrating, like the book as a whole, on the 1970s but also including titles which are relevant for the whole period in which the GDR has been in existence.

The editors wish to thank the Reimers Foundation in Bad Homburg and its director, Konrad von Krosigk, who generously sponsored this volume by giving us the opportunity to discuss the first version of the papers. We hope the result will be a more comprehensive volume and not just another book-binder's synthesis.

1 Power distribution and opportunities for participation: aspects of the socio-political system of the GDR

Hartmut Zimmermann

Preface

One of the chief factors which determines the distribution of power within a political system, together with the opportunities open to individuals and social groups to participate in decision-making processes, is the organisational structure of the system. This study therefore takes the organisations system of the GDR as its focal point. Political systems that are based on the well-defined and binding ideology of Marxism—Leninism must also be examined against the background of their own self-conception in order to permit a more precise determination of the constitutional principles governing the system and of the scope and limits for change built into it. The point of departure taken for this study is thus the self-conception of the theory of the state in the GDR, which has given a critical reception to the system theory in Western political science and is seeking new ways of analysing its own system. This section is followed by a brief outline of the fundamental organisational principles and techniques found in the political system, prior to an examination of the chief components of the system — party, state apparatus, people's representative bodies and mass and social organisations. Particular attention is paid here to attempts to involve as many of the population as possible in the political system in an organised form through the expansion of opportunities for participation. The concrete substance of different policies, however, falls outside the scope of this study; on this reference should be made to the other papers in this volume. Similarly, it has only been possible to cover the functions of the ideology and changes in its substance etc. in the framework of this study in so far as individual aspects of this are significant in the shaping of the political system. A further-reaching, critical ideological discussion of Marxism—Leninism would have gone beyond the bounds of the limited question being covered.

Discussions on the concept of the 'political system' in the GDR — the search for a more differentiated self-conception

In the interpretation and analysis of the political structure of its own society the GDR has increasingly come to use the concept of the 'political system', alongside the concept of the 'political organisation of socialist society' — a trend which began in the 1960s, coinciding with a critical adoption of a similar discussion in the Soviet Union.[1] Although the controversy about the definition and scope of these concepts has still not been finally settled, they nonetheless reflect a departure from reductionist, theoretically isolating and removed concepts of the role of the Marxist—Leninist party, the state and the function of the mass organisations. The discussion was started off by the realisation that the relatively global categories of 'dictatorship of the proletariat' and 'worker and peasant power', which had been in exclusive use until that time, were no longer sufficient for describing or indeed analysing the way the political structures of GDR society actually functioned or the way they were expected to develop in future. These older patterns of interpretation, which still make their mark today, place chief emphasis on the institutional and organisational aspects of the system and conceive the political machinery as being essentially directed from above, as a 'mechanism' which operates uniformly on the basis of clear lines of competence and function.

The weight that such views still hold today is evident, for instance, in the authoritative GDR text book on Marxist—Leninist theory of the state and law, which has a central chapter devoted to *The Mechanism of Socialist State Power.*[2] In line with the traditional approach, the term 'system' is avoided in this standard work and the term 'political organisation' used throughout. Nevertheless, it was obviously felt that even in this context some acknowledgement should be made of discussions in the Soviet Union and in the GDR, and a footnote suggests that the concepts 'political system' and 'political organisation' might be identical.[3]

Advocates of the 'system' approach, on the other hand, argue that there is a difference between the two concepts. Their main objection to the exclusive or predominant use of the concept of 'political organisation' is that it produces too narrow a view. It concentrates on the organisational and thus normative and legal side of the political superstructure and thereby neglects the informal interaction between individual organisations, the mutual relations between the political system and society, and the position of the individual within the political process. In contrast to the more static view inherent in the emphasis on institutionalised forms of political activity, the 'system' advocates are concerned with the 'dynamics of the working of the political process', its differentiation and the multiplicity of political and social factors that come into play, covering these themes in an 'integrative approach'.[4]

The influence of Western political science and sociology is evident in that the 'political organisational structure' and the official system of norms are rated only as parts (albeit central parts) of the political system, which have to be supplemented by 'political relations', 'political consciousness' and 'political culture'. According to these authors, it is only this wider view of the political superstructure that will allow the system to be perceived as a whole and permit a 'complex' description and analysis of its internal and external operating conditions. This emphasis on the dynamics of the GDR political system and its implications opens up the way for the Marxist—Leninist theory of the state to reinterpret (with recourse to Marx) the historical, i.e. the changeable and constantly changing features, tasks and influence of individual system components and their interaction.

Karl-Heinz Schöneburg, a leading legal historian and noted theoretician of constitutional law in the GDR, has given a very emphatic account of these views.[5] In his eyes, even the socialist state is still characterised by its separation from society and by the 'alienation of power from society'. However, its 'new quality', measured against the bourgeois state, lies in its 'capacity and necessity' to develop successively into an active power of society. Schoneburg does not specify whether complete reabsorption of the state into society ever will or can come about. He does, however, specifically emphasise that a reduction in the gap between state and society will in no way weaken the state.[6] From his further statements it seems that he expects the 'reconciliation' of state and society to come about through political assimilation, through the integration of society into the political system.

In Schöneburg's view, existing society is still socially differentiated and thus contains differences of interest and social contradictions. He therefore regards socialist political systems as 'forms of state-political development and solution of social contradictions'.[7] Abolishing private ownership of the means of production is not in itself, he feels, sufficient to bring about the formation of a uniform social interest.

Instead, this calls for the political system as the essential 'organisational form to fashion the collective interest of society into its concrete shape and produce the politically active subject of the revolutionary transformation'.[8] The social differentiation that is in evidence is seen by Schöneburg as stemming in part from the old class structures, which continue to live on even after private ownership of the means of production has been abolished. The 'alliance' of the various classes and strata, i.e. the integration of these social groups with their different interests into the socio-political organisation, is interpreted by him as a 'unity of contradictions' which undergoes constant change and requires constant redefinition. In Schöneburg's eyes, therefore, the chief task of the political system is to continue transforming society further along the road towards social unification.

Even in the present situation, though, Schöneburg sees not only 'stable common elements' existing between classes, strata and groups, but also continuing social differences, such as those between workers, co-operative farmers and the intelligentsia. He also maintains that there are 'social differences within these classes themselves that should not be overlooked'. In this view, therefore, the political system repeatedly produces politically relevant social differences during the very course of its transformation process. These are social differences which originate, for instance, in the division of labour, in the gap which still exists between town and countryside and in 'the different working conditions and qualifications of men and women'.

From these considerations, Schöneburg then proceeds to draw conclusions along two lines, which are significant both for the self-conception of the political system and for its analysis. Since the political system is both a product and a 'lever of social development', its concrete form at any one time can only ever be of a temporary nature – 'political systems of the ruling working class can ... never be conceived as abstract, ultimately unchangeable factors, in which at the most improved efficiency might produce a quantitative difference. It is much rather a question of comprehending their historical capacity and need for change as being determined by social laws and stages of social development'.[9] This emphasis on the social environment and its impact in the understanding of the structure and functioning of the political system, calls for ever new historicising analyses, which focus jointly on 'historico-genetic relationships and structural relationships'. Following on from social change (conceived as a revolutionary process directed according to plan and law) comes the 'internal class dialectic of the political system and its development and qualitative change as a whole, together with the individual progressive and regressive developments within the system, within the relationship of the system as a whole to its constituent elements and within these individual elements themselves'.[10] In this passage, particular attention should be paid to Schöneburg's statement that, even in a socialist system, progressive and regressive elements can obviously exist side by side. The standard applied in assessment, which Schöneburg himself does not expressly name but which has to be sought in the prevailing orientations of the party, will not be considered here.

The earnestness with which Schöneburg argues for a concrete, historical and ultimately sociologically-oriented analysis is evident, for example, in his suggestion that 'the legally fixed spheres of competence and the normative position of the individual parts within the political setting do not warrant conclusions about their actual functioning'.[11]

In this approach, the mediating link between state-organised political power and society is supplied by political organisations outside the state, i.e. by the mass organisations and social organisations in particular. However, Schöneburg goes beyond the prescribed organisational forms when he maintains that the political system 'in its entirety as well as in many of its individual parts ensures that the widest range of conscious, partly non-organisational and also spontaneous activities (in the sense of "seeds of consciousness") can be incorporated into the general context of political power by the party. Thus the various activities of groups or individuals will not constitute themselves separately, outside and beside the socialist forms of organisation'.[12] It will hardly be wide of the mark to take this to be a demand rather than the expression of an already practised openness of the political system *vis-à-vis* society. Schöneburg here tries to answer the problem that the available forms of participation and expression of interest are not sufficient to absorb and integrate the interest potential prevailing in society — either because they are too rigid and too ineffective, or because they are considered to be too undifferentiated. The fact that Schöneburg is well aware of the problems of existing forms of 'socialist democracy' is evident from his demand that the theory of the state 'should concentrate on analysing the actual form and content of participation in the exercise of power, its concrete contribution towards improving decision-making together with the implementation and control of decisions, and its impact on the development of a socialist state consciousness on the part of those concerned'.[13]

Nevertheless, it would be to misinterpret Schöneburg's concept of the 'political system' and that of the other participants in the discussion to regard them as 'revisionist demands'. On the contrary, Schöneburg in particular lays clear emphasis on the limits that remain to the 'perfection of socialist democracy'. In his view this 'cannot mean that the process of the overall strengthening of all the elements of the state and the political system can and must exclusively follow the further development of democracy'.[14] Accordingly, the advocates of the concept of the 'political system' in principle leave intact the fundamental axioms of Marxism—Leninism: Marxism—Leninism as a binding world outlook and instrument of scientific analysis; a belief in the laws governing the socio-historical process and the capacity and necessity for 'scientific politics' founded on this; the leading role of the Marxist—Leninist party as the centre of leadership in the political system; and the state and its associated system of norms as the chief instrument for the exercise of power and for social transformation.

The discussions on the concept of the 'political system' and its theoretical and practical political implications have not yet arrived at any conclusion which might be regarded as binding, even on a temporary basis, in either the Soviet Union or the GDR. Moreover, it has only been possible to mention individual aspects of these discussions here. I do feel, however, that the thread of the discussion is important for a number of reasons. Firstly, it shows that theoretical penetration of the GDR's political superstructure lags behind everyday political practice. Secondly, the controversy over such basic questions of ideological and theoretical self-conception makes it clear that political systems bearing the soviet stamp are 'on the move'. The 'dynamics' of the system are coming under critical examination not only from the political opposition and dissidents but also from the very groups of functionaries who form the mainstays of the established order, with an awareness of the problem aimed towards reform.

Fragmentary and controversial as the results of the discussions to date may be, they do nonetheless offer both to those involved and, even more so, to the 'outside' analyst a wide and demanding programme of research. This research would involve setting the political system in the context of its historical development and current socio-structural features, indicating the interplay of its system components in the process of decision-making and decision implementation, and highlighting the necessity and tendency towards change inherent in the system. No such analyses exist as yet — even in Western capitalist systems, where conditions are more favourable, this type of analysis has only reached its initial stages. In the case of the GDR, these analyses founder not only on grounds of their claims to universality and a lack of suitable methodology and instruments, but also on account of a lack of relevant information. The situation thus imposes conditions that set specific limits on any examination from outside. Despite this or indeed precisely for this reason, the reference to attempts within the GDR itself to reach a better understanding of its own system takes on its significance. It is intended as an incentive to set the individual aspects of the political system, as presented below, in a system context that has previously only been perceivable in outline form, and to illustrate the limited and temporary nature of any statements made.

The structural principles of the political system in the GDR

The processes of change within the GDR's political system and the system's marked differentiation cannot, or should not, hide the fact that its fundamental constitutional principles, safeguarded by ideology, stand unchanged. Without knowledge of these principles it is impossible to comprehend the interaction of the individual parts of the system, its inner coherence and the degree to which it can be controlled and dominated by the Marxist–Leninist party, the SED.

In Marxism–Leninism, politics is understood as the relationship of the various classes, strata and groups of a society to the political power, i.e. to the state.[15] The social structure of a society results in turn from the pattern of ownership of the means of production. Political power, i.e. the state, is basically always exercised in the service of one particular class, namely the ruling class. In capitalist societies this is the bourgeoisie, who own the capital, and in socialist countries, the working class.

These rather global statements call for greater concretisation and specification on several counts. Firstly, the view that political power is concentrated exclusively in the hands of the state is increasingly giving way to a more complex view now (in the interpretation of bourgeois parliamentary systems as well). This is shown up very clearly in the growing use of the concept of the 'political system', though it is already evident in the concept of 'political organisation' too. These concepts make it possible to include non-state political organisations and the concrete political behaviour of individual and social groups (i.e. behaviour directed at influencing the acquisition and exercise of power) in an analysis of the political superstructure, alongside state organisations. The state and the state-sanctioned system of norms still, however, retain their central position as the 'chief instruments' of the exercise and securing of power.

The concept of power itself should likewise be seen in a broader sense than simply political, i.e. state rule. Power also includes disposal of the economic resources of a society as the decisive basis for the exercise of political influence, and takes in 'ideological rule' too.[16] The stress laid on the power problem in the Marxist–Leninist concept of politics explains on a theoretical and ideological level why the 'power question', i.e. the accumulation and securing of power and the central control of all its resources and its application, is repeatedly declared to be the 'main issue' of the political system. This observation holds particularly true during crisis situations, when the party and its related political organisations are called upon to exercise particular watchfulness on the grounds of the need 'to secure the rule of the working class'. It is striking that Marxism–Leninism always identifies power with rulership, i.e. it conceives of power as institutionalised and exercised on a permanent and regular basis. One has to query here whether 'rulership' does not always simultaneously imply (or at least tend to imply) a hierarchic rulership structure and a perpetuation of the division between rulers and ruled.

The hierarchical power structures and the continued separation of the political superstructure from society are, moreover, also founded on other ideological and theoretical premises, on fundamental principles of organisation and on the actual situation, in particular the socio-structural conditions. The necessity that Lenin postulated in *What is to be Done?* for an ideologically conscious party removed from the working class, still holds good even after the new power configuration has been constituted. Although the working class forms the basis of legitimation for party action, the party invokes the 'objective class interest' in its work. This objective class interest, the party maintains, can only be established with theoretical ideological mediation and cannot be fashioned by a direct will and opinion moulding process fed by the empirical, day-to-day experience of the workers themselves. Additional justificatory criteria are drawn from the need for uniform organisational action, which similarly makes a centre of leadership and the centralisation of power inevitable.

This vanguard claim of the Marxist–Leninist party, first formulated under the specific conditions of a revolutionary movement in Tsarist Russia, is transferred to the totality of the new political system which emerges after the seizure of power. The party bases its continued claim to permanent leadership firstly on the argument that it alone has insight into the laws governing the overall socio-historical process, as Marxism–Leninism claims for itself, and secondly by maintaining that the settlement of the 'power question' in no way concludes the socio-political transformation process. Even after traditional property relations have been abolished the old class structures still live on and new differentiated social interest configurations constantly emerge, producing conflicting expressions of interest. The acquisition of power and its structural consolidation in the new organisational network does not therefore bring the socio-revolutionary process to a conclusion but merely creates better preconditions for it to be repeatedly set in motion again. The passages quoted from Schöneburg, illustrating his understanding of the socio-political system, testify to its nature as a process. The 'alliance' of the working class with other classes and strata does not, in the Marxist–Leninist view, mean prescribing a social status quo or negotiating one or several interest compromises on the basis of set rules. On the contrary, it is for the alliance partners themselves to change their working conditions, their attitudes and their behaviour and bring these more into line with the working class within the framework of and with the aid of the alliance party. The working class itself is likewise undergoing a process of change, moving towards the awaited communist man of the future with his all-round education and skills.

It is precisely these arguments that the party uses to reject any type of pluralist approach towards determining the collective interest of society: 'But even after the elimination of the exploiter classes, in the process of shaping a developed socialist society, the socialist state does not represent or realise a conglomerate of individual and group interests, or a mean derived from the different interests of the working population or different social groups of the working population'. Instead, the collective interest is derived from the 'requirements of social progress' and the 'requirements of the lawful development of society' which are ideologically fixed in the basic principles.[17]

The 'concrete' fashioning of the collective interest of society — the privilege and duty of the Marxist—Leninist party — is not, however, a matter which the party performs or indeed should perform for itself. The party's claim as regards the general line it adopts at any one time is, after all, precisely that it bears close relation to reality. To this extent (particularly in the case of recent developments) the party needs the 'functioning political system of socialist power' in order to recognise the 'manifold needs and interests of the working class, its various groupings and its alliance partners' and to be able to process these 'accordingly'. Expression of interest is thus not only possible but is a necessity. Two qualifications are called for at this stage, however. Firstly, interests can only be expressed within the prescribed organisational forms of the political system, and these are controlled by the party, and secondly, decisions on the weighting and consideration or non-consideration of particular interests rests exclusively with the party, and ultimately with the political leadership. In making their decisions the leadership will draw on insight founded on Marxist—Leninist historical philosophy and social theory as a yardstick for gauging the 'collective interest of society' — a yardstick which can never be fully resolved or verified in empirical, concrete terms.[18]

Expression of interest and interest integration thus very quickly come up against the boundary of the party. The party, as we shall see later, is always present with its political decision and control functions at all, even the lower, levels of the organisation structure, and is thus able to establish its claim to leadership when it comes to the assessment and selection of interests.

Nevertheless, it will be apparent that the confrontation that is taking place on all levels and in all parts of the system between individual and group interests on the one hand and the collective interest as represented by the party on the other, now contains elements of a dialogue or mutual relationship which were not present in this way in the Fifties or even in the Sixties. This still holds true, even though it has to be admitted that possession of power may be taken as 'clarified' (crisis situations apart) and hence that the party's will is assured. Although the party keeps to the basic statement of Marxism—Leninism on its socio-political system, according to which the elimination of private property has created a uniting basic interest for all members of society and for all groups, strata and classes, this postulated unity in principle needs to be constantly restated and brought to the attention of the people — it cannot be taken for granted but must be constantly recreated anew. Alongside this, though, differences of interest and contrasting interests still persist and keep emerging and these not only conflict with each other but also never become fully absorbed into the 'collective interest'. Conflicts of this nature are recognised and rated as 'non-antagonistic' contradictions (as opposed to the class antagonism in capitalist societies) and are hence considered as being basically resolvable.[19] There is now general agreement that they must be taken seriously, allowed for in concrete policy decisions and that every effort must be made to find a solution to them. Marxism—Leninism in the meantime has come to regard these contradictions as positive elements which further the development of society — as a 'source and driving force' of the social process. This view gradually gaining ground in the GDR of their society still being 'imperfect' and, even in the long term, being threaded with conflict, constituted the prerequisite for the upgrading of the various forms of participation in the political system and for extending the scope for expression that they offered.[20]

However, the emphasis placed on the 'non-antagonistic nature' of certain conflicts turns out to be not such a matter of principal as may have seemed at first sight. Hence, the statement that these contradictions 'do not necessarily intensify and culminate in conflict' also allows the reverse conclusion, i.e. that they may indeed intensify. Precisely when such a state comes about can be seen from the observation that conflict potentials in developed socialist society 'are *generally* [my italics — HZ] recognised in time by the leading organs in society' and that being so, 'they are solved according to plan'.[21] In other words, even apologists of the system conceive that it is possible, in a political system such as that of the GDR, for acute interest situations to be inadequately perceived or incorrectly assessed.[22]

The danger of failing to provide a timely and adequate reaction to unsatisfied interests must inevitably be considerable in a system where dissatisfaction can only be expressed individually or as views of small groups. Furthermore, the political system is still constructed in such a way that the party is able to endorse and integrate an opinion the very first time it is expressed. The scope, urgency and 'social might' of such conflict situations can never be made fully apparent, since there is no means of organising interests right through society from below, to a point where they can be represented either within or *vis-à-vis* the political system. Hence, when it comes to assessing the significance of interests, the top political leadership in the GDR system still remains dependent upon information collected within the organisational system and passed on to it. Apart from the fact that the selection, processing and aggregation of data in itself holds wide scope for error, it must be borne in mind that the different executive levels within the organisations each introduce their own interests into the process. From the executives' point of view it is much more satisfactory to report the pacification and solution of conflicts than to announce that conflicts are persisting or even coming to a head. Some scope for correction is assured by the fact that the information channels are many and varied and hence the specific situation or function of those concerned will necessarily ensure that a wide range of information is passed on to the top leadership. Thus, institutions concerned with internal and external security — the state security forces, National People's Army, the Police etc. — will naturally tend to emphasise the conflict potential, if only in order to justify their own existence or emphasise their own importance. The resultant 'pluralism of information' that reaches the top leadership will certainly provide a corrective balance. It must be stressed, though, that the actual 'upholders of the interests' do not become directly visible. Despite the multitude of information channels, this situation has led to the political leadership taking increasing recourse to opinion polls and, to some extent, to empirical social science research, as a basis for its decisions.[23]

The specific nature of Marxist—Leninist leadership results not least from its claim to pursue 'scientific' politics. 'Science' in this context means insight into the forces that govern the historical process — insight which Marxism—Leninism claims to possess. In this view, knowledge of social and political realities, i.e. 'empirical experience', is only one of many prerequisites for the process of decision-making. Afanasiev, a leading Soviet theoretician of scientific leadership activities ('Leitungstätigkeit') stated that 'the information used by the central organs of the party and the state is exceedingly generalised and highly theoretical. This information constitutes the point of departure and the basis for major policy decisions which affect the whole of socialist society and its main areas of activity and development'.[24] From this, GDR authors conclude that 'expressed in terms of the categories of the theory of cognition, the *relationship between the empirical and the theoretical* differs on the varying levels of leadership. At central leadership level, the theoretical component dominates the relationship and, for this very reason, it makes a particularly valuable contribution to the perception of social laws'. 'Theory' here does not mean a generalisation of empirical experience, but the 'scientific world outlook' of Marxism—Leninism, which has perceived the fundamental forces at play. It is, admittedly, conceded that by no means all the forces involved have been researched to date, and even less so the interaction of the various social laws, so there is a need for constant further development. The fundamental axioms are not, however, affected by this. These axioms include not least the statement that a cognition process of this type ultimately remains the prerogative of the party, on account of the greater capacity for theoretical insight that the party leaders hold. 'Institutionalised science' may indeed make a contribution towards researching social laws but 'the processes of perception inherent in the function of leadership' should not be 'identified' with the 'findings' of science.[25]

It is thus made clear once again that the 'theory' of Marxism—Leninism constitutes the most important basis for the party's claim to leadership. This ultimately evades empirical control, such as would be assured by the formation of a socio-political consensus from below to above. This repeated reference to the importance of Marxism—Leninism in the legitimation, structuring and functioning of the political system in the GDR will have to suffice for present purposes.[26] Marxism—Leninism remains unchanged as the fundamental justification for the leading role of the party. As a guideline for social action and 'revolutionary practice' it sees in the party the criterion for its scientific correctness. To this extent 'actual practice', i.e. the experience gained in the pursuit of a specific policy, channels feedback into Marxism—Leninism. The opportunities for correction that this opens up, however, are always simply interpreted as 'enrichment' and never as a revision of basic axioms that has been forced upon the theory by empirical experience – in particular when they relate to the specific function of the party.

The organisational task that confronts a Marxist—Leninist party in the overall political system consists essentially of the solution of two problems, which by no means necessarily coexist without conflict. Firstly, the party is concerned with controlling power structures at all levels and achieving a uniform exercise of power in line with its particular objectives. Secondly, it is necessary for society, with its social differentiation, to be integrated into this system in such a way that it can participate actively in the realisation of the party's policies, whilst having its interests incorporated or satisfied far enough to ensure that explosive conflicts that would tear the system apart are avoided. This dual task is a characteristic of 'democratic centralism' – the organisational and leadership principle that governs the structure and functioning of all parts of the political system. Democratic centralism embodies a generalisation of a wide range of practical organisational experience gained from the history of the Bolsheviks and the development of the state in the Soviet Union. Removed from its historical context, the organisational practice derived in this way forms part of the core of Marxism—Leninism and will remain valid at least until the ultimate socio-political goal is reached. Democratic centralism is therefore not only the structural principle of the system of political organisations, but its 'development principle' as well. This does not mean that modifications cannot be made to individual elements, as specific national, social, political or functional conditions may require, but it does set the binding framework within which changes must remain if they are not to fall victim to the party's verdict of 'revisionist' or 'deviationist'.

The basis for justification and, indeed, for shaping the system of organisations is the claim that 'victory of socialism and communism is only possible through strict, uniform planning and leadership of society and through the concentration of all social forces on solving the chief task emanating from the national economic plans'.[27] This then, it is maintained, requires a leading political centre, to ensure uniformity of action in all parts of the system.

Democratic centralism was originally developed in the organisational practice of Leninist parties and it is by the example of the Communist Party that it is still best illustrated today, even though democratic centralism has now become binding on all organisational forms within the political system.[28] Under democratic centralism the party as a whole is directed from an elected centre whose decisions are binding on all lower-ranking executive bodies and on all party members. The different executives are elected from below at periodic intervals and are accountable to the electoral bodies. The fact that decisions taken by the executives in office are binding leads to a strict organisational discipline. Divergent opinions may no longer be expressed, at least not once a higher-ranking executive body has taken a decision on the particular problem in question. The centralising effect of the subordination of the minority to the majority and 'the strictly binding nature of decisions of high bodies for lower bodies and members' is intensified by two further rules of organisation. First of all, the elected executives only meet at intervals. By far the majority of executive members have regular jobs in addition to serving on the executive. They therefore elect a smaller, full time body to perform the organisational work proper (in the party: at county ['Kreis'] and district ['Bezirk'] level this is the secretariat; at central level it is the Politburo and the Secretariat of the Central Committee). These bodies constitute the true political leadership, controlling the full-time party apparatus and competent to take decisions in the narrower sense of the term. Secondly, the ban on groups still holds good and hence deviant opinions and attitudes cannot join forces and form agreements. Criticism and opposition always remain a matter for the individual as a specific situation arises. Criticism and proposals are always greatly welcomed, though, and considerable use is made of this opportunity. The chances of actually having an opinion accepted by majority decision are however extremely slight, on account of the procedure applied, and it is ultimately left to the full-time executive to decide which of these opinions they wish to take up and which not. Since the executives in office always make the preparations for the next elections — both listing the candidates and determining political content — the continuity of person and political programme can normally only be broken or modified by controversy within the organ of leadership itself or by intervention from above (in the case of lower-ranking executives) or intervention from 'outside' (influence of the 'leading party', i.e. the Soviet Communist Party).

The dominance of centralist components in the political system is clear to see. Certainly the active participation of as large a number of members as possible is desired not only for programmatic reasons but also to ensure optimisation of the political line and to mobilise all human and material resources for achieving the goal. Despite this, the 'democratic' component basically remains limited to the 'influx' of the members' 'manifold experience' into the decisions of the higher bodies. If one looks beyond the party to society as a whole, however, one cannot fail to see that active participation of ordinary party members and citizens in the apparatus of the state, in the economy and in the social organisations, is coming to gain increasing weight. It is difficult to keep highly developed industrial nations functioning and capable of development on the basis of decrees alone. Their differentiated structure, their social problems and their development prospects, which frequently can only be discussed on a scientific or alternative basis, mean that they cannot be fully perceived or centrally steered solely from above. To this extent, the level of development that has now been attained is forcing onto the system a wider scope for expression and an increasing number of advisory bodies, since it is only these bodies that can put the political leadership in a position to formulate a policy commensurate with the actual state of affairs and to put this policy into practice.

The uniform concentration of political power, which is regarded as a necessity in Marxism—Leninism, leads to rejection of the principle of distribution of powers. Such a differentiated system as that of the GDR obviously cannot manage without a division of labour in decision-making processes, without delegation of competences, and without some degree of sharing of power. What is to be avoided though, is the feeling of an individual *raison d'être* for the different political functions (legislative, executive, judiciary), leading to mutual control of relatively autonomous system components, or even to the development of relatively autonomous sub-systems (state apparatus, parties, associations etc.), which repeatedly strive after an equilibrium of social and political forces within the political process. The postulate of the concentration of power (as opposed to the distribution of powers or 'pluralist' system configurations) is legitimated by the Marxist—Leninist theory of the state through the principle of the 'sovereignty of the people'. According to this theory, the people, now freed from class antagonism and able to constitute a social unity, also form a unity in their political superstructure. This highly theoretical-sounding statement has far-reaching consequences for the position of the individual citizen within the political system. Set against the background of this statement he is to conceive of himself as both a participant in power and simultaneously a subject of power. His rights (constitutional rights) are always at the same time his duties. Since the political system is 'his' system, and he forms a part of it, he cannot hold any rights *vis-à-vis* this system, only within it. Where there is a real and extreme imbalance of power in favour of the centre of leadership this interpretation of the sovereignty of the people tends to mean that an individual's catalogue of duties (i.e. the execution of decisions taken from above) figures more predominantly than his rights or his share in power. This observation is furthermore not countered by the Marxist—Leninist statement that the main direction followed in the development of the socialist state is the further unfolding of 'socialist democracy'. This, we are told, consists of 'increasingly comprehensive involvement of the citizens in state planning and control. The working population is to be won over to implementation of decisions taken by the party of the working class, to implementation of the laws and other statutory provisions, and their initiatives are to be developed purposefully towards goal fulfilment . . . Citizens will be consulted in the preparation of major decisions and kept informed on the realisation of decisions taken'.[29]

The unity of power is achieved by transposing democratic centralism from the party to the state and to all other organisations. In the course of transposition this organisational principle undergoes certain modifications. The most important of these consists in the laying down of the party's claim to leadership *vis-à-vis* the individual parts of the system, and the anchoring of this claim in the organisational structure. Whilst the state and the different social organisations admittedly each have their own centralised structure and a corresponding hierarchy of executive levels, they are also subject to the political direction and control of the party as well. At the same time, the individual parts of the system are ranked according to their importance as instruments for establishing the party's policies. Hence the state, which in a Marxist—Leninist system also holds a monopoly over might and legislation, and includes the economic sphere, constitutes the chief instrument of the party; the FDGB ('Freier Deutscher Gewerkschaftsbund'; Confederation of Free German Trade Unions), the trade union organisation of blue and white collar workers counts as the most important mass organisation, in front of the FDJ ('Freie Deutsche Jugend'; Free German Youth) – the social organisation of young people.

This brief study of the chief structuring elements of Marxist–Leninist policy on organisations would be incomplete without mention of cadre policy.[30] 'Cadres' is the term used for the persons who direct, on either a full-time or an honorary basis, the 'collectives', i.e. organised groups of people, or who take on socially influential advisory positions as 'experts'. Cadre policy or the cadre function is directed on the one hand at the recruitment, training and further education of top executive personnel, and on the other hand, to their deployment in appropriate positions.

The nomenclature is an important instrument of cadre policy, and is a catalogue of all the leading positions and functions, each of which comes under the responsibility of cadre departments both in the party apparatus and in the organisation to which the function belongs. These positions are classified under specific nomenclature ranks (I–III) as a function of the political significance attached to them. The nomenclature covers all the organisations in the political system, taking in the party, the state and economic apparatus, the cultural and educational systems and the mass organisations. It is impossible to occupy one of the leading positions listed in the nomenclature without the decisive co-operation of the party, whether this comes about through election, appointment or a contract of employment.

Originally, the quality of a cadre was measured first and foremost by his performance in party work, his loyalty to the party and his ability to comprehend and establish the particular party line at the time. The increasing complexity of the tasks to be resolved, however, has meant that specialist qualifications are gaining increasing importance too, so that all the leading positions of any relevance today are held by University or Technical College graduates. A highly differentiated continuous education system serves to keep the cadres' knowledge of their subject and their political knowledge up to date. A significant change in the style of leadership and hence also in the training and qualification of cadres has resulted from the fact that 'leadership' itself has become a subject of study in the management sciences such as organisational science, sociology and psychology.

Careful weighting of leading posts according to their political importance puts the party in a position to appoint non-members to posts of lesser importance. This enables the party to make use of their abilities and give them the opportunity to prove themselves. To this extent, cadre policy is not necessarily exclusive; it has definite integrative functions as well.

A further point is that even today the majority of next-generation cadres are supposed to be chosen primarily from among the working class. Tendencies towards self-recruitment are becoming increasingly apparent, however, and the children of University graduates have a greater chance of going to University themselves and thus of moving into cadre positions. Furthermore, the universally deployable cadre of the early years, whose party experience basically entitled him to take up any position that was assigned to him, has largely been superseded by the professionally qualified cadre.

The party, the state and social organisations within the political system

The party

In Article 1 of its constitution the GDR defines itself as a 'socialist state' and as 'the political organisation of working people in town and countryside under the leadership of the working class and its Marxist–Leninist party'.[31] In keeping with the logic of this statement, where the organisation of the state is subservient to that of the party, the constitution makes no detailed mention of the SED ('Sozialistische Einheitspartei Deutschlands': German Socialist Unity Party), of its objectives and organisational structure, or of the forms in which it exercises its direction of state and society. The SED puts itself above the constitution in deciding upon its programme and statutes entirely by itself.[32] Hence, the party defines itself as 'the highest form of socio-political organisation' and as 'the leading force of socialist society, of all organisations of the working class and the working population and of the state and the social organisations'.[33] The SED establishes this comprehensive claim to omnipresence and omnicompetence through its own closely-knit organisation network, and by obliging its members to think of themselves, in their capacity as party comrades, as active representatives of the collective political and social interest at all times and in all places.

The party is structured according to areas of work and according to territorial divisions. All permanently established enterprises, administrative departments, institutions and organisations which include at least three party members among their staff possess a basic organisation ('Grundorganisation' – GO). In enterprises this is called the enterprise party organisation ('Betriebsparteiorganisation' – BPO). Lone party members and members not at work come under a residential district party organisation ('Wohngebietsparteiorganisation' – WPO). A basic organisation having more than 150 members may be divided up into party organisation sections ('Abteilungsparteiorganisation' – APO). In line with the importance that Marxism–Leninism attaches to the economic sphere and, indeed, to work in general, the BPO is ranked highly in organisation policy terms, since it marks the anchoring of the party in the social work process. The remaining ranks of the organisational structure are essentially based on territorial divisions within the GDR.[34] The county administrative units have a county SED executive ('Kreisleitung' – KL) and the district administrative units a district SED executive ('Bezirksleitung' – BL). At the head of the party comes the Central Committee ('Zentralkomitee' – ZK), which for its part elects the secretariat for day-to-day party work, and the Politburo (PB) for the general work of leadership. Following the five-year plan rhythm that governs the national economy, party elections are held twice every five years up to district level and once every five years for the party as a whole. Small basic organisations (GOs) elect their executives once a year and GOs that are subdivided into party organisation sections share the same election rhythm as the counties and districts. In the smaller GOs, elections are held at members' assemblies; on all other levels these take place at delegates' conferences. Apart from electing executives for their own organisational sector, the assemblies also elect delegates for the next level of executive: the GO will elect delegates for the county, the county delegates' conference for the district and the district delegates' conference for the Party Congress.

The party executives brought into office by the party elections have a relatively large membership. GOs with more than 150 party members have an executive of 15 to 20 members, whilst counties and districts have executives of 60 to 100 members, plus 15 to 20 candidates for membership (see below). Secretariats are therefore set up at county and district level to deal with the day-to-day work of the party, i.e. to perform the true executive function. Whereas the elected executives meet only every three months or so (GO members' assemblies are held once a month), the secretariats are expected to meet in full session at least once a week. At the meetings of the elected executives the full-time executive officials report on their work since the previous meeting and announce the tasks on hand for the immediate future. In so doing, they specify the line of the party leadership as it applies to their specific regional, local or enterprise organisation. Comments on the reports are restricted primarily to exchanges of experience with other executive members in their particular functions and to binding statements on the future activities that will be required for the executive to fulfil the targets laid down by the secretariat in the working programme.

This outline of electoral procedures and everyday party life on the lower and middle echelons of the party structure calls for greater precision on a number of points in order to prevent any misunderstanding. The outcome of elections is largely determined in advance. The political content and formal organisational framework of the electoral procedure are laid down in the electoral directives issued at central level (Central Committee, Central Committee Secretariat, Politburo). Any discussion during the course of an election can thus only be focused on the best possible way of carrying out the 'line' that has been prescribed. The rule of procedure laid down in the statutes, which specifies that lower-ranking bodies and individual party members shall be bound by the decisions of higher executives, also continues to stand during the elections. The ban on forming groups — a prerequisite for making deviant opinions heard in big organisations — is a further factor which serves to confine criticism to the individual. In addition, certain minimum periods of party membership are required for a number of posts (county executive member: 2 years; district executive member: 3 years; county secretary: 3 years; district secretary: 5 years; Central Committee member: 6 years). Introduction of the status of candidate at the different executive levels also allows the party to try out potential leaders before they are fully admitted to the decision-making process. Candidates enjoy the same rights and obligations as full members but do not have the right to vote. They have thus not yet been admitted to the 'inner circle'. More effective than the principle of seniority, however, are the instruments of cadre policy. The lists of people standing for election are compiled by the cadre departments of higher-ranking executives, whilst the posts of secretary come under the party nomenclature. The appointment of a secretary thus requires the express approval of a higher-ranking executive. For the posts of First and Second County Secretary and district secretariat members, this approval has to come from the Central Committee or the Central Committee apparatus.

These different organisational practices serve to ensure the unity of party action and the closed nature of the organisation as a whole. Taken by themselves, however, they are not sufficient to explain how the party is able to assert its leading role throughout the overall political system. Whilst the internal functioning of the party is certainly an important prerequisite for the articulation of a clear-cut party will and for upholding this will in practice, actual realisation of the party's aims calls for suitable action by the other components of the political system and by society as a whole. The organisational practice of the SED is therefore not only directed inwards towards itself but is simultaneously focused on the other institutions and organisations in the system and on the prevailing socio-political environment (with the organised party members who work in these institutions and organisations serving to transmit the SED practice). The SED sees its essential political and organisational task here as consisting, on the one hand, of being omnipresent, exercising control and engaging in active participation, whilst, on the other hand, not becoming absorbed into the various parts of the system. As the organ which both formulates and represents the collective interest, the party must ensure that the individual tasks and interests of the various components of the system are integrated into the system as a whole and must seek to prevent any separate developments. This attempt on the one hand to devote party work to the specific features of individual areas in which the vast majority of party members work, and by whose results their individual performance is measured, whilst on the other hand ensuring that the 'collective will' prevails and that no separate developments emerge, constitutes the basic problem of practical party work at all levels of the party hierarchy, in particular at basic party organisation (GO) level.

The GOs or, to be more specific, their executives and secretaries, exercise political control over all proceedings in their organisational area and are expected to ensure that the general party line is followed and that party decisions and the decisions of state institutions are properly carried out. They have full rights of access to information to help them in this task — the secretary of the basic organisation attends the executive meetings of the enterprise, organisation or administrative department and has the right to inspect files. The party executive does not, however, have the right to intervene directly in the competences or responsibilities of the executive of the organisation concerned, or in the distribution of these competences. When it comes to political statements at party executive meetings or members' assemblies and to critical reports, the GO executive, which comes under the auspices of its particular SED country executive, remains tied to instructions from above. Although this marks an attempt by the SED to separate political responsibility from direct responsibility for the organisation concerned, the boundary nonetheless remains fluid — the cadres in the enterprise or administrative department are, after all, regarded as holding a political function as well. Added to this comes the fact that the SED GOs have an interest in ensuring that their particular organisational area achieves optimum results. Hence, complaints about a blurring of interests between the enterprise party organisation (BPO) and the enterprise executive are not infrequent. It is up to the higher-ranking executive to recognise these problems in good time and to redraw the line between party tasks and the tasks of the enterprise executive whenever this proves necessary.

All the same, it cannot be denied that the state institutions, enterprises and social organisations do carry weight of their own. They themselves form part of their own rigid hierarchy and hold direct powers of decision for matters within their own sphere. They do therefore have extensive practical experience and the corresponding specialist know-how built up from this experience. To this extent, there are certain pluralist, centrifugal tendencies inherent in the differentiated social structure and in the correspondingly aligned organisational structure with its division of labour, which are then reinforced by the self-interest found in all big organisations. To have direction and control solely from below, through the GO, and from the very top, through central party directives, would not be sufficient to counter this type of unwanted break-away development. For this reason, therefore, all the leading cadres of the chief state and social organisations are directly involved in party executive work at all levels by being made members of the executive in question. This principle applies right from the level of the GO, whose executive members include the chairman of the enterprise trade union executive ('Betriebsgewerkschaftsleitung' – BGL), the secretary of the Free German Youth ('Freie Deutsche Jugend' – FDJ) and, as a rule, the enterprise director ('Werkleiter'). The secretariats of the county executive (KL) and district executive (BL) include respectively the chairman of the county council ('Vorsitzender des Rates des Kreises') and the chairman of the district council ('Vorsitzender des Rates des Bezirkes'), the chairman of the regional planning committee and the chairmen of their particular regional trade union executive and Free German Youth (FDJ) executive.[35]

The co-ordination and control of the individual parts of the system through the membership of senior personnel from these individual institutions and organisations in the party's decision-making executives can be illustrated through the composition of the Central Committee (the broadly based elected body, which like county and district executives meets only at longer intervals) and the Politburo, which is the real leading organ. Table 1.1 gives a break-down of members and candidates of the Central Committee according to the areas in which they work full time, and the level of executive to which they belong. The table shows clearly how the SED Central Committee is a gathering of top functionaries from all organisations or sections of organisations that are regarded as especially relevant and it needs no broader interpretation.[36] For our purposes it may be sufficient to highlight one or two particular aspects. Overall it is apparent that the grass roots of society and individual political organisations are barely represented on the Central Committee. Only one full member (plus one candidate) of the 156 members (and 57 candidates) represents the members of the working class engaged in production. Even of the functionaries that can be attributed directly to the SED, only four members (and four candidates) come from executive levels below the district level; two of these are from enterprise party organisations (BPO).

Table 1.1
Members (and candidates) of the SED Central Committee elected at the 10th Party Congress according to organisational area and executive level[37]

PARTY

Central level: (Secretaries of the Central Committee, Staff of Central Committee Apparatus, Central Committee Scientific Institutions, central Party Press etc.)	40	(1)
First Secretaries of county ('Kreis') executives of central institutions (Ministry of State Security, Ministry of Foreign Affairs, Academy of Science)	2	(1)
Districts ('Bezirke')	21	(3)
Counties ('Kreise')	2	(2)
Enterprises	2	(2)
Veterans	6	
Total	73	(9)

STATE APPARATUS

Central level: Council of Ministers ('Ministerrat' – MR) (Chairman, First Deputy Chairman of the MR, President of the People's Chamber ('Volkskammer'), Secretary to the Council of State ('Staatsrat'))	4	(1)
Ministry of Economic Affairs and Planning Commission (including foreign trade, industry, agriculture, trade and distribution)	15	(4)
Foreign Policy (Ministry of Foreign Affairs, Friendship Societies, Ambassadors)	7	(3)
Defence	4	(4)
Ministry of the Interior, State Security, Justice; Worker and Peasant Inspectorate	5	(3)
Science, Education, Culture	6	(3)
Ministry of Health		(1)
Districts	3	(1)
Total	44	(20)

Source: Compiled from information given in *Neues Deutschland*, vol.36, no.92 of 17 April 1981, p.4f.

MASS ORGANISATIONS AND SOCIAL ORGANISATIONS		
Confederation of Free German Trade Unions ('Freier Deutscher Gewerkschaftsbund' – FDGB)	5	(3)
Free German Youth ('Freie Deutsche Jugend' – FDJ) 'Ernst Thälmann' Pioneers ('Pioneerorganisation 'Ernst Thälmann')	3	(1)
Writers Union ('Schriftstellerverband der DDR')	3	
League of Culture ('Kulturbund der DDR' – KB)	2	
Association of Composers and Musicologists ('Verband der Komponisten und Musikwissenschaftler der DDR')	1	
Democratic Women's League of Germany ('Demokratischer Frauenbund Deutschlands' – DFD)	2	
German Gymnastic and Sports Federation of the GDR ('Deutscher Turn- und Sportbund der DDR' – DTSB)	1	
Committee of Anti-fascist Resistance Fighters ('Komitee des Antifaschistischen Widerstandskämpfer der DDR')	2	
National Front ('Nationale Front der DDR' – NF)		(1)
German–Soviet Friendship Society ('Gesellschaft für deutsch-sowjetische Freundschaft' – DSF)		(1)
Journalists Union ('Verband der Journalisten der DDR' – VDJ)		(1)
Total	19	(7)
THE ECONOMY (EXCLUDING AGRICULTURE)		
Top level (General Directors of Enterprises etc.)	5	(2)
Middle level (Heads of Departments, Master Foremen etc.)	2	(8)
Lower level (Team Leaders)	1	(1)
Total	8	(11)
AGRICULTURE		
Top level	3	(5)
Middle level	1	
Total	4	(5)
SCIENCE		
Presidents of the Academies, University Chancellors, Technical College Chancellors etc.	5	(4)
Total	5	(4)
CULTURE		
(Theatre General Managers, President of the Academy of Arts etc.)	3	(1)
Total	3	(1)

Sum total of full members: 156
Total candidates: (57)

Moreover, full-time SED functionaries account for roughly half the Committee (47 per cent), followed by members of the state apparatus, (28.2 per cent of full members, and 35.1 per cent of candidates), almost all of whom have functions at the central level. Only three (plus one candidate) out of 44 members (and 20 candidates) come from the lower, district level. The counties and community authorities are not represented at all.

In assessing the composition of representatives of the party apparatus it should be borne in mind that all the First Secretaries of the SED district executives (15 plus one from the Wismut area executive, which is accorded the same standing) are members of the Central Committee. This strong representation shows the importance attached to these functionaries within the system as a whole. We may also conclude that regional interests and particular situations are expressed primarily through these functionaries.

The weakness of direct representation of economic interests in the Central Committee is astonishing. Only five full members (plus three from agriculture) hold functions at upper executive level (General Directors of Enterprises etc.), whilst there are 15 Ministers and Secretaries of State with responsibility for economic affairs on the Central Committee. It is clear that here too the state apparatus is given precedence over direct representation in the economic sphere.

It is also striking that the cultural sphere is relatively well represented, chiefly through representatives of the top leadership of cultural organisations, though also through top cadres from the Academy of Arts, theatre General Managers and the like. This is a reflection of the growing importance which this policy area gained during the 1970s, albeit in a conflict-ridden process. All in all, the representation of the mass and social organisations has been stepped up, even if only within certain limits. The trade unions and the Free German Youth predominate here, in keeping with their significance. Whilst it could perhaps be argued that the cultural intelligentsia is almost over-represented in quantitative terms, there are virtually no representatives of the industrial economic intelligentsia organisations, particularly the Chamber of Technology. This group is apparently considered to be so well integrated into the economic apparatus of the state and the scientific institutions (Academy, Universities), and also into the trade unions and cultural associations, that it can be neglected in direct representation. It is, nevertheless, striking that the strictly scientific field is so weakly represented as well, in spite of the fact that this field has been assigned a decisive role in the realisation of economic policy aims by the token of accelerated scientific and technical progress. Whilst the five full members (and four candidates) of the

Central Committee (University Chancellors, Presidents of the Academies etc.) are backed up by 6 representatives (plus one candidate) from central scientific institutions of the SED Central Committee, this is nonetheless a relatively small group in quantitative terms and is dominated by the social scientists, i.e. by the very 'administrators' and 'producers' of Marxism—Leninism.

The Central Committee of the SED is by statute of course the highest organ of the party between party congresses, but its true importance has to be seen relatively. Its work consists in the main of two to four meetings a year in which discussion is generally similar to that already briefly described for county and district meetings.[38] However, both the report from the Politburo, which is read out by a Politburo member, and the discussion papers presented at the meetings hold greater internal importance for the party. They represent binding guidelines for party work and hence for the functioning of the system as a whole. The results of the Central Committee plenary session are quoted in all statements, publications and declarations of intent, becoming generally more concrete as they pass down from one level to the next. But even beyond this, though, one must assume that the Central Committee can well become a vehicle for controversial discussion and a leading political force during times of crisis. This was the case in both Czechoslovakia and Poland and also in the GDR in 1953 and 1956—7, when the Central Committee showed a tendency towards revitalisation. Hence, an assessment of Central Committee composition should also consider the more general question of its potential to lead the party during critical periods.

Moreover, membership of the committee (including those with candidate status) has its own political weight. If a top cadre is on the Central Committee this simultaneously implies that his institution or organisation is regarded more highly. The Central Committee member himself will have preferential access to the political leadership, to the Central Committee apparatus and to the other political and social subsystems. This provides him not least with greater influence and a better chance of implementing his views, as well as with more information, in a system where information and the right to know is carefully apportioned according to rank of leadership and organisational area.

The Politburo, as the standing top leadership body of the party and the system as a whole, has a threefold function. This consists firstly in directing general party work, secondly in ensuring organisational coherence between the most important parts of the political system, and thirdly in laying down strategy for the system as a whole, whilst also monitoring and ensuring its day-to-day efficiency — in other words providing operative guidance. The composition of the Politburo with its 17 full members and 8 candidates is in keeping with its leadership function.³⁹ Responsibility for directing day-to-day party work rests with the ten-man Central Committee Secretariat. Their work involves, more specifically, the direction of Central Committee apparatus activity, the work of lower-level executives and apparatus and also the SED's external relations.⁴⁰ Eight of the secretaries are full members (Honecker, Axen, Dohlus, Felfe, Hager, Herrmann, Mittag, Verner) and two are candidates (Jarowinsky – trade and distribution; Inge Lange – women). The Chairman of the Central Party Control Commission (Mückenberger) is also to be counted as a party representative. The central Party Control Commission is responsible for keeping the party free of alien and harmful elements and is thus virtually equivalent to the head of a party judiciary.

The First Secretaries of the SED district executives (a favourite recruiting ground for Politburo leaders) are represented by the First Secretary of the Berlin SED district executive (Naumann), a full members, and the First Secretary of the Cottbus SED district executive (Walde), a candidate. The party press is also represented on the Politburo by the chief editor of the SED central daily newspaper *Neues Deutschland* (Schabowski), who is a candidate. The Council of Ministers ('Ministerrat') is represented on the Politburo by its Chairman (Stoph) and two First Deputy Chairmen (Krolikowski and Neumann), who are full members. In addition, equal status is accorded to those responsible for external and internal security, the Minister for National Defence (Hoffmann) and the Minister for State Security (Mielke). The Chairman of the State Planning Commission (Schürer) and the Minister for General Mechanical Engineering (Kleiber), on the other hand, hold only candidate status within the PB. Agriculture in the GDR is similarly represented through a candidate (Margarete Müller), the head of the Friedland Agro-Industrial Association for Plant Production. Other full members of the Politburo are the President of the People's Chamber (Sindermann) and the Chairman of the Confederation of Free German Trade Unions (Tisch). The Chairman of the Free German Youth (Kreuz) is a candidate of the Politburo.

The composition of the Central Committee and Politburo clearly shows up the aim of co-ordinating the political system and ensuring uniformity of action largely through integrating the heads of the various organisations and institutions personally into the top SED executives. The success of this measure depends on whether these various organisations and institutions themselves really perform the work allocated to them of integrating their organisation members within their particular area of the social system. However, the crises that have arisen in Soviet-type socio-political systems to date have been predominantly characterised by the fact that although people belonged to a large number of organisations they generally began to form groups and express their views not within but outside these existing institutions. This was clearly the situation in the GDR during the June 1953 strike. The significance of the SED's concern to achieve 'participation' and to expand 'socialist democracy', as the primary legitimation and integration strategy, becomes understandable against this background.[41] This is a point that will be taken up again later.

In addition, achievement of a political leadership position within the system as a whole is obviously related to one's ascent through the hierarchy of the big organisations, and this is controlled and manipulated by cadre policy. This career pattern has produced a specific type of political functionary, who is experienced in dealing with big organisations and has mastered both the written and empirical rules and norms of bureaucratic organisational practice. The preferred instrument of communication in these organisations is the written order, report or resolution. It is thus not direct speech or the capacity for direct political decision that are developed in this career; instead, the future leader learns to 'function' within a system of fixed roles and acquires the ability to observe and control the regularity of organisational procedures. These tendencies are strengthened and simultaneously given their specific political colouring through the political organisation language of Marxism—Leninism. All regulations, resolutions and analyses are cast in Marxist—Leninist terminology. This, however, is by no means a clear-cut terminology. It is the subject of constant redefinition according to the prevailing party line. Moreover, from the 1950s and 1960s onwards, the empirical and positivist theoretical sciences of the West began to enter the political language of official GDR statements (not only in the natural and technical sciences but in the social sciences too). Hence, we find a blend of terminology from varying scientific origins, with different interpretations, which is not always fully consistent.[42] It is essential for top leadership cadres at all levels to be able to decipher these documents and frame decisions for their own area of responsibility in this style of language. It is thus hardly surprising that no-one speaks off the cuff in GDR political life. Presentations, and even discussion contributions in decision-making bodies and all GDR organisation meetings, are always in document form before they are delivered; the speaker reads out a text that has been formulated and agreed to in advance.

The SED has a major integration function to perform within its own organisation, which can certainly be rated as a social integration function as well. In keeping with its traditional claim to be in the vanguard of the working class and the other major allied social groups it still makes high demands on every single one of its members. The individual party comrade is expected to be a moral and occupational model at his workplace and in all other social respects, always maintaining party discipline, ready to carry out every task the party may entrust to him, convinced of the correctness of Marxism—Leninism and able and willing to communicate this to others. A comrade is to act at all times as if the party were dependent upon him alone and is expected to subordinate his own interests to the social interest as represented by the party at all times. It is thus no wonder that an individual cannot just join the party directly but is instead 'solicited', has to provide references from two party members and serve a one-year candidacy before he can be entrusted not only with the obligations of party membership but with the voting and election rights that this brings too. These unchanged, strict requirements for membership lead to an individual party justice. Party sanctions include criticism, disapproval, warning, admonition, severe admonition and exclusion, with the attendant occupational and social consequences. The party member is subject to this authority not only in his behaviour in the party but (in principle at least) in his overall social behaviour as well.

This catalogue of requirements is orientated towards the model of a cadre party and is not without contradictions in relation to the real situation of the SED as a mass party. The SED has, in fact, never fully met the requirements of its statutes. Only a relatively small number of communists remained after the persecution of the Nazi period or emigration and stayed true to their convictions (the estimate is 50,000).[43] In the period between the call for the foundation of the party on 11 June 1945 and the congress which brought unification of the Communist Party with the Social Democrats on 20 April 1946, membership of the Communist Party grew to about 620,000. Together with the 680,000 or so SPD members they merged into the SED.[44] For many years the SED leadership saw one of its main tasks as the creation from above of a Leninist party out of this mass of members who had scarcely been politically socialised up until then (to say nothing of the newly enrolled members) and which contained groups of former Social Democrats and Communist splinter groups from the period of the Weimar Republic, which were quickly judged to be hostile. As time went on, it became apparent that sights repeatedly had to be set, and indeed still have to be set, on this particular goal. The party purges of the early years with their mass exclusions and persecutions have disappeared from the SED's current organisational practice. What has remained is a recruitment policy which differentiates candidates according to social origin and work, an ideological—political training system which covers the entire membership of the party, a periodic exchange of membership cards to eliminate inactive members and a cadre policy which is designed to provide a steady inflow and control of leadership personnel at all grades. There is also extensive control over the political and social behaviour of individual members, coupled with the sanctions open to party jurisdiction outlined above, though also with the opportunities that exist for political and social promotion.

At the time of its 10th Party Congress (11–16 April 1981) the SED had a membership of 2,069,629, together with 102,481 candidates. (The resident population of the GDR in 1980 was approximately 16.74 million, with 12.5 million over 18 years of age.) This means that some 17.38 per cent of the over-18 population were members of the party.[45] The percentage of SED members amongst the working population is higher than this average, at 21.9 per cent (the working population of the GDR in 1980 was 8.225 million, plus 492,000 apprentices). The fact that one in five of the working population belongs to the SED testifies to the SED's success in achieving one of its aims – namely the acquisition of new members in the youngest possible age bracket. At present members up to the age of 40 account for 42.5 per cent of party membership, whilst among the 18- to 25- year-olds one in seven is already a candidate member of the party. Even beyond these basic statistics, though, the SED has achieved a notably broad membership base within GDR society as a whole. Its membership breakdown is as follows: 57.6 per cent workers, 9.1 per cent white-collar workers, 22.1 per cent intelligentsia, 4.7 per cent co-operative farmers, 6.5 per cent other groups.[46] Women are said to account for 33.7 per cent of party members.

This positive picture does, however, call for greater precision on a number of points and needs to be put into perspective. The many problems associated with the allocation of individual occupations and positions to specific social categories are of less importance here. The party's success in integrating (at least formally) a broad social spectrum into its organisation will not really be affected by changes in terminology and the resultant recategorisations. What is more serious, though, is the fact that the high percentage of women among party members is not also found amongst the full-time cadres, i.e. the true positions of leadership in the party, or indeed in any other sphere of political life.[47] The equal status for men and women which has been largely achieved in occupational qualifications, as a result of a deliberate party policy to promote women, has not yet brought them effective equal status in politics. This certainly contains a potential for conflict which could change both society and the party as well.

A more important factor here, however, is the growing tendency towards 'scientisation' of the leadership, with the accompanying increase this brings in the number of academics at top cadre level, both in society as a whole and within the party itself. This process reflects the specific demands of a highly developed industrial society, in which science and technology have come to hold a key significance for the administration and further development of all social, economic and political spheres. Not only have scientific research and the application of research findings become major growth factors for the economy, but the social structures and relationships themselves, along with the organisational and political tasks that stem from them, have become objects of the social and organisational sciences and not only of Marxism—Leninism. The party's leadership itself needs scientific training in addition to its strictly party training if it is to be in a position to assert the party's claim to leadership in its day-to-day work with the specialists with leadership tasks in state administration, the economy, science, and cultural institutions. These more stringent demands on the party, or rather on its functionaries, explain why, even at the basic organisation level (GO), 64.5 per cent of secretaries are university or technical college graduates.[48] The figure for county and district secretaries is nearly 100 per cent. The announcement at the 10th Party Congress that university and technical college graduates in the meantime accounted for 34.1 per cent of party membership fits into this same context. (The proportion of graduates in the GDR working population is some 20 per cent.)[49] In assessing these figures, however, it must not be forgotten that the direct route from school to university or technical college, via military service, is not necessarily the standard route. In many cases students will have first undergone skilled worker training and been released for study to gain higher qualifications by the enterprise or organisation that employs them, on the basis of their performance at work. This would certainly appear to be the standard approach to a technical college education and also explains why there is such a high percentage (79.4 per cent) of fully qualified skilled workers among the SED membership.

Nevertheless, the fact remains that there is a close relationship between level of qualification (in particular university qualifications) and the chance of moving into a cadre position and being able to fulfil a political leadership role. It must, however, also be borne in mind that access to university is more difficult now. The number of study places has been reduced by 25 per cent since 1971 (new admissions in 1971 were around 44,000; in 1980 some 32,000) and political motivation or political cadre selection procedures are becoming increasingly important in the allocation of study places by schools, enterprises, the Free German Youth and similar. There is also a constant tendency towards self-recruitment in the intelligentsia — children of parents with a university or technical college background have a much better chance of being admitted to study themselves than do children from other social groups.[50] A course of study at a university or technical college is, however, only one of the prerequisites for becoming a cadre, a political leader. In addition to proving one's worth in a job there is also the advanced political specialist training to be served in one of the party's teaching establishments (or in an establishment run by the state, the Confederation of Free German Trade Unions or the Free German Youth etc.). Some of these courses last for several years, leading to an academic qualification as well. It is, in fact, this continuous education system that is the real recruiting ground for political leaders, and access to this system is solely through a co-opting mechanism (secondment or detachment on the basis of a cadre policy decision by the responsible party executive).[51]

This interrelationship between ocupational qualifications, political training, continuous political training and occupational and political trustworthiness, which is embedded in the cadre policy of the party apparatus, creates a clear gradation within the party membership, based on potential to influence decisions and the chance of obtaining a leading position. The mass of party members, and the members engaged in production work, simply constitute a recruiting ground for the next generation of leadership. As plain party members and production workers their participation in political and organisational decisions differs at most from other forms of 'socialist democracy' through their greater proximity to the decision makers. All the same, the demands on the average party member by his organisation are much higher than is generally the case in mass organisations with participatory functions. The party's most important instrument for inducing members to behave in a certain way is the party commission ('Parteiauftrag'). A party commission can, for instance, oblige members to initiate competitive campaigns or to support these with their participation, to develop certain activities in other organisations or to undertake similar tasks. In addition, it is virtually impossible for a party member to escape the mass party schooling, whose content is changed every year – the 'SED Party Training Year'. The extensive ideological and political training system is one of the most important instruments of integration into the overall organisation that the party has at its command.

The dual role of the SED, which is a cadre organisation and a mass party at one and the same time, is also evident in the 'party activist groups' ('Parteiaktive'). These groups are formed of party members who exercise functions in geographically definable areas (community, county, district, combine etc.) or specifically related areas (culture, education, health etc.). These activist groups constitute the politically active section of the party and have their own particular responsibilities, problems and tasks. At party activist group meetings, special reports are given by members of the leadership on the current situation, and a differentiated exchange of experience takes place, with problems frequently being discussed more openly than is normally the case in party gatherings. The activist group meetings do not, however, possess decision-making powers in the strict sense. They serve to ensure that party decisions are made known with appropriate speed and differentiation and offer advice on the best way of implementing these decisions in a given area. Where decisions are made at meetings of party activist groups these require the approval of the convening elected executive.

The traditional self-conception and organisation techniques of the SED are running into problems as significant aspects of the general social and political situation in the GDR change — and change not least as a result of the party's own policy. The party's ideology and functions are largely moulded by the experience of bitter struggles for power, resistance to the National Socialists and the period after 1945, when the SED was concerned with destroying the traditional socio-economic structure and replacing it with a new social and political system that the SED could dominate. These phases have now been concluded and GDR society, together with the political and economic organisations which go to make up its structure, have since then been engaged in the search for normality (a search which began in the 1950s, became evident in the 1960s and was above all apparent in the 1970s). Normality in this context means settling permanently into the new socio-economic and political system, which can now no longer be changed by revolutionary intervention, but only through gradual, tentative steps towards reform. This changed situation is manifested in a re-appraisal of the state of development achieved so far, the resultant prospects for the future and the tasks and policies that this will entail. The phase of socialism, which marks a preliminary transition to the classless communist society, and a phase to be run through rapidly, has now given way to the construction and expansion of developed socialist society — 'truly existing socialism'. The perfect society of the future seems to have moved into the distance and lost its legitimation force for present-day policies.[52] The need for the individual to prove his party loyalty in the revolutionary class struggle has given way to the need for exemplary achievement in the world of work. Social progress is no longer the result of fundamental intervention in the social structure but is tied to the mastering of the tasks of scientific and technical progress. It was not by chance that the 10th SED Party Congress proclaimed: 'Micro-electronics — our revolutionary barricade for the Eighties'. This catchphrase is a good example of the attempt by the SED to retain the revolutionary fervour of an 'heroic time of struggle' and to adapt it to a time when the main consideration is to secure and gradually improve the general standard of living — an improvement which is to be achieved through optimum economic performance, whilst the constantly emerging social problems are expected to be solved by the much more sophisticated but still only partly effective (to judge by the changes in ownership patterns) instruments of social policy.

We can only briefly indicate here the effects of this on the SED and the changing requirements that the party will have to face. Those generations within the party membership who remember the struggles of the Weimar Republic, the experience of illegality and the years of social restructuring have largely disappeared from the SED because of their age. The only area where they still dominate is the top party leadership in the Politburo. Of the 2,560 delegates to the 10th Party Congress who had voting rights, only 68 had belonged to one of the two workers' parties prior to 1945; 176 had joined the SED in 1946 when it was founded. The number of those who had played an active part in the resistance movement was similarly low, at 88 (26 of whom had been in prison or concentration camps).[53] For the party as a whole and the mass of the party's members direct experience of the class struggles has become part of history, an area of teaching and study in the party's training centres. In its place are experiences of their own social improvement, achieved through their own work performance, and by proving themselves both within and with the help of the party's structure and the socio-political system it dominates.[54] This interrelationship between career and party membership on the one hand encourages loyalty to the system to which the members owe their own rise, but on the other hand means that career aspirations are adapted to fit given organisational and political constraints. The SED admittedly tries to counter these tendencies by repeatedly putting cadres into situations where they have to prove themselves politically, by stepping up ideological schooling and by placing particular emphasis on the threat from the 'external enemy', who is trying to penetrate their country and who calls for constant watchfulness. Nevertheless, the party must also accept the pragmatic everyday behaviour of its members which is largely oriented towards personal advantage and prosperity, since this is clearly part of the achieved normality of the system and also stems from it.

Pragamtic tendencies are, moreover, also in evidence in the application of the SED's organisational principles. SED cadre policy cannot, after all, be oriented solely to party experience and loyalty as the decisive selection criteria. If the top leadership is to be effective it will need at least a minimum of respect, and human and technical qualifications in order to be able to activate the broad mass of party membership on a permanent basis and to assert its political leadership position and function as a control body towards the parallel leadership in enterprises, state institutions and the mass organisations. Furthermore, party work (even in its decisive elements) does not take place solely at official meetings and within the hierarchy of party bodies. Instead, there are a multitude of constant contacts and communications which make up everyday organisational life. Contact is by no means restricted to the flow from above to below — lower level executives certainly also take their problems of the moment to their immediate superiors and seek solutions to specific tasks. Leaders whose main activity is not in the party but in the economic, state or social sphere will also speak as party comrades within the party from the particular viewpoint of their work. In addition there are also frequently changing parallel interests, such as between individual enterprises and the regional state apparatus, between enterprise executives, party executives and the enterprise union executive. These can lead to (unplanned) interest associations which will favourably affect consideration in the decision-making process. Since the party executives are working in a highly differentiated industrial society, in which information and experience from very different fields are needed as much as specialised technical and scientific know-how, there are a large number of advisory bodies which become active both in the decision preparation phase and in decision implementation and control. Whilst these bodies have no formal decision-making powers they do have an important influence on the content of decisions. The arguments put forward by the experts frequently serve to further their own particular (and personal) interests. Moreover, since the GDR is a fairly compact geographic entity with organisational, education and training systems which, although differentiated, nonetheless intersect at various points, individual career and work paths will often tend to cross. This gives rise to a closely-knit network of informal relationships, all of which not only affect decisions of a political nature but personnel decisions too.

The problem complexes within the party and also within society as a whole which have been referred to in this outline of the structure and position of the SED are also found in the other organisations in the political system as well, albeit with the appropriate modification to the area in question. These problem complexes should always be kept in mind even when they are not specifically mentioned in the chapters that follow.

The state, apparatus of the state,
people's representative bodies

Alongside the party it is, of course, the state which plays a major role in determining the distribution of power and the opportunities for participation within the political system, and which also determines the way in which the political system functions. In rating the state as 'the main instrument of the working people, under the leadership of the working class, for the shaping of developed socialist society', the ideological theoretical self-conception of Marxism—Leninism also accords the state a clearly superior status within the overall network of political organisations.[55] The state and the state apparatus remain the decisive organisational forms of political power throughout the phase of 'socialist society'. The 'withering away of the state' — a central theory of Marxism, whereby there will be no need for a political power removed from society once the bourgeois class structures have been abolished, and hence the state will begin to wither away — is now not expected to come about in present-day Marxism—Leninism until that historical moment, some time in the indeterminate future, when the classless, i.e. 'egalitarian' society is accomplished.[56] Until that time, we are told, there will not only be no weakening of state-held political power but, on the contrary, this power will be strengthened and extended still further. The view prevalent in the 1960s in both the GDR and the Soviet Union to the effect that even at that time the mass organisations were taking over functions originally exercised by the state, i.e. that the gradual process of the 'withering away of the state' had already begun, has now been abandoned in the current discussion on theory of state.[57] This line of interpretation has been superseded by the thesis of further expansion of socialist democracy, i.e. further expansion of the various forms of participation.

This reasoning shows, on the one hand, that the leading role of the party and the concentration of political power in the hands of the state are both essentially fixed for the foreseeable future but, on the other hand, that the tasks and functioning of the state may well be subject to change in the view of Marxism—Leninism. There are two main factors conditioning such a change.

The first of these is the political system originally developed as the dictatorship of the proletariat, with the chief task of fundamentally transforming property relationships through abolition of private ownership of the means of production, and thus of transforming the class structures. In this task the working class (which in this context is always understood as being directed and represented by the communist party) also draws on the support of other big social groups and their organisations (in particular sectors of the peasantry and intelligentsia) within the framework of the so-called 'alliance policy' ('Bündnispolitik'). As the time interval since the expropriation and socio-political transformation phase proper increases, however, the 'enemy' within society disappears and alliance policy is extended to embrace all social classes, strata and groups. At the same time the social profiles of the original partners to the alliance also undergo modification: the peasants become co-operative farmers or workers in a state-controlled agricultural system, and the bourgeois intelligentsia is converted by changed recruiting and training mechanisms into a socialist intelligentsia. The working class is also affected by this process of social change — it increasingly emerges as a highly differentiated social group where training, income, activity and position within the social work process are all differentiating factors, giving rise to different interest configurations and different conscious attitudes.

Secondly, during the initial phase of shaping the political system state activity too is primarily focused on the tasks of power accumulation, internal and external assertion of power and destruction of the old property relationships and social structures. As time progresses, however, the task of bringing the economic resources now transferred into state hands into a workable and efficient production and distribution system moves to the fore. It has always been clear to Marxist and Marxist—Leninist theoreticians that the viability of their sociopolitical system would ultimately depend on success or failure in finding the optimum solution to economic problems and in establishing a more productive economic system than that of capitalism. Lenin expressed this in a phrase which is still felt to hold true today: 'It is the productivity of labour which, in the final instance, will be the most important and decisive factor in the victory of the new social order'.[58] This objective also involves a commitment to the technical and scientific progress, labour organisation, selection of commodities and consumer habits of the same 'capitalist enemy' who is normally fought against as a matter of principle. It is this linking of major socio-economic aspects of the system to the 'enemy' system, coupled with the failure so far to achieve the set target of higher labour productivity, that is one of the main reasons for Soviet-type systems being so prone to latent and manifest crises.

For a long time the central importance attached to the economic organisation tasks of the state, both in ideology and in practical politics, concealed the fact that the resultant identification of economic aims with socio-political aims was producing undesired social disparities, injustices and situations of need. In response to these conflict situations, which were clearly beginning to emerge within society, the GDR began in the 1960s to look for a relatively independent instrument that could be used to influence social structure and to correct the social conflict areas that were stemming from the economic process. Today, Marxist—Leninist social policy ('Sozialpolitik') is regarded as such an instrument (taking up the political line of the Soviet communist party). Since the 8th SED Party Congress in 1971, this social policy has been regarded as a part of the 'main task' ('Hauptaufgabe'), and as part of the general line to be followed by the SED, alongside and in close conjunction with economic policy, and standing at the centre of the political activity of the state.[59]

To keep an economy running smoothly not only presupposes that the interplay between institutions, organisations and individuals directly involved in the economic process can be properly calculated, but also requires a calculable and established normality in all social areas. Whilst the period of open political warfare was marked by direct and repeated political intervention, which did not ask after legal norms or simply gave these a new 'biased' interpretation to fit the form of conflict at the time, the gradual introduction of a formal and legal status for social relationships has been apparent for a number of years now.[60] The legislation passed in the GDR during the 1960s and 1970s shows that this process is not only affecting the economic sphere but is also having an impact on relationships between individual citizens (e.g. Civil Code, Family Law, Code on Civil Procedure), the distribution of competences within the political system and within the individual organisations themselves (discussion on administrative law),[61] and in some points, on relationships between citizens and state institutions (petition and complaints procedure, state liability legislation), which are becoming increasingly subject to legal norms. The leadership and control aspect of the legislation cannot be denied and the principles of unity and non-impartiality have similarly been maintained in the interpretation of the law, albeit in strict adherence to the wording of the legal norms ('socialist legality'), which in many cases leads to a 'positivist' interpretation of the law. Despite this, the fact of committing state activity to the legal form means that state activity becomes more predictable for the individual citizen and guarantees him certain minimum standards. The process of introducing a legal status makes it easier for the individual to settle into the given social and political structures.

The importance accorded to economic growth and technical progress has not left the cultural and educational function of the state untouched either. Originally, the education system was designed first and foremost to inculcate a particular view of the world and raise the general standard of education (with special attention focused on the social groups that had been underprivileged beforehand) and also to convey new 'socialist' patterns of behaviour, but now the emphasis is shifting towards an education whose contents can be directly utilised in the work process. The use of free time has become a major area, as in all highly industrialised societies, and here the traditional means of Marxist–Leninist cultural policy are failing in many respects to live up to the demands of a young generation, looking not only for entertainment and diversion but also for a more meaningful way of life than their workday routine.

These tendencies towards change which are arising from social and economic development have brought a more differentiated view of the functions of the state. Whereas earlier these functions were seen solely as comprising the securing of the new political order, both internally and externally, they have now come to include cultural and educational tasks, regulation of the level of work and the level of consumption (labour input, working hours, quantity and make-up of the supply of consumer goods), and the safeguarding of the socialist legal and property system and the rights and liberties of the citizen.[62] The increasing importance of social policy is indeed recognised in the GDR, though it has not so far been made into an independent area in the doctrine of the functions of the socialist state.[63]

Basically it may be assumed that this catalogue of tasks affects the work of all state institutions. This means that whilst the main focus in collective combines and enterprises is still on economic performance, the enterprise collectives are also subject to cultural and educational influence at the same time; there are internal security factors to be considered and foreign policy priorities to be observed in foreign trade etc. To this extent, a functional division of labour does exist within the GDR state apparatus on the one hand, but on the other hand, the functions of the individual institutions will inevitably overlap because of the overlap in the tasks they are called upon to perform. Nothing has so far come of the repeated call in GDR literature for a precise delimitation of competences for individual organisations and institutions, according to level of decision and area of work, which would provide greater efficiency (avoiding lengthy decision-making procedures and the passing off of awkward decisions to parallel organisations or higher executives etc.) and would also permit better control of decision-making processes (blurred areas of responsibility do not allow a comprehensive view of the decision-making process). This has foundered not least because of persistence in the view that state functions are inter-penetrating functions to be conceived as a unity.

The catalogue of functions, however, also makes it clear that all the tasks of the state remain intact — even those which could be considered outdated. The latter include in particular the function of repression, dating from the time of the struggle for power, which was originally only intended to be directed against the 'resistance of the overthrown exploiter classes'. Today, it is assumed (with particular reference to the developments in Czechoslovakia in 1968) that 'even when a stable (*sic*) socialist order of society has been established, the fundaments of socialism have been achieved and the exploiter classes no longer exist' it will still be possible for 'hostile forces' to attempt to influence internal political developments from outside and for there to be a 'revival of anti-socialist forces from within'. From this assessment of the situation it is then concluded that 'the function of repression is therefore not only necessary for the construction of the fundaments of socialism, but is still upheld during the period of the shaping of developed socialist society'.[64] For this reason, therefore, the instruments of repression are still to be found in the GDR state apparatus today. They come both in the form of legal norms (political penal law) applied appropriately by the courts to the case in question, and within the state institutions (police force, state security forces, public procurator's office). External and internal security are closely linked here. This juxtaposition means that military education and military service are always to be essentially conceived as an internal education and disciplining process within society, and not simply viewed in terms of their outward effect.[65]

The tendencies towards change and development that have been outlined above have also led to an ideological and theoretical reassessment of the 'essence' of the state in the GDR. According to the SED Programme of 1976, this essence consists in 'a form of dictatorship of the proletariat . . . which represents the interests of the entire people'.[66] This statement expresses the SED's persistence in its uncurtailed claim to leadership and also marks a declaration of intent to bring all social classes, strata and groups of society into the 'alliance policy' and to give due consideration to their interests when shaping the collective interest, in line with the party's own assessment of the prevailing situation. To this extent there is no big social group within GDR society that can be clearly rated as 'hostile', from the party's viewpoint, on the basis of socio-economic criteria.

This understanding of the state confronts the SED with a dual task. First of all it must integrate society as a whole both through and within the state, and at the same time it must uphold the instrumental character of the state as a decisive tool for the implementation of party policy. Solving the problems raised in this way becomes all the more important since the state too holds a monopoly over might and legislation in the GDR and additionally has all major economic resources at its disposal. Party resolutions are not therefore directly binding on society as a whole. They must first be converted into state acts of law and then channelled through the appropriate state action.[67] In addition to this is the fact that a wealth of direct experience is acquired during the course of practical state activity, that state functionaries have a high level of education[68] and that the state apparatus is directly responsible for its actions in a manner different from the party and is constantly confronted with the manifold interests of society. All of this leads to quite a natural competitive relationship developing between the state and the party. Whilst these tendencies of the state to develop its own *raison d'être* are restrained by the involvement of leading state functionaries in the party executives, by the application of cadre policy in the selection of personnel for the state apparatus and by the control exercised on the state apparatus from within by the SED basic organisations (GO), the tendencies cannot be ultimately eliminated because they are inherent in the system itself.[69]

Table 1.2

Composition of People's Representative Bodies

Deputies	People's Chamber		District assemblies		County and city assemblies		Community and (small) town assemblies		Borough assemblies	
	Number	%	Number	%	Number	%	Number	%	Number	%
By Mandate										
SED	127	25.4	722	25.4	4,997	18.4	58,430	34.3	689	17.3
DBD	52	10.4	291	10.2	1,874	6.9	13,493	7.9	128	3.2
CDU	52	10.4	283	10	1,942	7.1	10,024	5.9	245	6.2
LDPD	52	10.4	283	10	1,868	6.9	5,594	3.3	253	6.4
NDPD	52	10.4	283	10	1,919	7.1	5,268	3.1	255	6.4
FDGB	68	13.6	394	13.9	6,112	22.5	25,583	15.0	1,189	29.9
DFD	35	7.0	229	8.1	2,718	10.0	18,751	11.0	385	9.7
FDJ	40	8.0	255	9	3,873	14.3	17,256	10.1	659	16.6
KB (League of Culture)	22	4.4	100	3.5	730	2.7	1,788	1.0	90	2.3
VdgB/BHG (Farmers' Mutual Aid Association/Farmers' Trade Co-operative)	—		—		623	2.3	6,864	4.0	4	0.1
Consumer co-operative socs.	—		—		511	1.9	5,493	3.2	69	1.7
National Front	—				1	0	1,883	1.1	—	
Total	500		2,840		27,168		170,427		3,975	
According to sex:										
Men	332	66.4	1,765	62.1	15,831	58.3	111,079	65.2	2,359	59.3
Women	168	33.6	1,075	37.9	11,337	41.7	59,348	34.8	1,616	40.7
According to age:										
18 to 20	15	3.0	183	6.4						
18 to 24					5,873	21.6	22,863	13.4	856	21.5
21 to 25	25	5.0								
21 to 24			258	9.1						
26 to 30	20	4.0								
25 to 30			190	6.7	3,548	13.1	18,954	11.1	665	16.7
31 to 40	77	15.4	658	23.2	6,220	22.9	37,593	22.1	1,101	27.7
41 to 50	200	40.0	971	34.2	6,923	25.5	50,726	29.8	851	21.4
51 to 65	130	26.0								
51 to 60			531	18.7	4,168	15.3	33,565	19.7	438	11.0

61 and over / 66 and older	33	6.6	49	1.7	436	1.6	6,726	3.9	64	1.6
According to vocational training or first job:										
Workers	235	47.0	1,283	45.2	15,124	55.7	76,122	44.7	2,505	63.0
Members of agricultural co-operatives; small farmers, horticulturalists, fishermen	60	12.0								
Members of agricultural, horticultural and fishermen's production co-operatives			316	11.1	3,206	11.8	41,057	24.1	21	0.5
White-collar workers	127	25.4	1,066	37.5	7,465	27.5	42,303	24.8	1,283	32.3
Intelligentsia	76	15.2								
Traders, merchants			79	2.8	391	1.4	1,579	0.9	41	1.0
Independent traders, craftsmen, self-employed			64	2.3	407	1.5	3,133	1.8	52	1.3
Others	2	0.4	32	1.1	575	2.1	6,233	3.7	73	1.8
According to highest level of qualification obtained:										
of which, graduates from University	239	47.8	1,086	38.2	7,013	25.8	14,652	8.6	899	22.6
Tech. College	92	18.4	656	23.1	6,806	25.1	40,122	23.5	939	23.6

Source: Figures from *Statistisches Jahrbuch 1981 der Deutschen Demokratischen Republik*, published by the Staatliche Zentralverwaltung für Statistik, vol.26, Staatsverlag der Deutschen Demokratischen Republik, Berlin (GDR) 1981, pp. 385–93. Author's calculations. The figures given for the People's Chamber and the District Assemblies are from the 1976 election results, figures for the other assemblies are for the 1979 results.

The integration of social groups into state activity follows primarily via the people's representative bodies. Although these bodies are termed the 'highest organs of power' their true influence is very much less than this designation would lead one to believe. There are people's representative bodies at every level of the state structure (cf. table 1.2). They are brought into office by general elections (held every five years, with everyone over the age of 18 having the right to vote and stand for election). Votes are cast for single lists, which like the election programme are drawn up within the National Front ('Nationale Front der DDR' – NF). The programme is a general and popular version of the SED's overall line in every case. The National Front constitutes an appropriate vehicle for elections since, as a 'socialist people's movement' it already co-ordinates the activity of all political and social organisations in its committees before the actual constitutional processes come into play (right from the residential areas, through the community, county and district level and up to central level). The National Front does not therefore have individual membership; it embodies the 'People of the GDR' in what is already a politically structured form. The NF is backed up in its functions, which are essentially of an agitatory and propagandistic nature, by a small SED-dominated full-time apparatus and also by honorary work from representatives of the organisations it includes.[70]

The National Front was accorded constitutional status as an all-embracing form of alliance policy in 1968.[71] The parties and mass organisations working together within the National Front, however, have their own different roles when it comes to putting up candidates and thus in the allocation of seats. Only the associations which belong to the 'Democratic Block of Parties and Mass Organisations'[72] (SED, CDU, DBD, LDPD, NDPD, FDGB, FDJ, DFD, KB) are represented by their own groups in all people's representative bodies from the People's Chamber downwards. The Block is thus frequently referred to as the nucleus of the NF in GDR publications. It is clear from table 1.2, however, that the spread of organisations involved in the people's representative bodies widens below district level. In addition to the organisations listed above there then come the Farmers' Mutual Aid Associations and Farmers' Trade Co-operatives (VdgB/BHG), the consumer co-operative societies and, at community level, individuals who hold high social prestige and who are not ascribed to a particular organisation but to the NF in general. Even though the significance of membership of a particular organisation should not be overrated (the groups do not play an essential role in the people's representative bodies and the deputies of the mass organisations are often members of the SED as well) there is nonetheless an undeniable endeavour to achieve integration of as many wide and varied social interests and areas as possible, in line with the characteristics of the region in question. This same intention explains *inter alia* the lesser involvement of the Block parties at county and community level, as compared with their participation in the People's Chamber.[73] This cut-back in representation does not, however, affect all the Block parties in the same proportions. The relative strength of the CDU and DBD in rural areas ensures them a larger number of deputies in the rural community representative bodies than the LDPD and NDPD, which are more town-orientated.

Efforts to involve citizens in the political system at an early age, such as by their becoming deputies, have obviously proved successful — 14.7 per cent of deputies are under 25. This age group is most strongly represented at county level and in the city representative bodies (with 21.6 per cent and 21.5 per cent of seats) and most weakly represented in the People's Chamber with 8 per cent of deputies under 26. A similar picture emerges for women deputies: 35.9 per cent of all people's representative body members are women. In the county and borough assemblies they account for 41.7 per cent and 40.7 per cent of the seats respectively, whilst in the People's Chamber and the community assemblies the figures are 33.6 per cent and 34.8 per cent. Hence, two social groups that have traditionally been difficult to mobilise for political work and whose political ambitions often meet with resistance from the elderly or male population, have been admirably mobilised and integrated.

The figures on the breakdown of people's representative bodies according to the social origin of deputies (albeit very approximate figures) call for a more differentiated assessment. In terms of their share in the overall working population (1980: some 6.7 per cent),[74] the members of agricultural and horticultural co-operative societies (LPG and GPG) and the fishermen's co-operative society (PwF) would seem to be rather over-represented with their 11.1 per cent and 24.1 per cent of seats. The percentages given for the members of craft co-operative societies (PGH) and trading agents (private retailers and wholesalers who sell goods by order and for the state trading account) — namely 2.8 per cent and 0.9 per cent respectively — are virtually in line with their share in the total working population (1980: 1.8 per cent for PGH members and 0.3 per cent for trading agents). Other traders, self-employed craftsmen and the professions (constituting some 1.5 per cent of the working population in 1980, including assisting family members) have been given rather a generous share of deputies, with a percentage that varies from 2.3 per cent to 1.3 per cent of seats.

The percentage of blue- and white-collar workers is the most difficult percentage to evaluate. The very limited amount of information that the data on vocational training and first job provide has already been referred to in a previous context. The 1980 occupation statistics set the percentage of blue- and white-collar workers at 89.4 per cent of the working population. When it comes to the people's representative bodies, though, this percentage is only reached (and, in fact, surpassed) in the relatively small number of borough assemblies, which do not carry much weight (95.3 per cent). All in all, blue and white collar workers make up only 72 per cent of total deputies (72.4 per cent in the People's Chamber; 82.7 per cent in the district assemblies; 83.2 per cent in the county assemblies; 69.5 per cent in the community assemblies). If these figures are set against the figures for university and technical college graduates, it becomes clear that the number of blue-collar workers who still actually hold such deputy positions must be considerably lower. In terms of the total number of deputies, 34.4 per cent hold university and technical college qualifications (11.7 per cent and 23.7 per cent respectively). There is a positive correlation between the proportion of graduates and the level of decision-making, which results from the progressive decline in the proportion of deputies with university qualifications from the top downwards: in the People's Chamber, 66.2 per cent (47.8 per cent university, 18.4 per cent technical college); district assemblies, 61.3 per cent (38.2 per cent university, 23.1 per cent technical college), county assemblies, 50.9 per cent (25.8 per cent university, 25.1 per cent technical college), borough assemblies, 46.2 per cent (22.6 per cent university, 23.6 per cent technical college), community assemblies, 32.1 per cent (8.6 per cent university, 23.5 per cent technical college). These figures confirm that there is a high degree of vertical social mobility within the GDR and they also show that the path to higher educational qualifications frequently leads via skilled worker training, that access to participation in the political process is open especially to those who have attained a high level of formal qualification and, indeed, that it is precisely such persons who are expected to play an active role in the participatory structures. At the same time it is seen that a high level of education and specialised knowledge is vital for effective consultation in and control of state activity — essential functions of the people's representative bodies. One of the chief reasons behind this development, which after all disadvantages large groups of the population who do not possess these qualifications, lies in the complexity and the 'scientific' approach to the presentation of state decisions, particularly in the planning processes.

The conception of the state in the GDR, already outlined above, means that elections serve a fundamentally different purpose from elections in pluralist democratic societies. Elections in the GDR do not involve different parties and objectives competing for the approval of the electorate. Instead, they are designed to mobilise the whole of society to accept a single, given programme drawn up by the National Front and to which all candidates are equally bound. At the same time, they serve to motivate each individual to play his particular part in achieving the goals laid down. Elections are thus agitatorial, propagandistic campaigns designed to transmit programme content and to canvass support for the realisation of this programme content — wherever possible in the concrete form of self-commitment on the part of the workers' collectives. The fact of putting up candidates for election does serve a purpose in that it anchors the representative bodies in society on as broad a basis as possible. This is why successor candidates are nominated, over and above the seats available for election. The candidates have essentially the same rights and obligations as the full members to participate in the work of the people's representative bodies, except that they have no right to vote. When the lists of candidates are drawn up, care is taken to ensure that the leading role of the party is maintained in quantitative terms as well[75] and also to ensure that the lists comply with cadre policy (the members that the people's representative bodies have to elect to the executive councils ('Räte') are supposed to be — though do not strictly have to be — members of the people's representative bodies). The election meetings or electorate representative conferences at which the candidates are presented and confirmed, not only serve to propagate the election programme but are also intended to introduce the electorate to their future deputies.[76] In addition, proposals are put forward at these meetings and local grievances aired so as to give the future deputies some points of reference for their subsequent work and to ask them to speak out for specific local or regional interests in their work with the councils and their technical departments.[77]

The mediator function which clearly emerges from discussion processes of this type is a characteristic feature of a deputy's work. The deputy is expected to motivate citizens to active participation in achieving the goals set down by the state and at the same time play the complementary role of channelling feedback to the full-time state apparatus on attitudes, focuses of interest and dissatisfaction prevailing within his area of activity and discuss means of allowing for these factors in state activity. This profile of the deputy's function gives the rank and file of the electorate an indirect influence on the selection of candidates — a deputy must hold the direct confidence of the people and enjoy a certain standing in his own social environment if he is to be entrusted with proposals or if he himself is to campaign actively for topical causes. Deputies continue in their jobs or professions as a matter of principle (not least to keep them active within their social environment) and work on the people's representative bodies on a purely honorary basis.[78]

Viewed in this way, the election procedure proper simply marks the culmination of a mobilisation process; it serves to legitimate the system as a whole, along with the policy it pursues, and is intended to show up the unity of the people of the state and the unity of party, state and society, as postulated in Marxist–Leninist theory of state. The demonstrative, highly organised and open vote is thus still the rule and socio-political pressure is so strong that abstentions, invalidation of ballot papers and deletion of individual candidates occur only in isolated cases.[79] The election turnout and the number of valid votes cast is correspondingly high.[80] The consequence of this type of electoral procedure, however, is that it only achieves a limited legitimation effect amongst the electorate. The electorate generally approaches the elections with the feeling that nothing can be done anyway and that any deviation from the expected pattern of political conduct (such as the use of the polling booths) will be noted and could one day be held against them as evidence of opposition. Only in exceptional cases does the fact of participating in the election produce the desired effect of making the voter feel he has taken on a degree of responsibility for the whole by casting his vote.

The work of the people's representative bodies is fundamentally tied to the principles of democratic centralism. For the regional representatives (district and county assemblies, town assemblies, borough assemblies and community assemblies) it follows that 'under the leadership of the party of the working class, on the basis of the laws and statutory regulations in their territory, they shall realise state policy in close cooperation with the working people and the social organisations . . . '.[81] Although they are supposed to take their own decisions 'on all basic matters affecting their territory and the people who live there', the scope really open to them in decision-making will ultimately depend on how far organs above them make binding regulations. In keeping with the logic of the whole system, the people's representative bodies are likewise conceived as having their own hierarchical structure. Decisions taken at one level are binding on the next level down and higher-ranking people's representative bodies are also entitled to annul the resolutions of lower-level bodies if these are in contradiction with their own regulations.

The work of the regional organs of state focuses first and foremost on securing and improving the living and working conditions of the population (services, trade and supply, qualification and deployment of the labour potential, housing, cultural development etc.) and also on directing and planning for district-directed and local industry (which in 1980 accounted for 16 per cent of total industrial output).[82] They remain tied to the centralist structures in their work: 'In terms of the form of its state structure, the GDR is a unitarian state'.[83] As a consequence of this unitarian state principle, the executive levels ranked under the central government power are essentially responsible for performing the centrally-allocated tasks. In recent years, however, there has been a recognisable trend away from the implementation of centrally detailed measures towards the fulfilment and concretisation of more broadly formulated goals. The unity of the state budget has been maintained, however, and there is correspondingly little room for manoeuvre in financial matters at regional and local level. The ratio of central budget to local state organ budgets is currently in the order of 75:25.[84] Much of the executive work is in the hands of the counties, although the counties have less influence on long-term decisions than do the district councils. County councils have the major part of the budget allocated to regional organs at their disposal[85] and therefore largely determine what goes on in their territory. The importance of the county level is underlined by the fact that the party-leader, Erich Honecker, delivers a yearly speech of major importance to the first secretaries of the county executives of the SED.

The framework conditions and concrete terms of reference of the regional state organs are conditioned primarily by the degree of centralisation in industrial production and by the associated system of direction and planning for the national economy. The major part of industrial production (84 per cent) takes place in centrally directed People's Own Enterprises ('Volkseigene Betriebe' – VEB). Whilst the regional organs of state have no direct say in developments in these enterprises, the decisions taken on investment and also on the taking-up, closure or curtailment of production, are factors which affect regional infrastructure and have to be dealt with at the regional level. Enterprises that come under the control of the regional councils are in the main enterprises that deal in supplies and material and serve to meet the needs of the population in the region. Part of their output, however, will go to supply centrally directed VEBs and, in some cases, the regional enterprises themselves will be dependent on centrally directed VEBs for their raw materials and semi-finished products etc. As in any other economy that is characterised by a high degree of division of labour, this necessitates a large number of co-operation agreements and in the GDR, where the means of production are under state control, such agreements have to be passed through the appropriate political channels too. Experience to date has shown that the centrally directed enterprises have been better able to assert their interests than the regional organs of state. This is due to their economic weight, their importance as producers of export goods and to their closer proximity to the industry ministries, the planning commission and the appropriate departments of the SED Central Committee.

As a result of this situation, the regional enterprises are less well equipped with capital goods and the regional state organisations have to contend with the problems that arise from decisions taken centrally on economic development within their territory, over which they themselves have only limited influence. The grouping of VEBs into collective combines ('Kombinat') has also made co-operation between the specialised departments of the regional councils and the individual enterprise more difficult. Before this move the Associations of People's Own Enterprises ('Vereinigungen Volkseigener Betriebe' — VVB) had been largely responsible for direction and administration, while the enterprise itself remained the essential economic unit. The collective combines which have replaced the VVBs, and which now take in all the VEBs of a particular branch of industry throughout the whole of the GDR, are themselves defined as economic and co-operation entities — a factor which has curtailed the individual enterprise's scope for decision and its opportunity to conclude direct agreements with the regional state organs.[86]

The regional state organs are also, however, tied to the hierarchical structure of the state apparatus. This is governed by democratic centralism in the form of 'two-fold subordination' ('doppelte Unterstellung'). This organisational maxim means that not only are the individual departments subordinate to the regional council and its chairman, but also that the corresponding department on the next level up has the right to issue directives and exercise control. Hence the Council of Ministers has the right and obligation to direct and control the district councils and generally to secure the 'uniform action of regional councils in order to realise the policy of the socialist state'.[87] Decisions by the district councils which contravene existing legislation or other statutory regulations may be annulled by the Council of Ministers. The individual ministers enjoy this same right within their particular area of competence. The chairman of the Council of Ministers for his part controls the chairmen of the district councils; he directs them and can issue instructions to them. Conversely, the district councils 'shall be involved in the preparation of such decisions as affect the material, social and cultural requirements of their area'. The district councils possess similar rights and obligations of instruction, control and co-ordination towards the county councils and the county councils towards the community councils.

This outline of the hierarchical structure of the state will suffice to indicate the opportunities that exist and the limits that are placed on the activities of the state organs in the GDR. As has already been seen for the SED itself, the plenary sessions of the people's representative bodies are not of direct relevance to the decision-making processes proper. Their chief function is one of formal legitimation of cadre policy decisions taken elsewhere, and the sanctioning of resolutions that have already been prepared and definitively formulated.[88] The essential opportunity for deputies to influence decisions at the preparatory stage, to acquire information on the implementation and impact of these decisions and to exercise criticism, control and make suggestions, is provided by the commissions allocated to the specialised departments in all people's representative bodies.[89] In the exercise of their functions the commissions have the right to attend council meetings, to put forward written proposals and to invite to their meetings council members who hold responsibility for their area, or staff from specialised departments. The commissions do not, however, have the right to take decisions themselves which would commit the councils to specific action; they are consultative organs.

This limitation on the commissions' terms of reference largely explains their make-up. In addition to the deputies and their successor candidates, further experts are appointed to the commission and given the same rights as the deputies. This statutory provision underlines the integration function of the people's representative bodies and the endeavours of the state to involve as many citizens as possible in state activity, in a consultative capacity, without fundamentally restricting the decision-making powers of the full-time apparatus. Of the 204,410 deputies in the regional people's representative bodies in 1979, 164,709 were members of the commissions. In addition, these bodies comprised 57,758 successor candidates and 161,287 other members (total commission membership: 383,754).[90]

The People's Chamber ('Volkskammer' — VK) counts as the highest organ of power in the GDR. Its plenary sessions decide upon 'basic issues of state policy'.[91] This elevated status of the People's Chamber leads to a somewhat different formal structure from that of the regional people's representative bodies. The VK has a permanently elected Presidium, whose membership includes the president (Horst Sindermann, member of the Politburo of the SED Central Committee) and his deputy (Gerald Götting, Chairman of the CDU), one representative from each of the nine groups in the People's Chamber and the Secretary of the Council of State.[92] The People's Chamber has 15 standing committees to deal with the preparation of legislation and to monitor the results of legislative measures — 12 for individual policy areas, together with the citizens' petition committee, the standing orders committee and the mandate supervisory committee.[93] Only two thirds or so of VK deputies are members of a committee at the same time.[94] The activities of the other deputies are restricted to attendance at plenaries and agit-prop work in their workplaces, residential areas and National Front Committees, carried out in conjunction with deputies from other people's representative bodies in so-called deputy groups. The People's Chamber committees are entitled to involve successor candidates and experts in their work, either on a temporary or on a permanent basis.

At the plenary sessions of the People's Chamber, governmental declarations are confirmed and the budget, economic plans and draft legislation approved. The effort which has gone into upgrading the status of the People's Chamber has so far had no visible repercussion on the procedure or frequency of its meetings. There is still no discussion during meetings — the group spokesmen confine themselves to declarations of approval, which frequently amount virtually to a commitment on their part to fulfil the task on hand. Moreover, the number of VK meetings has been steadily declining since 1950. In the 7th legislative period from 1976 to 1981 it met only 13 times.[95] The influence of the VK on central decisions follows largely through the work of its committees. The feedback of information from the committees to the central government departments, which is based on the committee's own analysis of the effects of legislative measures and of the extent to which these are being observed, leads, in particular, to corrections being made in state activity and is also taken into account when new legislation is drawn up. The effectiveness of controls of this kind presupposes a certain experience of the mechanisms of power in the GDR too, and this can only be acquired through long-standing membership of the Chamber. There has also been a general reduction in mobility in the central leadership positions of the political system, most of which are held by persons who are deputies of the People's Chamber as well. On the whole, the number of persons elected to the VK for the first time is on the decline; in 1981 it was only 27.2 per cent.[96]

Beside its work on legislation, the other main legitimating function of the VK consists in the election of the Council of State, the Chairman of the Defence Council, the Chairman and members of the Council of Ministers and the President and members of the Supreme Court of Justice of the GDR and the Public Procurator's Office.[97]

The Council of State ('Staatsrat') functions as a collective head of state. It ratifies international agreements, the Council of State chairman appoints and recalls the diplomatic representatives of the GDR, and it is to the Council of State that foreign diplomatic staff present their credentials. The domestic functions of the Council of State, however, were greatly curtailed in comparison to what they had been in the 1960s by the 1974 modification of the constitution. In the 1960s the Council had the right to examine all draft legislation set before the People's Chamber, to convene meetings of the Chamber itself and to place binding interpretations on individual laws. The Council was also empowered to issue its own decrees and make decisions having legal force, which had only to be submitted to the People's Chamber for confirmation *ex post facto*. The Council of State thus assumed legislative and executive functions, which both lessened the power of the Council of Ministers and was starting to weaken the leading role of the party, i.e. the influence of the Central Committee apparatus.[98] The replacement of Walter Ulbricht as First Secretary of the Central Committee in 1971 brought this trend to a halt, although Ulbricht remained chairman of the Council of State right up to his death in 1973 and the constitutional modification which curtailed the powers of the Council was not passed until 1974. The Council of State now has the task of promulgating all legislation passed by the People's Chamber, receiving the oath of office from members of the Council of Ministers, ordering the regularly held elections, forming the chief electoral committee and giving continuous support to the work of the regional people's representative bodies. It also exercises the right of amnesty and pardon and endows state decorations and honorary titles, which are awarded by the chairman of the Council of State. The Council's tasks in the external and internal security of the GDR hold political weight; the Council of State nominates the members of the National Defence Council and if the need arises decides on a state of emergency, which is then proclaimed by the Council chairman.

Even though this means that the Council of State at present assumes predominantly representative functions, the composition of its membership nonetheless shows a certain analogy to the Politburo, in that the chairmen of the most important organisations are brought together again in an organ of the state. The 'alliance policy' aspect, i.e. the demonstrative display of the unity of the people in their head of state, plays a major role here. One very much desired side effect of the strong representation of SED Central Committee secretaries on the Council of State is that when these secretaries travel abroad, and particularly to non-socialist countries, or are engaged in negotiations with foreign guests of the state, they are not acting primarily in their capacity as top SED functionaries but first and foremost as representatives of the GDR state.

The Council of State elected for the 8th legislative period is made up of 25 members plus the secretary. The Chairman of the Council of State is the SED Secretary General, Erich Honecker. His seven deputies are: the chairman of the Council of Ministers, Willi Stoph; the president of the People's Chamber, Horst Sindermann; the Central Committee Secretary for Security, Paul Verner; and the chairmen of the four block parties (Manfred Gerlach, LDPD; Ernst Goldenbaum, DBD; Gerald Götting, CDU; Heinrich Homann, NDPD). The Council membership also includes four representatives of the Central Committee apparatus: secretaries Werner Felfe (agriculture), Kurt Hager (culture and science), Günter Mittag (economic affairs) and the head of the Central Committee department for constitutional and legal affairs,

Klaus Sorgenicht. The two former First Regional Secretaries of the SED, Alois Pisnik and Bernhard Quandt, who are both members of the SED Central Committee, represent the party tradition. The regional state apparatus is represented by the Chief Burgomaster ('Oberbürgermeisterin') of Potsdam, Brunhilde Hanke (SED), agriculture by the head of the Agro-Industrial Association of Friedland, Margarete Müller (PB candidate), and industry by the head of the Rostock Housing Construction Combine, Paul Strauss (member of the SED Central Committee). The working class, youth and women are represented by the chairmen of the appropriate mass organisations, whereby the trade unions, as the most important of the mass organisations, are granted two seats: Harry Tisch (Chairman of the FDGB, member of the Politburo), Johanna Töpfer (Deputy Chairman of the FDGB, member of the Central Committee), Egon Kreuz (First Secretary of the FDJ Central Council, Politburo candidate), Ilse Thiele (Chairman of the DFD, member of the SED Central Committee). The alliance policy aspect of the Council of State is additionally highlighted by the fact that each of the four block parties is allocated one member in the Council (3 are the chairmen of regional associations and one a member of the NDPD Presidium and Secretariat): Kurt Anclam (LDPD), Friedrich Kind (CDU), Werner Seifert (DBD), Rosel Walther (NDPD). The Secretary of the Council of State is Heinz Eichler (SED), who is simultaneously a member of the Presidium of the People's Chamber.[99]

Set against the strong representation of defence and security in the SED Central Committee and the Politburo, the Council of State at first sight appears as a highly 'civilian' head of state. The virtual absence of members responsible for defence matters (with the exception of the Secretary General and the Central Committee Secretary for Security) is all the more surprising since Article 73 of the Constitution expressly empowers the Council of State 'to take basic decisions on matters of national defence and security'. The concrete specification of this constitutional provision follows at the same point, though: the Council of State 'shall organise national defence with the aid of the National Defence Council'. The National Defence Council is thus 'the central organ of state . . . upon whom the uniform direction of defence and security is encumbent'[100] (and is accountable to the Council of State and the People's Chamber). The measures enacted by the National Defence Council are binding on all organs of state, including the Council of Ministers and hence, to this extent, the Council of Ministers only fulfils the 'defence tasks delegated to it', i.e. functions as an executive organ.[101] The chairman of the National Defence Council is the sole member elected by the People's Chamber; the other members (a minimum of 12) are nominated by the Council of State. Since the National Defence Council was set up in 1960, the position of chairman has always been held by the First Secretary or Secretary General of the SED Central Committee. The fact that one single person holds the three most powerful and prestigious positions within the GDR political system not only signifies an extraordinary accumulation of power but also marks an expression of the supremacy of the party both in domestic and external policies.

The true work of government is carried out by the Council of Ministers of the GDR. The focal points of its work are economic planning and the day to day direction of the economy. Since the means of production are for the most part owned by the people (*de facto* by the state), and the GDR abides strictly by the principle of a centrally directed and planned economy, economic processes have to be set in motion by political forces and be directed towards specified political aims. The state apparatus thus inevitably becomes an economic protagonist, although the enterprises themselves are not regarded as organs of state and their economic activity is not regarded as state activity.[102] Whilst state control penetrates right into the individual enterprises (enterprise directors are regarded as 'authorised representatives of worker and peasant power') the enterprises act 'on their own responsibility' in their economic dealings, on the basis of and within the framework of state directions. The Council of Ministers has the Planning Commission at its disposal for drawing up the one-year and five-year plans and also for monitoring implementation of these plans. Responsibility for individual sectors of the economy, for foreign trade, supplies to the population and similar, rests with the ministries concerned. Alongside this comes a wealth of cross-sector and co-operation work that has to be conducted at central level. This involves laying down the principles of the pricing and wage systems, laying down quality standards and developing and maintaining a uniform though at the same time differentiated legal system. In an economic system which is oriented towards growth and technical progress, science and research have come to gain increasing weight as growth factors as well. The planning, organisation and promotion of research have for a long time ranked amongst the most important tasks of the central state institutions. The same holds true for the cultural and educational institutions that serve (or at least also serve) the requirements of the economy. The national economic plan and fulfilment of this plan simultaneously determine the volume of the budget and, to a large extent, its allocation as well. This plethora of tasks explains the large membership of the Council of Ministers. Such an extensive and differentiated state administration can easily evade control, especially since the people's representative bodies do not have the right of direct intervention in state decisions and their commissions are chiefly orientated towards local problems of detail. In order to detect in good time any overstepping of competences or any non-fulfilment of obligations, the Council of Ministers disposes of the Worker and Peasant Inspectorate ('Arbeiter-und-Bauern-Inspektion' — ABI), in conjunction with the SED Central Committee. This inspectorate also checks that legal norms are observed, and serves to prevent any trends towards the development of an independent identity and any corruption within the individual state and economic institutions. The Chairman of the Worker and Peasant Inspectorate holds ministerial rank and is a member of both the Council of Ministers and the SED Central Committee. The organisation of the ABI follows that of the state itself and that of the individual sectors of the economy, such that it extends to practically all the state authorities, collective combines and enterprises. The full-time ABI functionaries are backed up in their work by a large number of honorary workers, the members of the ABI commissions and the People's Control Committees.[103] The ABI also works in close co-operation with the State Budget Auditors (part of the Ministry of Finance) and the GDR state bank, which monitors every stage of the nationalised economy to ensure that funds are put to legitimate use in accordance with the plan (money in circulation, investment capital, credit, etc.).

The Council of Ministers is supported in its work by the scientific institutions which fall directly under its authority. These include the Academy for Theory of State and Law, and the Institute of Politics and Economics, which is engaged in a running analysis of economic and political developments outside the socialist block, with particular focus on the Federal Republic of Germany. In addition to this, the State Planning Commission (and other Ministries too) have their own research institutes and advisory bodies, which influence the political decision-making process in an advisory capacity. When preparing decisions, the Council of Ministers is obliged to co-operate with the social organisations that will be affected by planned regulations and to seek their advice, as indeed are the individual Ministries, the independent state secretariats and other central departments.

The decisive substance of state activity is laid down in party resolutions. 'In the same way (as in the People's Chamber) the Marxist–Leninist Party shall also play the leading role in the Council of Ministers.' 'The activity (of the Council of Ministers) shall be directed towards the implementation of the policy of the party of the working class . . . It is a steadfast principle of the leadership work of the Council of Ministers that the substance of its measures and the organisational flow of its work shall always be co-ordinated with the activity of the party leadership.'[104]

This integration of state activity into the current policy of the SED is achieved through the intermeshing of party and state leadership, through joint resolutions passed by the Politburo and the Council of Ministers, through direct adoption by the Council of Ministers of party resolutions which are subsequently brought into force as state resolutions, and through the confirmation of state decisions by the Politburo.[105] Whilst this procedure is aimed at achieving co-ordination with the general party line on the policy to be followed, co-ordination in day-to-day ministerial work is assured by running consultations with the relevant department of the Central Committee apparatus. Here again, though, one must be careful not to take too schematic a view of the relationship between the central state and party apparatus. Although, in the event of conflict, the party is able to impose its view of the problem and its proposed solutions on the state apparatus, under normal circumstances the relationship will be one of co-operation based on the current political programme to which both sides have agreed.

The chairman of the Council of Ministers is always nominated by the strongest party (i.e. the SED in each case) and confirmed in office by the People's Chamber. The chairman, for his part, puts forward his deputies and the other members of the Council for election. Allocation of responsibilities to the members of the Council of Ministers rests with the chairman. This means that the functional composition of the government — a factor of considerable importance — is largely beyond even formal control by the People's Chamber. At present the Council of Ministers has 42 members, in addition to its chairman, Willi Stoph (member of the Politburo) and his two first deputies, Werner Krolikowski (member of the Politburo) and Alfred Neumann (member of the Politburo).[106] Nine of them hold the post of deputy chairman in addition to their specific functions. Amongst these deputy chairmen are the members of the Council of Ministers from each of the block parties: Manfred Flegel, Chairman of the State Contractual Court (NDPD), Hans-Joachim Heusinger, Minister of Justice (LDPD), Hans Reichelt, Minister for the Protection of the Environment and the Supply and Distribution of Water (DBD) and Rudolph Schulze, Minister of Post and Telecommunications (CDU).[107] Since the Council of Ministers is too large to work effectively in plenary session, a presidium has been created which comprises the chairman, his deputies and a further four members of the Council of Ministers. The presidium assumes the functions of the Council of Ministers between plenary sessions, it does the preparatory work on fundamental decisions and focuses the work of the Council of Ministers on fundamental conceptual matters.

The centralisation of the state apparatus, together with its closed nature and extensive decision-making powers, opens up the question of the means available to an individual citizen of the GDR to defend himself against state decisions which affect him, and which he feels curtail his rights.[108] The possibilities open to him in situations such as these (which are numerous since so many social areas are under state control) are indeed still very limited. A series of state decisions make provision for the 'complaint' ('Beschwerde') as a legal instrument for the person concerned. Providing the complaint is lodged within the appropriate deadline, the superior of the person concerned will check on whether it is legitimate and take a definitive decision. In all other cases, the citizen remains dependent on the 'petition' ('Eingabe'). This does not take any set form and may be submitted either to the people's representative body or to a state or party institution. A petition must be answered within four weeks of receipt by the state functionary responsible for its content area. Petitions may contain references to general problems, suggestions for improving the way in which the state administration operates or indeed individual complaints about cases of need or state decisions, in a bid to obtain relief. Decisions on petitions are again taken internally. In addition, the petitions are collected and evaluated at regular intervals so that conclusions may be drawn. Such conclusions may take the form of a decision to change or improve the way in which individual functionaries or departments operate, to make allowance for specific projects (kindergartens, services, etc.) in future planning or to modify statutory regulations that have figured particularly frequently in critical petitions.

The position of the individual in relation to organs of the state on the whole remains unsatisfactory, however. The continued implementation of this exclusively internal procedure for dealing with complaints is repeatedly justified on ideological, theoretical grounds — the socialist state is everybody's state. It does not pursue special interests but always achieves that which is possible within a given situation, that which is reflected in legal norms as being the collective interest of society. As a socialist state it is committed to observing these norms and committed to 'socialist legality'. Any violation of this socialist legality could only be an exception — an isolated incident to be dealt with by the administration internally. Moreover, citizens not only have the right, but also an obligation to participate in state activity by playing active roles in social organisations and the people's representative bodies etc. It is through their work that the prerequisites for better satisfaction of collective and individual needs are created. This argument may sound consistent from the ideological point of view but in practice it overlooks differences in interests, ignores the inertia of big administrations and will certainly only convince the individual citizen confronted with virtually opaque decision-making processes in the rarest of cases. The discussion on constitutional and administrative law bears witness to the fact that the problems of the citizen's relationship to the state have been duly acknowledged. Time and again appeals are made for 'care in dealing with petitions' and checks are carried out to ensure that the set procedure is observed. With the State Liability Law of 1969 it was nonetheless conceded that in isolated cases state functionaries might misinterpret statutory provisions, make the wrong decision and thereby inflict material damage on the citizen concerned. The state now has to bear liability for such cases.[109] Even here, though, decisions on whether a case fulfils the requirements and on how much compensation should be paid are an internal matter for the administration. The legal discussions are, however, still in progress. They have already brought recognition of the fact that even in a socialist legal system there are 'subjective rights' for the citizen and not simply uniform legal norms embodying both 'objective' and 'subjective' rights. The theory of law discussion has now reached the point where it allows the question of how a citizen can assert the 'subjective' rights he holds against the 'objective' rights that are embodied in the state institutions. In spite of this progress, there is not likely to be much of a change in the short term, since this would call for measures such as the introduction of an independent and controlling administrative judiciary, i.e. it would require an ideological reappraisal of the state within the GDR sociopolitical system.[110]

Mass organisations and social organisations

Any discussion of the basic structures of the political system in the GDR would be incomplete without an account of the mass organisations and the social organisations. These have already been mentioned on several occasions in conjunction with the SED, the people's representative bodies and the state apparatus. It should already have become clear that these organisations have two chief political functions to fulfil, which are by no means easy to reconcile. On the one hand, they are responsible for transmitting the will of the party to the social sphere in which they operate, and at the same time they are expected to speak out for the interests of their members. The social organisations thus play the role of intermediary between the political decision-makers and the social groups. To this extent, the same applies to the social organisations as has already been stated for the people's representative bodies, namely they constitute an essential instrument for the integration of society into the political system. It is therefore not by coincidence that right up until the 1960s the people's representative bodies themselves were rated in ideological theoretical terms as 'the most comprehensive mass organisation', embracing all social classes, strata and groups. This view has now been dropped so as to allow emphasis to be placed on the legitimatory function of the people's representative bodies for state leadership and state activity. Nevertheless, the grouping of the state forms of participation (people's representative bodies etc.) and the non-state forms of participation (social organisations) under the overall heading of socialist democracy shows that they are still taken together even in current ideological discussions. The significance of the social organisations for the system as a whole has been undeniably upgraded in this respect[111] and the function allocated to them of being solely a 'transmission belt' for the state and party in relation to their membership, as is found in Stalinist-type Marxism—Leninism, has been largely curtailed. They are now seen as an integral part of the political system and are expected to make an independent contribution towards stability, efficiency and further development of the system.

The functions of the social organisations can currently be summed up as follows:[112]

1. The 'transmission belt' function, i.e. the mass organisations propagate the goals of action set by the party or the state apparatus and attempt to mobilise their members to achieve these.

2. The function of representing their members' interests, i.e. of providing an organised and controlled framework within which the interests of the various social groups are supposed to be expressed, social needs and activities fulfilled (e.g. sporting and cultural events) and social conflicts aired and resolved. The task of keeping the expression and assertion of interests within the given system limits is assured by statutory regulations, the focus on the leadership role of the party and the effective action of SED party groups within the association, together with the specific organisational statutes of the mass organisations (democratic centralism, internal cadre policy within the organisations).

3. The educative function, i.e. the mass organisations are expected to make an essential contribution towards modifying the attitude and conduct of their membership to fit in with the prevailing shape of Marxism—Leninism, and in particular towards developing a 'socialist moral consciousness' and a 'socialist way of life'.

4. The cadre training function, i.e. leadership functions either in or on behalf of the mass organisations, are used for the trying out and selection of leadership personnel in positions that are generally of less relevance in political terms. The mass organisations thus act as a filter for selecting professionally qualified and politically tested next-generation cadres, and

simultaneously provide their members with the opportunity for social and political ascent.

5   The qualification function, i.e. depending on their particular terms of reference and field of activity, the mass organisations offer their members the opportunity to acquire additional professional qualifications and/or to improve their general education. This function is closely related to functions 3 and 4, without being identical to them.

6   A function as an instrument for control over society: the SED does not permit free formation of associations outside the mass organisations which it controls (the special status accorded to the churches and other religious communities is the only exception here). It endeavours to tie all social activity to the social organisations, so as to prevent the formation of spontaneous groups or communities of interest outside its organisational control.

7   A function as an instrument of 'social control': in order to prevent the misuse of power, any tendencies on the part of state or economic leadership to develop their own identity, and any fraud or non-observation of legal norms, the mass organisations have been allocated a legally standardised right to 'social control'. This right to control covers both the general misconduct of individual functionaries or groups of functionaries and also isolated cases where a person's rights have been infringed. It does not, however, allow the mass organisations to intervene directly in decision-making processes or in the personnel make-up of executives, but simply enables them to submit an appropriate report to the next highest state or party organ.

8   A function as an additional source of information providing corrective feedback: the proximity of the mass organisations to the various social groups means that they can provide the political leadership with additional information on the attitudes, wishes and dissatisfaction prevailing in society. This gives the leadership a further opportunity to correct their policy in time and to take account of these areas of conflict in their agit-prop work.

9   The consultative and advisory function: the decision-making areas for the political, economic and other leadership bodies in the GDR have become increasingly complex and in specialist areas the mass organisations allow such bodies recourse to the expertise of specific groups within their membership, so as to allow better-informed decision-making.

10 A function as an instrument of criticism and self-criticism: the members' assemblies, commissions, working parties and executives etc. provide a forum for controlled criticism directed towards individual questions. In addition, the leadership of the association and also economic and state functionaries can be called to account by these forums.

The functions listed here are not all fulfilled, or may be fulfilled to differing degrees, by each individual organisation. Moreover, the significance of the individual associations within the political system has to be rated differently. Their status is determined essentially by the socio-political relevance of their organisational area, the social groups they cover, the size of their membership and so on. As a generalisation it can be said that those organisations which are directly active in the labour process or in the education and training spheres or which include certain sections of the intelligentsia in their membership (engineers, artists) have gained both in the range of tasks allocated to them and in status since the 1960s — in particular since the 8th SED Party Congress in 1971.

Membership of the mass organisations is basically voluntary. It does, however, constitute a precondition for social ascent and is taken as evidence of a minimum degree of loyalty to the system (in particular membership of the Free German Youth, the trade unions and the DSF). Personal records contain information on membership and functions held in social organisations by way of evidence of social activity. In addition, membership of a mass organisation brings certain advantages (e.g. FDGB and FDJ vacation service; financial benefits in cases of need; participation in further training courses) and access to party, state and economic leaders. Moreover, any interests and hobbies which call for a club-like setting can only be pursued through the organisational forms provided by the mass organisations system: folklore in the FDGB or the Free German Youth, philately and numismatics in the League of Culture of the GDR, rabbit and poultry breeding in the Gardeners, Settlers and Small Animal Breeders' Association and sport in the DTSB. This organisation of society right down to the last detail should not, however, be overrated. Nowadays joining one or more of the organisations is only regarded as a conscious political act in exceptional cases. As a rule it is seen as quite the normal practice, either because 'everyone' joins trade unions or because to practise sport one naturally joins the DTSB. At the lower levels in particular, much of what goes on in the mass organisations is of a general club-like nature rather than of a political nature.

The Confederation of Free German Trade Unions enjoys a clearly raised status amongst the mass organisations. As a trade union it is directly present in the labour process and its membership covers almost the entire active core of GDR society.[113] In all more recent legislation the FDGB is expressly named as the chief interlocutor of central and regional councils. It provides the largest contingent of deputies after the SED. The anchorage of the FDGB in the political system through the intermeshing of SED and FDGB staff — a highly important factor from the power angle — has already been covered in a previous context.

The weight of the FDGB, however, stems less from demonstrative references in legal texts and programmatic declarations and more from its tasks within the enterprise. The Labour Code ('Arbeitsgesetzbuch' — AGB), which came into force on 1 January 1978, clearly strengthened the rights of the enterprise union organisations ('Betriebsgewerkschaftsorganisationen' — BGO) and their executives ('Betriebsgewerkschaftsleitungen' — BGL).[114] The chairman of the BGL (and only he) is entitled to attend meetings of the plant management and inspect the enterprise files, in the same way as the secretary of the enterprise party organisation. The enterprise union organisation constitutes the vehicle for all forms of participation within the enterprise.[115] These have little impact during the plan compilation stage but play a significant role in the operative phase when plan implementation and plan fulfilment are the concern. In questions relating to enterprise social policy, to cultural activities and also to the fixing of workers' bonuses, the enterprise union executives not only have rights of participation but rights of co-determination as well. The enterprise union executive has similar rights in individual labour law, particularly when it comes to the dissolution or modification of existing employment relationships. Despite this, union activity within the enterprise still operates in two directions. On the one hand it is directed towards plan fulfilment, towards the realisation of the goals set for the enterprise and towards propagating all aspects of the current party line, yet on the other hand, it has to be guided by the direct interests of the enterprise workforce and attempt to ensure optimum satisfaction of these interests within the possibilities open to the enterprise. In addition, the enterprise union organisation is also responsible for seeing that the enterprise management observes the legal norms. From this it becomes clear that the possibilities open for union work within an enterprise depend to a decisive extent on the nature of the planning and management system. One factor here is the principle of individual management ('Prinzip der Einzelleitung'), whereby only the enterprise director is empowered to take economic decisions that are binding on the enterprise.[116] A second factor is the position of the enterprise within the general hierarchy of economic direction. As the number and scope of decisions that can be taken within the enterprise diminishes, so the significance held by the forms of consultative participation within the economic sphere is weakened.

The formation of collective combines, which has already been mentioned above, has considerably curtailed the scope for decisions within the enterprise.[117] Furthermore, the level of bonus payments and the resources to be set aside for the cultural and social fund is essentially determined by the enterprise's results. Since the chief decisions on investment and product range are generally taken at levels above the enterprise, the enterprise is left with no direct influence on matters which are decisive for an optimum organisation of the production process and thus for optimisation of its own economic situation. This likewise curtails the scope of the enterprise union executive for satisfying the wishes of the workforce.

It is necessary to mention at least some of the problem areas encountered within enterprises in order to allow a realistic assessment of the significance and the opportunities for trade union participation. The extensive tasks of the trade union and the commissions and subdivisions of the enterprise union organisations set up to deal with these, explain the proportions that honorary union activity has taken on within the enterprise. At present there are more than 2.1 million honorary union functionaries in enterprises. This figure will give some idea of the integration and mobilisation capacity of the union movement. Even after allowance is made for those persons counted more than once (not infrequently one person will hold two or more honorary functions) and for the fact that elected functionaries are sometimes strikingly casual in their approach to organisational duties, the figures nonetheless highlight the significance of big organisations like the FDGB for actively involving large groups of society in the political system. The degree of mobilisation within the FDGB is admittedly particularly high, but the same is found in the other organisations as well, albeit to a lesser extent. The commitment that an individual feels when taking on such a function is difficult to judge. The answer to this question will only be found when the motives that prompt an individual to take on a function within the FDGB or other organisation are known (occupational and social ascent; readiness to do something for his colleagues; an expression of political conviction; consequence of social or political pressure etc.). In the last analysis, however, the importance that an honorary functionary position holds for an individual is likely to be gauged by what he can actually achieve through his work and whether he feels that his input bears an acceptable relationship to the result (honorary work is carried out predominantly in spare time).

The limits on participation and the fact that it is restricted to individual criticism, consultation and the putting forward of proposals have already been covered in various contexts in this study. Here we need only add that an organisation like the FDGB is also governed by the principles of democratic centralism, displays a corresponding degree of centralisation and bears the stamp of the SED as far as cadre policy and organisational policy are concerned. Although the FDGB is divided up into 16 industrial trade unions ('Industriegewerkschaften' — IG) and other trade unions ('Gewerkschaften' — Gew) these are not independent associations that have joined together to form a federation. Instead, they only exercise functions specific to their particular branch of industry, they direct the enterprise union organisations (BGO) in their organisational area and hence assume more of the character of out-of-house specialist departments. Resolutions of the FDGB Presidium are binding on the industrial and other trade unions, and the county and district boards of the individual unions are not only subordinate to their own central board but, on all matters of general trade union policy, to the FDGB county or district boards as well. The presidium also decides upon the demarcation of organisational areas and has the power to disband or merge individual trade unions and create new associations.[118]

The power of the organisation is not identical to the power of its members in the GDR either. Despite the evident increase in the significance and functions accorded to the FDGB, the scope for its members to express and assert their interests from below upwards still remains severely limited. Whilst this observation does not lessen the fact that trade union functionaries are able to articulate and uphold their members' interests, the members themselves remain distrustful of these decision-making processes because essential aspects are concealed from them, thereby preventing them from following through their own role in the decision-making process. To this extent it has to remain an open question as to how far the members conceive of the FDGB as their own interest association.

This somewhat more detailed outline of the FDGB and the fundamental problems that have been revealed are found again in the other social organisations, with the appropriate modification to their specific areas. We shall only be able to take a brief look at a few selected associations here. Figures for the most important organisations are given in table 1.3.

Alongside the trade unions it is primarily the Free German Youth (FDJ) and the 'Ernst Thälmann' Pioneer Organisation, which shares part of the FDJ staff, that call for particular attention from the party's viewpoint. These are conceived essentially as educational organisations, designed to school a young generation of socialists and communists in close organisational co-operation with state educational and training establishments. The SED is making increasing efforts to win over the 'best' FDJ members as candidates to supplement its own ranks at as early an age as possible. (As a rule the 'best' members will be those who

Table 1.3

Membership figures for parties and selected mass and social organisations

'Sozialistische Einheitspartei Deutschlands' (SED)[1] (Socialist Unity Party of Germany)	2,172,100
of which: Candidates	102,110
'Demokratische Bauernpartei Deutschlands' (DBD)[2] (Democratic Farmers' Party of Germany)	95,000
'Liberal-Demokratische Partei Deutschlands' (LDPD)[2] (Liberal Democratic Party of Germany)	75,000
'National-Demokratische Partei Deutschlands' (NDPD)[2] (National Democratic Party of Germany)	84,000
'Christlich-Demokratische Union Deutschlands' (CDU)[2] (Christian Democratic Union of Germany)	115,000
'Freier Deutscher Gewerkschaftsbund' (FDGB)[3] (Confederation of Free German Trade Unions)	8,806,754
'Freie Deutsche Jugend' (FDJ)[4] (Free German Youth)	2,300,000
'Pionierorganisation "Ernst Thälmann"',[5] ('Ernst Thälmann' Pioneer Organisation)	1,507,211
of which: 'Jungpioniere' (Young Pioneers) (1st to 3rd year at school)	574,448
'Thälmannpioniere' (Thälmann Pioneers) (4th to 7th year at school)	932,763
'Gesellschaft für Sport und Technik' (GST)[6] (Society for Sports and Technology)	approx. 500,000
'Demokratischer Frauenbund Deutschlands' (DFD)[5] (Democratic Women's League of Germany)	1,400,000
'Kulturbund der DDR' (KB) (League of Culture of the GDR)	226,593
'Vereinigung der gegenseitigen Bauernhilfe/Bäuerliche Handelsgenossenschaften' (VdgB/BHG)[7] (Farmers' Mutual Aid Association/Farmers' Trade Co-operatives)	approx. 300,000
'Verband der Konsumgenossenschaften der DDR' (Konsum)[8] (Consumers' Co-operative Societies of the GDR)	4,442,488
'Gesellschaft für Deutsch-Sowjetische Freundschaft' (DSF)[3] (German–Soviet Friendship Society)	5,700,000
'Verband der Kleingärtner, Siedler und Kleintierzüchter'[9] (Gardeners', Settlers' and Small Animal Breeders' Association)	1,127,382

'Volkssolidarität'[5] (People's Solidarity)	2,029,387
'Deutsches Rotes Kreuz der DDR' (DRK)[10] (German Red Cross of the GDR)	1,277,707
of which: 'Jugendsanitäter' (young medical orderlies) (10–14 years)	74,170
Members over 14	633,703
Friends of the DRK	569,834
'Deutscher Turn- und Sportbund der DDR' (DTSB)[11] (German Gymnastics and Sports Federation of the GDR)	3,139,333
'Kammer der Technik' (KDT)[12] (Chamber of Technology)	243,826

1 *Volksarmee*, 1981, no.20, p.7. Figures are for the 10th SED Party Congress, 11–16 April 1981.
2 *Staat und Gesellschaft in der DDR* (Study Series: *Landeskunde DDR für Ausländer*), VEB Verlag Enzyklopädie, Leipzig 1981, p.136. Figures for 1977.
3 *Statistisches Jahrbuch 1981 der Deutschen Demokratischen Republik*, published by the Central Statistical Office of the GDR, Staatsverlag der Deutschen Demokratischen Republik, Berlin (GDR), 1981, p.395. Figures for 1980.
4 *Staat und Gesellschaft in der DDR*, op.cit., p.137. Figures for 1978.
5 *Statistisches Jahrbuch 1981 der DDR*, op.cit., p.396. Figures for 1980.
6 *DDR-Handbuch*, published by the Federal German Ministry for Intra-German Relations, 2nd revised and enlarged edition. Verlag Wissenschaft und Politik, Cologne, 1979, p.469. Figures for 1977.
7 Ibid., p.450. Figures for 1978.
8 *Statistisches Jahrbuch 1981 der DDR*, op.cit., p.397. Figures for 1980.
9 Ibid., p.398. Figures for 1980.
10 Ibid., p.342. Figures for 1980.
11 Ibid., p.42. Figures for 1980.
12 Ibid., p.398. Figures for 1979.

have proved themselves in elective functions within the FDJ and have achieved good results in their training.) The Free German Youth is by no means an organisation for the élite of the young generation, however. On the contrary, it aims to take in all young people up to the age of 25 in all social spheres. The FDJ thus makes an effort to exercise an organising influence on young people through schools, universities and colleges, apprentice training establishments and the national people's army, reaching out into their leisure activities as well by providing youth clubs, sports facilities, discotheques and the young people's travel service, etc. It does, however, see itself faced with growing difficulties here. On the one hand, the range of leisure activities offered by the FDJ is no longer sufficient to satisfy the increased demands of young people today and, on the other hand, the substance of what it offers does not meet up to the young people's expectations. Most young people, without being opponents of the system, prefer to follow Western tastes and fashion trends. The impulsive protest behaviour of young people and their longing for something different and out of the ordinary is coupled to a weariness at having to move within organisational structures right from their earliest childhood.

In educational and training establishments the level of organisation is high, at close on 100 per cent. Since the assessment of the FDJ executive also plays a vital role in deciding upon admissions to university and the allocation of training places for particularly sought-after subjects, young people who are anxious to succeed in life can hardly afford not to join in the activities arranged by the youth organisation. Once young people have completed their schooling, studies or apprenticeships, a sharp fall is registered in the degree of participation.[119] Measured against the FDGB, the FDJ plays a considerably smaller role within the enterprise. Admittedly, the efforts being made to harness the enthusiasm and desire to succeed of young people by giving them specific youth assignments under the political and agitatorial auspices of the FDJ, are meeting with a measure of success. These are, however, by their very nature short-lived functions, which cannot be carried out without the responsible co-operation of adults and which remain fully integrated into the executive structures of the enterprise. Despite this though, above and beyond the political implications, the intensity with which the young generation is being encouraged, as is reflected by the many different forms of youth policy, is meeting with an overall positive reception. The awareness that much is being done for young people in the GDR and that this kind of policy is a good thing, is widespread in GDR society, even outside the party.

The Democratic Women's League of Germany ('Demokratischer Frauenbund Deutschlands' — DFD) enjoys surprisingly low status, in view of the party's policy towards women, which is aimed at equality between the sexes. The comparatively small membership of 1.4 million (there are 4.5 million women in the FDGB) is in itself proof of this. The relatively weak position of the DFD is ultimately due to the form in which the SED has pursued its policy towards women. Work conducted in the enterprises to promote women has always had its organisational foothold in the SED itself or in the FDGB. The DFD has played no part at the workplace. Its chief tasks, following on not least from the traditions of bourgeois women's movements, have been to change traditional role concepts, particularly those of housewives, so as to win them over to taking up work; to promote the expansion of services in residential areas so as to relieve working women; to realise the concept of alliance policy in winning over women with predominantly middle-class values for the construction of the new socio-political order; and to maintain international contacts with particular focus on the World Peace Movement.[120] The fact that the DFD nonetheless provides a considerable number of deputies, particularly at regional and community level, and is also represented on the Council of State and on the SED Central Committee, is due to a number of factors. First of all it provides evidence of the status accorded to the policy of equality of the sexes, which so far, however, has not led to anything like equal representation of men and women in full-time leadership positions. Secondly, the working wife urgently requires an improvement in the facilities and services available in residential areas, in view of the only very gradual change that is coming about in role distribution within the family. Thirdly, the SED has not changed its alliance policy concept in principle to date — the concept which in organisational policy terms is manifested in the make-up of the Democratic Block and the National Front — and to this extent it is still orientated towards the ideas that governed the composition of the people's representative bodies at the end of the 1940s.

The League of Culture ('Kulturbund' — KB), like the Democratic Women's League, is also still operating under the conditions under which it was founded. Set up in 1945, the League of Culture was intended to bring together the bourgeois intelligentsia into their own association through the application of a very broad culture concept, which although democratic, still bore the traits of the cultured bourgeoisie ('Bildungsbürgertum'). Its aim was to win this social group over for the construction of an initially anti-fascist democratic community and then a socialist community. In addition, it had the further task of awakening understanding for Russian, i.e. Soviet cultural development in a German public which was still strongly influenced by the anti-Bolshevism of National Socialism. This task of integrating the 'old' intelligentsia remained the chief focus of League of Culture activity until the end of the 1950s. Looking back, it has to be concluded that the League's efforts were not without success. Relatively early on, however, different areas of activity within the League of Culture began to gain their own organisational identity and this led to a permanent loss of function and a lasting curtailment of political significance for the League. The Society for the Study of the Culture of the Soviet Union was founded as early as 30 June 1947, and in 1949 it changed its name to the German—Soviet Friendship Society ('Gesellschaft für Deutsch-Sowjetische Freundschaft — DSF'). At the beginning of the 1950s specialised associations for the artistic intelligentsia began to be founded — the Writers' Association (1952), the Association of Plastic and Graphic Arts (1952), the Association of Composers and Musicologists (1952), the Architects' Association (1952), the Libraries' Association (1964), the Theatre Association (1966) and the Film and Television Association (1967). In addition to these there is the Artists' Union, which is a member of the FDGB, and within which the employed wage earners of the cultural sphere are organised. These specialised organisations currently constitute the chief bodies that represent the interests of the different groups of the cultural intelligentsia, and the decisive instruments of cultural policy. The League of Culture lost the majority of its functions in the general adult education sphere to the Urania association, which was founded on 17 June 1954 under the title 'Society for the Dissemination of Scientific Knowledge'. Since then Urania has dominated the sphere of popular science lectures (in 1980 it arranged nearly 400,000 events which attracted more than 12 million participants).

Although this loss of functions incurred through the founding of other associations has robbed the League of Culture of the monopoly it was originally given in the cultural sphere, it has not been left entirely devoid of functions. The traditional concept of culture on which the League was originally founded and which has been repeatedly confirmed and consolidated by the SED itself through its high regard for the 'classical cultural heritage', has retained its attraction — and not only for the intelligentsia. In the clubs that are run by the League of Culture for the intelligentsia (in 1980 there were 147 such clubs) where lectures are held, exhibitions arranged, League of Culture Study Groups meet and 'cultural companionship' is fostered, the traditions of bourgeois society are showing their capacity to live on under a different guise. Nowadays the League of Culture is involved not only in general cultural and educational activity but also in interest and study groups (e.g. protection of nature and the environment, local history, Esperanto, numismatics, photography, aquarium-keeping, terrariatology) and special-purpose cultural organisations (Society for the Preservation of Monuments, the Bibliophiles' Association — known as the 'Pirkheier Society', the GDR Philatelists' Association), all of which come under the League's umbrella. The representation of the League of Culture in the People's Chamber and in the people's representative bodies derives from the organisation's history on the one hand, and on the other the League remains the sole cultural organisation representing the cultural sphere within these organs. The weak representation of the League in regional and local people's representative bodies, however, highlights the limits on its scope for political activity.

The DSF ('Gesellschaft für Deutsch-Sowjetische Freundschaft' — German—Soviet Friendship Society) merits special mention in the context of politico—cultural organisations. With its 5.7 million members, the DSF constitutes the second largest mass organisation, in terms of membership figures. Despite this, however, membership of the society is largely a formality, viewed as a duty and as evidence of the right civic-minded attitude, which is also expected to include an appreciation of the importance of the ties between the GDR and the Soviet Union. Although membership of the DSF only entails the assumption of organisational duties in exceptional cases, this says little about the impact of the DSF on the GDR public in general. In 1980, for instance, the organisation held nearly 1 million events with 23.6 million participants. It is not so much the lectures proclaiming the achievements and intentions of the Soviet Union in the political, scientific and social development spheres that appeal to the general public but rather the cultural performances instead. This example should serve to show that not only are the economic and political circumstances in the GDR different from those found for example in the Federal Republic of Germany, but the cultural situation differs essentially as well, and this cannot fail to have an effect over the long term. It is precisely these influences which carry particular weight in the GDR's development of its own socio-cultural profile.

Ever since GDR economic and social policy accorded prime status to accelerated scientific and technical progress for the future development of the country, the technical intelligentsia have been assigned a key role to play. Not only have their numbers increased several times over, but their organisation, the KDT ('Kammer der Technik' — Chamber of Technology) has gained increasing importance as well. The KDT has enterprise organisations ('Betriebssektionen') in all the larger VEBs and also in the universities and research institutes.[121] It is increasingly being involved, in a consultative capacity, by the SED district and county bodies in the preparation and implementation of rationalisation and modernisation measures. The organisational structure of the KDT is divided into a large number of different sub-sectors, in line with differentiation within the engineering professions and within engineering in general. This enables the KDT, with its specialised technical and subject know-how, to become involved at central government level, within the specialised ministries and the Planning Commission, in the planning of future technical development, the laying down of technical standards and so on. Both the KDT and the five technical and scientific societies ('wissenschaftlich-technische Gesellschaften' – WTG) which come under its central organisation are members of international scientific associations. Representatives of the KDT travel to congresses abroad and, in return, the organisation itself is holding an increasing number of professional congresses in the GDR. Like all the specialised and professionally-orientated social organisations, the KDT is one of the associations which is growing in importance.

The Block Parties play a specific, even if limited special role within the organisations system.[122] They have committed themselves to the leading role of the SED and its programme as the binding principle of their own work and their task lies in influencing and integrating the remaining members of social groups with a middle-class and religious outlook. They thus constitute a firm part of the organisations system and do not differ in principle from the other mass organisations. To this extent, the term 'party' is hardly an accurate reflection of their functions – the only feature reminiscent of a party is their representation on the full-time executive bodies of the state (albeit a very weak representation) and the fact that the SED exerts its cadre policy influence on the block parties in a different way from those associations where the SED is directly present with its own members.

Despite this, the block parties have certain peculiarities which distinguish them from the mass organisations to a sufficient degree for them to be termed 'special types' of social organisations. These particular features essentially fall into three groups.

Firstly, their origins are distinct. Whilst all other mass organisations have always been under strong SED influence right from the outset, the CDU and LDPD remained autonomous parties for a lengthy period of time and were only transformed into their current form in a gradual process. The NDPD and DBD differ in this respect, since they both owe their existence to a political decision taken by the SED and SMAD ('Sowjetische Militäradministration in Deutschland' – Soviet Military Administration in Germany). All the same, though, their scope for decision-making and the substance of their policies has also changed over the course of their history.

Secondly, the block parties are concerned with social groups and strata that mainly bear the traits of the previous social order, which, in SED understanding and policy, has been or, indeed, is still to be overcome (primarily the petit bourgeoisie and the middle classes).

Lastly, the block parties serve to integrate and convert value systems that are foreign or hostile to Marxism—Leninism, along with the sociopolitical goals that go with them. These are to be adapted to the SED's goals over the course of time within the framework of an alliance concept. Although no time limit has been placed on this alliance concept, in the SED's historical perspective it is a fundamentally finite concept.

The essential difference between the block parties and the mass organisations is thus founded on the SED's concept of social development, which places a shorter time limit on the tasks the block parties are to perform. The parties are, as it were, a relic of historic ages past. This view explains why the SED will not permit the block parties to increase their membership at will and also why it excludes them from certain social fields altogether (e.g. independent youth work, enterprise work in the VEBs). The SED leadership has, however, always made it clear that it is not thinking of disbanding these organisations within the foreseeable future. The reason for the continued application of this organisational strategy lies not least in the fact that social behaviour patterns and values still persist in politically, socially and economically relevant groups even though property ownership has been transformed.

These general remarks need to be put into perspective for the individual parties concerned. In terms of the aspects mentioned above, the CDU would appear to hold considerably more importance than, for instance, the NDPD. The religious commitment of a not inconsiderable sector of GDR society has proved to be of a lasting nature (a sector which cannot be clearly classified under particular social classes, strata or groups). The NDPD, on the other hand, was set up to influence former NSDAP members and 'nationally' though not religiously orientated sectors of the petit bourgeois, which have now largely disappeared. The DBD remains an important instrument for integrating co-operative farmers into the political system, since the SED has not been as successful as it would have wished in establishing itself in organisations in rural areas. The LDPD, whose membership is orientated primarily towards the urban petit bourgeoisie (retail traders, craftsmen, small businessmen) lost much of its original sphere of influence in 1972 when all remaining private industry and manufacturing crafts were brought into state ownership. There are still traditional branches in the trade and craft sectors, however, for which the LDPD remains the responsible organisation.

It is not possible to cover the full organisations system in detail in a study of this kind. The examples given will suffice to give an impression of the multiplicity of organisations which is nonetheless found in the GDR, and show up the differentiation in the internal organisation structure of the various associations. It must also be remembered that there is extensive intermeshing and overlapping of personnel between these social organisations and that they are increasingly concluding agreements and long-term contracts to work together on the performing of joint tasks. Entitlement to conclude such agreements no longer rests exclusively with the central boards but has been granted to lower-level executives, right down to enterprise level. All in all, this results in an extraordinarily close-knit organisational network, in which the boundaries between social functions and political functions have become fluid and where the scope for comprehensive control and direction (i.e. by the party) is beginning to shrink.

In conjunction with the organisations system, the special role played by the churches and the religious communities should at least be pointed out. These are the only big organisations to have retained their autonomy. It is one of the particular features of the GDR that it is predominantly characterised by Protestantism, in contrast to the other COMECON states. The SED has thus been unable to draw on the experience of the other ruling communist parties in matters of church policy.[123] In the 1950s and 1960s the SED attempted to force the Protestant church out of public life and decimate its membership through atheist propaganda, attacks on the all-German ties of the Protestant Churches of the GDR, the introduction of the initiation ceremony ('Jugendweihe') and discrimination against practising Christians in schools, universities and at work etc. It only met with partial success, however. Although the Association of Protestant Churches of the GDR was founded on 10 September 1969, thereby causing these churches to withdraw from the All-German Protestant Church in Germany, special relations were still maintained beyond the state boundaries. There has been a considerable drop in church membership but the external pressure now being exerted on church members has given them an even greater feeling of belonging together. At all events, a dying out of the church would not appear to be imminent (estimated and no doubt exaggerated figures for 1978: Protestant church: 7.645 million; Roman Catholic church: 1.283 million; Free Churches, sects etc.: some 220,000). The political leadership of the GDR responded to this situation, which in its eyes was unsatisfactory, with a modification of its assessment of the situation as of 1971. This change in church policy was in line with the fundamental reorientation of SED policy in respect of the future prospects for the development of GDR society. These are now viewed as much more long term, complex and threaded with conflict than had been believed in the 1960s. The SED came to the conclusion that religious attitudes would continue to exist for the foreseeable future in their then current denominational form. The churches for their part likewise sought a defined position within the socio-political system of the GDR, which they had now come to regard as a permanent system, and coined the new binding formula of 'the church in socialism', as an expression of their changed view of themselves. The gradual and conflict-ridden advances of church and state in the 1970s culminated in the Chairman of the Council of State, Erich Honecker, receiving the leaders of the Protestant Church on 6 March 1978.

This new policy towards the churches represents a step backwards for the political leadership of the GDR, in that the church is now being allowed back, or allowed for the first time, into areas from which it was previously deliberately driven out or held back. These areas include new housing settlements, television, pastoral care in prisons, state hospitals, homes for the elderly and youth work. The new situation is also bringing a large number of unsolved problems and open questions for the church itself. It is in danger of being used as a haven for dissident groups and thus of becoming politicised. The main concern as far as the church is concerned is to establish a theological definition and grounding for itself as 'the church in socialism'. Furthermore, active church members continue to be predominantly old people, still largely drawn from the middle classes, with middle class attitudes and conduct. In addition, the new church policy by no means implies that the relationship between church, state and party will be free of conflict either now or in the future. The fundamentally different concept of peace held by the church is causing the SED great difficulty even now in areas such as schools, on the question of military education. The political significance of the SED's attempts to establish a well-ordered relationship with the churches lies not least in the fact that for the very first time, the party is permitting a calculated articulation of differences of opinion in public. The positive attitude that this embodies towards the feasibility of achieving 'integration through dissent', is new to the political leadership and until very recently would have been regarded as alien to the system, if not outrightly hostile.

Conclusions and further-reaching considerations

This study began with an examination of the discussion on the theory of state in the GDR. This is a discussion which is currently seeking for concepts which will allow the increasing complexity of the political organisations network to be recorded and analysed in theoretical and practical terms in its social setting, whilst at the same time leaving the 'unrelinquishable' political principles of Marxism—Leninism intact. The critical impetus inherent in discussions of this type even in highly ideologised political systems, such as that of the GDR, thus remains clamped within a narrow evolutionary framework. The need to make better allowance for the wide and conflicting range of interests within GDR society and to view the solving of conflicts of interest positively, as an opportunity for social progress, is now appreciated. The solutions proffered, however, are still marked by the fear that any expression of interest which is not caught up by the organisations system and kept under party control from the time it first emerges, could go too far and thereby endanger the constitutional principles of the system as a whole and threaten its very existence.

From the description of the organisational structures and the multiple intermeshing of the party, state apparatus and social organisations (which Georg Klaus called a 'multi-loop servo-mechanism', in the language of cybernetics) it is clear that Marxist–Leninist theory of state simply sets out to interpret everyday pragmatic political life *ex post facto* and relate it back to Marxism–Leninism. The claim made in the ideology about pursuing scientific politics, which implies that Marxist–Leninist theory processes the results of socio-economic practice as they happen and from this draws scientific conclusions which are applied to determine the next step to be taken by the political leadership, has so far failed to materialise.

Despite this, the question still remains as to what results this evolutionary policy has in fact shown so far — the policy that is manifest in the programmatic theory of further expansion of 'socialist democracy' and in the 'ever increasing involvement of the broad mass of the working population' in the political process — and what prospects it holds for the future. It is impossible to give a conclusive answer at this point. This is not only because of the difficulty inherent in any political prognosis of formalising and passing judgement on complex socio-political phenomena through their selection and weighting; as far as this particular study is concerned, it must be pointed out that it set out solely to trace the intermeshing between the different organisations. The social environment has thus only been covered in passing and the concrete substance and results of policies have been almost totally excluded. Added to this comes the fact that our knowledge of the true attitudes held by GDR citizens stems from occasional meetings with individuals and from critical reading of publications both from and on the subject of the GDR. These sources in themselves are fragmentary and haphazard and, more especially, they give no indication as to the breadth and intensity of wishes, interests and values, how they rank amongst themselves and how, and in which situations they join together to provide motivation for a certain course of action. For this reason, statements on situations and development trends can only be of a hypothetical and temporary nature and are intended more as a challenge for further research than as the secured findings of past research. With this reservation, a number of additional aspects of the internal and external situation in the GDR need to be briefly included in the study at this point in order to allow a better understanding of certain problem areas in the political system.

Not the least of these aspects is the experience that members of society and, indeed, the political leadership in the GDR have gained in attempts to fundamentally modify their own system, and the experience which they have assimilated into their own 'situation consciousness' as a result of the failing of similar undertakings in other socialist states — 17 June 1953, the movements in Hungary and Poland in 1956, the end of the Prague Spring in 1968 and the strikes and signs of breakdown within the political system in Poland, with its climax to date in the imposition of martial law on 13 December 1981. These developments, which were watched in the GDR in the hope that they might be the run-up to different forms of socialist society (with the exception of the recent events in Poland) have led to the widespread view that fundamental change is not possible in the foreseeable future. The exposed situation of the GDR in political and military strategic terms, together with the visible military presence of the Soviet Union, are clear proof to the GDR population of the limited scope for manoeuvre they possess in political matters. The population thus welcomed the policy of détente since it at least brought a certain relief from the pressures of domestic policy and relaxed the isolation of the GDR from its environment at a number of points.

The political leadership, for its part, tends to find its distrust of the people of the GDR and their loyalty strengthened by developments in other socialist states. All the instruments created to offer the political system both internal and external protection have not only been maintained but have also been further expanded. The leadership is however making increasingly sparing use of them, and by making this clearly apparent, is opting more for a deterrent effect than for direct repression. The shock of 1953 is obviously still making itself felt, since even the political leadership feels that the severity of repressive and expropriation measures and the compulsory increase in labour norms at that time went too far.

The political leadership is in difficulty with the repressive side of its political system, both in theoretical and also in practical terms, since this (as we have seen) draws its justification from the struggle for power and the need to secure power during the expropriation phase and from the crushing of the old social order. Furthermore, the concentration of power within the party and in the party leadership is legitimated by the need to complete the different stages of development rapidly and to proceed towards the classless society of the future. Neither of these bases for legitimation still exists in its previous form today — even according to official party texts the foundations of socialist society had been laid by the early 1960s at the latest. Since the end of the 1960s and the start of the 1970s the current stage of construction of developed socialist society has been viewed as a long-term process threaded with conflict, and the communist society of the future on the horizon has lost much of its legitimating power for present-day policy. The emphasis which has been placed on social policy as the chief socio-political instrument since 1971 has highlighted this trend towards a more pragmatic reform policy. It has also brought changes in the legitimation of present-day policies, however. These policies can no longer be justified by the promise of a better tomorrow, but must prove their worth here and now by raising the standard of living and resolving social conflicts etc. After an initial measure of success in the first half of the 1970s, the policy of the 'main task in its unity of economic policy and social policy' has been meeting with increasing difficulty. The increase in the price of raw materials, the world-wide recession and the growing political and economic difficulties within COMECON itself have left their mark on the GDR economy. Although the GDR is managing well in this difficult situation, the economic growth rates it has achieved so far are no longer sufficient to permit an improvement in the range of goods on offer or an increase in the social services, but are simply enough to secure and maintain the achievements of the GDR to date.

A poor economic climate of this type weighs particularly heavily on the GDR. In contrast to the other states of the same type the GDR has so far only been able to define its identity on the basis of its specific socio-political structure. The GDR cannot claim (at least not indisputably) to be the political expression of an independent nation. Although the SED has been speaking of the end of a common national identity with the Federal Republic of Germany since the beginning of the 1970s, it claims for itself no more than the progressive 'creation of a socialist German nation', i.e. a historical process that is still going on. The formula first used by Honecker to define the GDR citizen — 'nationality: German, citizenship: GDR' — which found its way in modified form into the 1976 SED programme, is a fairly accurate reflection of this intermediate situation. It has to remain to be seen how far the GDR's efforts to take over the whole of German history and make the GDR appear to be its conclusion will be successful from the legitimation point of view. Like the fixation on the Federal Republic of Germany as the enemy and the virtually exclusive yardstick by which the achievements of the GDR are measured, attempts of this kind always reawaken memories of the common features of the two Germanies and thereby point to conceivable alternatives to the continued existence of the GDR. In the long term, however, the very fact that the two German states have gone their own way since 1945 and their societies have acquired increasingly different experiences will probably lead them to orientate themselves towards different futures.

There are, however, also a number of aspects of the GDR system which are rated positively in GDR society. These include the extensive social security, especially the lack of unemployment, and certain aspects of youth and education policy. In addition, the political system is able to support some of its requirements on traditional values prevailing in society — the high regard for work, order and self-discipline. An authoritarian, though social patriarchalism is also not new to German history.

These various — and by no means exhaustive — general aspects of the situation in the GDR have to be taken into account in order to arrive at a better understanding of the problems of the political system. This system is characterised by its efforts to take as many areas of society as possible, with all their facets, into the organisations system, whilst leaving intact the distribution of power, on which the Marxist—Leninist theory of dictatorship of the proletariat is based. At first sight it would seem that both these aims have been achieved to a surprising degree. Virtually every GDR citizen is a member of at least one, and in most cases more than one organisation. In view of the amount of honorary work involved in the social organisations, most people will not be able to avoid taking on some kind of function on the lower level and will thus have become caught up in the ideological schooling by this stage at the latest. The party has maintained its key political position as the decisive power throughout the organisations system (as this study has attempted to show), not letting the state apparatus in its many and varied aspects slip out of its control.

The picture is not, however, so simple or harmonious as this might suggest. The party has so many other different organisational connections with its members and individual parts of organisations that it can only create the unity and the necessary distance from individual social fields and political institutions (upon which it has to pass judgement) in the decision-making process. It is not only because the SED is a mass party but also very largely because it is so tied into the organisations structure that it is now finding itself increasingly playing the role of co-ordinator, an indispensable body for deciding between conflicting interests and proposals, instead of applying itself and its wide range of powers to point the way forwards for the political system and for society.

The political system in its complexity also displays a number of other particular features which have the effect of strengthening the special role of the party without, however, in the final instance widening its scope for decision. It is a feature of all big organisations with a hierarchic and centralised structure that the lower levels do not use their powers to their fullest extent if the decisions to be taken fall outside the usual framework or if the decision taken could offend either the people concerned or higher-ranking bodies. Queries addressed to higher-ranking executives, which swamp them with individual cases, slow down the decision-making process without appreciably improving the final result. The blurring of responsibility at individual levels and the possibility of involving the central bodies, which exists in all big organisations, explain the cumbersome nature of the apparatus, while further means of postponing outstanding decisions, or seeking decision routes which appear as the optimum to those concerned, are provided by the overlap in the terms of reference of the different executive channels (between the various state departments, between state and economic executives, between the individual social organisations, and between the mass organisations and state or economic executives). From the citizen's point of view it is not only (and perhaps not even chiefly) the 'omnipotence' of the functionaries that makes bureaucracy so hard to bear, but rather the slowness and obscurity of what goes on both within and between the big organisations. In this situation the party virtually offers itself as an organ to take the final decision, just as it also has the task of jolting the other institutions in order to keep them moving. At all events, functions of this type have very little in common with the role of a revolutionary party which is concerned with keeping in motion a dynamic process leading to the classless society.

There are also various aspects to the integration of GDR citizens within the different social organisations, the people's representative bodies and similar, which need to be rated differently. Where an individual derives direct benefit from his membership (e.g. by being able to pursue his own interests in his spare time or having promotion made easier or, indeed, made possible at all) he will accept the requirements of membership as a fair price. Alongside this, there is a widespread attitude of 'taking what comes' within GDR society. It must after all be remembered that 48.9 per cent of the population was born in or after 1945, and that 64.7 per cent of the population is under 50, and these people have spent their entire active life in the Soviet occupied zone or the GDR. For them the organisations structure of the GDR is normality and although they may find it tedious on many occasions they have nonetheless become used to it and come to terms with it. The organisational constraints, on the other hand, and the agitatorial slogans in what is regarded as empty or false ideological language are felt to be excessive. In these cases 'settling down' means placing greater emphasis on private life, as a sphere set apart from the political world, where one can be on one's own without this implying that one is necessarily opposed to something.[124] The consequences that this type of attitude, which is widespread in the GDR, holds for the political system are not clear-cut. On the one hand, a large number of social activities are conducted in these private corners and conflicts which have arisen in the public sphere are discussed and argued over, thereby relieving the pressure on the political system. On the other hand, though, the energy absorbed in the private sphere is lost to the political and economic process — labour as an accomplishment for society is moving into second place in the catalogue of values and only arouses interest in so far as it is essential for the satisfaction of personal needs. Complaints in official GDR publications about declining work morale and labour discipline bear witness to this. At the same time the integration capacity of the organisations system is being undermined and the hoped-for flow of information from the expansion of consultative participation opportunities (information on social attitudes, suggestions for improvement, and self-commitment) is failing to materialise.

These observations lead on to the question of whether the forms of 'socialist democracy' to date are in fact capable of supplying what the political leadership expects from them at all. The information and criticism function will remain extremely limited so long as expression of interest is caught up by the organisations structure with its stamp of democratic centralism the very moment it occurs. The urgency and social power of interests can never be portrayed in this way. At all events, the political leadership cannot establish the priorities that exist within society in this manner. For the individuals participating in the discussions, on the other hand, this practice has meant that they are not forced to take on different and competing aspirations in their arguments — they are only ever confronted with the already-defined 'collective interest of society'. It is this fact of specific individual interests meeting up with the collective interests of society, as institutionalised in the organisations, at such an early stage which explains why limited dissatisfaction can remain concealed or scarcely visible for a long period of time and why, when it has found its way into the open, it rapidly assumes the proportion of a widespread, general protest, which starts to organise itself outside the political system and is capable of provoking a crisis in the system. As a rule, however, things are different (at least in the GDR). Since it is only in exceptional cases that those involved in the participation process can conceive of their criticism, proposals and suggestions actually leading to changes in leadership behaviour and modified political, social and economic aims, they tend to become resigned. What began as an enthusiastic commitment develops into a burdensome exercise of duty which is only carried out in so far as is absolutely necessary to avoid political trouble or to obtain material gratification through bonus payments.

The fact that this study is restricted to a consideration of different problem areas within the organisations system and society of the GDR may disappoint those who were looking for a clear-cut judgement of development trends in the GDR. In my opinion, however, this kind of ambivalent approach does not represent a shying away from assessment or decision. It is, I feel, inherent in the very situation of the GDR. Despite the cumbersome, restricted and ambiguous nature of the processes of change in the GDR, it has proved possible to show up a certain movement in the political system. The further prospects of this movement will be conditioned not least by the development of political and economic aspects of East–West relations and also by the situation both in and between the socialist states.

Notes

1   In the 1960s the concept 'system' was closely related to the then current influence of cybernetics and the transfer of systems concepts from cybernetics to the social sciences, in particular by Georg Klaus. Cf. Ludz, P.C., *Parteielite im Wandel. Funktionsaufbau, Sozialstruktur und Ideologie der SED-Parteiführung. Eine empirisch-systematische Untersuchung (Schriften des Instituts für Politische Wissenschaft, vol.21)*. Third revised edition, Westdeutscher Verlag, Cologne and Opladen 1970, in particular p.312 ff. In the theory of state it was mainly Heuer, U.-J., *Demokratie und Recht im neuen ökonomischen System der Planung und Leitung der Volkswirtschaft*, Staatsverlag der Deutschen Demokratischen Republik, Berlin (GDR), 1965, who attempted to move in a new direction, partly following Georg Klaus. Both positions were criticised at the end of the 1960s on the grounds that they were ultimately weakening the leadership role of the party and diminishing the importance of democratic centralism. Uwe-Jens Heuer made a further contribution to the present discussion with his publication *Gesellschaftliche Gesetze und politische Organisation*, Dietz Verlag, Berlin (GDR), 1974. Here he partly corrected his earlier position but on some points went further. Examples of more recent publications are Luge, C. and Mand, R., 'Politisches System des Sozialismus, Recht, Demokratie, gesellschaftliche Organisationen', in *Staat und Recht*, vol.28, 1979, no.3, p.232 ff; Baumann, H., 'Zu einigen Grundfragen der Theorie der politischen Systeme', in *Staat und Recht*, vol.29, 1980, no.2, p.155 ff; Will, R. and Wippold, W., 'Staatsform und Form der politischen Organisation der sozialistischen Gesellschaft', in *Staat und Recht*, vol.29, 1980, no.10, p.877 ff;

Schöneburg, K.-H., 'Methodologie staatstheoretischer Forschungen über politische Systeme sozialistischer Macht', in *Staat und Recht*, vol.30, 1981, no.3, p.254 ff. These papers also form the basis of the present analysis. An account of the discussion in the Soviet Union can be found in Schroeder, F.C., *Wandlungen der sowjetischen Staatstheorie (Beck'sche Schwarze Reihe*, vol.193), Verlag C.H. Beck, Munich, 1979. The same author's 'Falsche Übersetzung russischer rechts- und politikwissenschaftlicher Bücher in der DDR', in *Deutschland Archiv*, vol.12, 1979, no.2, p.174 ff, documents attempts to adapt relevant Soviet publications to the internal discussion in the GDR by changing the terminology in translation.

2   *Marxistische—leninistische Staats- und Rechtstheorie. Lehrbuch*, published by the Institut für Theorie des Staates und des Rechtes at the Akademie der Wissenschaften der DDR, 3rd revised edition, Staatsverlag der Deutschen Demokratischen Republik, Berlin (GDR) 1980, p.356 ff.

3   Ibid., p.250. See also under 'politische Organisation der sozialistischen Gesellschaft', in *Kleines politisches Wörterbuch*, 3rd revised edition, Dietz Verlag, Berlin (GDR), 1978, p.699 ff.

4   See especially Luge and Mand, op.cit. (Note 1), p.233, and Baumann, op.cit. (Note 1), pp. 155 and 159 ff.

5   Schöneburg, K.-H., op.cit. (Note 1). Schöneburg is also co-author of the text book quoted in Note 3.

6   Ibid., p.260 f.

7   Ibid., p.256.

8   Ibid.

9   Ibid., p.255. In another passage of his article Schöneburg says 'It is thus important for the function of the political system that it can never be orientated towards a simple reproduction of the status quo, balancing the existing contrasts in society, or solely stabilising existing power relationships. On the contrary it is much more a matter of reproducing what exists by way of a transitional stage in a broader reproduction, of protecting what has been achieved as a necessary part of qualitative development and change and of revealing and resolving social contradictions so that the historical process can be consciously and deliberately fashioned'; ibid., p.262.

10 Ibid., p.256 f.

11 Ibid., p.263.

12 Ibid., p.261.

13 Ibid., p.262.

14 Ibid., p.263.

15 'Politik', in Klaus, G. and Buhr, M. (eds), *Philosophisches Wörterbuch*, eleventh edition, vol.2, VEB Bibliographisches Institut, Leipzig 1975, p.941 ff.; 'Politik', in *Kleines politisches Wörterbuch*, op.cit. (Note 3), p.693 ff.

16   'Macht', in *Philosophisches Wörterbuch*, op.cit. (Note 15), p.733 ff.; 'Macht', in *Kleines politisches Wörterbuch*, op.cit. (Note 3), p.542.
17   An example of this and following comments may be found in Weichelt, W., 'Zur Realisierung der gesamtgesellschaftlichen Interessen durch die politische Organisation des Sozialismus', in *Staat und Recht*, vol.30, 1981, no.4, p.290 ff.
18   Cf. ibid., p.293; 'The problem consists . . . not in the balancing of interests but in careful determination of the concrete requirements of the governed progress of society at the time together with the state measures required for its realisation'.
19   On the discussion on contradictions see the paragraph 'Marxistische Konflikttheorie in der Sowjetunion und in der DDR', in Ludz, P.C., *Ideologiebegriff und marxistische Theorie. Ansätze zu einer immanenten Kritik*, Westdeutscher Verlag, Opladen, 1976, p.213 ff.
20   The concept 'developed socialist society' used in the Marxist–Leninist theory of communist social formation expresses the idea that this is a society that has definitively broken with the previous form of society but has not yet reached the stage of a 'perfect' communist society. Of special significance is the shift in time scales as compared with the 1950s and 1960s when, according to the Soviet Party in its party programme, the time was then right for a start on the transition to communism. Cf the statement on this made by Leonid Brezhnev at the 16th Soviet Communist Party Congress: 'Rechenschaftsbericht des Zentralkomitees der KPdSU und die nächsten Aufgaben der Partei in der Innen- und Aussenpolitik', in *Neues Deutschland*, vol.36, 24 February 1981, p.11. On the subject of the preparation of a new party programme Brezhnev says 'our development of communism will be accomplished via the stage of a developed socialist society. That is . . . a necessary, *long historical period, which follows the laws of history* (my italics H.Z.) in the development of a communist social formation. This is the conclusion that the party has drawn and refined over the past few years and must, at all events, be reflected in due form in the party programme'.
21   Cf. Buhr, M. and Kosing, A., 'Widerspruch', in *Kleines Wörterbuch der marxistisch-leninistischen Philosophie*, 2nd revised edition, Dietz Verlag, Berlin (GDR), 1974, p.302 ff., particularly p.304 f.
22   Götz Dieckmann, Director of the Faculty of History and Holder of the Chair for the History of the International Labour Movement at the SED party university: 'In the developed socialist society there is no class antagonism. If, however, rifts occur in society as a result of a one-sided policy, mistaken priorities in economic policy, shortcomings in ideological work or other reasons . . . , if the party does not correctly express class interests in its policy (not the group interests of certain

parts of the working class but real class interests), then contradictions arise, which can expand into serious social conflicts'. In the same context, Roland Bauer, a member of the SED Central Committee, spoke of the 'apprenticeship fee we paid in 1953'. This reference contains the admission that it was a mistaken SED policy that led to the riots of 16 and 17 June 1953. Cf 'Die Partei und die Gestaltung des entwickelten Sozialismus. Kollektives Interview der DDR', in *Probleme des Friedens und des Sozialismus*, vol.24 (1981), no.6, pp. 731 and 734.

23 Roland Bauer commented only recently on the problem of 'how the party learns from the masses and takes their reaction to (party) decisions and actions into account'. Bauer's use of the phrase 'takes into account' illustrates the point I make in the text. The specific instruments he names for establishing opinions are: (1) the published resolutions and documents of the party and state, together with the ensuing discussions; (2) experience gained in party members' assemblies, reports by activists on their direct encounters with the population, the assessment of petitions from citizens submitted to party executives, state executives and the mass media; (3) the experience of leading party functionaries gained at party meetings or in 'discussions with specific circles of the population'; (4) sociological surveys, 'which produce certain results, e.g. quantifiable comparative data, which is welcome'. Cf. *Die Partei und die Gestaltung des entwickelten Sozialismus*, op.cit. (Note 22), p.732 f.

24 Afanasiev, V.G., *Soziale Information: Leitung der Gesellschaft*, Staatsverlag der Deutschen Demokratischen Republik, Berlin (GDR), 1976, p.80.

25 Loose, W. and Schumann, M., 'Sozialistische Demokratie und Erkenntnis gesellschaftlicher Gesetze', in *Dreissig Jahre DDR. Aktuelle Fragen der Entwicklung von Staat, Recht und Demokratie (Aktuelle Beiträge der Staats- und Rechtswissenschaft*, no.205), Selbstverlag der Akademie für Staats- und Rechts-wissenschaft der DDR, Potsdam-Babelsberg 1979, vol.1, p.31 ff, here p.40.

26 The meshing of the 'scientific approach' with the 'leading role of the party' is illuminated *inter alia* by the following comments: 'The question as to the recognition or non-recognition of the leading role of the party in socialist society thus inevitably changes into the question of the recognition or non-recognition of objective laws'. '. . . the question of the leading role of the party (is) part, and a very important part, of the question about the scientific conception of socialism.' Cf. *Die Partei und die Gestaltung des entwickelten Sozialismus*, op.cit. (Note 22), pp. 726 and 727.

27 Cf. 'Zentralismus' in *Philosophisches Wörterbuch*, op.cit. (Note 15), p.1323.

28 On the following see 'Demokratischer Zentralismus' and 'Souveränität', in *Kleines politisches Wörterbuch*, op.cit. (Note 3), p.158 f. and p.789.
29 Cf. *Verwaltungsrecht. Lehrbuch*, published by the Akademie für Staats- und Rechtswissenschaft der DDR, Potsdam-Babelsberg, Staatsverlag der Deutschen Demokratischen Republik, Berlin (GDR), 1979, p.165.
30 On cadre policy in the GDR, cf Glaessner, G.-J., *Herrschaft durch Kader. Leitung der Gesellschaft und Kaderpolitik in der DDR am Beispiel des Staatsapparats (Schriften des Zentralinstituts für sozialwissenschaftliche Forschung der Freien Universität Berlin*, vol.28), Westdeutscher Verlag, Opladen 1977, especially p.218 ff. and p.291 ff.; Glaessner, G.-J. and Rudolph, I., *Macht durch Wissen. Zum Zusammenhang von Bildungspolitik, Bildungssystem und Kaderqualifizierung in der DDR. Eine politischsoziologische Untersuchung (Schriften des Zentralinstituts für sozialwissenschaftliche Forschung der Freien Universität Berlin*, vol.30), Westdeutscher Verlag, Opladen 1978, especially p.27 ff. See also under 'Kader', 'Kaderarbeit', 'Kaderpolitik', 'Kaderprogramm' in *Kleines politisches Wörterbuch*, op.cit. (Note 3), p.420 f.
31 Cf. *Die DDR-Verfassungen*, edited and with introduction by Herwig Roggemann (*Quellen zur Rechtsvergleichung: Aus dem Osteuropa-Institut an der Freien Universität Berlin. Die Gesetzgebung der sozialistischen Staaten: Einzelausgabe*, No.7), 2nd revised and enlarged edition, Berlin-Verlag, Berlin 1976, p.114.
32 'Programm der Sozialistischen Einheitspartei Deutschlands' and 'Statut der Sozialistischen Einheitspartei Deutschlands', in *Protokoll der Verhandlungen des IX. Parteitages der Sozialistischen Einheitspartei Deutschlands im Palast der Republik in Berlin 18 bis 22 Mai 1976*, Dietz Verlag, Berlin (GDR) 1976, p.209 ff. and p.267 ff.
33 'Statut der Sozialistischen Einheitspartei Deutschlands', op.cit. (Note 32), p.267. Individual references from the statute will not be given in the remainder of the text. On the structure and functioning of the SED cf. also Neugebauer, G., *Partei und Staatsapparat in der DDR. Aspekte der Instrumentalisierung des Staatsapparats durch die SED (Schriften des Zentralinstituts für sozialwissenschaftliche Forschung der Freien Universität Berlin*, vol.29) Westdeutscher Verlag, Opladen 1978, p.26 ff. and ibid., 'Veranderungen in der Organisationspolitik der SED', in *Der X. Parteitag der SED. 35 Jahre SED-Politik. Versuch einer, Bilanz. Vierzehnte Tagung zum Stand der DDR-Forschung in der Bundesrepublik Deutschland 9. bis 12. Juni 1981* (Edition *Deutschland Archiv*) Verlag Wissenschaft und Politik, Köln 1981, p.112 ff.

34   There are also county executives in a number of big enterprises (collective combines) and also in the National People's Army and the Railways, for instance, which have their own party organisations extending over the entire territory of the GDR. GOs and APOs are sub-divided into party groups once they have reached a certain size. In 1980 there were 52,226 GOs, 22,947 APOs and 89,516 party groups. Cf. Neugebauer, G., 'Veränderungen in der Organisationspolitik', op.cit. (Note 33), p.117; in addition the information in Fricke, K.W., 'Im Vorfeld des X. SED-Parteitages. Bilanz der Parteiwahlen 1980/81', in *Deutschland Archiv*, vol.14 (1981), no.4, p.338 ff., especially p.339.
35   On the composition and terms of reference of the SED executives cf under 'Grundorganisationen der SED', 'Kreisparteiorganisationen der SED', 'Bezirksparteiorganisationen der SED', in *DDR-Handbuch*, published by the Federal Ministry for Intra-German Affairs, 2nd completely revised and enlarged edition, Verlag Wissenschaft und Politik, Cologne 1979, p.496 ff., p.616 ff., p.212 ff.
36   For an interpretation of the personnel decisions taken at the 10th SED party congress see Fricke, K.W., 'Signale nach innen'. Der X. Parteitag der SED', in *Deutschland Archiv*, vol.14 (1981), no.5, p.499 ff. and Kuppe, J. and Kupper S., 'Parteitag der Kontinuität' in *Deutschland Archiv*, vol.14 (1981), no.7, p.714 ff. In addition, Schwarzenbach, R., 'Zur "führenden Rolle" der SED', in *X. Parteitag der SED. Gesellschafts- und wissenschaftspolitische Aspekte* (vol.1981, no.4) published by the Institut für Gesellschaft und Wissenschaft (IGW) at the University of Erlangen-Nuremberg, Erlangen 1981, p.11 ff. For comparisons with the composition of earlier SED Central Committees see Ludz, P.C., *Parteielite im Wandel*, op.cit. (Note 1), p.151 ff. and running accounts in the periodical *Deutschland Archiv*.
37   The classification in the table is based on that in *Neues Deutschland* for the organisational areas and executive levels of the individual full members and candidates. It may be assumed that these data are focused on chief functions. Despite this, decisions had to be taken in a number of cases that were not clearcut and these could also have come out differently. The 'veterans' group, for instance, includes persons such as Abusch and Gotsche, who as writers could equally well have been classified under the cultural sphere. The same applies for Hilde Benjamin, who is still listed as a Professor at the Academy of Constitutional and Legal Science of the GDR, and could thus have been classified under the science sphere. The decisive factor in including her under 'veterans' was that she has given up her true leadership function in the meantime, on account of her age, and her present activities can be regarded as being on a more or less part time basis. On the other hand, persons who from the age point of view could have been listed under 'veterans' are still included under 'mass and social organisations'.

One of these is Hans Jendretzky, Chairman of the FDGB group in the People's Chamber, together with Käthe Kern, Chairman of the DFD group in the People's Chamber, and executive members in the Committee of Anti-Fascist Resistance Fighters. These reclassifications would not, however, produce a significant difference. A further point which could be questioned is the classification of scientists from the Central Institute for Socialist Economic Management, the Academy of Social Sciences, the Institute of Marxism–Leninism and the party university, under the organisational area 'Party — Central Level'. The classification selected here was based on the wish to show up the direct representation of full-time party organs in the Central Committee. The group of party scientists includes 6 full members and one candidate of the SED Central Committee. This makes it roughly as strong as the 'Science' group (5 full members and 4 candidates) which takes in persons from scientific institutes who are not directly assigned to the party.

38 Roland Bauer, op.cit. (Note 22), p.733, has pointed out that the public is not, after all, given full information on the work of the Central Committee: 'We take it for granted that plenary sessions of the Central Committee are held regularly and that at each Central Committee plenary a report is first given by the Politburo on its work since the previous plenary ... *With the exception of certain inner-party details* (my italics – H.Z.) everything is reported in full in *Neues Deutschland* and other newspapers; the same procedure is followed for the discussion contributions'. In view of the significance attached to precisely these 'inner-party details', this statement allows us to assume that a Western observer will not have enough material on which to base a definitive assessment of the course of Central Committee meetings.

39 Cf. on the composition of the Politburo: *Neues Deutschland*, vol.36, no.92 dated 17 April 1981, p.5 – The Chairman of the Central Revision Commission (ZRK), Kurt Seibt, is neither a member of the Central Committee nor the Politburo. Nevertheless, he is still to be included in the central party leadership. The revision commissions that exist on all levels of party organisation monitor the observance of organisational regulations, especially the observance of party resolutions, as well as the financial and administrative side of party work.

40 The full-time 'apparatus' of the Central Committee and the district and county executives cannot be discussed in detail here. (Party work in the GO is largely voluntary.) Little is known about the size or detailed breakdown of the apparatus. The number of full-time employees in the Central Committee apparatus (not including the central education and research institutes) is estimated at more than 2,000 and they work in more than 40 departments or working groups. The Central Committee departments are the party's organisational units

which, according to their terms of reference, are in constant contact with state institutions (the ministries, the Planning Commission and so on) and the mass organisations working with them in a controlling and directing capacity. They prepare material, analyses and personnel decisions for the Central Committee Secretariat and for the Politburo, direct the lower-ranking specialist departments of the district executives (estimated number of full-time personnel in the district executive party apparatus: 180–250 in each district) together with the GOs in the collective combines, the county executives in the central state institutions etc. The importance of the apparatus is reflected in the fact that, by statute, the heads of department have to be confirmed in office by the elected members of the party executives, and hence, at central level, by the Central Committee itself. All the same, 17 of these departmental heads and one deputy departmental head from the Central Committee apparatus are currently either full members or candidates of the present Central Committee. See on this the appropriate headings in *DDR-Handbuch* (Note 35), Neugebauer, G., *Partei und Staatsapparat* op.cit. (Note 33), p.59 f. and p.212 f. and also Kuppe, J. and Kupper, S., 'Parteitag der Kontinuität', op.cit. (Note 37), p.715 f.

41 On the 'legitimatory' aspects of participation cf von Beyme, K., *Economics and Politics within Socialist Systems. A Comparative and Development Approach*, Praeger, New York 1982, pp. 394 ff.

42 The problem of the parallelism or limitations of varying and unclear terminology in the official language of the GDR has been examined by Peter Christian Ludz in his book *Mechanismen der Herrschaftssicherung. Eine sprachpolitische Analyse gesellschaftlichen Wandels in der DDR*, Carl Hanser Verlag, Munich/Vienna 1980.

43 Cf. Staritz, D., *Sozialismus in einem halben Land. Zur Programmatik und Politik der KPD/SED in der Phase der antifaschistisch-demokratischen Umwälzung in der DDR* (*Politik* No.69), Verlag Klaus Wagenbach, Berlin 1976, p.40, Note 23.

44 On the question of the 'unification' see Staritz, D., op.cit. (Note 43), p.60 ff. for further references. On developments in membership and on the question of the mass party in the early days of the KPD/SPD/SED's history and the measures taken to convert them into a Leninist party see Stern, C., *Die SED. Ein Handbuch über Aufbau, Organisation und Funktion des Parteiapparates* (*Rote Weissbücher* No.14) Verlag Rote Weissbücher, Cologne 1954, p.152 ff; this is an older work but is still well worth reading and contains valuable material. Ibid., *Porträt einer bolschewistischen Partei. Entwicklung, Funktion und Situation der SED*, Verlag für Politik und Wirtschaft, Cologne 1957, p.46 ff.

45   This and subsequent information on the current social structure of the party is based on *Volksarmee*, vol.1981, no.20, p.7; Honecker, E., 'Bericht des Zentralkomitees der Sozialistischen Einheitspartei Deutschlands an den X. Parteitag der SED', in *Neues Deutschland*, vol.36, no.87, dated 12 April 1981, p.12 f, together with data from the *Statistisches Jahrbuch 1981 der Deutschen Demokratischen Republik*, published by the Central Statistical Board, vol.26, Staatsverlag der Deutschen Demokratischen Republik, Berlin 1981.

46   Classification under the individual large social groups is difficult in a number of respects. Officers, full-time party functionaries and state functionaries, for instance, are frequently counted under the working class despite their university qualifications and leadership functions. The sociological concept 'intelligentsia' is just as disputed and hence just as unclear as that of 'white collar worker'. Honecker lists the 480,970 members of the intelligentsia in the SED as 125,000 engineers and economists, 117,000 teachers and education workers, 19,000 working in the cultural sphere. On the more recent discussion of terminology and social structure see Erbe, G., *Arbeiterklasse und Intelligenz in der DDR. Soziale Annäherung von Produktionsarbeiterschaft und wissenschaftlichtechnischer Intelligenz im Industriebetrieb? (Schriften des Zentralinstituts für sozialwissenschaftliche Forschung der Freien Universität Berlin*, vol.38) Westdeutscher Verlag, Opladen, 1982.

47   For instance, there are only 19 full members and 5 candidates of the Central Committee elected by the SED at its 10th Party Congress who are women, out of a total of 156 full members and 57 candidates. See also the analysis conducted up to 1971, which is still basically relevant, by Gast, G., *Die politische Rolle der Frau in der DDR (Studien zur Sozialwissenschaft*, vol.17) Bertelsmann Universitätsverlag, Düsseldorf 1973. More recent information on selected areas is to be found in Lemke, C., 'Frauen in leitenden Funktionen. Probleme der Frauenpolitik in der DDR', in *Deutschland Archiv*, vol.14 (1981), no.9, p.970 ff.

48   On this see 'Grundorganisationen und Parteisekretäre', in *Neuer Weg. Organ des Zentralkomitees der SED für Fragen des Parteilebens*, vol.36 (1981), no.7, third cover page, and Neugebauer, G., 'Veränderungen in der Organisationspolitik', op.cit. (Note 33), p.121 ff.

49   There is no precise information available on the number of university and technical college graduates in the GDR population as a whole or in the working population. The percentage of the working population with university or technical college qualifications amongst the working population with vocational qualifications within the socialist economy is given at 6.67 per cent and 12.14 per cent respectively = 18.81 per cent for 1980.

50   Cf. for instance, the references given in Zimmerman, H., 'Politische Aspekte in der Herausbildung, dem Wandel und der Verwendung des Konzepts "Wissenschaftlich—technische Revolution" in der DDR', in *Wissenschaftlich—technische Revolution und industrieller Arbeitsprozess. Neunte Tagung zum Stand der DDR-Forschung in der Bundesrepublik 8.—11. Juni 1976. Deutschland Archiv*, Special Issue, p.33, note 39. Whilst at the beginning of the 1970s there was an attempt to reduce the number of students from intelligentsia families (though this did not meet with widespread success), in more recent publications the trend towards self-recruitment within the intelligentsia is clearly rated more positively, from the efficiency angle. Cf Zimmerman, H., 'Zu einigen politischen Aspekten des X. Parteitages der SED' in *Der X. Parteitag der SED*, op.cit. (Note 33), p.31 ff.

51   Cf. Glaessner, G.-J., *Herrschaft durch Kader*, op.cit., and Glaessner, G.-J. and Rudolph, I., *Macht durch Wissen*, op.cit. (both Note 30). A survey of the current schooling system may be found in 'Die marxistisch—leninistische Aus- und Weiterbildung der Mitglieder und Kandidaten der SED', in *Neuer Weg. Organ des Zentralkomitees der SED für Fragen des Parteilebens*, vol.35 (1980), no.23, third cover page.

52   On the most recent Soviet interpretation of the state of development attained and future prospects see the quotation from Brezhnev's speech in Note 20. For more details on this problem see the works given in Note 50 and Zimmermann, H., 'The GDR in the 1970s', in *Problems of Communism*, vol.XXVII (1978), no.2, in particular p.21 ff. (revised and updated version: ibid., 'Die DDR in den 70er Jahren. Zu einigen Aspekten der innenpolitischen Situation der DDR', in Erbe, G., et al, *Politik, Wirtschaft und Gesellschaft in der DDR. Studientexte für die politische Bildung*, 2nd revised and enlarged edition, Westdeutscher Verlag, Opladen, 1980, in particular p.39 ff.).

53   Mückenberger, E., 'Bericht in der Mandatsprüfungskommission an den X. Parteitag', in *Neues Deutschland*, vol.36, no.89 dated 14 April 1981, p.4. Figures on the age structure of SED membership for the beginning of 1980 (?): 23.1 per cent younger than 30; 42.2 per cent younger than 40; 65.1 per cent younger than 50. Data taken from 'Zusammensetzung der Mitgliedschaft der SED', in *Neuer Weg. Organ des Zentralkomitees der SED für Fragen des Parteilebens*, vol.35, (1980) no.18, third cover page.

54   A highly developed system of awards in the GDR plays a particular role in the formation of a new meritocracy, which has been proven within the existing socio-political system. The orders and other awards convey both social and political prestige, which does not, however, necessarily coincide with the prestige the individual really enjoys in the eyes of his peers. The correlation between awards received and

socio-political upward mobility can be illustrated, for example, by the make-up of the delegates of the 10th SED Party Congress. Of the 2,560 delegates with the right to vote, 2,216 had received high state awards. These included 108 holders of the Karl-Marx Order ('Karl-Marx Orden'), 19 holders of the Star of International Friendship ('Stern der Völkerfreundschaft'), 938 holders of the Fatherland Service Medal ('Vaterländischer Verdienstorden'), 59 holders of the National Prize ('Nationalpreis'), 420 holders of the Banner of Labour Order ('Banner der Arbeit'); 4 delegates held the title Hero of the GDR ('Held der DDR') and 101 the title Hero of Labour ('Held der Arbeit'). (Data from Mückenberger, E., op.cit., Note 53.) On the awards system in the GDR see Bartel, F., *Auszeichnungen der Deutschen Demokratischen Republik von den Anfängen bis zur Gegenwart*. Militärverlag der Deutschen Demokratischen Republik, Berlin 1979.

55 SED Programme, op.cit. (Note 32), p.237. On the state of the discussion regarding theory of state and law in the GDR see in addition to the text books already cited — *Marxistisch—leninistische Staats- und Rechtstheorie* (Note 2) and *Verwaltungsrecht* (Note 29) — the Soviet reference work that has bearing on the discussion: *Marxistisch—leninistische allgemeine Theorie des Staates und des Rechtes*, vol.3 (*Der sozialistische Staat*) Staatsverlag der Deutschen Demokratischen Republik, Berlin 1975, and also *Staatsrecht der DDR. Lehrbuch*, published by the Academy of Constitutional and Legal Science of the GDR, Staatsverlag der Deutschen Demokratischen Republik, Berlin 1977, and *Einführung in die marxistisch—leninistische Staats- und Rechtslehre*, published by the Academy of Constitutional and Legal Science of the GDR, Dietz Verlag, Berlin 1979. The running discussion is also to be found in the periodical *Staat und Recht* published by this same Academy. I also owe thanks to Walter Völkel who gave me access to his as yet unpublished paper on the development and phases of the discussion on theory of state in the Soviet Occupied Zone/GDR from 1945 to 1977. This provided me with many ideas though it is not possible for me to repeat or discuss his highly differentiated considerations within the context of this essay.

56 On the question of the 'withering away of the state' see *Marxistisch—leninistische allgemeine Theorie des Staates und des Rechtes*, op.cit. (Note 55), in particular p.333 ff. The following internal social prerequisites are now being given for the transition to 'communist self-administration' (op.cit. p.349): 1. Plentiful supply of material and cultural commodities; 2. standardised ownership forms, giving uniform communist ownership; 3. overcoming of the class differences that still prevail between workers and peasants and the associated elimination of the essential differences between town and countryside; 4. elimination of the essential differences between intel-

lectual and physical labour; 5. (for the Soviet Union) complete elimination of residual nationalist feeling and increasing rapprochement of all nations and nationalities; 6. shortening of the working day; 7. a high level of culture for all members of society; 8. the disappearance of social phenomena such as criminality and violation of the law in general; 9. the all-round development of democracy and the instilling of the firm habit of participation in self-administration into the population as a whole; 10. the imparting and anchoring of the communist moral outlook within all citizens. Added to this comes the foreign policy condition that 'socialism will have been victorious and found a firm footing throughout the world', 'and thereby the causes that lead to war have been eliminated' (op.cit., p.351).

57   Cf. *Marxistisch—leninistische allgemeine Theorie des Staates und des Rechtes*, op.cit. (Note 55), p.343 f.

58   Lenin, V.I., 'Die gross Initiative' (1919) in *Werke*, vol.29 (March—August 1919), p.416. The same essay contains evidence of further fundamental views held by Lenin, which have remained effective right through to the present: his belief in scientific and technical progress, in the capacity and necessity to take over capitalist technology, and in large-scale production as the most productive form of industrial organisation. He thus speaks for instance (op.cit., p.412 f.) of the need to lead 'the masses of the working population . . . on to the path towards creation of a new social bond, a new labour discipline, a new labour organisation, which combines the last word in science and capitalist technology with the mass amalgamation of consciously working people, bringing socialist mass production into existence'.

59   Cf. the article by Helga Michalsky in this book and for more details on my own view: Zimmermann, H., 'Sozialpolitik als Gesellschaftspolitik?' in *DDR-Report*, vol.9 (1976), no.12, p.749 ff.

60   A brief survey of the legal system in the GDR may be found in Brunner, G., *Einführung in das Recht der DDR (Schriftenreihe der Juristischen Schulung*, no.29.) Second revised and enlarged edition, C.H. Beck'sche Verlagsbuchhandlung, Munich 1979, especially p.24 ff. Examples of the 'biased' re-interpretation of norms in the hand-down Bourgeois Civil Code (BGB) in the early years may be found in Pfarr, H.M., *Auslegungstheorie und Auslegungspraxis im Zivil- und Arbeitsrecht der DDR (Schriften zur Rechtstheorie,* no.30), Duncker and Humblot, Berlin 1972, p.77 ff.

61   On the discussion on administrative law see Ziegler, U., 'Zur Diskussion um Verwaltungsrecht und Verwaltungsrechtswissenschaft in der DDR', in *Deutschland Archiv*, vol.7 (1974) no.10, p.1036 ff. The results achieved so far are set out in the text book *Verwaltungsrecht*, op.cit. (Note 29). This also contains valid statements on the possibilities for petitions and complaints open to the citizen and on state liability law etc.

62 Cf. *Marxistisch—leninistische allgemeine Theorie des Staates und des Rechts*, op.cit. (Note 55), p.98 ff. In the prevailing opinion of the GDR theory of state the task of regulating working hours and consumption is seen solely as a sub-function of economic and organisational state activity (cf. *Marxistisch—leninistische Staats- und Rechtstheorie*, op.cit. (Note 2), p.317). Reference should also be made to differentiation in the foreign policy functions of the socialist state: defence against attack from outside; co-operation and mutual aid between the socialist states; support for developing countries and liberation movements; the 'struggle for peace, for peaceful coexistence of countries with different social orders'.

63 Cf. *Marxistisch—leninistische Staats- und Rechtstheorie*, op.cit. (Note 2), pp. 317 and 319. For the Soviet Union, which according to Marxist—Leninist contexts, has already reached the higher stage of development of the 'state of the whole people' it is assumed that a chief internal function of this type 'providing members of society with a wide range of social services' (social policy) already exists (op.cit. p.326 and *Marxistisch—leninistische allgemeine Theorie des Staates und des Rechts*, op.cit (Note 55), p.120).

64 Cf. *Marxistisch—leninistische Staats- und Rechtstheorie*, op.cit. (Note 2), p.312 ff.; *Marxistisch—leninistische allgemeine Theorie des Staates und des Rechtes*, op.cit. (Note 55), p.112 f. The different effects and scope of repressive measures during the different development phases of the GDR system are not, however, reflected in the Marxist—Leninist Theory of State and Law. During the early years, depriving certain groups subject to expropriation of their rights and the persecution of these groups may eliminate specific resistance and hence obstacles to growth. At least, repression of this kind can be ideologically and theoretically grounded in the context of Marxism—Leninism. Conflicts such as those in Czechoslovakia or the current conflicts in Poland, however, result predominantly from the failure of their systems. The repression measures are thus directed against the new socio-political structures that the communist parties, i.e. the communist party leadership itself, has created, and against the dissatisfaction that has arisen from this. The application of internal and external means of repression may secure the distribution of power and the existence of the system (for the short term) but it cannot bring about elimination of the reasons behind the conflict. These measures are first used to secure the very factor that has given rise to the conflict — a political, economic and social system that does not satisfy the manifest needs of large social groups. If there is no self-criticism, taking in the principles of the system itself, by way of follow-up to the repression measures, then this will result in a further drifting apart of political system and society (withdrawal into private life, orientation

solely towards direct personal advantage, opportunist conduct etc.).
65   Cf.the article by Gero Neugebauer in this book.
66   SED programme, op.cit. (Note 32), p.237. An evaluation of such Marxist–Leninist concepts really calls for a detailed analysis of the functions of ideology in political systems of the soviet type, in particular in the GDR. Such an analysis is not possible here, however, and a reference to the following functions of Marxism–Leninism will have to suffice: 1. the function of masking the true power structures; 2. the function of legitimating the leading role of the party and its policy; 3. the scientific, analytical function (analyses of social and political conditions are still carried out essentially with the aid of Marxism–Leninism and their results cast in the concepts of Marxism–Leninism); 4. ideological statements do not restrict themselves to reflecting the status quo but always contain directions for changing the status quo as well. They are programmatic formulae relating to the more satisfying future which will allegedly be definitely achieved if party policy is carried out; 5. ideology still functions as the most important means of linguistic communication within the political system; it is, as it were, the 'system language'. It goes without saying that the masking and legitimatory functions cannot be fully reconciled with the scientific and programmatic functions and hence that a mixture of different intentions will be found in every ideological statement. Despite this, a critical ideological analysis of Marxism–Leninism is necessary before statements can be made on how the party rates itself and on its future intentions.
67   Party resolutions form 'the foundation of all state activity. They determine the directions, the specific tasks and aims of the application of state power, they ensure that state activity is conducted according to plan and with resolve and they constitute the chief form in which the party of the working class realises its steering and guiding role vis-à-vis the socialist state. *Party resolutions do not however represent a substitute for the state will formation process* (my italics – H.Z.) but instead develop its class foundation, give state activity its class orientation and determine its political line. The steering and guiding role of the Marxist–Leninist party of the working class in state activity continues to be realised through the basic organisations of the party in the state organs and the practical state activity of the party members'. (*Marxistisch–leninistische Staats- und Rechtstheorie*, op.cit. (Note 2), p.245).
68   On the social make-up and level of education of state cadres: 'Over 60% of the leaders and scientific staff of the central organs of the state apparatus come from the working class in terms of their social origin. Almost 50% of them have been workers themselves. Ninety-six per cent have technical college or university qualifications. In the district and county councils more than 75% of members are workers and

peasants in terms of their social origin. For the burgomasters of the towns and communities the figure is more than 88%, of whom more than 80% have previously been workers themselves. Ninety-nine per cent of district council members and 94% of county council members hold university or technical college qualifications, as do 36.1 per cent of their staff. One in three deputies and almost one in four burgomasters in the GDR is a woman'. (*Verwaltungsrecht*, op.cit. (Note 29), p.162).

69 Fundamental work on this problem area: Neugebauer, G., *Partei und Staatsapparat in der DDR*, op.cit. (Note 33). Although some of the facts are now out of date, Richert, E., *Macht ohne Mandat. Der Staatsapparat in der sowjetischen Bezatzungszone Deutschlands* (*Schriften des Instituts für politische Wissenschaft*, vol.11), second enlarged and revised edition, Westdeutscher Verlag, Cologne and Opladen 1963. This still retains its significance through a comprehensive account of all the problems of the GDR political system. From the angle of constitutional law see *Die DDR-Verfassungen*, op.cit. (Note 31) and the detailed comments on the constitution (albeit without consideration of the far-reaching constitutional modifications of 7 October 1974) by Siegfried Mampel, *Die sozialistische Verfassung der Deutschen Demokratischen Republik. Text und Kommentar*, Alfred Metzner Verlag, Frankfurt a. Main, 1972.

70 On the organisational structure of the National Front see 'Aufbau der Nationalen Front', in *Neuer Weg. Organ des ZK der SED für Fragen des Parteilebens*, vol.36 (1981), no.3, third cover page. (According to this source, 335,000 citizens work in the 17,500 NF committees; 147,000 of these are SED members, 70,000 belong to block parties and 118,000 do not belong to any party.) See also *Deutsche Demokratische Republik. Handbuch*, VEB Verlag Enzyklopädie, Leipzig 1979, p.276 ff. especially p.278. In addition to the SED and the four block parties 26 associations are named as working within the NF. The NF developed out of the People's Congress Movement ('Volkskongressbewegung'), a mass movement initiated by the SED in 1947, which (with the participation of the parties and mass organisations of the Soviet occupied zone, though also of the KPD (German Communist Party) and some groups and persons from the Western zones) supported the German policy of the party and sponsored three German People's Congresses for Unity and a Just Peace ('Deutsche Volkskongresse für Einheit und gerechten Frieden') held in its name. The second People's Congress elected the German People's Council ('Deutscher Volksrat') as the 'leading organ' and this Council worked out a draft constitution on the basis of a directive from the SED, which was then passed (13 March 1949). This draft was definitively accepted by the third People's Congress (30 May 1949), which was the first to be elected

on the basis of uniform lists by the population of the Soviet occupation zone who held the right to vote. The Third German People's Council established itself as a provisional People's Chamber on 7 October 1949 and brought the first constitution of the GDR into force. On the same day the National Front of the Democratic Germany ('Nationale Front des demokratischen Deutschland') established itself out of the People's Congress Movement on the basis of a resolution from the party board (later to become the Central Committee). In order to stress the alliance character of the NF and emphasise its formal status above the parties, the Presidents of the NF to date have been natural scientists not belonging to a party: 1950—1981, the Chemist Prof. Dr Erich Correns, and as of 1981, the Chemist Prof. Dr Lothar Kolditz.

71   Article 3 of the 1968/74 GDR Constitution reads: 'The alliance of all the forces of the people finds its organisational expression in the National Front of the German Democratic Republic. In the National Front of the German Democratic Republic the parties and the mass organisations unite all the forces of the people in working jointly towards the development of socialist society. In this way they bring all citizens to live together in a socialist community according to the principle that each bears responsibility for the whole'. (*Die DDR-Verfassungen*, op.cit. (Note 31), p.115).

72   The stages of SED alliance policy are reflected in the history of the 'block'. When parties were permitted to form under Order No.2 dated 10 June 1945 from the Soviet Military Administration in Germany (SMAD), the KPD (Communist Party) was set up on 11 June 1945, the SPD on 15 June 1945 (the KPD and SPD merged to form the SED on 21/22 April 1946) the CDU on 22 June 1945 and the LDPD on 5 July 1945. In view of the desperate social and economic situation and the expected difficulties in building up a democratic Germany after the war and overcoming National Socialism, these parties joined together to form the Block of Anti-Fascist, Democratic Parties ('Block der antifaschistisch-demokratischen Parteien'). Each party retained its own individuality but pledged to work with the others in resolving outstanding tasks and to make efforts to evolve a joint policy. This determination was expressed in the commitment that block resolutions could only be passed unanimously. In view of the support offered by the Soviet Military Administration in Germany (SMAD) first to the KPD and then later to the SED, this commitment to co-operation and unanimity above all curtailed the scope for political action held by the bourgeois parties. Despite the pressure being exerted upon them the CDU and LDPD resisted attempts to make them follow the line of the SED and this led to a block crisis in 1948. In order to highlight the minority position of the old bourgeois parties and to extend the SED's influence in social areas in which it would hardly have

been able to gain a foothold before, the DBD was founded as a Farmers' Party on 29 April 1948 and the NDPD founded as a party for former petty Nazis and the nationally-orientated middle classes on 25 May 1948. The DBD was taken into the block along with the FDGB on 5 August 1948 and the NDPD admitted on 7 September 1948. By way of preparation for the founding of the state of the GDR (National Socialism was deemed definitively overcome and the 'anti-fascist democratic phase' concluded) the block was renamed the Democratic Block of Parties and Mass Organisations ('Demokratischer Block der Parteien und Massenorganisationen') on 17 June 1949. The FDJ (6 July 1950) and DFD (13 June 1952) also became block members as did the League of Culture, at a later date. The originally bourgeois parties are referred to as block parties in official GDR language on the basis of their block membership. There are block committees not only on central but also on district and county level.

73 A further explanation for the relatively weak participation of the block parties in the lower-level people's representative bodies lies in their proportionally lower membership figures, which make it difficult for them to take part in all forms of participation. Cf also table 1.3.

74 Cf. on the social data concerning the working population, information on the socio-economic structure of the working population in *Statistisches Jahrbuch 1981*, op.cit. (Note 45), p.90. This table, however, only contains figures for the proportion of LPG members (6.5 per cent) and not for the GPG or PwF. The latter can probably be put at approximately 0.2 per cent.

75 It has already been pointed out that deputies elected to represent mass organisations are frequently members of the SED as well. For this reason cross-faction party groups are set up within the people's representative bodies which are under the direction of the regional party executive in question and are intended to ensure uniform action of SED members in the people's representative bodies. Only occasional, regional data are available on the true proportion of SED members. It should however be pointed out that it is in line with the integration function assigned to the people's representative bodies for them to have a larger number of non-party deputies. As an example of the work that a party group performs in a county council see the report from the county of Marienberg, in the Karl-Marx-Stadt district (of the 105 deputies and 30 successor candidates, 74 belong to the SED) by Helmut Ziegner, 'Erfahrungen bei der Verstärkung der führenden Rolle der Partei in den Volksvertretungen', in *Die Einheit von Volk, Partei und Staat — Verfassungswirklichkeit in der DDR. Protokoll der Wissenschaftlichen Konferenz der Akademie für Staats- und Rechtswissenschaft der DDR und des Rates des Bezirks Karl-Marx-Stadt am 26.6.1979 in Karl-Marx-Stadt (Aktuelle Beiträge der Staats- und Rechtswissen-*

schaft, no.206), Selbstverlag der Akademie für Staats- und Rechtswissenschaft der DDR, Potsdam-Babelsberg 1979, p.121 ff.

76   Very little use is made of the statutory means available for rejecting candidates. The cases that have occurred involved moral objections ('disorderly conduct', 'lacking work ethic' etc.) as the reason for the candidates being eliminated. It would appear that there are more cases where deputies are dismissed or resign their posts. However, there have been no known cases where this was attributable to an initiative on the part of the electorate from below. See on this point the empirical study of the activity of regional people's representative bodies by Schaarschmidt, G. and Sternkopf, W., *Zur weiteren Vervollkommnung der Tätigkeit der Tagungen, der Kommissionen und der Abgeordneten der örtlichen Volksvertretungen (Aktuelle Beiträge der Staats- und Rechtswissenschaft*, no.208) Selbstverlag der Akademie für Staats- und Rechtswissenschaft der DDR, Potsdam-Babelsberg 1979, p.122 ff. On the statutory framework and the procedure to be observed see *Kommentar zum Gesetz über die örtlichen Volksvertretungen und ihre Organe in der Deutschen Demokratischen Republik v. 12. Juli 1973*, Staatsverlag der Deutschen Demokratischen Republik, Berlin 1977, 2nd revised and enlarged edition, p.98 f.

77   Recommendations and proposals of this kind are not binding on the deputies. They have the legal status of petitions ('Eingaben') and the executive organs decide on these under their own responsibility. Different from these, however, are the electors' commissions ('Wähleraufträge'), upon which more stringent requirements are placed. A group of persons wishing to issue an electors' commission must be representative of their electoral area, both in size and make-up, and must be called upon by the NF committee or an enterprise union executive. Even the electors' commission is only binding when it is accepted by the people's representative bodies, i.e. after it has received the consent of the councils. See *Staatsrecht der DDR*, op.cit. (Note 55), p.304 ff.

78   Meetings of people's representatives at community and county level are frequently held in the evening, i.e. in the deputies' free time. Where this is not the case, deputies must be released from their enterprises, administrations etc. on full pay; their employment relationship may only be terminated with the agreement of the people's representative body. The deputies also receive expense allowances or a lump-sum payment and free travel on public transport within their area of activity. Cf. *Kommentar zum Gesetz über die örtlichen Volksvertretungen*, op.cit. (Note 76), p.95 ff. and *Staatsrecht der DDR*, op.cit. (Note 55), p.312 ff. This also contains statements on the immunity and indemnity of deputies and also on their right to refuse to give evidence on matters confided to them in their capacity as deputy, unless criminal acts are involved.

79 The statutory provision allowing individual candidates to be withdrawn from the list would only be effective if a candidate received less than 50 per cent of the total valid votes cast. In such a case he is deemed not elected. No case of this type has so far become known. Cf *Staatsrecht der DDR*, op.cit. (Note 55), p.352.

80 In the election to the People's Chamber on 14 June 1981, the election turnout was 99.21 per cent; 99.98 per cent of votes cast were valid; the percentage of 'no' votes was 0.14 per cent. See also the table, which also summarises previous results, in Schneider, E., 'Die Wahlen zur Volkskammer der DDR (1981) und zum Obersten Sowjet der UdSSR (1979)', in *Zeitschrift für Parlamentsfragen*, vol.12 (1981), no.4, p.494.

81 *Kommentar zum Gesetz über die örtlichen Volksvertretungen* op.cit. (Note 76), p.23.

82 In Honecker, E., *Bericht des Zentralkomitees der SED*, op.cit. (Note 45), p.8.

83 *Staatsrecht der DDR*, op.cit. (Note 55), p.255.

84 'The state budget is a multi-layer system of territorially and functionally structured part budgets which correspond to the democratic centralism of the structure of the state in socialism. Its uniform structure is characterised by the fact that the budgets of all people's representative bodies at the different state executive levels in ascending order constitute part of the budget of the next state executive level up.' Quotation from *Sozialistische Finanzwirtschaft. Hochschullehrbuch*, Verlag Die Wirtschaft, Berlin 1981, p.119. On the terms of reference and rights of the local people's representative bodies in planning and directing their finances see ibid., p.340 ff. Since the state budget of the GDR can only be touched on briefly in this study, reference should be made to the detailed account given by Haase, H., *Grundzüge und Strukturen des Haushaltswesens der DDR (Berichte des Osteuropa-Instituts an der Freien Universität Berlin*, no.117), Eigenverlag des Osteuropa-Instituts, Berlin 1978, and the essays by Haase, H. and Buck, H., in *Deutschland Archiv*.

85 'The budgets of the county councils have particular weight in volume terms within the district budgets . . . they focus above all on expenditure for education, the health and social services system and culture. They are closely connected with the local utilities network and with the construction, trading and transport enterprises run at county level, which are very important in maintaining the standard of living and make a significant contribution towards realisation of the budget.' *Sozialistische Finanzwirtschaft*, op.cit. (Note 84), p.123.

86 'The responsibility of the local organs of state for resolving state tasks in their territory is closely connected to the overall responsibility of the collective combines for the economy, which is linked to essential

territorial prerequisites and conditions. This relates to the utilisation of sites and social labour capacity, requirements for territorial resources such as water, energy, transport and telecommunications, and also to the development of cultural and intellectual life and the satisfying of the social needs of the working population . . . The wide geographical distribution of the collective combine enterprises and their production plant alone is connected with new conditions . . . In order to live up to these requirements, two things are essential: a longterm concept for the work of the central state organs with central state decisions on basic issues involving the active participation of the local councils and collective combines and trusting cooperation between the local organs of state and the collective combines.' *Staatliche Leitung und Planung im Territorium,* Staatsverlag der Deutschen Demokratischen Republik, Berlin 1980, p.126 f.

87   See section 1,6; section 8,4; section 12,5 of the 'Gesetz über den Ministerrat der Deutschen Demokratischen Republik' (Law on the Council of Ministers of the GDR) dated 16 December 1972 and reproduced in 'Die Staatsordnung der DDR', adapted and introduced by Herwig Roggemann (*Quellen zur Rechtsvergleichung aus dem Osteuropa-Institut an der Freien Universität Berlin. Die Gesetzgebung der sozialistischen Staaten,* vol.5), Berlin Verlag, Berlin 1973, p.201 ff. Also sections 9, 10, 11 and 12 of the 'Gesetz über die örtlichen Volksvertretungen und ihre Organe in der DDR v. 12.7.1973', in *Kommentar zum Gesetz über die örtlichen Volksvertretungen,* op.cit. (Note 76), p.64 ff.

88   The local people's representative bodies do not have a permanent presidium or a permanent executive. Instead, each meeting elects an executive to act at the next meeting, with the council chairman generally being a standing member of this executive. This practice is justified on the basis of the unity of power of the legislative and executive. This weak organisational structure without doubt prevents the people's representative bodies from developing into an instrument of control and from developing a weight of their own as an overall body. The district representative bodies are supposed to meet at least once every three months and the other people's representative bodies at least every two months (cf *Kommentar zum Gesetz über die örtlichen Volksvertretungen,* op.cit. (Note 76), p.48 ff.). The observance of this prescribed meeting frequency seems to have improved – in 1974/75 only 63 per cent and 72 per cent respectively of the towns and communities investigated held the required number of meetings. In 1976/77 the percentages were 80 per cent and above. In small communities, in particular, which have only a small number of commissions and where the meetings are held in the evenings and are not to go on too long, this meeting frequency is even surpassed. On the other hand, the

attendance of deputies and successor candidates at plenary sessions is on the decline — 182 people's representative bodies were investigated with a total of 14,060 deputies and 2,329 successor candidates from county level down to the communities. The figures show that in 1974/75 deputy attendance was 78 per cent; 1976/77 74 per cent (72 per cent and 67 per cent respectively for the successor candidates). No significant differences emerge between urban and rural communities or between the different decision-making levels. Cf. Schaarschmidt, G. and Sternkopf, W., *Zur weiteren Vervollkommnung* op.cit. (Note 76) p.36 ff.

89 On the commissions see *Kommentar zum Gesetz über die örtlichen Volksvertretungen*, op.cit. (Note 76), p.79 ff. and also Schaarschmidt, G. and Sternkopf, W., *Zur weiteren Vervollkommnung*, op.cit. (Note 76), p.70 ff. The full-time state apparatus is permanently present on the commissions as it is in the meeting executives of the people's representative bodies: the position of secretary to the commission, a post which is important for the preparation and assessment of meetings, is generally held by a member of the competent specialist department's staff. He is frequently a member of the commission as well.

90 *Statistisches Jahrbuch der DDR 1981*, op.cit. (Note 45), p.394.

91 On the People's Chamber see the essay by Schneider, E. (Note 80), and also Neugebauer, G., 'Die Volkskammer der DDR', in *Zeitschrift für Parlamentsfragen*, vol.5 (1974), no.3, p.386 ff. and Lapp, P.J., *Die Volkskammer der DDR (Studien zur Sozialwissenschaft*, vol.33), Westdeutscher Verlag, Opladen 1975. See also Articles 48—65 of the 1968/74 GDR Constitution in *Die DDR-Verfassungen*, op.cit. (Note 31), p.131 f.

92 The allocation of the position of President of the People's Chamber to a member of the Politburo of the SED Central Committee in 1976 served *inter alia* to upgrade the People's Chamber both inside and outside the country. Until then, Johannes Dieckmann (LDPD) had been President from 1949 up to his death in 1969, followed by Gerald Gotting (CDU) until 1976.

93 Five Secretaries of the SED Central Committee are also Committee Chairmen: Committee for Foreign Affairs: Hermann Axen; for National Defence: Paul Verner; for Industry, Building and Transport: Günter Mittag; for Trade and Supply: Werner Jarowinsky; for National Education: Kurt Hager. The local people's representative bodies have no equivalent of the People's Chamber 'Citizens' Petitions Committee'. The introduction of complaints committees in the local people's representative bodies for a trial period from 1969 to 1974 was abandoned. No reasons were given but presumably it was feared that this type of institutionalised control over the state administration could lead to the

local people's representative bodies developing their own self-interests.
94   See the figures in Lapp, P.J., *Die Volkskammer der DDR*, op.cit. (Note 91), p.153 f. according to which there is a rising trend in the number of People's Chamber deputies engaged in committee work.
95   Cf. table 14 in Schneider, E., *Die Wahlen zur Volkskammer der DDR*, op.cit. (Note 80), p.503.
96   Cf. table 13 in Schneider, E., *Die Wahlen zur Volkskammer der DDR*, op.cit. (Note 80), p.502.
97   In addition to the relevant articles of the Constitution see the reports of the first and second meetings of the People's Chamber in the 8th legislature on 25 and 26 June 1981 in *Neues Deutschland*, vol.36, no.150 and 151 dated 26 June and 27/28 June 1981. The following data on the composition of the Council of State and the Council of Ministers are drawn from these sources. A further source was *Staats- und Parteiapparat der DDR. Personelle Besetzung Stand: 22.7.1981*, compiled by the Gesamtdeutsches Institut, Bundesanstalt für gesamtdeutsche Aufgaben, Selbstverlag Bonn 1981. It is in keeping with the unity of power principle that the full-time judges and the members of the jury are elected and count as organs of the unified state power. The judges and jury members for the district courts are elected by the district representative bodies and the judges for the county courts by the county representative bodies. For the social courts (dispute commissions in enterprises, arbitration commissions in residential areas — these constitute the first instance for disputes resulting from labour relationships and minor criminal offences) and also for the jury members on the county people's representative bodies, elections are held in the enterprises and residential areas. Compared with this the Public Procurator's Office ranks as a 'unified organ', with only the Public Procurator having personal legitimation through his election by the People's Chamber. See on this *Staatsrecht der DDR*, op.cit. (Note 55), p.279 f., p.329 ff., p.421 ff., and also Lohmann, U., 'Das Rechtswesen', in *Politik, Wirtschaft und Gesellschaft in der DDR. Studientexte für die politische Bildung*, second revised and expanded edition, Westdeutscher Verlag, Opladen, p.192 ff.
98   Cf. Neugebauer, G., *Partei und Staatsapparat in der DDR*, op.cit. (Note 33), in particular p.131 ff. A comparison of the text of the 1968 Constitution with the amendments of 1974 may be found in *Die DDR-Verfassungen*, op.cit. (Note 31), p.162 ff.
99   Of the 26 members of the Council of State (including the secretary), 18 belong to the SED and 8 to the block parties. The SED members include 8 full members of the Politburo and 2 candidates of the Politburo together with 5 ordinary members of the SED Central Committee. Five Council of State members are women.

100 On the terms of reference and status of the National Defence Council under constitutional law see *Staatsrecht der DDR*, op.cit. (Note 55), p.349 ff.; quotation: p.350.
101 See section 6 of the 'Gesetz über den Ministerrat', op.cit. (Note 87), p.205.
102 On the people's own collective combines, enterprises and other economic institutions the *Marxistische—leninistische Staats- und Rechtstheorie*, op.cit. (Note 2), p.365 states: 'They are state-owned enterprises, subordinate to state organs, and have multiple links with other state organs, with whom they cooperate closely. With a view to directly realising state tasks in respect of the satisfaction of the material needs of society in particular, the people's own enterprises have several features in common with the state institutions, although they again differ essentially from these on account of their economic activity'. These formulations are not imprecise by chance. In particular, they make no attempt to differentiate between state leadership and planning activities in the economic sphere and the 'economic activity' of the enterprises, on the basis of specific criteria. This lack of concrete specification conceals an unresolved theoretical problem, which at its heart marks a central political problem: the relationship between the base and the superstructure within Soviet-type Socialist systems. In the view of Marxism—Leninism, the base (i.e. property relationships, the level of development of productive forces and the ensuing production relationships) determines the superstructure (i.e. party, state, ideology etc.) and its functions. In capitalism, the base cannot ultimately be controlled and drives capitalist societies from one crisis into another, thereby opening up the possibility and the need for the transition to socialism (assuming there is a Marxist—Leninist party as a 'consciously' acting leadership). Without basically calling into question the conditional relationship between the base and the superstructure, Marxism—Leninism postulates a new and changed role for the superstructure in socialist societies — claiming that with the aid of Marxism—Leninism it has proved possible to perceive and make use of fundamental social and economic laws. The transition to socialism and communism is thus, it is claimed, not a spontaneous process but a process which calls for 'conscious' leadership through the elements of the superstructure, i.e. the party, state and ideology. These deductions are used *de facto* to justify the leading role of the party and the hierarchical structures of the political system. If the state were now to be allocated increasing functions taken from the economic basis (as individual state theorists and political economists in the GDR have done) it would, in the view of Marxism—Leninism, increasingly lose its designated role as an instrument of leadership towards the base.

103 The ABI commissions are made up of representatives of the SED, the state and the chief mass organisations. There are ABI commissions on every level of the state structure, right down to county and borough level and also in the collective combines, enterprises and co-operatives. In the communities and residential areas there are People's Control Committees ('Volkskontrollausschüsse'). Their members are put forward by the competent SED party executive and by the executives in the chief mass organisations and then elected in enterprise or residential area assemblies (cf 'Organisationsstruktur der Arbeiter-und-Bauern-Inspektion der DDR', in *Neuer Weg. Organ des Zentralkomitees der SED für Fragen des Parteilebens*, vol.36 (1981), no.1, third cover page). In 1980 the ABI had 17,939 commissions and 6,336 People's Control Committees with a total membership of 233,168 (cf. *Statistisches Jahrbuch der DDR 1981*, op.cit. (Note 45), p.395). On the terms of reference and rights of the ABI see *Staatsrecht der DDR*, op.cit. (Note 55), p.374 ff.
104 *Staatsrecht der DDR*, op.cit. (Note 55), p.354 and p.363.
105 Idem, p.363.
106 The 42 members of the Council of Ministers (excluding the chairman and his two first deputies) are not all ministers managing their own specialist departments. On the contrary, many of the Council of Ministers members are heads of other central state institutions with some institutions being represented more than once: Chairman of the ABI; Head of the Office for Youth Questions; chief Burgomaster of Berlin; President of the GDR State Bank; Chairman and two secretaries of state from the state planning commission; chairman of the state contractual court; permanent representative of the GDR in COMECON; first deputy and secretary of state to the minister for foreign trade; secretary of state for labour and wages. Of the total of 45 members in the Council of Ministers, one is a woman. On the intermeshing of personnel between the different levels of the central state apparatus and the SED Central Committee, see table 1.1. For an analysis of the composition of government in the first 20 years of the GDR see Hoffmann, U., *Die Veränderungen in der Sozialstruktur des Ministerrats der DDR 1949 bis 1969 (Mannheimer Schriften zur Politik und Zeitgeschichte*, vol.1) Droste Verlag, Düsseldorf 1971.
107 The representation of the block parties in the Council of State and the Council of Ministers is largely conditioned by history (cf Note 72). The representatives of the block parties have only exerted a noticeable influence on political decisions in very isolated cases, when acting as spokesmen for individuals or for residual bourgeois groups (crafts, retail trade). Apart from this the block parties recognise the SED's claim to leadership and recognise its programme as binding on their work as well. The Ministers of the block parties are to a large extent

isolated in their positions. Among the many secretaries of state and deputy ministers in almost all of the ministries only the Ministry for District-Controlled Industry and the Food Industry has one secretary of state from the LDPD, the Ministry of Justice one deputy minister from the LDPD and the Ministry of Finance one deputy minister from the LDPD (since December 1981). The CDU provides the President of the Supreme Court. (For sources cf Note 97.)

108 Cf. on the following the section 'Die verwaltungsrechtliche Stellung des Bürgers', in *Verwaltungsrecht*, op.cit. (Note 29), p.187 ff.

109 The emergence and current practice regarding the state liability law is covered by Lörler, S., *Das Staatshaftungsrecht und seine Anwendung (Aktuelle Beiträge der Staats- und Rechtswissenschaft*, no.238), Akademie für Staats- und Rechtswissenschaft der DDR, Eigenverlag, Potsdam-Babelsberg, 1981.

110 As an example of the significance that the rediscovery of the subjective rights of the citizen has or can have in terms of administrative law, see Bönninger, K., 'Zu theoretischen Problemen eines Verwaltungsverfahrens und seine Bedeutung für die Gewährleistung der subjektiven Rechte der Bürger', in *Staat und Recht*, vol.29 (1980), no.10, p.931 ff. Bönninger proposes that administrative procedure be brought further into a legal framework in all its details so that the citizen is given increased legal security through the rules of procedure having legal form. The citizen should then receive a legal status of his own and his own procedural rights in order to allow him to exert influence on decision-making. The fact that Bönninger pleads for the individual to be allowed to have a lawyer represent him can be regarded as a preliminary form of legal control over administrative decisions. This proposal also bears witness to the trend towards putting political activity in the GDR on a firmer legal base. Although it makes the conduct of the state institutions more calculable for the individual, it also presupposes that the individual has knowledge of the law and is capable of applying this knowledge.

111 See for example the section 'Staatliche und nichtstaatliche Formen sozialistischer Demokratie', in *Marxistisch—leninistische Staats- und Rechtstheorie*, op.cit. (Note 2), p.303 ff. An attempt at an overall survey of the social organisations that exist in the GDR together with their terms of reference may be found in *Die gesellschaftlichen Organisationen in der DDR. Stellung, Wirkungsrichtungen und Zusammenarbeit mit dem sozialistischen Staat*, Staatsverlag der Deutschen Demokratischen Republik, Berlin 1980.

112 The following is based on an extensive analysis of my own, extracts of which are published in *Gutachten zum Stand der DDR- und vergleichenden Deutschlandforschung*, sponsored by the working circle on Comparative German Research under the chairmanship of

Peter C. Ludz, Federal German Ministry for Inner-German Affairs, Eigenverlag, Bonn 1978, p.232 ff.

113 For 1979 there are more exact figures available on the social make-up of the FDGB membership. According to these figures, the FDGB had 8,700,564 members in 1979. These included 1,365,663 (15.7 per cent) under 25 years of age and 4,411,703 (50.7 per cent) women. On the basis of social groups the membership divided up into 4,653,164 (53.3 per cent) workers, 1,772,203 (20.4 per cent) employees, 933,522 (10.7 per cent) members of the intelligentsia, 1,359,675 (15.6 per cent) pensioners and temporarily non-working members. (In assessing the proportion of employees, it must be remembered that a number of occupations which count as employee relationships in the Federal Republic of Germany are classified as worker relationships in the GDR. The figures cannot therefore be compared directly.) Cf. *Parteilehrjahr der SED 1980/1981. Studienhinweise für die Teilnehmer der Seminar zu Theorie und Politik der weiteren Gestaltung der entwickelten sozialistischen Gesellschaft in der DDR (4. Studienjahr)*, Dietz Verlag, Berlin 1980, p.94.

114 The currently valid labour legislation provisions, including the AGB (Labour Code) may be found in *Arbeitsgesetzbuch und andere ausgewählte Rechtsvorschriften. Textausgabe mit Anmerkungen und Sachregister*, published by the Secretariat of State for Labour and Wages, Staatsverlag der Deutschen Demokratischen Republik, Berlin 1980. For a more detailed political assessment of the AGB from my viewpoint see Zimmermann, H., 'Neues Arbeitsgesetzbuch in der DDR verabschiedet', in *Die Quelle. Funktionärszeitschrift des Deutschen Gewerkschaftsbundes*, vol.28 (1977), no.9, p.351 ff.

115 Cf. the comprehensive account and analysis in Belwe, K., *Mitwirkung im Industriebetrieb der DDR. Planung, Einzelleitung, Beteiligung der Werktätigen an Entscheidungsprozessen des VEB* (*Schriften des Zentralinstituts für sozialwissenschaftliche Forschung der Freien Universität Berlin*, vol.31), Westdeutscher Verlag, Opladen 1979.

116 The expectations that the director of a VEB has to live up to together with his rights and responsibilities are summarised in *Leiter — Kollektiv — Persönlichkeit. Handbuch für die sozialistische Leitungstätigkeit*, 4th completely revised edition, Verlag Die Wirtschaft, Berlin 1979. Results of an empirical investigation are presented in Ladensack, K., *Arbeits- und Lebensweise der Leiter, Analysen, Probleme, Hinweise*, Verlag Die Wirtschaft, Berlin 1981.

117 Co-operation between the BGOs of the individual enterprises in the collective combine has not yet been definitively settled. At present the chairmen of the enterprise union executives meet together within the collective combine at regular intervals for consultations and co-

ordination work. Since a number of the collective combines include enterprises from different branches of industry, several different wage agreements are often in force within a single combine. If these were to be standardised to give a single wage agreement for each combine this would require the organisation areas of the industrial trade unions to be redefined. The individual BGOs are currently headed by different industrial trade unions within one and the same combine. There is also confusion regarding the power of the combine executives to decide on the deployment of productive forces within the enterprises. On the one hand the collective combine directors are responsible for the optimum utilisation of labour, yet on the other hand the labour contracts (plus the labour assignment specified in them) are concluded with the individual enterprises. Modifications to labour contracts are governed by the fixed regulations of the AGB and co-determination by the BGL. The authority of the combine directors to issue instructions to the enterprise directors, which is embodied in the principle of democratic centralism, is in contradiction to this. Current discussions are tending towards the idea of strengthening the collective combine vis-à-vis the individual enterprise. If this were to result in a definitive regulation, it would most certainly curtail the enterprise's right to co-determination.

118 For more details on the organisational structure and tasks of the FDGB see the leading article 'FDGB (Freier Deutscher Gewerkschaftsbund)' in *DDR-Handbuch*, op.cit. (note 35), p.351 ff. On the current position of the FDGB in the political system of the GDR from the viewpoint of its Chairman — Harry Tisch, 'Rolle und Aufgaben der Gewerkschaften bei der weiteren Gestaltung der entwickelten sozialistischen Gesellschaft und der allseitigen Stärkung unseres Staates', in *Staat und Recht*, vol.31 (1982), no.1, p.3 ff. On the current situation of the FDGB: Zimmermann, H., '3. FDGB-Kongress 1950 — der FDGB dreissig Jahre danach', in *DDR Report*, vol.13 (1980), no.12, p.781 ff.

119 Glaessner, G.-J., 'FDJ und Jugendpolitik', in Erbe, G., et al, *Politik, Wirtschaft und Gesellschaft in der DDR*, op.cit. (Note 52), p.166 f.: 'The youth of the working class is regarded as the core of the association, but the social composition of the FDJ shows a completely different tendency. Whilst scholars, students, apprentices and officers and longer commissioned soldiers in the National People's Army are organised up to a level of about 80% in the FDJ, only some 50% of workers who have completed their apprenticeship are members of the FDJ, only 40% of the unskilled workers and only 20% of the young LPG farmers and workers on people's own estates from the age of 14 to 25 years. From these figures it can be deduced that the FDJ is particularly strong in those areas where membership is a condition of professional advancement'. On the situation of young people and youth

policy in the GDR: *Jugend im doppelten Deutschland*, published by Walter Jaide and Barbara Hille, Westdeutscher Verlag, Opladen 1977.

120 The current composition of the DFD membership still reflects its original task, albeit in somewhat modified form. The membership comprised 72.2 per cent women at work and 27.8 per cent housewives. The age structure of the membership is as follows: 21.5 per cent under 35 years old; 43.9 per cent between 35 and 55 years old; 34.6 per cent 55 years old and above. The relatively high proportion of non-working and older women together with the restriction of organisational activities to the residential area constitute the characteristic features of the DFD and distinguish it from other associations which operate in the enterprise. Cf *Statistisches Jahrbuch der DDR 1981*, op.cit. (Note 45), p.396.

121 In 1980, 219,176 of the 264,204 KDT members (which include 30,765 women) were organised in enterprise organisations. The KDT takes in predominantly technical college and university graduates though highly qualified skilled workers and masters with particular technical interest may also be admitted to the organisation. Of the KDT membership 61,655 (including 6,513 women) had university qualifications and 139,191 (including 17,113 women) had technical college qualifications. Cf *Statistisches Jahrbuch der DDR 1981*, op.cit. (Note 45), p.398.

122 The following is based on a detailed analysis of my own, extracts of which are published in *Gutachten zum Stand der DDR- und Deutschlandforschung*, op.cit. (Note 113), p.267 ff.

123 On the history of SED church policy and on the situation of the Protestant churches cf Dahn, H., *Das Verhältnis von Staat und Kirche in der SBZ/DDR 1945 bis Anfang der 70er Jahre* and Wensierski, P., 'SED-Kirchenpolitik und die Rolle der Kirchen in der DDR. Thesen', in *Der X. Parteitag der SED. 35 Jahre SED-Politik. Versuch einer Bilanz*, op.cit. (Note 33), p.173 ff; and 164 ff; Zimmermann, H., 'Kirche im Sozialismus — Zur Situation der evangelischen Kirche in der DDR', in *DDR Report*, vol.12 (1979), no.1, p.5 ff. Sources, documentation and analyses on the development of the churches in the GDR are published constantly in *Kirche im Sozialismus. Materialien zu Entwicklungen in der DDR*, by the Berliner Arbeitsgemeinschaft für kirchliche Publizistik und *epd Dokumentation, Informationsdienst der Zentralredaktion des Evangelischen Pressedienstes*, published by die Gemeinschaftswerk der Evangelischen Publizistik e.V. Frankfurt am Main.

124 Günter Gaus, the first head of the Federal German Representation to the GDR Government (1974—1981) spoke in this context of GDR society as a 'society of private corners'. Cf. Gaus, G., *Texte zur deutschen Frage. Mit den wichtigsten Dokumenten zum Verhältnis der*

beiden deutschen Staaten (*Sammlung Luchterhand*, vol.383), Hermann Luchterhand Verlag, Darmstadt and Neuwied, p.26 f.). Garton Ash, T., '*Und willst du nicht mein Bruder sein . . .* ' *Die DDR heute* (*Spiegel-Buch*, vol.15) Rowohlt Taschenbuchverlag, Reinbek b. Hamburg 1981, p.82, speaks of the 'dual lives of GDR citizens'. Although Ash in his impressionistic book adopts a much more critical approach to the GDR than Gaus, he too comes to the conclusion: 'It is an attitude of adaptation, of public conformity that belongs to the dual life of the GDR citizens. As long as the state can guarantee a minimum of security and as long as the "subject" mentality persists and GDR citizens continue to think in the categories of "in our country" and "duty", there will be no danger to the security of the state — not even from the strongholds of unwillingness in Berlin'.

2 Economic system and economic policy: the challenge of the 1970s

Jürgen Strassburger, Free University, Berlin

Introduction

At the VIIIth SED (Sozialistische Einheitspartei Deutschlands — Socialist Unity Party) Party Congress in 1971 the 'Main Task for the Further Development of a Socialist Society' was proclaimed ('Hauptaufgabe zur weiteren Gestaltung der entwickelten sozialistischen Gesellschaft'). This was a socio-economic framework providing binding orientation data and directives for central planning and control by the state, the organs of state power in the districts, regions and cities, and the control organs in the various sectors of the economy, in enterprises and combines.

The IXth Party Congress in May 1976 decreed that the policy laid down by the SED in 1971 for the realisation of the 'Hauptaufgabe' should be continued. The directive for the development of the economy between 1976 and 1980 passed by the Congress states: 'The Main Task accepted by resolution of the VIIIth Party Congress to increase further the material and cultural standard of living of the people through a swift development of production, greater efficiency, scientific and technological progress and further growth in the productivity of labour is to be pursued in its dual aspect as a consistent long-term strategy'.[1]

Before discussing the 'Main Task' as a central socio-economic and political concept for the 1970s and efforts to realise it I would first like to give a brief outline of the general questions to be considered in this chapter and the approach adopted.

The main concern is a political and sociological analysis of the economic policy in the German Democratic Republic. In contrast to studies based on quantitative economic research attention here focuses on qualitative aspects. Quantitative issues play a part where they can serve as a yardstick for the success or failure of qualitative changes in economic policy and/or organisation.

A discussion of the economic policy and economic system of the German Democratic Republic during the 1970s seems appropriate not only because we can now look back on the decade as a whole but also because of the developments which took place during that period. There is general agreement among West German economists that at the beginning of the 1970s, personally with the change from Ulbricht to Honecker (in May 1971) and politically with the VIIIth SED Party Congress in June 1971 a change in direction occurred of which the policy of the 'Main Task' formed the programmatic centre.

The 'Main Task' is expressly stated to be a long-term strategic plan: a deliberate move away from the reform policy of the Ulbricht era. Since the VIIIth Party Congress it has been the 'constant point of reference for all measures of economic, social and cultural policy'.[2]

In addition to examining what is actually 'new' in this ideological and programmatic concept for the 1970s and so outlining the changes which have taken place I shall discuss the question of which social and economic problems the new policy was designed to tackle and solve. The answers will in themselves be an indication of the reasons for the change. We shall see that the main causes were not the change in personality from Ulbricht to Honecker but the need for reaction to serious economic and social problems which had emerged at the end of Ulbricht's regime.

A brief outline of economic policy and the economic development in the GDR from its inception to the beginning of the 1970s will make this clearer. It will also provide some basic information for an understanding of how the economic system evolved and developed.

The initial economic situation[3]

After the collapse of the Third Reich and the end of the Second World War on 8 May 1945 the Allied Control Council assumed supreme power in Germany on 5 June 1945. The Potsdam Conference (17 July to 2 August 1945) confirmed the commanders of the armed forces as the supreme powers in Germany, each responsible for the zone occupied and 'jointly in their capacity as members of the Control Council in questions affecting Germany as a whole'. On the basis of the individual responsibilities of the occupying powers the occupied zones were absorbed into the different spheres of influence and power despite the agreement to treat Germany as a political and economic unity. With the first phase of the Cold War, which set in soon after the end of hostilities, tension between the Soviet Union and the Western allies grew, playing a major part in the subsequent division of Germany.

The very first 'reforms' carried out by the Soviet occupation forces in their zone in 1945 and 1946 marked the beginning of fundamental changes in the economic and social structure. (Changes were made in the legal system, the administrative system, in education, land ownership and industry.) Divergence in the development of East and West Germany was strengthened by the proclamation of the two-zone Economic Council in the West in May 1947 and the formation of the German Economic Commission in the Soviet occupied zone in June of that year. With the break-up of the Allied Control Council in March 1948, the inclusion of the Western zones in the plan for economic aid for the reconstruction of Europe in 1948 (the Marshall Aid Plan resulting from the Paris Conference of July to September 1947) and finally the separate currency reforms (in the West on 20 June 1948 and in the East on 23 June 1948) the division of the old German economic area was final.

At the same time the political unity of Germany, so far as it had been maintained in joint organs of the occupying powers, came to an end. Under the influence of the Soviet occupying forces the SED took over in the Eastern zone, thus creating the prerequisite for the establishment of an economic and social system which saw itself as the opposite of the economic and social orders in the capitalist states.

The political leadership of the SED, the gradual nationalisation of the means of production and the construction of a centrally planned, administered and controlled economic system provided the political and institutional framework for the transition to the 'Socialist planned economy'.

The system of planning and control of the economy which began to emerge after 1948 was characterised by:[4]

    (a)   central planning in units of quantity;
    (b)   prices fixed by the state and in force for long periods;
    (c)   obligations on the part of enterprises to produce planned quantities;
    (d)   a state monopoly of foreign trade.

Even before the plans put forward in 1948/49 covering all economic activity for several years there had been a number of attempts at economic planning, although these were mainly limited to individual regions.[5] These initial steps were taken under the direction and control of the 'SMAD' (Soviet Military Administration for Germany), with the organisation in the hands of the newly formed German administrative organs, specifically the Land Administrations for Labour and the Economy.

At the beginning of economic reconstruction, as the East German economist Selbmann tells us, there were two over-riding tasks:

> 1. The general revival of the economy: first and foremost simply to meet the most essential requirements of the people and secure a basic existence . . . the most important thing was to get production going again.
>
> 2. What we in the Soviet occupied zone in the first months after the collapse of the Fascist regime called the 'reorganisation of the economy'. Basically it was the beginning of the change in economic organisation and in the conditions of production in large sectors of industry.[6]

The initial conditions for economic and especially industrial revival in the Soviet occupied zone, later the GDR, were, as we shall see, very much worse than in the Western zones. The territory occupied by the Russians had, on a pre-war basis (base year 1936) accounted for 30 per cent of the total volume of industrial production in the German Reich but the direct and indirect[7] effects of the war had destroyed altogether roughly 40 per cent of capacity (destruction in the Western zones amounted to about 20 per cent). Altogether in what is now the German Democratic Republic more than 1,500 major and 800 small and medium-sized plants had been destroyed.[8] The damage to transport had been equally devastating.[9] How bad the situation in agriculture was can be seen from the decimation of livestock: over pre-war levels 900,000 cattle, 3,000,000 pigs and 1,100,000 sheep had been lost.[10] Agricultural efficiency was further impaired as the loss of livestock brought shortages of organic manures while the destruction of factories caused a further shortfall in chemical fertilisers.[11] Inevitably this affected harvests. Last but not least the stock of agricultural machinery and equipment has been reduced by about 30 per cent through war damage.[12]

A further burden on the Soviet occupied zone was the fact that it had to shoulder almost the entire volume of reparation payments to the Soviet Union. As tension grew during the Cold War the Western occupied zones evaded most of the regulations agreed at the Potsdam Conference with regard to reparations to the Soviet Union. The Russians therefore exacted the amounts agreed with the Allies exclusively from the territory they had occupied.[13] These payments had been fixed at 10 billion dollars in 1933 prices.

They were made by removing entire plant, parts of plant or equipment[14] and in the form of transfers from current production. When the removal of plant ceased in the spring of 1948 further payments were only exacted in the form of production goods. The enterprises which had originally been selected for removal but were then transferred to Soviet ownership (they were known as 'Sowjetische Aktiengesellschaften' — SAG enterprises) played a major part in these transfers. Although payments from current production were certainly a milder penalty than the loss of entire plant they still proved a heavy drain on the economy, causing[15] a loss of national income, a reduction in the raw materials base as long as the material used to make the goods was not substituted in full, a loss of export capacity, and a reduction in consumption, either immediately or over the longer term, according to whether the goods taken were consumer or capital goods.

It may be taken that the SAG enterprises worked exclusively to provide reparation payments in 1946. After 1947 the quantity of transfers was reduced and some products in the consumer goods sector were actually exempted.[16] They then helped to improve supply for the population.

The main categories of goods for reparation payments after 1947 were mechanical engineering and electrical engineering products, precision and optical instruments. It has been estimated in the West that reparation payments amounted to 25 per cent of the total production of the Soviet occupied zone up to 1953.[17]

The return of the SAG enterprises to German administration and the government of the GDR (after October 1949) and their subsequent nationalisation was carried out in four stages. The last 33 of originally 196 enterprises were handed over to the GDR government in January 1954.[18]

In contrast to the loss of capacity through the removal of plant, which the workers could only compensate to a very small extent through improvisation and greater input,[19] the reparation payments from current production, although they clearly constituted a heavy burden on the economy, did have some positive effects on economic development in the GDR, as some East German economists see it: firstly they helped to prevent unemployment and created a greater demand for qualified workers; secondly the enterprises were supplied with raw materials from the Soviet Union to fulfil the reparation orders and some of the material, cotton for example, was allowed to be used for home consumption. But the GDR economists see the main advantage of this form of reparation in that it created industrial orders which required a high standard of technology and entailed the production of quality goods, thus making a not inconsiderable contribution to the reconstruction of the domestic economy.[20]

But in addition to war damage and reparation payments there were further factors which had a negative effect on the reconstruction process. Until 1945 the economic area of what is now the German Democratic Republic was closely interlinked with the Western parts of the former German Reich. There was a considerable degree of self-sufficiency in agriculture and the food industry, but all other sectors were dependent on supplies of raw materials and energy from the West. So the East German industrial structure was imbalanced, with an under-developed basic materials sector (including energy) and a highly-developed and highly specialised manufacturing industry (tools and textile machines, precision and optical instruments, electrical engineering). In 1938 the share of what was later the territory of the GDR in the total production of iron ore in the Reich was only 1.3 per cent. Its share of coal mined was 1.9 per cent and of coke production 0.8 per cent in the same year.

With the high percentages registered by the manufacturing sectors (in 1938 tool machines accounted for 34.5 per cent, sewing machines 51.3 per cent, textile machines 66.7 per cent, office machinery 61.7 per cent, cameras, according to construction and quality between 50.8 per cent and 79.0 per cent, handbags and watches 88.2 per cent of total production in the Reich) this imbalance presented a major problem to the industrial structural policy of the GDR.

Certainly there could be no thought of rebuilding industry along the lines of pre-war production. On the contrary a far-reaching and extremely costly restructuring process was needed to create an independent industrial basis by strengthening the basic materials and capital goods sectors. At the same time the complete disruption of the traditional foreign trade links required a reorientation towards Eastern Europe, which was technically and economically relatively under-developed. This adjustment too was hardly possible without frictional losses.

The change in the economic order

In September 1945 a land reform was carried out. Two and a half million hectares (1 hectare is about 2.5 acres) of land which had been taken from former landowners and 600,000 hectares which had belonged to Nazi leaders or the state were put into a land fund. From this about 500,000 persons, former agricultural workers, landless peasants, re-settlers and small farmers were given enough land to ensure a basic existence. About one third of the total amount of land confiscated was handed over to the Länder (the district and local authorities) for administration.

Of even greater importance for future developments than the land reform was the industry reform which began at the end of 1945. On the basis of Orders No. 124 and 126 of the SMAD of 30 and 31 October respectively, the entire property of the German state, the National Socialist Party and its officials and the former German Wehrmacht was confiscated. Some of the enterprises — generally heavy industrial plants — were, as already explained, turned into Soviet-controlled enterprises. The rest was handed over to the German administration in March 1946.

To further the nationalisation of industry a referendum was held in Saxony at the suggestion of the Communist Party. The proposal was that all enterprises and plants which had worked for war production or which belonged or had belonged on 8 May 1945 to Nazi criminals, active Nazis or war criminals should be confiscated without compensation.[22] With a turn-out of 93.7 per cent, 77.6 per cent of voters approved the proposal and 16.5 per cent voted against. The percentage of invalid votes was 5.8. Similar enterprises and plant were then also confiscated in the other Länder of the Soviet occupied zone (but without a referendum). This created the essential basis for the establishment of a new economic order.

The most urgent task was to get industrial production going again, repair war damage and ensure supplies to the population. At the same time a new industrial and production structure was needed.

The economic aims were therefore to create and expand an independent basic materials industry, and to increase the production of capital goods. This was only possible with a deliberate neglect of the services sector and the production of consumer goods.[23]

The beginning of the two-year plan for 1949–50 and the transition to overall economic planning marked the beginning of investment to counteract the effects of the war. The Federation of Nationalised Enterprises ('Vereinigung volkseigener Betriebe' — VVB) was allowed 50 per cent of its amortisation for general repairs while the remaining 50 per cent had to be handed over to the state and was used to finance investment which was in the interest of the economy as a whole.[24]

The two-year plan for 1949–50 was fulfilled, as was the following five-year plan for 1951–55.[25] But although production targets were met economic and social problems multiplied. The policy of reconstruction and construction was largely to the detriment of supplies to the population and the standard of living dropped further and further behind that of the Federal Republic of Germany.

As a result a growing number of people began to leave the GDR.[26] In the period immediately following the war the number of inhabitants in the Soviet occupied zone had risen steadily through the stream of refugees from former Eastern German territories but after 1948 it began to drop steadily. In May 1939 what is now the GDR including East Berlin had a population of 16.745 million; the peak was reached in 1947 at 19.102 million inhabitants. But despite an excess of births of 915,432 and an inflow of released prisoners of war and people from former Eastern territories the number of inhabitants had dropped to 17.136 million by the end of 1962.[27] So between 1947 and the building of the Berlin wall on 13 August 1961 the GDR had lost more than three million people, a large number of them skilled workers, members of the technical intelligentsia and university and technical college graduates. This mass emigration brought an increasing shortage of manpower.

A drain of these proportions would have weakened any economy. It was a particular blow to the GDR as the economy was still in the phase in which growth was largely being achieved through the expansion of labour-intensive production; only in a few cases was it possible to make good the loss of labour through work intensification and rationalisation.

All the available reserves of labour, especially women, were mobilised.[28] But this brought further problems for economic policy: it was no longer possible to pursue the target of economic growth through increasing the number employed. To counteract the effects of the constant outflow of labour and disruption to the production processes the second five-year plan (for 1956–60) was broken off in 1959 and replaced with a new seven-year plan. The aim of this, the 'Main Task for the economy', was to bring per capita consumption of all major foodstuffs and consumer goods up to or higher than the level of the Federal Republic by 1961. It was hoped to achieve this through a maximum increase in labour productivity and production in all sectors of the economy through the optimum in scientific and technological development while at the same time lowering costs.

It soon became clear how unrealistic these hopes were. At the end of the 1950s private consumption per inhabitant of the GDR was in real terms between 25 and 30 per cent below that of the Federal Republic.[29]

Catching up with the Federal Republic would have entailed strong economic growth and at the same time an increase in consumption. But material shortages were such that the two together were unattainable. 'The planned increase in every kind of consumption was soon to seem like pulling at every side of a blanket which was too small.'[30]

In fact the imbalance caused overall growth rates to drop. New supply difficulties arose and together with the final collectivisation of agriculture in 1960 brought a further strong rise in the flood of refugees to the West. The building of the wall in Berlin finally put an end to that aspect of the problem.

The economic reforms (NÖS/OSS)

State economic policy reacted to the failure of the seven-year plan by formulating the economic plan for the year 1962: this de facto buried the 'main economic task' to which such hopes had been attached and reformulated the aims for the development of private supply independent of the seven-year plan. This had far-reaching consequences for economic policy and economic organisation: the leaders of the GDR had to admit that the way the economy was organised and the current system of planning and control had ceased to be effective after the largely successful conclusion of the period of reconstruction and construction. There is general agreement among Western economists that the Soviet system of planning adopted by the GDR in the phase of industrial expansion had proved an extremely effective growth instrument but that the effectiveness of a centralist system, which works mainly with material balances and plans, declines with the degree of development of an economy. A major factor in this case was that the quantity planning which largely favoured capacity expansion (quantitative material planning and extensive growth) brought a constant decrease in the degree of utilisation of production capacities.[31] With the reserves of labour exhausted the need arose for a system which would ensure proportional and optimal growth based on qualitative factors (work intensification, growth in efficiency and labour productivity).

The structure of economic planning and organisation up to 1963 did not fulfil these requirements for three reasons:

1 Quantitative planning largely ignored economic factors and led to investment mistakes with ensuing structural disequilibria.

2 The rigid price system brought distortions in the price structure. The result was a waste of raw materials and other supplies and delays in the absorption of scientific and technological innovation into production methods.

3 The bureaucratic and centralised decision-making structure which forced enterprises to meet targets which were often uneconomic whatever the price reduced the overall economic rationality of the plan (at least in its programmatic elements) to a 'rationale of target requirements' which was socially and economically irrational.[32]

In view of the economic situation there had been repeated demands in the 1950s for a reform of the system to cope with the transition from the phase of extensive to a phase of intensive growth. At the end of 1962 under the impact of the ideas on reform put forward in the Soviet Union by the economist Liberman and the open discussion on them, a discussion on reform broke out in the GDR as well.[33] At the VIth SED Congress in January 1963 Ulbricht announced comprehensive economic reforms, large sections of which were oriented to ideas put forward during the Liberman discussion in the USSR. On 11 July 1963 the Council of Ministers in the GDR passed a resolution on the 'Guidelines for the New Economic System (NÖS — Neues ökonomisches System) of Planning and Control of the Economy'.

In addition to the demand for scientifically-based performance criteria and planning and a redistribution of the functions and powers of the apparatus of economic administration and planning, the new system provided for the application of a complete system of 'economic levers' to replace the former instructions and regulations. The economic levers were to be effective on two levels: firstly that of enterprises and the industry-based Federations of Nationalised Enterprises (VVBs) and secondly that of the individual worker.

At plant level costs, prices, turnover and profits were to act as direct levers; at the level of 'the personal material interests of the people' wages and premiums were to be the direct levers and wage funds and premium funds the indirect levers.

The whole complex was to be so adjusted as to create a uniform and co-ordinated system organically linked with the plan and working in the same direction.

Of equal importance was the expansion and strengthening of the functions of the VVBs which instead of administrative organs became a kind of Socialist concern, head economic organs of their industries.

The shift of some decision-making powers to enterprises was often interpreted by Western writers as a decentralisation of the economic system. Damus has pointed out that the decentralised planning system of the GDR only transferred decisions downwards after 1963 insofar as 'this did not call in question the existing decision-making structures'.[34] Accordingly she sees the measures resolved in 1963 as an instrumentalisation of the lower decision levels as compared with the 'negation' of their competence before 1963, and calls this an 'indirectly centralised' rather than a 'directly centralised' planning system.[35]

With the beginning of the economic reforms of 1964 came a number of measures to improve the efficiency of the GDR economy. They were mainly to enable enterprises to be steered indirectly through monetary instruments:[36]

1 A revaluation of industrial fixed assets as per 30 June 1963.

2 A reform of industrial prices in three stages, the first of which began in 1964.

3   A change in investment financing (in 1964) in the form of greater participation by enterprises.
4   Introduction of interest payable on enterprises' own funds to be financed from earnings; this was called a 'production fund levy'.
5   Correction of planning and balance sheet methods.

The immediate effect on the economy of the introduction of the new system was extremely positive: in the first five years after the reforms economic growth was consistently at 5 per cent. But even so this did not solve all the problems. The 'scientifically-based leadership' did not come up to expectations nor did the economic levers prove adequate to co-ordinate central and enterprise interests. There was also considerable lack of clarity over the rights and relations of the VVBs and VEBs ('Volkseigene Betriebe' — People's Own Enterprises) to each other and their position with regard to the superior economic organs. The handling and processing of the large amount of new enterprise data caused problems and resulted in inadequate reporting and information flows with consequent disruptions to the planning process.[37]

The basic economic policy for the NÖS was contained in the 'Outlook Plan 1964 to 1970 for the Development of the National Economy of the German Democratic Republic' accepted by the VIth SED Party Congress at the beginning of 1963. The plan, which was never given legislative force, was highly unrealistic in its planning data. It was emphasised that the data were only to serve as guidelines and would be adjusted as time went on. The designation of a long-term plan as a guideline only was in keeping with the experimental nature of the new reform period.

In December 1965 Ulbricht announced at the 11th meeting of the SED Central Committee that the reforms would go on, outlining the target with these words: 'With the new economic system of planning and control we shall build up a real Socialist economic system in the German Democratic Republic on the bases of the economic laws of Socialism'.[38]

The reforms were to be continued on the basis of a new outlook plan for 1966—70. But numerous difficulties prevented the conclusion of industrial price reform which had been envisaged for 1 January 1966 and also delayed the resolution on the outlook plan itself. After a year's delay the industrial price reform was concluded on 1 January 1967. The new outlook plan, again covering five years, was announced in legislative form.

It was only now that the full effects of the economic levers in use up to then became apparent and enterprises were able to assess the extent, type and origin of their costs and consequently their profitability ... It was clear that the measures used so far had not led to a complete system which could for example ensure the development and manufacture of new products or a high return on investment.[39]

To counteract this the reform policy was continued.

The transition from the New Economic System (NÖS) to the Economic Socialist System (ÖSS) in 1967–68 has been very differently interpreted in the Federal Republic. While some writers see the measures of 1967/68 as a back-down from the reforms, others — as we shall see, rightly — see the period from 1968 to 1970 as the phase of greatest 'decentralisation'.[40]

If one considers the two major components of the economic reform concept of the phase from 1963 to 1970, namely:

(a) The transfer of essential economic decisions on the organisation of goods production from the economic authorities to the production units themselves (VVBs, the combines and the VEBs); and

(b) The steering of state production units primarily through financial instruments (reform of price plans, credit, interest, production fund levies and so on) and financial incentives (profit-sharing schemes for the workers, premiums, piece work and so on)[41]

we can say that the measures taken in 1967 and 1968, namely:

(a) The direction of enterprises exclusively through financial performance requirements (target data on expected profits, profit levies to the state, yield on capital, permissible borrowing levels and so on) and financial investment and income incentives; and

(b) The transfer of responsibility for purchasing and sales from the planning authorities and state distribution offices to the enterprises themselves

were fully in conformity with the aim which had been announced as early as 1963 to orient enterprises to profit maximisation as the decisive criterion for rational operations in conformity with the plan.[42]

This was to prevent disruptive conflicts of aims among producers between the fulfilment of binding production targets on the one hand and profit maximisation on the other and to end the struggle over the negotiation of 'soft' plans (easy to fulfil) between the planning authorities and the enterprises.[43]

To ensure that the enterprises, which were now even more independent of direct central planning decisions, were not left entirely to their own initiative basic principles of structural policy were established after 1968[44] which limited the extent of decentralisation and in some cases were actually in contradiction to it.[45] But implementation of these principles naturally affected the system of economic planning: a long-term structural policy concept was developed based on long-term macro-economic prognoses as the main instrument for economy policy decisions, from which in turn 'structural determinants' were derived. In contrast to economic planning hitherto, which had been rather of the nature of 'expectations that the targets set by the political leaders would be met'[46] the structural policy concept derived from prognosis planning was an attempt to make the decision-making process more institutional and put it on a more scientific basis.[47] In content the structural policy concept was designed to make the products, processes and technologies (the structural determinants) which were regarded as of decisive importance for economic growth, and hence were to be given priority in development, the orientation point for planning for the current and future years. The main focus of attention would be balance sheet decisions, contracts, order research and so on.[48]

In keeping with the outlook plan which had been declared the main steering instrument of the economy the products listed as 'structural determinants' were to be manufactured in greater quantities. With the establishment of such priority areas in the manufacturing programme and a concentration of economic potential in the form of various groupings of enterprises the economic policy-makers in the GDR hoped to be able to force economic growth.

But steering instruments were needed for the implementation of these aims to orient the activities of enterprises to the development aims laid down by the state authorities. For this more recourse was had to direct central steering instruments in the form of state pronouncements on basic economic proportions and binding and detailed data on the structural determinants.

Buck has given a very telling characterisation of this phase of the ÖSS (1968–70) and its effects:

> This kind of economic steering, aimed on the one hand at bringing about an economic upswing through making enterprises more independent and on the other at implementing state views on the priority areas for production, investment and foreign trade policy, carried an inherent conflict of aims and inevitably bore the seeds of even sharper controversies between the central and decentral decision-makers. The conflict between the freedom to take initiatives in production on the one hand and state efforts to

concentrate scarce resources on the other contributed further to the increasingly imbalanced growth structure in 1969/70 as well.[49]

The imbalance was mainly the result of the fact that it never proved possible to harmonise the economic policy concept and its structural determinants with the concurrent trend to greater independence for certain economic sectors or enterprises.[50] The expansion of certain sectors enforced by the state entailed additional investment, which drew resources off from other areas. Soon the building industry, for example, could no longer meet the demands being made on it.

A further reason for the failure of the state-supported sectors to meet their targets was a shortage of raw materials and semi-manufactures from sectors which had not been stepped up to the same extent.[51]

Precisely when, according to the programme, specific sectors of the GDR economy should have been among the world leaders with their products and the thesis of 'Overtaking without stopping at the same level' was the dominant theme new bottlenecks emerged to hamper both short and long-term growth:[52] in technical infrastructure (energy supplies, transport); in supplies and reserves for production; in spare parts and repairs; and in the supply of goods and services to the people. Moreover the degree of foreign indebtedness rose rapidly.

After a number of discussions on the rapidly worsening economic situation and a revision of the targets of the economic plan for 1970 the reform policy introduced in 1963 was *de facto* ended by the consultations of the 14th Meeting of the SED Central Committee in December 1970.

Assessments in the Federal Republic of the reform phase largely agree that this period of development brought major changes and did have some successes. It is emphasised particularly that with the announcement of the NÖS the Stalinist idea of maximal economic growth was largely replaced by the concept of optimising economic growth.[53] This is an implicit recognition that the GDR succeeded during this period in establishing an economic and planning organisation which proved effective even under conditions of intensively expanded production without at the same time entailing a return to the methods of a market economy.

However, it did entail some ideological 'opening' of the Socialist political economy towards 'bourgeois' methods. Some examples of this are:[54]

(a) the development of optimisation methods of planning with the help of econometric models;

(b) the use of electronic data processing to make the information system more effective;

Table 2.1
Indicators of Economic Development in the GDR 1966 to 1970

	Real growth over preceding year in per cent					Total growth 1966–70	
	1966	1967	1968	1969	1970	Actual	Plan
Produced national income	4.9	5.4	5.1	5.2	5.6	29	28–32
Industry:							
Gross production	6.3	6.8	6.0	6.8	6.0	36	37–40
Net product[1]	5.0	5.6	6.0	6.3	6.1	33	–
Productivity of labour[2]	6.4	6.5	5.2	6.3	6.3	34	40–45
Construction							
Building and pre-fabricated production	5.3	9.5	9.9	6.5	5.9	43[8]	40
Net product	6.5	7.4	11.0	8.1	5.7	45	–
Labour productivity	5.3	6.2	2.3	-1.1	2.9	16	35–40
Agriculture:							
Net product	4.8	6.2	-0.8	-7.0	5.6	9	–
State production per hectare:							
beef cattle	6.4	6.1	5.2	2.3	0	22	16–20
milk	6.3	3.0	5.5	0.7	-0.8	15	23–28
eggs	-1.0	3.9	3.0	5.4	9.2	22	–
grain	-2.4	0.5	1.4	1.9	9.8	11	–
Transport, post, telecommunications	3.6	2.3	5.4	2.5	8.2	24	–
Trade							
Net product	5.2	4.6	4.6	8.5	4.0	30	–
'Social consumption'	6.0	7.9	10.9	7.0	4.4	41	25[7]
'Individual consumption'	3.9	4.3	3.6	5.7	3.8	24	23[7]
Turnover retail trade (estimate)[3]	4.1	3.9	4.9	6.0	4.3	25	23[7]
food, beverages and tobacco	4.3	4.3	4.6	5.3	3.5	24	18[7]
industrial goods	3.9	3.4	5.3	6.9	5.4	27	29[7]
Gross investment in fixed assets[4]	7.3	9.2	10.3	15.4	7.3	60	48–52
Foreign trade turnover[5]	9.2	4.9	6.7	15.2	13.9	60	38–46
Exports	4.4	7.8	9.7	9.5	10.3	49	–
Imports	14.4	2.0	3.5	21.5	17.6	73	–
Income of the population[6]	3.4	3.2	5.0	5.0	3.4	22	23[7]

Sources: *Statistische Jahrbücher der DDR*; calculations by the DIW, Berlin (cf. *DDR-Wirtschaft. Eine Bestandsaufnahme*, tables in appendix); *Neues Deutschland* of 19 June 1971.

1 Including producer crafts but not construction industry.
2 Gross production per worker and white collar worker (excluding apprentices).
3 Growth at current prices.
4 Not including general repairs.
5 Total imports and exports including trade with the Federal Republic but not including services; in foreign exchange Marks at current prices.
6 Net money income (nominal).
7 These figures are not in the published text of the Outlook Plan; they were given by the President of the Council of Ministers, Stoph, at the VIIIth SED Party Congress.
8 Including statistical projections of construction volume quoted since 1969, as well as steel and metal construction and exports, total construction volume has increased by 48 per cent.

From: Mitzscherling, P., 'Die Wirtschaft der DDR', in Hühmann, H.H. (ed.), *Die Wirtschaft Osteuropas zu Beginn der 70er Jahre*, Stuttgart, Berlin, Cologne, Mainz, 1972, p.63.

(c) the use of cybernetics and systems theory methods to optimise steering;

(d) the development of a 'Socialist theory of commerce'.[55]

Despite the problems of the years 1969/70 most of the quantitative targets for economic development were met during the period 1966 to 1970 (see table 2.1). However, when comparing the targets with the actual data it should be borne in mind that the targets were not made public until 1967 and that constant changes in the price system and new methods of compiling statistics make comparison very difficult.[56]

The ideology of the reform phase and social problems

With the orientation of economic policy to an intensive utilisation of production factors[57] technical progress, scientific and technological experience and knowledge inevitably came to be of greater and greater importance.

The possibility of using new sources of energy (nuclear power), changes in the production processes through mechanisation and automation, the use of electronic data processing equipment in the production and information process and so on seemed to the GDR leaders to offer the hope of achieving the 'Communist society' within the foreseeable future.[58]

It seemed as if it would be possible to eliminate heavy physical work, level out the differences between physical and intellectual work, remove social differences — especially between rural and urban areas — and guarantee that all social requirements could be fulfilled.

These clearly Utopian expectations came to form the concept referred to as the 'scientific-technical revolution' (WTR). In contrast to the existing and newly developing social differentiation together with the divergences in social interests Ulbricht put forward the thesis of the 'Socialist society in the GDR' which was becoming more and more clearly established: the image of a harmonious, basically satisfied people. The reality was different.

The use of material incentive systems to stimulate individual achievement (wages, premiums etc.) was not new to workers in the GDR. Since the state had come into existence attempts had been made in enterprises — generally in vain — to establish an effective wage-performance differential. These efforts had been frustrated not only by the resistance of the workers but also because it proved virtually impossible to interest the enterprise leaders in the implementation of an effective co-ordination of work norms and performance pay rates because their attention had to focus on meeting plan targets, cost what this might, and because of the increasing shortage of labour. The wage system which had been instigated in the 1960s was in any case so complicated that few workers had any real grasp of it, but it did enable both works management and skilled workers to negotiate particularly favourable pay rates. A completely unplanned differentiation of the entire wage system developed and, as the reform policy went on, no more fulfilled the function of stimulating individual performance (a role it was increasingly expected to fulfil) than any of the other economic functions of wages (the allocation function, qualification incentives and so on). At the same time the personal will to perform was inhibited by factors beyond individual control: lack of material, inadequate supplies, unsatisfactory or insufficient tools and spare parts, faults in the machinery and equipment and so on. All these had a negative effect on work motivation.

But even more important than these implications of the wage system would appear to be the fact that the appeal to the material interests of the individual can only be effective if there is a sufficient supply of consumer goods which he can purchase with the extra money he earns. Certainly the orientation to the consumer habits and the standard of living of 'bourgeois' societies, i.e. first and foremost the Federal Republic, was in keeping with the interests of the majority of the people in the GDR. But the fact that this aim was not being achieved despite all the efforts they were making was bound to have a demoralising effect in the end. It was not possible to use the extra pay to acquire a better standard of living. Hence the system of material incentives lost more and more of its expected effect as an 'economic lever'.

Other hopes that had been placed in the production sphere also proved illusory. The improvements that had been expected from automation and mechanisation did not materialise to the extent envisaged. It did not prove possible to eliminate physical work — especially in the subsidiary and auxiliary production spheres — nor could the amount of 'creative' work with the expected higher requirements in terms of qualification levels be increased.[59] In fact changes in technological conditions brought new problems in addition to the already existing difficulties: de-qualification, monotony, mental stress with physical under-utilisation and so on.[60]

To obtain an adequate yield on the increasingly costly and elaborate plant and equipment a growing number of enterprises switched to shift work. But supply bottlenecks and the inadequate infrastructure (transport problems, peak hour congestion, shortages in the supply of services) increased the social problems this brought. In addition to the physical and psychological effects of shift work on individual workers the new arrangements put an even greater burden on families.[61]

The mobilisation of all available reserves of labour to cope with the shortage of manpower had particularly affected women. Almost all the women who were capable of working were integrated into the production process. This had a positive effect on their qualification and training level and greatly improved their social opportunities. But it did not eliminate the still very traditional views on the different roles of men and women so that despite the programmatic emphasis on emancipation women generally found themselves carrying the double burden of a job and caring for the family, often with physical and psychological stress.[62]

The number of creches and kindergartens was increased but there were still severe shortages of services and other supplies which, together with inadequate housing, made the burden for women a heavy one. The number of divorces rose markedly and the birth-rate showed a steady decline. It was not until the 1970s that measures could be taken to alleviate this situation but the problems have by no means all been solved.

Economic organisation and economic policy in the 1970s

The abandoning of the reform policy which, as already shown, was decided during the consultations at the 14th meeting of the Central Committee in December 1970 brought the following measures:[63]

1. Powers of decision on the production programme were largely removed from the production units (VVBs, combinates, VEBs). Production was again primarily steered by central requirements expressed in terms of value (money) and quantity. The one-sided orientation of enterprises to profit maximisation was replaced by an absolute target for net earnings laid down in the plan.[64] This was to prevent enterprises concentrating solely on meeting irrational targets and ensure consideration for economic operations and the quality and sales prospects of their goods despite the abandonment of profit maximisation.

2. Powers of decision on replacement, rationalisation and completion investment were also taken from enterprises or very much reduced by the establishment of preconditions.

3. The financial scope of enterprises (use of financial reserves, borrowing) was reduced by tying the utilisation of earnings more to the fulfilment of quantity targets. This was to prevent enterprises expanding or investing in directions which were not in conformity with the plan.

The transfer of these powers from the lower (VEB) and middle (VVB and some combines) level of decision-making to the higher state economic apparatus (the Council of Ministers, the state Planning Commission, the industrial ministries) marks the return to a direct central steering of economic units. These increasingly became only the implementation organs of central control.

The price system was particularly affected by changes in economic organisation and planning. Where during the reform phase an attempt had at least been made with the industrial price reform to use prices as an active and efficient means of stimulating production, this was now abandoned. In 1971 an industrial price stop was introduced, all the measures to make prices more dynamic were ended and experiments with the formation of 'fund-related prices' broken off. A system of application and confirmation was introduced for new or more highly developed products operated by the state Price Office. 'This made prices once more a passive element in planning from which no real impulses to greater efficiency could be expected.'[65] The effects of this drastic form of price planning were to make the problem of achieving an economic production process and of modernising production almost insurmountable.

What induced the political leaders and economic leaders of the GDR to break off the reform experiment at the end of 1970?

Firstly, and there is general agreement on this particularly among economists in the Federal Republic, the reason was the negative effects on the economic system in 1969/70. The steering capacity of the economic mechanism was not adequate to fulfil the structural policy aims, prevent shortages in supplies of capital and consumer goods and achieve an effective internal production organisation in enterprises or co-ordination above enterprise level.

Secondly — as has already been pointed out — it did not prove possible either to achieve the promised social levelling between the different groups (particular problem groups were women, pensioners, shift workers, unskilled workers) or to satisfy the consumer needs of the population.

The great hopes which had been placed on economic reforms and the concept of the scientific and technical revolution both for the social and the economic situation were reduced to a mockery by reality.

However, it cannot be denied that this — so far the last — manifestation of the revolutionary and Utopian element in Marxism—Leninism aroused a positive echo, especially among some younger academics and technologists.[66] But among the bulk of the population the discrepancy between the ideological and programmatic proclamations and the reality of everyday life brought a growing lack of interest in political and social matters and caused many to retreat into the private sphere.

The situation certainly did not constitute a threat to the system but the strikes in Poland at the end of 1970 would appear to have strengthened the resolve of the party and economic leaders to abstain from further experiments and '. . . to give priority to securing the internal stability of the political system even if this had to be at the expense of greater economic growth'.[67]

So there were political, social and economic reasons for the abandonment of the reform policy. Accordingly at the beginning of the 1970s there was not only a change in the planning and steering mechanisms but at the same time a deeper change in the ideological and programmatic image projected by the party and its leaders. A large number of decisions and regulations, laws and orders during the period from December 1970 to mid-1971 laid the basis for planning techniques and organisation for the coming five-year period. But in view of the difficult economic situation initially only an 'operative', short-term, one-year plan was drawn up for the year 1971, in contrast to the outlook plans covering five-year periods which had been the former practice.

While the five-year plan for the period 1971–75 was still being worked out the leadership passed from Ulbricht to Honecker. At the 16th meeting of the SED Central Committee on 3 May 1971 Erich Honecker officially took over as First Secretary of the SED Central Committee. At the same meeting a draft was accepted for a directive for the five-year plan, which was then passed at the VIIIth SED Party Congress in June that year with very few alterations. In December 1971 the People's Chamber of the GDR finally passed the necessary legislation for the new five-year plan.

The main economic policy goal of the plan was to eliminate existing disequilibria: to secure and strengthen the energy and raw materials basis, expand the technical infrastructure, strengthen the supplier industries and reduce external indebtedness by stepping up exports.[68] That the main concern was really consolidation and no longer economic growth at any price could be seen from the cautious targets for growth rates. The produced national income was to rise by 5 per cent per year, industrial goods production by 6 per cent. The construction industry was expected to reach an annual growth rate of 5 per cent and absolute priority was to be given to housing.

There was a particularly drastic reduction in the growth rates for gross capital investment. These were to be only 3 per cent per year. (From 1964 to 1967 the average annual increase in gross capital investment had been 8.8 per cent, from 1968 to 1970 10.8 per cent.)[69]

To achieve 5 per cent annual growth in national income with such a low level of investment enterprises were told to achieve an optimal combination of maintenance and renewal of plant and equipment and expansion of the means of production. Expansion of the basic stock (of production means) was only permitted if every means of improving existing technical equipment, all possible repairs and rationalisation had been carried out. Instead of the 'Main Task' announced at the VIIIth Party Congress to increase the material and cultural standard of living of the population an average annual increase of private consumption of 4.1 per cent was planned.

The main difficulty in this plan was that efforts were to be made to improve the standard of living of the population and at the same time foreign debts were to be reduced by increasing exports. The conflict in aims brought new but temporary bottlenecks in 1971. It proved possible to overcome these in the course of the planning period, in part by correcting the targets. 'Over the five-year period as a whole the GDR did succeed in meeting most of the quantitative targets established in the plan. In many areas the development actually proved better than the economic leaders had expected.'[70] The produced national income, for example, grew by 5.4 per cent per year from 1971 to 1975 instead of 5 per cent as planned (see table 2.2). The total volume of investment rose by 5.4 per cent per year instead of 3 per cent as planned. The positive overall achievement was partly due to the fact that although the number of inhabitants dropped (from 17.1 million to 16.9 million) the number of persons of working age increased during the period from 58 per cent to 60 per cent of the total population so that the number of persons at work could be increased.

The improvement of the standard of living and of consumption which the VIIIth Party Congress had announced as the aim was very largely achieved. Turnover in the retail trade rose by 28 per cent. Per capita consumption of many basic foodstuffs reached the level of the Federal Republic. The equipment of private households with consumer durables was also greatly improved (see table 2.3), as was the supply of housing. This was a central point in the socio-political programme of the SED. But although much has been achieved in the housing sector it cannot be said that the supply problem, which is still acute, has been overcome (see table 2.4).

In keeping with the overall positive figures in the GDR current account a number of socio-political measures were introduced during the five-year period (these included higher pensions, longer maternity leave, reductions in working time for mothers with full-time jobs, support for young married couples through loans, child allowances to increase the birth-rate).[71]

Further economic policy measures had to be introduced to counteract the effects of the international rise in prices which was having its full effect in the GDR by 1975 at the latest. They were aimed at intensifying production, i.e. at achieving optimal utilisation of capacity by increasing the productivity of labour, rationalisation and cost

Table 2.2
Gross national product according to sectors

	1970	1971	1972	1973	1974	1975	1970	1975	Growth 1970/75 in per cent	
	in billions of Marks in constant prices, base 1975						per cent		total	annual average
Industry[1]	64.5	67.9	71.4	75.7	80.5	85.5	57.5	59.1	32.6	5.8
Building industry	8.5	8.9	9.3	9.7	10.1	10.7	7.6	7.4	25.9	4.7
Agriculture and forestry	14.5	13.9	15.3	15.4	16.4	16.0	12.9	11.1	10.3	2.0
Transport, post and telecommunications	5.6	6.0	6.1	6.4	6.7	7.3	5.0	5.0	30.4	5.4
Internal trade	16.0	17.0	18.1	19.1	20.5	21.2	14.2	14.7	32.5	5.8
Other producer sectors	3.1	3.2	3.3	3.5	3.7	4.0	2.7	2.8	29.0	5.2
All producer sectors	112.2	117.0	123.4	129.8	138.0	144.7	100.0	100.0	29.0	5.2
Minus statistical adjustments	2.7	2.5	2.5	2.5	2.1	2.3	–	–	–	–
Gross national product	109.5	114.5	120.9	127.7	135.8	142.4	–	–	30.0	5.4

1 Including producing crafts but not construction crafts.

Sources: *Statistisches Jahrbuch der DDR 1977*, p.74 (errors through rounding up of figures).

From: Cornelsen, D., 'DDR', in Höhmann, H.H. (ed.), *Die Wirtschaft Osteuropas und der VR China 1970–1980; Bilanz und Perspektiven*. Stuttgart, Berlin, Cologne, Mainz, 1978, p.64.

Table 2.3
Stock of selected consumer durables
(number per 100 households)

	1960	1965	1970	1975	1980[4]
Private cars[1]	3	8	16	26	–
Motorcycles[1,2]	–	33	42	50	–
Radios[3]	90	87	92	96	–
TV sets[3]	17	49	69	82	97
Electric fridges	6	26	56	85	100
Electric washing machines	6	28	54	73	80

1 Not including vehicles largely used for business purposes or by the administration.
2 Including scooters and mopeds.
3 Licensed sets.
4 Plan (cf. ND of 15 January 1976, p.9).

Source: *Statistisches Jahrbuch der DDR 1976*, p.312.

From: Cornelsen, D., 'DDR', in Höhmann, H.H. (ed.), *Die Wirtschaft Osteuropas und der VR China, 1970–1980: Bilanz und Perspektiven*, Stuttgart, Berlin, Cologne, Mainz, 1978, p.69.

Table 2.4
Selected data on housing construction in the GDR

	Completed housing units Total	modernisation[1]	of which		
				new building	
			total	pre-fabricated	individual
		in 1000s		percentage	
1966–70	364.0	67.3	296.7	90.8	–
1971	86.8	21.8	65.0	88.1	3.4
1972	117.0	47.5	69.6	86.6	3.5
1973	125.8	45.0	80.7	84.3	6.4
1974	138.3	50.0	88.3	79.6	10.8
1975	140.8	44.8	96.0	80.1	11.7
1971–75	608.7	209.1	399.6	83.3	7.7
1976–80[2]	750.0	200.0	550.0	–	10.0

1 Including conversions and extensions.
2 Five-Year Plan.

Source: *Statistisches Jahrbuch der DDR 1976*, p.157; Gesetzblatt der DDR, Part I/1976, p 528.

From: Cornelsen, D., 'DDR', in Höhmann, H.H. (ed.), *Die Wirtschaft Osteuropas und der VR China 1970–1980: Bilanz und Perspektiven*, Stuttgart, Berlin, Cologne, Mainz, 1978, p.68.

reductions. The 'intensification complex' also and to a significant extent included efforts to achieve a more effective form of planning and control.

A planning order was issued together with framework guidelines for the year's planning by enterprises and combines. Both were intended to make planning more lucid. The main aim, however, was to increase the authority of the five-year plan over the annual targets: the figures for each year were predetermined sections of the targets in the five-year plan.

At enterprise level changes in the form of planning had their counterparts in detailed regulations on proof of efficiency and means of calculating the productivity of labour.

There were also movements in the price system. The rise in the prices of imported raw materials caused changes in domestic prices designed to ensure economical use of the raw materials. But as it was not permitted to pass these increases on in consumer prices state subsidies had to be given to compensate enterprises for higher costs (reductions in levies, state price compensation funds and so on). At the beginning of 1977 new prices were also fixed for sales of goods between enterprises. But again these could not be passed on to the consumers and they brought further state price support procedures.

The economic principle of stable consumer prices which is still being followed for the current five-year period conflicts, however, with the aim of the increases introduced in prices for raw materials and trade between enterprises: ensuring economical and rational use of the materials and the achievement of a more economical income and expenditure account. A further change in price policy still did not prove adequate to solve this problem: enterprises were able to keep their prices for new and further developed products constant up to 1980 if they could save costs by cutting their consumption of raw or other materials or introduce other rationalisation measures to save costs. Robert Havemann, a critic of the regime from within the GDR, gives a drastic account of the situation: 'The low-price system [of export and consumer goods prices] is the economic system of real Socialism. It makes really rational economic planning virtually impossible. The economic achievements both of individual enterprises and of the economy as a whole are so distorted through the financial procedures involved and presented so wrongly that any economic planning on the basis of the figures in enterprise accounts and banks would certainly be mis-planning'.[72]

As long as a transition to market prices is prohibited because of the disruptive effects this would have on the system the faults in the price system will entail repeated changes not only in price planning but in the entire economic mechanism as well. The price increases for consumer goods of the 'higher categories' which began at the end of 1979 are not a solution to the price problem. The price problem creates in the GDR as in all the economies of the Soviet Socialist type a constant 'inherent pressure to reform'.[73]

The five-year plan for 1976–80 which was passed in legislative form by the People's Chamber of the GDR in December 1976 is also cautious in its growth orientation. With the exception of gross capital investment the planned growth rates are actually lower than those achieved in the previous planning period (see table 2.5).

Table 2.5

	1971–1975		1976–1980
	Plan	Actual	Plan
Produced national income	4.9	5.4	5.1
Industrial goods production	6.0	6.5	6.1
Gross investment	3.0	4.0	5.2
Retail trade turnover	4.1	5.1	4.0

Source: Cornelsen, D., 'DDR', in Höhmann, H.H. (ed.), *Die Wirtschaft Osteuropas und der VR China 1970–1980: Bilanz und Perspektiven*, Stuttgart, Berlin, Cologne, Mainz, 1978, p.85.

These extremely cautious targets are realistic insofar as economic policy in the mid-1970s was facing the following problems:

1. Largely due to price increases on the world market the GDR was showing a growing trade deficit although its foreign trade was increasing.[74] To counteract this export efforts were to be stepped up.

2. More investment was needed to expand domestic production capacity.

3. The policy of the 'Main Task' introduced at the VIIIth and confirmed at the IXth Party Congress in 1976 to achieve a constant improvement in the living and working conditions of the population had to be maintained, as workers expected a steady improvement in the supply of goods, services, and social services in return for the greater demands that were being made upon them at work.

Although this five-year period has not yet come to an end it may be taken that the GDR has and will largely achieve the quantitative targets set. But this does not mean that the basic economic and social problems have been solved. For the whole of the period of economic development under review here we can say that it was a proven instrument of economic policy to counteract economic difficulties, undesirable developments and even crises by changing the overall mechanism of planning and control and the economic organisation itself. In the 1970s more attention was devoted to a second factor in the efforts to combat economic difficulties: human labour. The more comprehensive organisation of 'Socialist competition' increased the intensity of work and put more pressure on individual workers to increase their performance and their own productivity. After a long period of development the planning year 1974 brought greater efforts to apply the concepts and knowledge of labour economics to planning in the enterprise. The methods and instruments of 'scientific work organisation' (WAO) not only created the prerequisites for higher performance (work study and work organisation) but also provided a more penetrating definition of the conditions for the minimum performance required (work study and work classification).

Parallel to this development in May 1976 a resolution was published on the implementation of a wage reform.[75] This was to reduce the percentage of earnings dependent on performance (about 10 to 30 per cent) but at the same time be a more direct reflection of the work done.[76]

This greater pressure on the individual worker gives the policy of the 'Main Task' in its 'unity of economic and social policy' a further dimension: the social policy measures announced at the same time as the wage reforms are not simply a nice present from the party and the state, they are the necessary prerequisite to maintain the individual's will to perform; they are not only the result of performance but its precondition. 'The creation of the will to perform which is necessary politically and economically to secure the necessary readiness over the medium term is one of the main functions of social policy in the GDR.'[77]

From the ideological and programmatic point of view the changes introduced at the VIIIth Party Congress and confirmed at the IXth are seen as the expression of the move to a more realistic policy. Short-term expectations in connection with the scientific and technical revolution have given way to a more sober assessment of the speed and possibilities of scientific and technical progress. During this re-orientation process the political leaders have become more aware of the problems inherent in the possibilities and limits of the creation of 'progressive' work organisation and the greater development of the personality through automation and mechanisation. The use of new technologies is an experimental area with largely undetermined outcome. At the same time empirical social research has come to play a larger role and the search for practicable instruments of socio-political intervention has determined whole research programmes.[78] The revolutionary and Utopian hopes of rapid social and economic improvements have given way to a position based on expectations of a long-term, conflict-ridden process of socio-structural change.[79]

But this means that the increase in individual responsibility for greater efficiency in social production by increases in personal productivity at work can no longer be bound up with immediate hopes for the future. The material interests of the individual in relation to the present thus remain the only incentive. It is in keeping with the condition of 'real Socialism' for the 'revolutionary aim' of Socialism to be integrated into the bureaucratically foreshortened calculations of efficiency and in this way to be 'dispersed'.[80] At the same time there is a risk that the 'emancipatory interest of the worker in the production process' which was once politically desirable may be reduced to 'a material egoistic interest in the given rationality of the [existing] system'.[81]

Neither reform of the planning and control system nor changes in economic organisation will affect this. As the events in Poland now show, the only solution is real political and economic co-operation and codetermination by the workers.

The outlook[82]

The beginning of the 1980s has been characterised by a wave of link-ups above individual enterprise level. The formation of combinates (roughly comparable to 'trusts' in the West) to replace the old VVBs is to help improve the efficiency of the economic system.[83]

While in the control hierarchy as it has been up to now (Ministries of Industry – VVBs – VEBs) the VVBs were the main organ of coordination between state control (the ministries) and the individual plants (VEBs) this function is from now on to be exercised by the new combinates. Like the old VVBs the combinates are directly responsible to the ministries and act on instructions from the minister concerned. However – and this is a major distinction from the VVBs – in all questions concerning the development of the combinate the General Director has sole powers of decision, i.e. his powers within his combinate have been extended with regard to the powers of the ministry. Powers can now be transferred to the combine which are formally still in the hands of the state administration, i.e. the ministries.

From theoretical discussions among economists in the GDR and a number of statements by leading politicians it is clear that the formation of the combinates and the resultant changes in the planning, control and organisational structure are intended to alleviate problems in the economic system and altogether ensure greater economic efficiency. The expectations placed in the combinates have been formulated in the Order on Combinates which outlines their role in the economy and their responsibilities:

(a) securing production to meet requirements and meeting the targets for quality, quantity and value set in the state plans;

(b) developing new products with a high standard of technology and science and putting these into production at short term; at the same time the percentage of top quality products in terms of science and technology, function, design and products which serve to lower costs must be steadily increased;

(c) organisation of the production process of the combinates in the most rational and effective way with the use of the most modern technologies and with minimal expenditure on construction;

(d) constant expansion of production, especially through rationalisation investment with a falling percentage of construction expenditure;

(e) fulfilment of the improvement in the relation between expenditure and results, reduction in costs with at the same time an increase in value through greater quality production as laid down in the plan;

(f) organisation of an effective sales activity, especially for exports together with the appropriate customer service;

(g) continuous improvement of the conditions of work and the standard of living of the workers, especially those on material production.

The simplification of the multi-stage control system which the formation of the combinates has brought about is to improve the efficiency of the information flow and information processing. The direct co-operation between the Minister and the General Director of the combinate is designed to reduce bureaucracy and superfluous reporting.

How far the development of the combinates and the appropriate changes in the economic organisation of the GDR are likely to achieve this it is still too early to say. The Order on the People's Combinates, Combinate Plants and People's Plants of 8 November 1979 came into force on 13 November 1979. Further orders, largely concerned with planning methods and contractual implementation conditions, will have to follow if conflicts which are already becoming apparent are to be settled and clearly defined areas of competence in planning, control and instruction marked out.

Only the coming five-year period, from 1981 to 1985, will show whether the experiment of the combinates has succeeded and the ambitious economic and social aims have been fulfilled.

Notes

1   Direktive des IX. Parteitages der SED zum Fünfjahrplan für die Entwicklung der Volkswirtschaft der DDR in den Jahren 1976–1980. Berlin (DDR), 1976, p.16.
2   Zimmermann, H., 'Die DDR in den 70er Jahren. Zu einigen Aspekten der innenpolitischen Situation der DDR' in Erbe, G., et al., *Politik, Wirtschaft und Gesellschaft in der DDR. Studientexte für die politische Bildung.* Second revised edition, Opladen 1980, p.41.
3   For the following cf. also Strassburger, J., 'Das Wirtschaftssystem in der DDR' in Erbe, G. et al., op.cit. (Note 2), p.241 ff.
4   For the following points see Mitzscherling, P., 'Die Wirtschaft der DDR' in Höhmann, H.H. (ed.), *Die Wirtschaft Osteuropas zu Beginn der 70er Jahre.* Stuttgart, Berlin, Cologne, Mainz, 1972, p.53.
5   Cf. inter alia Selbmann, F., 'Anfänge der Wirtschaftsplanung in Sachsen' in *Beiträge zur Geschichte der Arbeiterbewegung 14* (1972) 1, p.76 ff.
6   Ibid., p.76.
7   'Indirect war damage' includes deliberate destruction by the German army itself. On 19 March 1945, for example, just before the end of the war – the order was issued to destroy all transport, supply, production and communications plant or equipment which might be used for military purposes before it fell into enemy hands.
8   Cf. Barthel, H., *Die wirtschaftlichen Ausgangsbedingungen der DDR. Zur Wirtschaftsentwicklung auf dem Gebiet der DDR 1945–1949/50,* Berlin (GDR) 1979, p.44.
9   After the war only 40 per cent of the pre-war means of transport was still available in the Soviet-occupied zone. About 1,500 bridges, including 970 railway bridges, had been destroyed by enemy action and the German army. The rolling stock of German railways remaining in 1946 in what is now the GDR was about 60 per cent of the 1936 stock. About 18,000 kilometres of road had suffered heavy damage. Cf. Barthel, H., op.cit., p.44 f.
10 Cf. Grüneberg, G., *Von der gegenseitigen Bauernhilfe zur sozialistischen Landwirtschaft,* Berlin (GDR), 1965, p.13.
11 In September 1945 the Leuna-Werke, for example, was only producing 25 per cent of the quantity of nitrogen it had produced before the war. In the autumn of 1945 the Piesteritz nitrogen works had not been able to resume production owing to war damage. Cf. Barthel, H., op.cit., p.49.

12   Ibid., p.48.
13   The Soviet Foreign Minister Molotov stated at the meeting of the Council of Foreign Ministers on 17 March 1947: 'Even the resolutions passed a year ago in the Control Council on reparations from the Western zones are not being implemented. Naturally the Soviet military administration took and is taking measures in its zone to coordinate its reparation plan with the resolutions of the Berlin [he is referring to the Potsdam Conference] and Crimea Conferences [Yalta]. In the Soviet zone industrial plant and goods from current production have been handed over. Certain enterprises have also been transferred to Soviet ownership'. Molotov, W.M., *Fragen der Aussenpolitik. Reden und Erklärungen, April–June 1948.* Moscow, 1949, p.370. Quoted from Barthel, H., op.cit. (Note 8), p.96. The enterprises which had been transferred to Soviet ownership were the 196 firms which later became known as SAGs (Sowjetische Aktiengesellschaften) and remained in Soviet possession for some years.
14   There are widely divergent data on the number of plants which were partly or wholly removed. GDR sources state that 676 plants were removed from the Soviet occupied zone, among them 311 aircraft works, 140 munition factories, 129 weapons factories and 14 tank works (e.g. Doernberg, S., Stulz, P., *Deutschland 1945–1949*, Berlin (DDR), 1959, p.32 f. and Barthel, H., op.cit., p.96) but Western sources give 1372 plants removed or partially removed, mainly mechanical engineering plant, steel works, chemical plant and optical industry works. (Inter alia Nettl, J.P., *Die deutsche Sowjetzone bis heute*, Frankfurt/M., 1953, p.35 and Weber, H., *Von der SBZ zur DDR. 1945–1967*, Hannover (2nd edition) 1966, p.25.
15   On the following points see Barthel, H., op.cit., p.104.
16   Cf. *Neues Deutschland*, edition B, no.14 of 16 January 1947. Quoted from Barthel, H., op.cit., p.104.
17   Cf. Stolper, W., *The Structure of the East German Economy*, Cambridge/Mass. 1960, p.5 and Dietz, R., *Die Wirtschaft der DDR 1950–1974. Forschungsberichte des Wiener Instituts für internationale Wirtschaftsvergleiche beim Österreichischen Institut für Wirtschaftsforschung* no.37, October 1976, p.6, and Weber, H., op.cit. (Note 14), p.25.
18   Cf. Barthel, H., op.cit., p.102.
19   Barthel reports that the following measures were taken to counter the difficulties caused in the GDR by the removal of the plant:

> (a) the restoration of machinery which had been destroyed or badly damaged from the ruins left by the war;
> (b) re-utilisation of old machinery and equipment which had been taken out of service and improvements to increase the efficiency of the old machines;

 (c) a redistribution of machinery in keeping with the plans for the economy to ensure even utilisation;
 (d) new production of plant and equipment.
20 On this aspect of the reparation payments see Zahn, L., *Reparationen und 'Reparationen'.* Die Arbeit 4. (1950) 9, p.428. Zahn admits that it seems contradictory to argue that there was a positive effect from the reparation payments in the form of transfers from current production, and goes on: '. . . but this recognition will force the contradictory truth upon all those who see the reparation payments as an obligation which we could not avoid', loc.cit. Krause, W., *Die Entstehung des Volkseigentums in der Industrie der DDR*, Berlin (GDR), 1958, p.103 f. Barthel, H., op.cit., p.103 f.
21 Cf. Archiv der Staatlichen Zentralverwaltung für Statistik, no.154, Paket Nr. 47, quoted from Barthel, H., loc.cit. p.182.
22 Cf. Weber, H., op.cit., p.28.
23 While for example in 1936 in the territory that is now the GDR about 68 per cent of the produced national income was directly available to supply the needs of the population only 47 per cent of the consumed national income was available to the population in 1947. Cf. Archiv der Staatlichen Zentralverwaltung für Statistik, no.135, Paket Nr. 131 and 43, quoted from Barthel, H., loc.cit., p.146.
24 Cf. Rumpf, W., *Die neue Finanzpolitik*, Berlin (GDR) 1950, p.23. On the general development of investment activity in the GDR see Dietz, R., op.cit., p.30 ff and in more detail for the period 1950 to 1963; Thalheim, K.C., *Die Wirtschaft der Sowjetzone in Krise und Umbau*, Berlin 1964, p.39 ff.
25 Cf. Mitzscherling, P., op.cit., p.53.
26 In addition to the purely economic incentives, many people left the GDR because they were not prepared to accept the political system.
27 Cf. Thalheim, K.C., op.cit., p.123.
28 Apart from the social side effects the policy of mobilising labour reserves, especially women, was extremely effective: the GDR today has one of the highest employment ratios in the world at c. 52 per cent (FRG 45 per cent). (Ratio of persons employed to total population.)
29 Cf. Deutsches Institut für Wirtschaftsforschung Berlin (ed.), *Handbuch der DDR-Wirtschaft*, Hamburg, 1977, p.26. In its 7-year plan the GDR followed the Soviet plan which, inspired by Krushchev, set comparable aims with regard to the USA.
30 Ibid.
31 Cf. Dietz, R., op.cit., p.54. The overall economic growth rate dropped from 11 per cent in 1959 to 6 per cent in 1960 and finally to 4 per cent in 1961.
32 On these arguments see Mitzscherling, P., op.cit., p.53.

33 On the relation between the discussion in the Soviet Union and the developments in the GDR see Thalheim, K.C., op.cit., p.49 ff.
34 Damus, R., *Entscheidungsstrukturen und Funktionsprobleme in der DDR-Wirtschaft*. Frankfurt/M., 1973, p.50. Thalheim has given a similar interpretation of the reforms: Thalheim, K.C., op.cit., p.75.
35 Cf. Damus, R., op.cit., p.50 f.
36 Cf. Mitzscherling, P., loc.cit., p.56 f.
37 At the Eleventh Meeting of the SED Central Committee in December 1965 Ulbricht said: 'We still have insufficient control of overall economic processes in our planning and balances' and demanded a higher quality of planning. Ulbricht, W., *Probleme des Perspektivplans bis 1970*, Berlin (GDR), 1966 (second edition), p.10 ff.
38 Ibid.
39 Mitzscherling, P., loc.cit., p.58.
40 Cf. Damus, R., op.cit. (Note 34), p.64 ff; Mitzscherling, P., op.cit. (Note 4), p.58 ff. and Buck, H., 'Umkehr zur administrativen Befehlswirtschaft als Folge nicht behobener Steuerungsdefekte der Wirtschaftsreformkonzeption' in Gleitze, B., Thalheim, K.C., Buck, H., Förster, W., *Das ökonomische System der DDR nach dem Anfang der siebziger Jahre*, Berlin, 1971, p.78 ff.
41 Cf. Buck, H., loc.cit., p.78.
42 Ibid., p.79.
43 Ibid.
44 Cf. *Beschluss des Staatsrates der DDR über weitere Massnahmen zur Gestaltung des ökonomischen Systems des Sozialismus* of 22 April 1968. Gbl. der DDR, Part I, no.9, p.223 ff. and the *Beschluss über die Grundsatzregelungen für komplexe Massnahmen zur weiteren Gestaltung des ökonomischen Systems des Sozialismus in der Planung und Wirtschaftsführung für die Jahre 1969 und 1970* of 26 June 1968. Gbl. der DDR, Part II, no.66, p.433 ff.
45 Buck, who gives impressive evidence to support his thesis of the further decentralisation in the phase from 1968 to 1970 and hence the continuance of the reform policy of the years 1963 to 1967, actually concedes 'that some of the economic policy reorganisation measures adopted in these years were contradictory and can therefore be interpreted as a gradual increase in *general recentralisation*', Buck, H., op.cit., p.78.
46 Mitzscherling, P., op.cit., p.59.
47 Deutsches Institut für Wirtschaftsforschung, Berlin (ed.), *DDR-Wirtschaft. Eine Bestandsaufnahme*, Frankfurt/M., 1971, p.83.
48 Ibid.
49 Buck, H., loc.cit., p.82.

50   Buck shows by his analysis of credit policy that the economic leaders were facing a virtually impossible task 'in attempting to establish organic links between central planning and planning on their own responsibility by the Socialist goods producers [the enterprises] by the use mainly of finance policy steering instruments'. Buck, H., op.cit., p.82 ff.
51   On this cf. Cornelsen, D., 'DDR', in Höhmann, H.H. (ed.), *Die Wirtschaft Osteuropas und der VR China 1970—1980: Bilanz und Perspektiven*, Stuttgart, Berlin, Cologne, Mainz, 1978, p.59, and Zimmermann, H., op.cit., p.21.
52   On the following points see Cornelsen, D., op.cit., p.59.
53   Cf. Thalheim, K.C., 'Die neue Phase des ökonomischen Systems des Sozialismus', in Gleitze, B., Thalheim, K.C., Buck, H., Förster, W., op.cit., p.55.
54   On the following points see ibid., p.55 f.
55   On this last aspect see the detailed account in Forster, W., 'Das ökonomische System der DDR nach dem, Anfang der siebziger Jahre. Betriebswirtschaftliche Konsequenzen', in Gleitze, D., Thalheim, K.C., Buck, H., Förster, W., op.cit., p.109 ff.
56   On this problem see Mitzerschling, P., op.cit., p.62.
57   Here it should be emphasised that the transition from the extensive to the intensive improvement of production is not based only on subjective decisions, it is objectively necessary at a particular point of development to ensure further effective growth. Hence I argue that the economic reforms in the GDR in 1963 were a belated reaction to objective requirements which had already arisen by the end of 1958. For more detail see Strassburger, J., 'Wissenschaftliche Arbeitsorganisation in der DDR (II)', *Deutschland-Archiv*, 8 (1975), 6, p.626.
58   On this and the following argumentation see Zimmermann, H., op.cit., p.16 ff and Zimmermann, H., 'Politische Aspekte in der Herausbildung, dem Wandel und der Verwendung des Konzepts "wissenschaftlich-technische Revolution" in der DDR', *Deutschland-Archiv*, Special issue 1976, p.17 ff.
59   Cf. Strassburger, J., 'Einige Aspekte der Wirkung des wissenschaftlich-technischen Fortschritts auf die materiellen Arbeitsbedingungen in der industriellen Produktion der DDR', *Deutschland-Archiv*, Special issue, 1976, p.95 ff.
60   Ibid.
61   In more detail see Strassburger, J., 'Ökonomische und soziale Probleme der Schichtarbeit', *Deutschland-Archiv*, Special issue 1978, p.71 ff.
62   On the problems and achievements of women at work in the GDR see Helwig, G., *Zwischen Familie und Beruf. Die Stellung der Frau in beiden deutschen Staaten*, Cologne, 1974.

63   See Buck, H., op.cit., p.96 f, Cornelsen, D., op.cit., p.60 f and Mitzscherling, P., op.cit., p.80 f.

64   Net profits are calculated from gross profits minus production fund levy. The production fund levy was introduced during the NÖS and constitutes a levy payable by plants to the state for the production means provided by the state. Since 1971 it has been 6 per cent of the value of the basic stock (production means). With the constant changes in the price system and the faults this still has (see above) the production fund levy has never been able to fulfil its real function of inducing plants to be economical with their basic stock and so increase productivity. On the production fund levy see Bundesministerium für innerdeutsche Beziehungen (ed.), *DDR-Handbuch*, Cologne, 1979 (2nd edition), p.862 f.

65   Cornelsen, D., op.cit., p.61.

66   Cf. Zimmermann, H., op.cit., p.22.

67   Ibid., p.22. Cornelsen, D., op.cit., gives a similar argument, p.62.

68   Cf. Cornesen, D., op.cit., p.62. The foreign trade relations of the GDR are not discussed here as they are dealt with in the chapter by H.D. Jacobsen.

69   Cf. Dietz, R., op.cit., p.31. The average annual growth rates for the national product were 5.0 per cent and 5.3 per cent during the same period.

70   Cornelsen, D., op.cit., p.63 and for the following data ibid., p.64 ff.

71   Here I can only give an indication of the aims and effects of social policy in the GDR. There is a more detailed discussion of this in the chapter in this book by H. Michalsky.

72   Havemann, R., 'Der reale Sozialismus hat abgewirtschaftet', in *Stern-Magazin*, no.36 of 28 August 1980, p.182. These are extracts from a book by Havemann which will shortly be published in the FRG.

73   Cf. Mitzscherling, P., op.cit. and Leptin, G., 'Bilanz der Wirtschaftsreform in der DDR', in Höhmann, H.H., Kaser, M.C., Thalheim, K.C. (ed.), *Die Wirtschaftsordunungen Osteuropas im Wandel. Ergebnisse und Probleme der Wirtschaftsreformen. Vol.I. Länderberichte: Ausmass und Bedeutung der institutionellen Veränderungen* Freiburg im Breisgau, 1972, p.108.

74   In 1975 the GDR's foreign trade percentage was about 25 per cent, nearly as high as that of the FRG.

75   Cf. 'Gemeinsamer Beschluss des Zentralkommitees der SED, des Bundesvorstandes des FDGB und des Ministerrates der DDR über die weitere planmässige Verbesserung der Arbeits- und Lebensbedingungen der Werktätigen im Zeitraum 1976–1980' of 27 May 1976, in *Sozialversicherung und Arbeitsschutz 22 (1976)*, 6, p.9 ff.

76   On wage reform see Zimmermann, H., 'In der DDR wird das Lohnsystem reformiert', in *Die Quelle*, 1977, vol.3, p.114 ff. and Strassburger, J., 'Ein neues lohnpolitisches Experiment? Aspekte der Neuordnung der Grundlöhne in der DDR', *Deutschland-Archiv 9*, (1976), 9, p.950 ff.
77   Strassburger, J., 'Neue Grundlöhne in der DDR. Ein Beitrag zur Einheit von Wirtschafts-, Sozial- und Lohnpolitik', *DDR-Report 10* (1977), 7, p.411.
78   Cf. Zimmermann, H., op.cit., p.41.
79   Quoted from Zimmermann, H., op.cit., p.40.
80   Belwe, K., *Mitwirkung im Industriebetrieb der DDR. Planung — Einzelleitung — Beteiligung der Werktätigen an Entscheidungsprozessen des VEB*, Opladen 1979, p.63.
81   Ibid.
82   This passage includes part of my contribution to Erbe, G., et al. op.cit. (Note 3), p.259 f. The basic concept has been formulated in Melzer, M., Scherzinger, A., Schwartau, C., 'Wird das Wirtschaftssystem der DDR durch vermehrte Kombinatsbildung effizienter?' in Deutsches Institut für Wirtschaftsforschung Berlin (ed.), *Vierteljahreshefte zur Wirtschaftsforschung Heft 4*, 1979, p.365 ff. A detailed discussion of the problems of the combinates can be found in Melzer, M., Erdmann, K., 'Probleme der Kombinatsbildung in der DDR — Volkswirtschaftliche und betriebswirtschaftliche Aspekte' in Forschungsstelle für gesamtdeutsche wirtschaftliche und soziale Fragen (ed.), *FS-Analysen 8*, 1979, p.25 ff.
83   Fundamentally the expectations placed in the formation of large enterprises is not a new development. Ulbricht used almost the same words when announcing the formation of the VVBs as Honecker used to describe the combinates which have now replaced them: 'The VVB is responsible for the production process of the enterprises which belong to it, from the establishment of requirements to the evolution and implementation of technical progress, from research to the use of new technology, from production to sales and the achievement and distribution of the target earnings. So the VVB acts independently and in its own responsibility in the planning, implementation and control of the state functions entrusted to it and takes a key position in the direction of industry'. From the speech by Walter Ulbricht at the economic conference of 24 June 1963, in *Neues Deutschland*, 26 June 1963, p.6.

3 Foreign trade relations of the GDR

Hanns-Dieter Jacobsen, Foundation for Science and Politics, Ebenhausen, Saarland

Introduction

Foreign trade relations have been of major importance for the political and economic development of the GDR, for at least two reasons. Firstly during the 1950s and 1960s foreign trade played a major part in East Germany's efforts to achieve international recognition as a state; secondly it also made a decisive contribution to putting the economy on a relatively high level of development.

Since the wave of international recognition of the GDR between 1969 and 1973 the importance of foreign trade relations has not diminished. But since the economic crises of 1973 and after (the GDR is poor in natural resources and has been badly hit by the rise in world prices for fuel and other raw materials) the context in which this policy operates has changed and it is clear that the GDR is orienting its foreign trade relations increasingly only to economic considerations.

The field of tension between continuity and change is the main focus of this chapter; attention concentrates on historical and political issues as well as economic aspects.[1] The first section contains a discussion of the theoretical basis of the GDR's foreign trade relations and the modifications undergone by the Soviet system, which was initially transferred *in toto* to the Soviet Occupied Zone, as it then was. The second section considers the scope the GDR has for independent action in this field and examines the question of how far, with its strong dependence on foreign trade, the GDR has been able to use this policy not only to further its economic development but also to achieve what was originally its main concern and gain international recognition as a state. The last section discusses the relation between co-operation and delimitation, concentrating firstly on the deteriorating economic situation and the tight-rope which the GDR has to tread between integration into COMECON and relations to the West; secondly it discusses the internal social and ideological problems which have arisen as foreign trade policy has become more and more oriented to considerations of efficiency only.

The Soviet system and the role of foreign trade in a 'small' socialist economy

After the recent discussion on the role of foreign trade in a planned economy there is now general agreement that a system of this nature *cannot* be characterised by a tendency to national self-sufficiency or autarchy.[2] In the Soviet Union, which was for a long time the only planned economy, the system did in fact give rise to a 'trade aversion',[3] and foreign trade degenerated to a 'stop-gap'. The size of the country and its immense wealth of resources made autarchy or independence possible[4] and foreign trade played only a minor role in efforts to raise the general standard of living. The imposition of the Soviet economic system on the people's democracies of Eastern Europe — and hence the GDR as well — after the Second World War meant that in these countries too foreign trade was accorded little significance, at least at first. But it was quickly apparent that a largely schematic transfer of the mechanisms and methods of Soviet economic planning to countries which were inadequately provided with natural resources and had only very small domestic markets was not feasible.

The difficulties arose as the GDR and other East European states succeeded in raising their level of economic performance. East Germany, Hungary, Czechoslovakia and the other Eastern European states are extremely dependent on efficient foreign trade. They have to import nearly all the raw materials they need for their manufacturing industries and they require sales markets abroad if they are to produce goods of international standard.

It was only at the end of the 1950s in the context of general economic reforms that foreign trade came to be accorded a new function in the GDR and was adjusted to the country's real needs.[5] In both the theory and the practice of economic policy it ceased to be a stop-gap and came to be recognised as one of the major factors which could contribute to growth in a Socialist economy as well.[6]

This had an immediate effect on the foreign trade policy of the

GDR. Restriction of the range of goods produced at home and specialisation mainly on 'intelligence-intensive products'[7] showed a readiness to participate in the international division of labour within the framework of the 'Socialist world economic system', in other words COMECON, and to a certain extent within the world economy as a whole. This then also entailed an increasing dependence on imports and on products which could no longer be manufactured at home, and created dependence on foreign markets for goods which could only be produced in large numbers or with such research and development expenditure that the domestic market no longer sufficed to justify the outlay or absorb the quantity.

The economic situation in the GDR, which has a high degree of industrialisation and few raw materials, meant that foreign trade relations were indeed necessary to provide sales markets for high technology products and at the same time guarantee a supply of raw materials at favourable prices.

The foreign trade monopoly held by the state and practised in the GDR on the Soviet pattern since 1949[8] provided the instrument for the implementation of foreign trade and foreign policy aims. It was defined in the Act on Foreign Trade, in force since 9 January 1958 and laid down in the Constitution, which had been in force since 6 April 1968 (Article 9, para. 5).[9] The Act on the Council of Ministers of the GDR of 16 October 1972 contains provisions on the exercise of the monopoly: section 5, subpara. 4 states that the Council of Ministers 'guarantees maintenance of the state monopoly in foreign economic relations, including trade and foreign currency'.[10] So the foreign trade monopoly covers a number of powers: it includes besides trade (the Ministry for Foreign Trade, foreign trade enterprises and so on), foreign currency and the conversion of the Mark (the Ministry of Finance, the Bank for State and Foreign Trade etc.), planning co-ordination, transport and other matters.[11]

Hence political decision-makers in the GDR had enough institutional levers at their disposal to be able to use foreign trade relations over the shorter term as well for other than purely economic purposes. But the development of a consistent strategy proved difficult, especially since in the period immediately after the war all efforts had to be concentrated on supplying the people in the Soviet Occupied Zone and revitalising the economy, which had completely broken down.

*The initial consolidation in the period
immediately following the war*

Proclamation No.2 of the Allied Control Council of 20 September 1945 stated that trade relations between Germany and other countries had come to an end on the day of unconditional surrender, 8 May 1945. But some days before, on 9 September 1945, the Soviet Military Administration (SMAD) had announced the establishment of a 'Foreign Trade Administration' in their zone. Until the GDR was founded in 1949 this institution formed the central organ of planning, administration and approval for the conclusion and implementation of foreign trade agreements.[12]

By 1949 a number of other institutions had been founded which were engaged in the organisation of foreign trade for the Soviet Occupied Zone and the gradual restoration of foreign trade functions to German hands. They were to ensure 'production for the international exchange of goods to secure the import of the raw materials needed for reconstruction' (guideline on economic policy issued by the Communist Party on 7 January 1946) and thus help to 'lay the basis for the re-integration of Germany into international trade through the export of consumer goods and the import of the necessary raw materials and food, partly with the help of international goods credits' (Principles and Aims of the SED, passed at the congress at which the party was founded, 21–22 April 1946). But although these postulates would appear to be directly related to the needs of the Soviet Occupied Zone there can be no doubt that the implementation of foreign trade measures was subject to Soviet directives. This applied particularly to trade between the Soviet Occupied Zone and the USSR itself: the East Germans not only had to make considerable reparation payments but also accept extremely unfavourable conditions regarding both the type of goods exported to the Soviet Union (high quality goods in short supply) and prices (frozen at 1944 export levels).

This clearly determined the aim of foreign trade policy as far as its major area was concerned: a reduction or if possible cessation of reparations in the form of the removal of plant or transfers of goods from current production, and then the achievement of more favourable conditions in trade with the USSR.

It was not until after the uprisings of 17 June 1953 that the first aim was fully achieved. On 22 August 1953 the Soviet Union stated that it was prepared to waive further reparations from the GDR and return the remaining 'Soviet enterprises' (SAGs) to the Germans. The second aim was also only achieved – at least in part – in the early 1950s in the trade agreements which the GDR began to conclude with the Soviet Union.

Nevertheless the complex relations with the Soviet Union remained one of the main problems in foreign trade relations for the GDR, and it remains so today. The Soviet Union exercised a dual role as occupying power and guarantor of internal and external security in the GDR, and the East Germans had to establish their own economic interests against this force.

It is therefore not surprising that even in the early stages of its development the Soviet Occupied Zone and then the GDR, when it was still not in a position to pursue an independent foreign trade policy, began trying to establish economic contact with the other zones in Germany and West European countries in addition to its relations to the Soviet Union and the new 'people's democracies' in Eastern Europe. But scope for this was extremely small: the growing conflict between East and West, which brought increasing economic discrimination against East European countries by the West,[13] and the rise in world prices for raw materials as a result of the Korean War, drove the GDR further into the arms of the Soviet Union and other East European states. After its foundation on 7 October 1949 the GDR was given diplomatic recognition by the Soviet Union and the other East European states; long-term trade agreements were concluded with these countries at government level and finally on 29 September 1950 the GDR became a member of the Council for Mutual Economic Aid (COMECON), although this was not at the time of major significance.

The GDR thus became completely integrated into the 'Socialist world economic system' and this created the main framework for its foreign trade activities.

GDR foreign trade policy up to the beginning of the 1960s: the first attempts at diversification

When in 1955 the government of the Federal Republic of Germany made the claim which it had been propounding since 1949, to be the sole representative of the German nation abroad, as a major principle of its foreign policy and threatened to break off diplomatic relations with any state which recognised the GDR, efforts to achieve international recognition became the main element in East German foreign policy. Trade policy was the most important instrument in the battle against what came to be known as the 'Hallstein doctrine', especially since few potential partners were really interested in direct bilateral relations beyond trade.[14] Generally it can be said that in the 1950s and 1960s foreign trade relations, although they made a decisive contribution to supplying the raw materials the GDR needed, were made subordinate to the aim of achieving political recognition; in other words, political aims had priority over economic interests.

But as, despite intensive efforts, the GDR was only rarely able to conclude trade agreements on government level with either Western industrialised countries or developing countries, it evolved a graded range of instruments to be used on a lower level. These would ultimately lead, it was hoped, to the conclusion of government agreements and where possible the establishment of diplomatic relations.

Table 3.1
GDR foreign trade turnover 1949–1981
(in millions of foreign exchange Marks)
Regional structure of GDR foreign trade
(in percentage of foreign trade turnover)

Year	Total foreign trade turnover (mill.M)	USSR	Rest of COMECON	Other socialist countries	Developing countries	FRG	Other Western industrial countries
1949	2,702.2	37.7	27.2	0.0	0.3		34.7[1]
1950	3,677.8	39.7	32.6	0.0	0.4	16.0	11.3
1951	5,545.2	45.6	27.9	2.7	1.1		22.7[1]
1952	6,348.1	42.3	28.0	4.8	1.5		23.4[1]
1953	8,190.1	45.7	25.4	0.4	0.7		21.7[1]
1954	10,020.5	48.2	20.3	7.6	1.4		22.5[1]
1955	10,389.3	38.2	25.8	8.1	2.9	10.9	14.1
1956	11,562.1	40.9	24.8	7.4	3.4	11.0	12.5
1957	14,566.4	44.6	21.9	6.8	3.9	11.3	11.5
1958	15,194.5	42.7	22.6	8.6	4.4	11.3	10.3
1959	17,466.0	44.9	23.6	7.5	3.6	11.1	9.3
1960	18,487.4	42.8	24.8	7.0	4.3	10.3	10.8
1961	19,034.6	43.8	27.1	4.1	4.8	9.2	11.0
1962	20,098.5	48.9	26.0	4.1	3.6	8.3	9.1
1963	21,182.9	48.6	25.9	4.1	3.5	8.6	9.5
1964	23,373.6	46.6	25.7	4.1	3.8	9.4	10.4
1965	24,693.2	41.1	28.3	4.4	4.5	9.5	12.2
1966	26,963.8	41.5	26.7	5.0	4.6	10.2	12.1
1967	28,286.1	42.0	27.4	4.8	4.5	9.0	12.3
1968	30,172.6	42.6	28.9	4.5	4.1	8.7	11.2
1969	34,760.8	41.1	27.5	4.1	4.2	10.0	13.1
1970	39,597.4	39.1	28.2	4.3	4.0	10.2	14.2
1971	42,240.6	38.1	29.1	4.4	4.1	10.2	14.1
1972	46,782.4	37.7	30.2	3.2	3.2	10.3	15.5
1973	53,501.7	34.6	31.3	2.8	3.4	9.2	17.1
1974	64,012.7	31.4	29.6	3.1	5.0	9.4	21.5
1975	74,393.6	35.7	30.6	3.5	4.4	8.7	17.2
1976	85,456.5	32.5	31.4	3.2	4.6	8.6	19.7
1977	91,726.3	35.4	32.5	3.5	4.9	8.5	15.2
1978	96,879.4	36.0	32.7	3.3	5.2	8.2	14.5
1979	108,844.6	36.1	29.7	3.0	5.2	8.0	16.0
1980	120,100.8	35.2	27.2	3.8	6.1	8.4	19.1
1981	132,926.9	37.5	25.9	3.2	4.9	8.3	20.2

1 Data for the Federal Republic of Germany and other Western industrialised countries together.

Sources: Annual Statistics (*Statistische Jahrbücher*) of the GDR, current issues.

The Foreign Trade Chamber of the German Democratic Republic established on 14 November 1952 played a major part in this task. Its work included not only 'the establishment, extension and cultivation of economic relations with foreign trade and economic organisations'[15] but 'initially also functions beyond the normal activities of a foreign trade chamber, such as the conclusion of trade agreements'[16] with Western countries which did not recognise the GDR.

However, these efforts only met with very limited success. As table 3.1 shows, the Soviet share of trade with the GDR had risen to nearly 50 per cent by the beginning of the 1960s, while the share of Western industrialised countries (including inter-German trade) had dropped slightly. Only with the developing countries had some increase proved possible. The GDR leaders assumed that with the integration of the main West European countries into the Atlantic Alliance their own foreign trade activities should concentrate on neutral countries such as Sweden, Finland and Austria and the 'anti-Imperialist nation states' especially those in Asia and Africa.[17] The declaration of intent, which generally went with the trade relations, to 'help' the new independent countries in Asia and Africa to build up their economies was a good way of disguising the real aim of 'buying' international recognition through supplying goods and giving technical aid. The conclusion of trade agreements, preferably at government level, were the first steps in this direction. The GDR did not succeed in achieving international recognition but by the end of the 1950s it had concluded government agreements with Egypt, India, Indonesia and some other countries on the exchange of goods and payments.[18]

To counteract the effectiveness of the activities of the GDR in the Third World and prevent it from acquiring nation status the Federal Republic also developed a 'graded range of instruments', in which granting or not granting economic or development aid to these countries played a decisive part.[19] The GDR was at a disadvantage compared with the Federal Republic here because it had far fewer economic resources available for aid. Moreover, some developing countries such as Egypt and India exploited the conflict between the two German states to their own advantage, conferring their political favour on one or other depending on the improvement in economic terms which could be offered.[20]

The other focal area of GDR foreign trade policy was Scandinavia, the states immediately adjoining the Baltic, and Norway. On 2 September 1957, for example, the GDR began a major diplomatic offensive, offering all the Baltic states bilateral or multilateral agreements to expand economic, transport and cultural relations and as from the summer of 1958 it organised a 'Baltic Week' in Rostock every year to improve sports and cultural relations with the countries adjoining the Baltic and with Norway and Iceland, which also participated.[21]

*The New Economic System and the shift
in the functions of foreign trade policy*

In the 1960s the GDR leaders intensified their efforts at diversification. However, changes in the internal and external framework conditions for economic development in the GDR had a considerable effect on the role of its foreign trade relations.

The enforced concentration of economic policy on heavy industry and import substitution brought serious economic problems at the end of the 1950s and in the early 1960s; these included growing shortages in supplies to the population, failure to meet targets and so on. It seemed that the economic system was no longer adequate to meet the demands being made on it. The second five-year plan (for 1956 to 1960) was replaced in 1958 by a seven-year plan with projections up to 1965 and the hardly realistic aim to 'catch up and overtake West Germany in the productivity of labour' was proclaimed.[22] The aim was not achieved and the seven-year plan in turn was broken off in 1963.[23] Even before this there had been extensive discussions on possible modifications to the economic system; these culminated in the announcement of the 'New Economic System of Planning and Control' (NÖSPL) in the summer of 1963, which certainly constituted a break with the 'dogmatic insistence on an economic policy which is clearly obsolete'.[24] The transition from extensive to intensive production which took place in the GDR as in other East European states at this time, the general orientation to criteria of efficiency, to qualitative rather than quantitative target data and new and more flexible methods of planning and control brought a change in the functions of foreign trade as well.

It was recognised that foreign trade could no longer only serve to obtain the raw materials which the GDR needed for production and to create the prerequisites for large-scale, and hence more profitable and rational production methods through growing sales; it also had to help 'solve those economic problems which we cannot solve alone and for which we need the exchange of goods and economic and scientific and technological cooperation'.[25] After 1963 this brought more intensive efforts to expand trade relations not only with the other COMECON states but also with Western countries and put these as far as possible on a longer-term basis.

This intensified the conflict between the two main functions of foreign trade relations: to achieve international recognition (this entailed a readiness to use economic resources which were urgently needed at home) and to support the production process in the GDR. The change in internal conditions narrowed rather than widened the scope for the use of foreign trade as an instrument of foreign policy, although its relatively highly developed economic potential and greater efficiency made the GDR a more attractive trading partner to many countries than other East European states.

Two events marked the change in internal conditions relating to foreign trade relations. Firstly the building of the Berlin wall on 13 August 1961 and the sealing of the frontier with the Federal Republic of Germany put an end to the drain of people and particularly highly qualified workers to the West, and no doubt helped to stabilise the domestic economy, but it did untold damage to the international reputation of the GDR. The second event of major importance was the further integration of the GDR to the COMECON organisation. This brought with it the 'Basic Principles of the International Socialist Division of Labour'[26] and the intention expressed by the Soviet Union to move beyond planning co-ordination to joint planning within COMECON.

Socialist integration versus international division of labour — elements in the GDR foreign trade strategy

A large part of the discussion on the foreign trade relations of the COMECON countries since the 1960s has been devoted to the question of whether their trade with the West should be seen as a substitute for economic integration within COMECON or whether the two can be seen as complementary.[27] It is difficult to answer this question, partly because this would entail an analysis of a number of factors inherent in the systems which hamper East—West economic relations (foreign trade monopolies and structural bilateralism in the East and cyclical fluctuations in the West), but also because the development of political relations between East and West is a decisive factor in determining the potential for East—West economic relations. The GDR provides virtually a model example of this, with its foreign trade relations largely conditioned during the 1960s and even more in the 1970s by its relations with the Soviet Union on the one hand and with the Federal Republic of Germany on the other. Within this field of tension the GDR did succeed in establishing a balance which, albeit extremely fragile, was highly advantageous to itself.

Economic relations with the Soviet Union and the other COMECON states

Even if, as table 3.1 clearly shows, the Soviet Union remained the constant factor in foreign trade relations for the GDR throughout the 1960s, it became more and more apparent that the GDR was concerned at least to keep the general orientation of its foreign trade with that country within limits. The GDR leaders covered their flank for a cautious approach to relatively greater economic independence by repeated assurances of their 'unbreakable ties of friendship' with the Soviet Union, which were anchored among other things in the constitution of 1968 (Article 6, para. 2). In fact the GDR succeeded in achieving a considerable drop in the Soviet Union's share of its foreign trade turnover, which had been 50 per cent in 1963: this fell during subsequent years, reaching a minimum in 1974 at 31.4 per cent. It did not prove possible to maintain this figure, largely because the prices for raw materials supplied by the Soviet Union rose markedly. In 1981 the Soviet share of GDR foreign trade was 37.5 per cent.

The share of trade with the other COMECON states rose slightly but not to the same extent: since the beginning of the 1970s this has been fluctuating around 30 per cent. So within the group of European COMECON countries the distribution has shifted slightly — as table 3.2 shows — in favour of the smaller countries, at least until the end of the 1970s.

We have already indicated that the process of integration into COMECON had an increasing influence on developments within the GDR. The resistance put up by Rumania to comprehensive plans by

Table 3.2
Foreign trade turnover of the GDR with the Soviet Union and the other European members of COMECON 1960–1981 (in millions of foreign exchange Marks);
Regional structure of GDR foreign trade with the European COMECON states (in percentage of foreign trade turnover)

Year	Total foreign trade turnover (mill. Marks)	of which (in percentage)					
		USSR	Bulgaria	Poland	Rumania	Czechoslovakia	Hungary
1960	12,557.9	63.0	4.1	9.8	3.4	13.5	6.3
1966	18,298.2	61.1	4.9	10.0	3.5	13.9	6.7
1969	23,767.7	60.1	5.3	10.2	3.5	13.8	7.0
1972	31,420.9	56.3	5.3	12.2	4.3	13.9	7.9
1974	38,268.0	52.5	5.7	13.2	5.2	14.5	8.9
1976	53,696.9	51.7	5.2	13.9	5.7	14.0	9.5
1977	61,133.2	53.1	5.3	11.8	5.8	13.7	9.4
1978	65,167.9	53.6	5.1	12.5	6.0	13.7	9.2
1979	70,012.6	56.1	4.9	11.4	5.6	13.0	9.0
1980	73,654.6	57.8	5.1	10.5	5.3	12.6	8.6
1981	82,314.6	60.6	4.9	8.9	5.0	12.3	8.3

Source: Annual Statistics (*Statistische Jahrbücher*) of the GDR, various issues.

the Soviet Union to raise the process of economic unification within COMECON, which had only just begun, to the level of joint planning for national economic development, and create a joint planning organ for this,[28] is symptomatic of the attitude of the East European people's democracies and the GDR as well. In rejecting the Soviet initiative, which would certainly very greatly have increased its influence in Eastern Europe, the Rumanians emphasised the 'national sovereignty of a Socialist country';[29] this would have been very considerably reduced by the formation of a joint economic planning organ.[30] There is much to suggest that the Rumanians and the concept which was not pursued further by the Russians, won at least the tacit approval of the other East European states.[31]

Serious conflict appears to have broken out repeatedly between the GDR and the Soviet Union but not only over the general aims of the 'international Socialist division of labour' but also over the five-year and one-year plans and the negotiation of bilateral trade agreements. The GDR seems to have claimed that it was being forced into a position of economic disadvantage, to which the Soviet Union replied that it could not carry the burden of political and military obligations alone. The suicide of Erich Apel, then Chairman of the Planning Commission of the GDR and leader of negotiations with the Soviet Union, on 3 December 1965, one day before a trade agreement between the two countries was signed, is generally taken as a sign of the strain on the GDR leaders. Even if there has never been any official confirmation of the link between the negotiations and Apel's death the coincidence of the two dates suggests that he may have acted 'for his country's terms of trade'.[32]

But relations between the GDR and the other East European states are by no means free of conflict either. At least in its relations to the Soviet Union the economic interests of the GDR do not in principle differ from those of its East European neighbours. But the GDR is by far the most highly developed and internationally competitive of these countries and the advantages it derives from its trade with the Federal Republic, which gives indirect access to the markets of the EEC and is treated by the West Germans not as foreign trade but as trade within Germany, are the cause of considerable ill-feeling.[33] Particularly the less developed COMECON countries have repeatedly insisted on adherence to the postulate formulated in the 'Basic Principles' of 1962 and again in the 'Complex Programme' of 1971 that there should be 'adjustment of the state of development'. The GDR has always refused a real transfer of economic resources or a price structure in favour of these countries, although it has on occasions admitted that the exchange relations between itself and the other East European members of COMECON are to the disadvantage of the latter.[34]

The alternative postulated by the GDR is a process of fundamental integration beyond foreign trade and including the production process (e.g. the establishment of joint enterprises). The GDR argues that there should be an orientation towards 'the proper structures' and that a long-term structural policy should be developed, providing for 'the choice of production sites according to international criteria', in other words, meeting the requirements and development aims of the other COMECON states.[35] But the integration process as it has been realised so far does not reflect this. Roughly since the mid-1970s it has been clear that the far-reaching aims of the 1971 Complex Programme (e.g. internal convertibility of COMECON currencies) would not be realised owing to the immense price increases for fuel and raw materials on world markets; this has somewhat reinforced the already strong tendency to bilateralism among the COMECON countries. The co-ordination of economic plans is still one of the main instruments of COMECON integration but the announcement in the 'Long-Term Programmes and Targets' of 1978 and 1979 that efforts were to be concentrated on major bottlenecks such as energy supplies, major food items and industrial consumer goods, together with mechanical engineering and transport, suggests that there are more concrete problems to be solved first. This has enabled the GDR to retain some scope for independent economic action which it has used to further its own interests and aims, including the expansion of its trade relations with the West.

Economic relations with the Federal Republic of Germany and the other Western industrialised countries

Relations with the Federal Republic of Germany have always occupied a special place in the GDR's trade with the West. The motives generally given for relations between Communist countries and the West[36] have been particularly well satisfied by the 'inner-German' trade between the two states. These relations are a unique phenomenon. Although trade between East and West Germany has all the characteristics of cross-frontier transactions it is regarded by the Federal Republic not as international but as the internal movement of goods. The reasons for this are political. The Federal Republic sees its trade relations with East Germany as one of the few remaining links holding the two Germanies together. And although the GDR is in all other respects stubborn in its insistence on its national sovereignty it has so far given no indication that it is prepared to do without the advantages which this special treatment in trade affords. The benefits are many:[37] a protocol annexed to the EEC Treaty, for example, states that agricultural imports from the GDR to the FRG are exempt from levies and manufactured goods are exempt from customs duties, so that the GDR is not subject to the regulations governing trade between the EEC and third countries. Nor is 'inner-German' trade subject to the joint trade policy of the EEC countries; it is handled autonomously by the Federal Republic. The GDR also derives advantages from the mutual interest-free credit facility arranged between the two states and which so far only the East Germans have utilised.[38] The GDR and its foreign trade organs have increased the possible benefits of these preference structures by making internal adjustments. That structural changes have been made has been confirmed by empirical studies. Roughly since the mid-1960s the structure of GDR exports to the FRG has differed considerably from that of exports to comparable OECD countries[39] and this is a direct result of the conditions of 'inner-German' trade.

These examples show that it is one of the maxims of the GDR to utilise advantages offered in international trade even if this goes contrary to political principles — in this case acceptance of treatment as a 'home market' by the Federal Republic — when it is apparent that the political objective is not going to be achieved. On the other hand the GDR is making obvious efforts to reduce the economic influence which the FRG exercises or could exercise upon it. 'Inner-German' trade is felt to be a potential source of pressure particularly with regard to the question of free access to West Berlin, regulations on visits by West Berliners and West Germans to the GDR and the matter of 'keeping the German question open'. Accordingly the GDR is concerned not to let its indebtedness to the Federal Republic and other Western countries grow too high although, like other COMECON countries, it has made extensive use of Western credit facilities in recent years.[40]

As table 3.1 shows, the share of inner-German trade in total foreign trade turnover for the GDR has rarely exceeded 10 per cent since the beginning of the 1960s; since the beginning of the 1970s there has actually been a slight decline (to 8.3 per cent in 1981). But there has been a considerable increase in trade with other Western industrialised countries (from about 10 per cent at the beginning of the 1960s to 20 per cent in 1981). This is due to the increase in trade with the USA and Japan and other NATO countries such as Great Britain and France.[41] But the share of neutral states, such as Austria and Sweden, which were formerly given preference, has dropped slightly.[42]

Of West European states which are members of alliances France and Great Britain have been the GDR's first choices for foreign trade policy activities and it has succeeded in building up a considerable degree of organisational and institutional ties with these countries. In 1959, for example, a trade representation was opened in Great Britain and the first chamber agreement concluded. In the pursuit of its political aims (international recognition) and economic goals (long-term trade agreements) the GDR made to Britain, as it had done to France and Denmark, offers (such as a multiple increase in bilateral trade within a few years)[43] which it was hardly in a position to fulfil as this would have far overstrained its industrial capacity. After the establishment of diplomatic relations with Britain and France in 1973 the GDR cut back imports from these countries, despite previous assurances to the contrary, causing considerable ill-will.[44]

Among neutral countries Austria was the focus of most GDR activity in the 1960s. Austria's neutral status left both countries considerable scope although Austria made it plain that the Federal Republic of Germany was by far its more important trading partner and there could be no question of recognising East Germany. But a factor which facilitated relations between Austria and the GDR was that as integration within the EEC increased Austria, which was not and could not become a member, aimed to expand its trade with Sweden (like itself a member of EFTA). The shortest transport routes lead across the GDR and the offer of access to these proved attractive to Austria which in turn offered the GDR certain economic advantages (such as most-favoured nation treatment in 1968).

Sweden was also one of the GDR's prime targets for trade activity during the 1960s. The GDR participated, for example, in the Göteborg international trade fair 'often despite disparities in economic performance'.[45] Representations of the Foreign Trade Chamber of the GDR, which were opened in Sweden in 1957, did not have consular or diplomatic status but they were of considerable importance as economic footholds in the country. The political gains from all these efforts, however, were meagre: Sweden not only refused to accede to GDR demands for international recognition but also refused to conclude the long-term trade agreements which the GDR so greatly desired.

An assessment of the development of foreign trade relations between the GDR and Western industrialised countries in regard to the two main aims pursued by East Germany, namely raising its political status or actually achieving recognition as a state, and integration in the international division of labour, shows that despite considerable material expenditure this policy did not result in recognition as an independent state. However, the GDR certainly succeeded in expanding its foreign trade. Since the beginning of the 1970s, when the 'wave of recognition' began after the Basic Treaty was signed between the Federal Republic of Germany and the GDR, one quarter of its foreign trade has been with Western industrialised countries (including the FRG). This figure has since remained largely constant.

Table 3.3
Foreign trade turnover of the GDR with
Western industrialised countries 1960–1981
(in millions of foreign exchange Marks)

Share of selected Western industrialised countries
(in percentage of foreign trade turnover)

Year	Total foreign trade turn-over (mill. Marks)	of which (in percentage)								
		FRG	France	GB	Italy	Netherlands	Austria	Sweden	Japan	USA
1960	3,897.2	49.1	2.9	6.7	2.7	4.6	4.2	4.7	0.2	1.0
1966	6,005.5	45.9	4.8	5.6	3.3	4.5	4.2	4.1	0.9	2.4
1969	8,028.9	43.5	3.8	4.3	3.6	4.1	2.7	4.6	1.4	1.6
1972	12,048.7	40.1	7.6	6.2	3.2	5.3	3.1	3.7	2.4	2.5
1974	19,790.7	30.3	4.6	8.1	3.3	8.3	4.4	4.1	1.3	2.9
1976	24,208.1	30.4	6.9	10.8	2.9	4.8	3.5	4.8	0.7	9.3
1977	21,758.4	35.6	4.9	6.0	2.7	5.6	4.0	5.5	1.1	3.8
1978	22,005.4	36.2	6.2	6.4	4.3	5.1	3.8	4.9	1.8	4.9
1979	28,283.4	30.8	7.0	7.5	4.1	5.2	3.9	3.6	4.7	4.8
1980	32,959.8	30.6	6.6	5.3	3.0	5.3	5.9	4.5	3.2	5.8
1981	37,840.7	29.2	8.5	4.5	3.3	5.8	6.8	4.2	2.6	3.6

Sources: Annual Statistics (*Statistische Jahrbücher*) of the GDR, various issues.

The role of the developing countries

The developing countries' share of the GDR's foreign trade has, as table 3.1 shows, seldom been more than 4 to 5 per cent. Relations with these countries, especially those which chose a 'non-capitalist path' were, like relations with Western industrialised countries, at first made to serve the dual purpose of ensuring supplies of raw materials, food and so on for the GDR and contributing to the enhanced political status of the country through 'contractual agreements on state and government level, as are usual in international relations and indeed indispensable'.[46]

But even in the 1950s it was clear that the GDR was concentrating its attention on certain focal points in the Third World. These were mainly in Asia and Africa, with India and Egypt playing the major roles. In 1960 these two countries accounted for nearly 50 per cent of the GDR's total trade with Third World countries (see table 3.4); in 1972 the figure was still nearly 40 per cent and it only dropped after that date to just on 14 per cent in 1981.

The political importance attached to these countries can be seen from the diplomatic activities of the GDR. India especially, with its leading position in the non-aligned world, was regarded as a pace-maker and possible multiplier for the GDR's international reputation and hence made one of the main trading and co-operation partners in the

Table 3.4
Foreign trade turnover of the GDR with developing countries 1960–1981
(in millions of foreign exchange Marks)

Share of selected developing countries (in percentage of total)

Year	Total foreign trade turnover (mill. M)	in Asia (in percentage)						in Africa (in percentage)					in Latin America					
		India	Indonesia	Iraq	Iran	Lebanon	Syria	Egypt	Algeria	Angola	Ethiopia	Libya	Argentina	Brazil	Chile	Colombia	Mexico	Peru
1960	791.3	16.0	2.6	1.9	1.5	1.7	1.8	33.1	0.1	–	–	0.6	2.4	12.9	0.0	1.7	0.4	0.0
1966	1,249.1	17.3	9.5	1.0	1.4	2.2	1.5	21.5	0.2	–	–	0.3	0.7	7.9	0.3	5.9	0.5	3.6
1969	1,442.7	16.6	0.4[1]	1.9	1.9	2.0	2.9	21.7	1.6	–	–	0.4	–	15.1	0.2	4.8	0.7	2.8
1972	1,494.0	13.8	–	8.4	0.1	2.3	5.4	26.4	4.1	–	–	0.3	0.4	13.3	1.7	3.0	0.7	3.0
1974	3,167.1	10.1	0.7[2]	20.5	1.2	2.0	5.2	19.8	2.6	–	–	0.3	0.9	6.7	5.6[3]	1.6	1.1	5.3
1976	3,918.3	8.9	0.7	19.9	2.5	1.7	8.9	14.3	3.1	0.0	0.0	1.6	1.1	12.7	–	3.1	1.0	5.2
1977	4,504.1	7.5	0.9	13.2	2.7	0.8	7.6	12.1	2.2	5.2	6.2	–	3.8	10.3	–	3.4	1.0	5.2
1978	5,027.7	9.4	0.8	14.4	3.2	1.1	8.1	8.8	6.4	4.6	6.3	0.3	3.0	10.1	–	2.0	1.0	3.1
1979	5,670.1	6.7	1.2	16.1	2.8	1.1	7.7	9.2	4.4	5.5	1.1	1.0	5.2	8.3	–	3.0	1.6	3.4
1980	7,331.2	6.0	1.0	20.5	7.5	1.5	5.3	4.2	7.4	3.8	1.8	6.8	3.0	8.2	–	3.0	2.9	0.5
1981	6,542.3	9.1	1.4	10.9	9.3	1.9	6.6	4.5	3.8	3.0	1.0	7.6	3.6	10.1	–	2.2	4.0	0.9

1 1970
2 1975
3 1973

Sources: Annual Statistics (*Statistische Jahrbücher*) of the GDR, various issues.

Third World.⁴⁷ Relations with Egypt were also designed to have a multiplier effect, this time in the Arab world. Here in addition to expanding trade and co-operation the GDR took the rather unusual step for a Communist country of offering long-term capital aid.⁴⁸ The visit paid by Walter Ulbricht to Egypt in 1965 — his only state visit outside the Communist world — was a clear sign of the importance the GDR attached to this region.

These efforts brought some successes at the end of the 1960s. An Asian country broke the ice: Cambodia was the first non-Communist country to recognise the GDR, in May 1969. It was followed a few weeks later by the Arab states of Iraq, the Sudan, Syria, South Yemen and Egypt. That promises of economic aid in the form of trade expansion and presumably technical aid as well had been a major factor in the decisions by these countries (and others which followed), which had to accept a deterioration in their relations to the Federal Republic, can be seen from the case of the Central African Republic, which broke off relations with the GDR a few months after first establishing these on the grounds that no aid worth speaking of had been forthcoming from the GDR.⁴⁹

Generally it can be said that the volume of trade and co-operation agreements concluded by the GDR with under-developed countries was modest and remained concentrated on certain crucial areas. The East Germans achieved their main diplomatic successes where they were able to offer development aid in the form of credits, technical aid and in some cases even military aid. An analysis of the GDR's foreign trade shows that some of the main trading partners in the Third World (such as India and a few Latin American countries such as Brazil, Columbia and Peru) are not among those which opened diplomatic relations with the GDR before the 'wave of recognition' began in 1972. But of those countries which did recognise the GDR before 1970 nearly 90 per cent had received capital aid between 1954 and 1970.⁵⁰ So the GDR's development aid policy paid off, albeit late.⁵¹

Co-operation and delimitation in the GDR's foreign trade relations

The full integration of the GDR into the international community of nations, which took place as from 1972/73 as diplomatic relations were established with almost every country in the world, caused yet another shift in the functions of its foreign trade. The subordination of this to purely political ends, which had been a policy for a time and entailed considerable economic losses, could be reduced and in some cases ceased altogether. International recognition of the GDR meant that foreign trade policy could be oriented to purely economic considerations and the GDR was able to exercise this policy more in keeping with its 'natural' function within its own economic system.

But the scope for utilising this economic independence, which had been so hardly won from its two main trading partners, the USSR and the FRG, was dealt a severe blow by the increases in the prices for fuel and other raw materials on the world market after 1973/74. As the GDR could not increase its export prices to the same extent the price rises brought not only a deterioration in its terms of trade but also higher borrowing from the USSR and Western industrialised countries. The trade deficit grew. As the external problems served to increase internal problems which were already manifest they brought not only far-reaching changes in the domestic economy (the economic reforms of 1979/80, aimed at making the economy more efficient by the creation of combinates in industry with greater decision-making powers) but adjustment processes in foreign trade as well. To prevent its shortage of convertible currency from affecting its trade with the West the GDR has, for example, been trying for some years to engage in barter transactions and thus prevent money having to change hands at all, but this has provoked a growing negative reaction from Western countries. Again, like other COMECON countries, the GDR no longer seems to object to economic co-operation in the form of specialisation between GDR enterprises and Western firms or division of labour in the production of certain series of goods or certain ranges, as it did in the early 1960s.[52] But it is clearly not yet prepared to engage in more far-reaching forms of co-operation such as joint production or joint ventures, obviously regarding the political risk as too high and fearing that the precarious balance, in any case, between economic cooperation with the West and political protection at home would be jeopardised to an even greater degree than it is already.

For the attempts to make use of the advantages of the international division of labour both within COMECON and with Western industrialised countries exposed the economy and society of the GDR to greater disturbance from outside. That was already clear in the early 1960s, when a 'stop disturbances now' campaign was conducted to eliminate the dependence of the GDR on supplies largely from West Germany. Although this attempt failed ultimately and was broken off in 1962 it remains symptomatic of the basic desire of the GDR leaders to shield themselves economically and even more so politically as far as possible from influence from the capitalist world. But as economic ties with the West have grown this influence has inevitably grown as well, facing the GDR leaders with difficult, if not indeed insoluble problems.

The disturbance potential results from the interaction of the following factors:

(a) cyclical fluctuations and inflationary developments in the world economy, which affect the GDR through its external channels;

(b) the need to adjust planning to the often short-term fluctuations in demand in the West;

(c) dependence on Western technology and on decisions by individual Western companies;

(d) dependence on the foreign and foreign trade policy of Western governments (embargoes, credit controls and so on);

(e) adjustment of the export structure to Western demand, which can lead to an orientation to 'capitalist fashion trends' rather than 'Socialist consumer patterns' not in keeping with the development of a 'Socialist mentality' and a 'Socialist society' in the GDR.

In their desire to maintain what they regard as a stable social development and hence protect their Marxist—Leninist claim to power while utilising their economic relations with the West it is only to be expected, in the face of the many and complex economic and political disturbance factors, that the GDR leaders will make use of political delimitation measures in an attempt to control possible erosion processes: political delimitation is being used more and more as the counterpart to economic co-operation with the West.[53]

However, at present it is not possible to see clearly where the main points of focus will lie in future political and economic decisions. On the one hand it is becoming clear that the GDR is prepared to accept demonstration and penetration effects as a result of the intensification of economic relations with Western countries and is shifting its delimitation measures to other spheres (e.g. limiting the number of Western visitors by raising the amount of money which has to be converted at the frontier — the 'Zwangsumtausch'). This is substantiated by the changes mentioned earlier in the attitude to certain kinds of economic co-operation which go beyond pure trade. On the other hand — and the data for the years since 1976 point in this direction (see table 3.1) — over the longer term a stronger re-orientation of the GDR's foreign trade to the Soviet Union is very likely. There are not only political reasons for this, although the Soviet entry into Afghanistan has brought a noticeable cooling of relations with the West and the strikes in Poland have brought greater efforts at delimitation in East Germany. But price increases on the Western markets for raw materials have both made the GDR more dependent on supplies from the Soviet Union (particularly for oil, 85 per cent of which comes from this source) and brought even greater shortages of hard currency, which again has drastically reduced imports from the West.

These developments show yet once again that small countries like the German Democratic Republic, particularly if they are at the border between East and West, have only limited scope for independent economic and political action and cannot avoid the effects of external events or can do so only to a limited extent.

Notes

1   For a more detailed discussion of this, see Jacobsen, H.A., Leptin, G., Scheuner, U., Schulz, E. (eds), *GDR Foreign Policy*, Armonk, New York, London, 1982.
2   For a long time this was one of the basic concepts of Western economists. Cf. for example Thalheim, K.C., *Grundzüge des sowjetischen Wirtschaftssystems*, Cologne, 1962, p.135; Kiesewetter, B., *Der Ostblock — Aussenhandel des östlichen Wirtschaftsblocks einschliesslich China*, Berlin, 1960, p.15 and p.234; Kruse, A., *Aussenwirtschaft*, Berlin, 1958, p.507; Pryor, F.L., *The Communist Foreign Trade System*, London 1963, p.23 ff. The counter argument was presented very forcibly and at an early stage by Lerner, A.P., *The Economics of Control*, New York, 1944, p.381.
3   On this concept see Brown, A.A., 'Towards a Theory of Centrally Planned Foreign Trade', in Brown, A.A., Neuberger, E. (eds), *International Trade and Central Planning*, Berkeley and Los Angeles, 1968, p.62. Inter alia 'trade aversion and autarchy are very different concepts . . . Autarchy is a policy of self-sufficiency . . . Trade aversion implies to some extent an opposition to trade in general.' This hostility to foreign trade can, for instance, be caused by the emergence of price and quantity variations on world markets which threaten the achievement of targets.
4   The concept 'capacity for autarchy' relates the scope for foreign trade to the size of the domestic market of a country and its possession of resources. The concept 'capacity for independence' goes much further: this is determined by the state of development and the development potential of a country at a particular point in time (productivity, resources, size of the domestic market, capacity utilisation in industry and so on), and a country's ability to break off, reduce or substitute relations with another country and its ability to keep the relative costs of interdependent relations down to a minimum.

5   The process was extremely difficult. As the Torrens-Ricardo theorem of the comparative advantages of foreign trade was rejected as a 'theory of capitalist exploitation' (cf. Wilczynski, J., 'The Theory of Comparative Costs and Centrally Planned Economies', in *Economic Journal*, vol.75 (1965)) there were at first only very few and extremely cautious indications of calculations of economic rationality. Kohlmey, G., *Der demokratische Weltmarkt*, Berlin (GDR), 1955, may be taken as an early example. The same author has made a pioneering contribution to discussion on the theory of foreign trade in the GDR. Cf. inter alia Kohlmey, G. (ed.), *Aussenwirtschaft und Wachstum*, Berlin (GDR), 1968.

6   We do not want to go into this in more detail here. Cf. Nattland, K.H., 'Theoretische und praktische Aspekte des Zusammenhangs zwischen Aussenhandel und Wirtschaftswachstum in der DDR', in Förster, W. and Lorenz, D. (eds), *Beiträge zur Theorie und Praxis von Wirtschaftssystemen*, Berlin, 1970, p.297 ff; Dietsch, U., *Aussenwirtschaftliche Aktivitäten der DDR*, Hamburg 1976, p.47 ff.

7   This expression was first used by Walter Ulbricht at the Vth SED Party Congress (10—16 June 1958). He went on: 'The demand for the right kind of specialisation means under the economic conditions prevailing in the German Democratic Republic — and which are partly the result of our lack of raw materials — that within the framework of the international Socialist division of labour and cooperation we should concentrate on those production programmes which require a high degree of intellectual and scientific work'. Minutes of the Vth SED Party Congress (*Protokoll des V. Parteitages der Sozialistischen Einheitspartei Deutschlands*, Berlin (GDR), p.88).

8   On 22 April 1918 foreign trade was nationalised by decree in the Soviet Union and by mid-1925 it had been made a total monopoly of the state. Cf. Freymuth, K.-D., *Ursprung und Grundlegung der sowjetischen Aussenhandelsorganisation* (1917—1921), Berlin, 1967, p.87 ff; Carr, E.H., *Socialism in One Country 1924—1926*, vol.1, Middlesex, 1970, p.475 ff.

9   *Gesetzblatt der DDR I/1958*, p.89.

10   *Gesetzblatt der DDR I/1972*, p.253 ff.

11   Lemper, M. and Maskow, D., *Aussenwirtschaftsrecht der DDR*, Berlin (GDR), 1975, p.21 f.

12   On the chronology of these measures see Förster, W., *Das Aussenhandelssystem der Sowjetischen Besatzungszone Deutschlands*, Bonn, 1957, 3rd edition, p.17 ff.

13   Largely by the formation of the NATO Coordinating Committee (COCOM) in November 1949. The committee, to which all the NATO countries except Iceland and Japan belong, draws up embargo lists of strategic goods, which are not to be exported to Communist countries

or into the Communist power sphere. Cf. Adler-Karlsson, G., *Western Economic Warfare 1947–1967*, Uppsala, 1968; Wiles, P.J.D., 'On the COCOM Embargo' in Gumpel, W. and Keese, D. (eds), *Probleme des Industrialismus in Ost und West*, Munich, Vienna, 1973, p.383 ff.
14 Cf. Gasteyger, C., *Die beiden deutschen Staaten in der Weltpolitik*, Munich, 1976, p.69.
15 Section 4 of the 'Satzung der Kammer für Aussenhandel der DDR', 10 April 1953, in *Der Aussenhandel*, vol.3, no.19 (1953), p.445.
16 Murgott, E., 'Vielfältige Förderung der Aussenwirtschaftsbeziehungen der DDR', in *Sozialistische Aussenwirtschaft*, vol.22, issue 10 (1972), p.33.
17 Cf. Ulbricht, Walter 'Der zweite Fünfjahrplan und der Aufbau des Sozialismus in der Deutschen Demokratischen Republik', in *Protokoll der Verhandlungen der 3. Parteikonferenz der SED*, 24–30 March 1956, vol.I, Berlin (GDR), 1956, p.142.
18 Cf. Hofmann, O. and Scharschmidt, G., *DDR-Aussenhandel gestern und heute*, Berlin (GDR), 1975, p.108.
19 On this see Lamm, H.S. and Kupper, S., *DDR und Dritte Welt*, Munich, Vienna, 1976, p.53 ff.
20 Cf. End, H., *Zweimal deutsche Aussenpolitik. Internationale Dimensionen des innerdeutschen Konflikts, 1949–1972*, Cologne, 1973, p.130.
21 Cf. Eymelt, F., *Die Tätigkeit der DDR in den nichtkommunistischen Ländern, II. Die Nordischen Staaten*. Forschungsinstitut der DGAP, Bonn, 1970, especially pp. 26 ff.
22 'Gesetz über den Siebenjahrplan 1.10.1959', *Gesetzblatt der DDR* I/1959, no.56, 17 October 1959, p.705.
23 On this see the article by Jürgen Strassburger in this volume.
24 Ulbricht, Walter, 'Neue Fragen des ökonomischen Systems der Planung und Leitung der Volkswirtschaft', from the speech 'Das Programm des Sozialismus und die geschichtliche Aufgabe der SED', given at the VIth SED Party Congress, 15–21 January 1963, in ibid., *Zum ökonomischen System des Sozialismus in der DDR*, Berlin (GDR), 1969, p.107.
25 Hofmann, O. and Scharschmidt, G., *DDR-Aussenhandel*, op.cit., p.38. On the discussion at the time see inter alia, Jarowinsky, W., *Grundprobleme der Aussenwirtschaftsbeziehungen in der zweiten Etappe des neuen ökonomischen Systems der Planung und Leitung*, Berlin (GDR), 1966, chapter 3: 'Die Rolle intensiver Aussenwirtschaftsbeziehungen als Wachstumsfaktor der Volkswirtschaft', p.22 ff.
26 In *Neues Deutschland*, no.164, 17 June 1962, p.5 f.
27 This discussion was taken up again recently by Brabant, J.M.v., *Socialist Economic Integration*, Cambridge, 1980, p.274 f.

28   Cf. Khrushchev, N., 'Wesentliche Fragen der Entwicklung des sozialistischen Weltsystems', in *Probleme des Friedens und des Sozialismus*, no.9/1962, p.729 ff.
29   Some of the documents are summarised in Thalheim, K.C., 'Das Wirtschaftswachstum der Donaustaaten unter dem Einfluss von Zentralplanung und Ostblockintegration', in *Der Donauraum*, vol.10, H 1/2, 1965.
30   Accordingly the complex programme of 1971, in which the economic integration of COMECON was projected for the next 15 to 20 years, contains a clear rejection of the formation of supra-national institutions: 'Socialist integration will develop on the basis of complete freedom of will and does not entail the creation of supra-national organs'. 'Komplexprogramm für die weitere Vertiefung und Vervollkommung der Zusammenarbeit und Entwicklung der sozialistischen ökonomischen Integration der Mitgliedsländer des RGW', in *Dokumente RGW* Berlin (GDR), 1971, p.16. On the problems behind this statement, see Jacobsen, H.D., 'Internationale Produktion und Supranationalität im RGW', in *Deutschland Archiv*, vol.9, 1976, no.6, p.606 ff.
31   Even an intensive evaluation of statements by leading GDR politicians from the period immediately after the proposal from Khrushchev yields no indication of support for the Soviet initiative. On the contrary, a later assessment of this phase is: 'On isolated occasions at the beginning of the 1960s it was proposed to further the international Socialist division of labour through the creation of an international planning organ which should be endowed with appropriate and far-reaching powers . . . But in practice especially it appeared that the possibilities of property organised on the basis of the individual state . . . were by no means fully utilised'. A collective of writers under Kohlmey, G., *RGW—DDR 25 Jahre Zusammenarbeit*, Berlin (GDR), 1974, p.122.
32   Wiles, P.J.D., *Communist International Economics*, Oxford, 1968, p.241.
33   Cf. Scharpf, P., *Europäische Wirtschaftsgemeinschaft und Deutsche Demokratische Republik*, Tübingen, 1973; Biskup, R., *Deutschlands offene Handelsgrenze. Die DDR als Nutzniesser des EWG-Protokolls über den innerdeutschen Handel*, Berlin, 1976.
34   Cf. for example Huber, G., 'Aussenwirtschaft und Wirtschaftswachstum' in Maier, H., Schilling, G. and Steinitz, K. (eds), *Zu Grundfragen der sozialistischen Wachstumstheorie*, Berlin (GDR), 1968, p.243.
35   Cf. Kohlmey, G., 'Wahl von Produktionsstandorten und internationale Mobilität von Produktivkräften in der Wirtschaftsintegration der RGW-Länder', in *Wirtschaftswissenschaft*, vol.21, issue 9, 1973, p.1301 ff.

36   Cf. Baumer, M. and Jacobsen, H.D., 'CMEA and the World Economy' in *East European Economies Post-Helsinki*, Joint Economic Committee, US Congress, 95th Congress, 1st session, Washington DC, 1977, p.1003 ff.
37   Cf. Lambrecht, H., 'The Development of Economic Relations with the FRG', in Jacobsen, H.A. et al. (eds), *GDR Foreign Policy*, op.cit., p.322 ff.
38   Since 1974 this facility has provided for a maximum amount of DM 850 million by the end of 1981. If no new agreement is concluded, the amount would be reduced in accordance with an earlier agreement to DM 200 million.
39   Cf. S. Nehring, 'Präferenzen und DDR-Exportstruktur im innerdeutschen Handel' in *Weltwirtschaftliches Archiv*, vol.114, no.2, 1978, p.339 ff.
40   While net indebtedness was only 1.2 billion US dollars at the end of 1971, it had risen to 8.4 billion dollars by the end of 1979. The GDR's share of the net indebtedness of European COMECON countries, however, dropped from 24 per cent (in 1971) to 13 per cent. National Foreign Assessment Center, *Estimating Soviet and East European Hard Currency Debt*, ER 80-10237, Washington DC, June 1980, p.7.
41   Relations with France appear to have particular importance for the GDR. For the period up to 1985 large-scale co-operation projects with French firms (in the motor industry, for railway compartments and so on) are planned. Cf. 'DDR spielt verstärkt die französische Karte', in *Süddeutsche Zeitung*, 4 September 1980.
42   Here a remark on the GDR's foreign trade statistics is appropriate: since the mid-1970s the GDR has been the only COMECON country not to publish foreign trade data broken down according to imports and exports but only in terms of total turnover. So we can only make assumptions from these balances, as in the case of the USA and Japan, where imports will probably be very much higher than exports.
43   Cf. Dietsch, U., *Aussenwirtschaftliche Aktivitäten der DDR*, op. cit., p.113 ff.
44   Cf. Schulz, E., 'Der Aussenhandel als aussenpolitisches Instrument der DDR seit der internationalen Anerkennung' in *DDR-Report*, no.11/12, 1974, p.654.
45   Dietsch, U., *Aussenwirtschaftliche Aktivitäten der DDR*, op.cit., p.181.
46   Ulbricht, W., 'Die gesellschaftliche Entwicklung in der DDR bis zur Vollendung des Sozialismus', *Schlussansprache auf dem VII. Parteitag der SED*, 17–22 April 1967, 4th edition, Berlin (GDR), 1970, p.27 f.

47 Cf. Lamm, H.S. and Kupper, S., *DDR und Dritte Welt*, Munich, Vienna, 1976, p.178 ff.
48 Lamm and Kupper, op.cit., p.162 ff., with acknowledgement of the difficulty of interpreting the source material, these authors believe that the GDR granted Egypt development credits to the amount of between 150 and 200 million US dollars up to 1971.
49 Cf. the survey given by Thieme, S., *Die Tätigkeit der DDR in nichtkommunistischen Ländern, VIII. Schwarzafrika*. Deutsche Gesellschaft für Auswärtige Politik, Bonn, 1972.
50 Lamm and Kupper, op.cit., p.273.
51 In more detail see Plate, B.v., *Die Aussenwirtschaftsbeziehungen der DDR zu den Entwicklungsländern und die Neue Weltwirtschaftsordnung*, Ebenhausen, 1979, p.30 ff.
52 Cf. Schmidt, M., 'Wirtschaftsbeziehungen zwischen sozialistischen und kapitalistischen Ländern im Lichte neuer weltpolitischer und -wirtschaftlicher Prozesse' in *IPW-Berichte*, vol.5, no.8, 1976, p.3 ff.
53 In more detail see Jacobsen, H.D., 'Kooperation und Abgrenzung in den wirtschaftlichen Beziehungen zwischen Ost- und Westeuropa' in Zellentin, G. (ed.), *Annäherung, Abgrenzung und friedlicher Wandel in Europa*, Boppard am Rhein, 1976, p.438 ff.

4 Military policy in the GDR
Gero Neugebauer, Free University, Berlin

Military policy is often seen as only concerned with the deployment of military means for security purposes and is therefore regarded as an area which should be analysed in the context of foreign policy and defence. However, this is to neglect its internal functions. These are not limited to military matters but extend into many other aspects of society as well. The programme of the Socialist Unity Party of the German Democratic Republic (SED) lays great stress on the relation between the external and internal functions of military policy, which is concerned with all those measures which will contribute to ensuring 'peace and security':

> The military defence of Socialism is guaranteed by the service of the people of the German Democratic Republic in the National People's Army, the Border Brigades or another branch of the armed forces, by Socialist pre-military education and training, especially for young people, by the education of our people to a state of revolutionary alert in loyalty to their Socialist homeland . . . by continual strengthening of the Works Combat Groups, by the activities of the Society for Sport and Technology, by expanding Civil Defence and a comprehensive orientation to security in every sphere of society.[1]

The significance of military policy for society as a whole was also stressed by Heinz Hoffmann, GDR Minister of Defence:

> We must organise the defence of our Socialist homeland by the whole of our Socialist society and maintain ourselves in readiness. Like the economy, the improvement of the material and cultural standard of living of our people, this must be an object of care and responsibility for all levels of state leadership, in all spheres of activity and for every citizen.[2]

So military policy covers all those measures, not only military but political, social and economic as well, which serve the construction and maintenance of the national system of defence. The core of this system is the National People's Army (NVA). The army's function is not limited to the territory of the GDR. In the view of the SED it is international, because the GDR is a member of the Warsaw Pact and hence has to make a contribution to the defence of Socialism generally. The NVA is part of the military organisation of the Warsaw Pact and, in keeping with the political nature of the organisation and its treaty, national decisions on military policy are strongly dependent on decisions made in the alliance. That means that they are strongly dependent on the Soviet Union. The international implications of military policy in the GDR and the area it covers at home can be seen from the structure of the national defence system and its many ramifications. The following may be taken as the main components of the system:

> The National People's Army (NVA) with staff, units and troops;
>
> other armed forces (organs of defence and security):
>
> (a) Armed police squads ('Bereitschaftspolizei');
> (b) The police force;
> (c) State security forces;
> (d) Works Combat Groups;
> (e) Civil Defence Units;
>
> Leading organs of the party apparatus and of the state apparatus;
>
> Institutes of education and research:
>
> (a) Military institutions (the F. Engels Military Academy, officers' training colleges and so on);
> (b) Institutes of military science;
> (c) Schools for the armed forces;
> (d) Central Combat Group schools;
> (e) Soviet military academies and schools;
>
> Socialist pre-military training and education:
>
> (a) General schools;

(b) Universities, colleges and technical schools;
(c) Commissions for Socialist military education (part of the state apparatus);
(d) Mass organisations (e.g. Free German Youth, Young Pioneers, Trade Unions, Society for Sport and Technology, German Red Cross of the GDR and so on);
(e) Reservist work;

The defence network, consisting of:
(a) The army's logistic system;
(b) Recruitment and mobilisation;
(c) The armaments industry;
(d) Military research and development;
(e) Transport and communications;
(f) Health care.

An assessment of the function of military policy within the political system of the GDR may therefore begin with the military sphere but it must include other areas as well. Nor can it be limited to the present — it must cover the whole development of this policy sphere in the GDR, showing which of the elements in its inception are still effective today, what changes have occurred and how these should be evaluated.

The development of a military power

Even before the German Democratic Republic was founded the SED Politbureau demanded, in March 1949, that the German people should be able to give the Soviet Union military support in case of an attack by the United States of America.[3] But the armed forces available at that point of time in the Soviet occupied zone were not adequate for military action in the case of an East–West conflict: hence the military defence of the Soviet occupied zone (and the German Democratic Republic when it was founded in October 1949) was the responsibility of the Soviet Army. The declaration of the paramilitary units (Kasernierte Volkspolizei — KVP) — 'People's Police' stationed in barracks — as 'National Defence Forces' in 1952 hardly changed the situation, although both in their organisation and equipment these forces were more like military units. The declaration served a purpose in foreign policy: it was a reaction to attempts by the Western powers to integrate the Federal Republic of Germany into the European Defence Community. The strengthening of the 'national armed forces' was to provide training for cadres for the future army. Some former members of the Wehrmacht, who had been re-schooled in Soviet anti-Fascist camps as prisoners of war, played an important part in the top organs. But they were by no means so prominent as the former Wehrmacht officers in building up the West German Bundeswehr.

In 1955 the GDR became a member of the Warsaw Pact, which had been founded under the leadership of the Soviet Union partly as reaction to the entry of the Federal Republic into the North Atlantic Treaty Organisation (NATO). When joining the GDR undertook to make a military contribution to the Pact in the form of a national army. Between May 1955 and February 1956 the first units of the NVA were formed from former units of the KVP. In January 1956 the People's Chamber of the GDR passed legislation on the formation of the National People's Army but did not make military service compulsory as it was in the Federal Republic. Conscription was not introduced until 1962, partly as a result of the greater demands being made on the People's Army within the Warsaw Pact.

In contrast to those of the other member countries, the People's Army units were immediately placed under the Warsaw Pact Supreme Command. They were quickly supplied with Soviet weapons and equipment and right from the start the structure and leadership followed decisions by the Supreme Command in strict adherence to Soviet military and organisational principles. Soviet military specialists were delegated to the staff and units of the National People's Army as advisers and as early as August 1957 the first joint manoeuvre was held by units of the Soviet armed forces in Germany and the NVA. In 1958 the Warsaw Pact confirmed the incorporation of NVA troops in the Pact forces. The integration was accelerated by manoeuvres which after 1961 were also held together with troops from other member countries. It was de facto complete in 1965 with the integration of the NVA in the First Strategic Force of the Warsaw Pact. Since then the National People's Army has been one of the strategic action forces of the Warsaw Pact. The air defence forces are part of the alert system of the Warsaw Pact, i.e. they are permanently ready for action. The People's Navy is under the joint command of the fleets of the Warsaw Pact and operates in the Baltic together with the Soviet Red Banner fleet and the Polish fleet of warships.[4]

But where co-operation with staff and units of other Warsaw Pact forces mainly takes the form of occasional delegations and participation in joint manoeuvres, co-operation between staff, troops and units of the NVA and the Soviet forces in Germany is very close.[5]

The organisation and strength of the National People's Army and the other armed forces

The National People's Army consists of three branches: the land forces, the air force and air defence forces and the People's Navy. The branches have various categories of weapons and services. The NVA is not a structural copy of the Soviet army. It has no atomic weapons but it can operate carriers. A survey of the development of the army over the years will show that the main build-up was during the 1960s:

Table 4.1
Strength of the National People's Army (in 1,000 persons)

1962	1964	1966	1968	1969	1970	1972	1974	1976	1979
85	106	122	126	137	129	131	145	157	159

Source: The International Institute for Strategic Studies, The Military Balance, London, annually.

The expenditure on defence shows a very much more dynamic development:

Table 4.2
Defence spending in the GDR (in millions of Marks)

1962	1964	1966	1968	1970	1972
2,820.7	2,735.0	3,200.0	5,765.0	6,733.0	7,625.0

1974	1976	1977	1978	1979	1980
8,732.5	10,233.0	7,868.0	8,261.0	8,674.0	9,403.0
		3,155.0	3,312.0	3,474.0	3,683.0

Source: K.W. Fricke, 'Der Verteidigungshaushalt der DDR' in *Deutschland-Archiv* 2/1977, p.165. Up to 1974 calculations are from actual figures, after 1976 target figures, after 1977 break-down into expenditure on national defence and expenditure on public safety, law and protection of the border. Data for 1976: GB1. I, 1975, no.46, p.746; for 1977: GB1. I, 1976, no.47, p.536; for 1978: GB1. I, 1977, no.37, p.419; for 1979: GB1. I, 1978, no.42, p.462; for 1980: GB1. I, 1979, no.45, p.462.

173

The GDR Border Brigades have a special status. On the one hand they are not part of the NVA and so they would, for instance, not be affected by negotiations on reductions in troop strengths. On the other hand the head of the Border Brigades is one of the representatives of the Minister for National Defence. The Border Brigades are to provide military support in case of war. In times of peace they secure the frontier of the GDR, mainly with the Federal Republic of Germany and West Berlin. In 1979 their strength was 46,500.[6] The People's Police are responsible for public law and order. The paramilitary units stationed in barracks, the *Volkspolizei-Bereitschaften*, who constitute a kind of security police force, are part of this organisation. Figures for their strength vary between 18,000 and 25,000.[7] Of the other police forces — the municipal police, traffic police, criminal police, transport police — only the last, and here mainly the active units, have military functions. It is their duty to keep transport routes open and ensure the mobility of military forces in the hinterland. Readiness to combat enemy forces in the hinterland of the GDR is one of the most important tasks.

The Combat Groups have been in existence since 1953. They were formed after the events of June 1953 showed that the police forces were not adequate to secure law and order in plants and enterprises. They are composed of workers from plants, the administration and the co-operatives who have already done their military service. The original task of only protecting plant and buildings has been extended since 1970. In the case of military conflict the Combat Groups now have active and defence duties to perform alone or together with the 'Bereitschaften'. They are trained along the lines of the National People's Army by officers and NCOs of the 'Bereitschaften'. Figures for the strength of the Groups vary between 350,000 and 500,000 men.[8] The name 'Armed Organs of the Working Class' is designed to indicate both their military character and their proximity to the SED. Finally there is the Watch Regiment of the Ministry for State Security (more than 5,000 men), whose task it is to protect government buildings and institutions.

Another element in the central core of the national defence system is the Civil Defence Forces, who date back to the year 1958, when the GDR began building up her civil air defence. Since 1977 civil defence has been under the Ministry for National Defence. Until that date it fell within the sphere of the Ministry for Internal Affairs. The forces (about 15,000 cadres strong) are to help defend the territory of the GDR and keep the march routes for troops and units open. One of their main activities is air defence and work in times of national disaster. Service in the civil defence counts as military service.[9]

The conditions and forms of Socialist 'Wehrerziehung' — pre-military education and training

The SED has not limited its military policy to building up the army and the other armed forces. It has been and still is concerned to establish a close relation between security and social policy, by devoting as much attention to the political and moral condition of the forces and the ideological aspects of military service as to measures concerned with the material and social basis of national defence. In the years following the establishment of the People's Army the political and ideological education of the people within the framework of military policy concentrated on the question of the nation, Socialist patriotism and protecting the GDR in alliance with the Soviet Union. When, after the building of the Berlin wall in 1961 and the reorganisation of the Warsaw Pact forces, the role of the People's Army was re-defined, the national question was tacitly ignored where it touched on the question of the army and national unity. Attempts were made to legitimise the political function of the armed forces as guarantors of the Socialist German state on the basis of the existence of a class enemy, conquered within the GDR but still threatening from outside. The national character of the army was further emphasised by designating it 'the army of the Socialist state of the German nation'. In any envisaged hostilities it would not have to fight Germans but 'representatives of the Imperialist system'.[10] Within the framework of the policy to develop a national consciousness in the GDR the attempt was made at the same time to define the relationship between the army and society not only as a political relationship but a national one. This was and is still being done through preservation of national traditions linking the history and achievements of the NVA with revolutionary events in German history (the peasants' war in the Middle Ages, the wars of liberation in 1813/14, the March revolution of 1848 and the November revolution of 1918) as well as with leading figures in the German and international labour movement and Prussian history (Clausewitz, Scharnhorst, Gneisenau and others).

The SED lays great stress on the relation between 'Socialist patriotism' and 'Socialist internationalism', and the international character of the NVA as part of the military defence system of Socialism. The fact that up to 1969 it was the government of the Federal Republic which more or less took the offensive in demanding reunification and restoration of a united Germany within the 1937 borders, which would have meant the dissolution of the GDR, made it easier for the SED to maintain that there was an external threat. The other Warsaw Pact countries supported East Germany in this and the existence of the army was used to legitimate the GDR state system.

After the conclusion of the treaties between the Federal Republic of Germany, the Soviet Union and the People's Republic of Poland in 1970, the Treaty on the Bases of Relations between the two German States in 1972 and the beginning of the policy of détente, the SED clearly felt the need to step up its political and ideological education work in the military policy sphere. This is still based on the assumption that it is the long-term aim of the West to undermine the existence of the Socialist camp. The attempts by the Federal Republic to insist that there is still only one German nation are seen as an attack on the policy of the GDR in developing her own national identity and they are certainly a major factor in the handling of the policy. It is apparent that since 1970–72 efforts have been stepped up to intensify political and ideological work as part of the relation between military and social policy and to create the sense of national identity which the SED needs to legitimate its military policy. Defence expenditure has been stepped up on the grounds that there is still a danger of open military hostilities in Europe because of the 'abrupt turns and changes' in Western policy, the contradictions inherent in the Imperialist system and the worldwide conflict between Socialism and Imperialism. This is also intended to destroy 'illusions' on the policy of détente and possibilities of reducing tension, and maintain the image of the enemy to increase the readiness of the population, especially young people, to defend their country. 'Socialist pre-military education and training' serves as an important instrument of this policy.[11]

As early as 1957 it was stated at a scientific SED conference that the system of propaganda to induce the population, and especially young people, to defend their country, was a major factor in military policy.[12] In 1971 the Minister of Defence demanded that 'all citizens, whether young or old, men or women, should to a very much greater degree be induced to show an attitude and mentality oriented to the defence of our country in times of peace and in any possible hostilities'.[13] In the education of the Socialist personality the system of values should be so structured that loyalty to the political and social constitution of society meant a readiness to make a personal contribution to its military defence. So measures within the framework of Socialist military training are not only designed as physical and mental preparation for military service, i.e. they do not only affect young people but all age groups and social areas. Most important are the institutions of education and training and the organisations which mainly recruit young people, i.e. the Free German Youth (Freie Deutsche Jugend – FDJ) and the Society for Sport and Technology (Gesellschaft für Sport und Technik – GST).

Socialist pre-military education and training is designed to educate young people to a readiness and ability to engage in military service and enable them to acquire an outlook and approach commensurate with military policy and the moral attitude this entails. This is in complete identification with the policy of the ruling party and the state. Special measures which mainly serve as preparation for military service are carried out by the Society for Sport and Technology which was established solely for this purpose.[14] More general measures, especially in the education sphere, are carried out in the general and vocational schools and the technical schools, colleges and universities and in plants. These measures are not only for young people during their education and training but also adult men and women. They are graded and differentiated to meet the requirements of the different age groups, and they range from the aim to establish understanding of the reasons for military expenditure and the consequences for the individual and society, to the need to participate in certain organisations, for instance civil defence. The work of the institutions and organisations, including the National People's Army, in military education and training, is co-ordinated and directed by the Commissions for Socialist Military Education and Training which have been established on the lower and middle levels of administration (the districts and local authority areas).

The Society for Sport and Technology trains about 200,000 16 to 18 year olds every year, i.e. it prepares them for military service. Military sports activities are for the older groups. The measures for young people are based on the natural interests of these age groups and linked to military purposes. The opportunities offered by the GST for young people to learn to drive a car or ride a motorcycle, use radio equipment, parachute, go in for motor sports or sailing and rowing are an incentive to many. Young people are then subject to a barrage of propaganda to make them consent to stay in the army longer. Compulsory military service lasts for 18 months. Afterwards young people are expected to serve in the Combat Groups or Civil Defence units as NVA reservists. But the realities of civilian working life soon diminish any enthusiasm that might originally have been present. The competent political bodies try to keep interest in military activities alive with propaganda and mobilisation campaigns and offer material incentives (reimbursement of expenses) to encourage participation.

The organisation and scope of Socialist pre-military education and training show that this is mainly directed to young people during the education and training process, but no definite information is available on how effective it actually is. In addition to the usual reports of success we can find indications that all does not go according to plan. There are complaints, for instance, that young people have insufficient grasp of the aggressiveness of Imperialism, that they have no real image of the enemy or that they are insufficiently politically motivated. The introduction of the special subject 'Military education' at school in

1978 for pupils in the 9th and 10th years at the general polytechnical schools (4 double hours in a school year and 12 teaching days of 6 hours each in a camp) can be interpreted as a sign that so far it has not proved possible to encourage enough 14 to 16 year olds to take up a career in the army.[15] And the fact that there are still conscientious objectors in the GDR, although no state or social bodies advocate this course of action, shows that it has not proved possible to achieve a total mobilisation of young people for the military policy aims of the SED.[16]

The SED continues to use Socialist pre-military education and training to convince its citizens that the political and social system of the GDR is worth defending and requires a personal contribution from them. Probably these means will have little real effect on the political and moral attitudes of the people as long as the immediate environment remains relatively peaceful and their interests are concentrated on the economic and socio-political situation. They will only be convinced that a military and defence apparatus is necessary when the external situation justifies the SED's military propaganda. It is an essential element in the self-legitimation of the military to argue that an external threat exists in peace time as well and that the system is in danger and needs to be defended. For these reasons the SED argues that the army exercises functions such as 'Protecting Socialist achievements', 'developing international patriotism' and 'developing love of the Socialist Fatherland'. This gives it a particular value in the eyes of the political leaders, both as a pillar of the existing social order and an instrument to influence Socialist behaviour.

The party and the army

The impression that large sections of society in the GDR are dominated by military concepts and principles could give rise to the assumption that the military have acquired independent weight, indeed almost an autonomous life. But an examination of the relation between political and military bodies will show that the party's claim to play the leading role in military matters has never at any point been called in question. The SED has used three main ways of implementing and strengthening its claim to military leadership.

Firstly the military have been made subordinate to party political institutions right from the start. All major military questions which the GDR has the power to decide are handled by the Politbureau of the SED Central Committee. The Security Commission of the Politbureau, the Secretary for Security Matters and the Security Department of the SED Central Committee play an important part here. Since 1960 military and security policy matters have been handled by these bodies and their decisions have been implemented by the GDR National Defence Council as the top state organ of military policy. The Chairman of the National Defence Council is the Secretary-General of the SED Central Committee; the Council itself consists of at least 12 persons. The Ministry of Defence, which contains among others the main staff of the People's Army, is sub-divided into several grades of administrative departments. It is responsible for implementing the decisions taken by the party and state organs on the military level. The dominant role of the party is underlined by its staff policy: the functionary responsible for building up the military sector, Willi Stoph, was a member of the SED Central Committee Politbureau and it was this institution which appointed him Minister of Internal Affairs (from 1952 to 1955) and then Minister of National Defence (from 1956 to 1960). The establishment of the National Defence Council of the GDR in February 1960 then made it possible among other measures to appoint H. Hoffmann, an expert in military affairs but not of equal political experience, as Minister of Defence.[17]

Secondly members of the party have been and still are entrusted with military functions. When the People's Army was still being built up this meant that party functionaries were given a military training and were then appointed officers. The attempt to establish the principle of 'collective counselling' in the early years of the army between army officers and the relevant party leaders in the army divisions and units led to some collisions between the military need to develop and train an army and political requirements.[18] But by 1960 the party leaders had come to the conclusion that the new commanders of the People's Army were sufficiently qualified both militarily and politically and that the principle of unity between political and military leadership had been achieved. Since that date the commanders have been responsible both for military and political work with their troops, while the Politofficers have remained at their side as 'representatives of the commander for political work'. The party also exercised an influence on the selection and training of the officer corps in order to implement the SED's idea of an officer with class characteristics, i.e. one who came from the working class and was a loyal member of the SED. As a result of this policy about 99 per cent of the officers of the People's Army are members of the SED. Socially the majority of them do come from the working class.[19]

The system of politorgans and party organisations established by the SED in the People's Army constitutes the third way in which the party has underlined and strengthened its leading role in the armed forces.

There are no politorgans below the level of the regiment. In the batallions and companies the representatives of the commander for political work are responsible for directing party work and controlling

Table 4.3
The structure of party organs in the military sphere

Organisational level	Politorgan	Party organisation
Ministry of National Defence	Main political administration	Party district
Branches of the armed forces	Political administration	Party local area
Division	Political department[1]	Party local area
Regiment	Polit-representative (Central party leadership)	Party regiment organisation
Battalion	Polit-representative	Basic organisation
Company	Polit-representative	Party group

1 In the military academy and the officers colleges as well.

the implementation of the party's decisions. At all levels the heads of the politorgans are at the same time the first secretaries of the appropriate party organisation. Hence the head of the Main Political Administration of the People's Army is at the same time First Secretary of the overall NVA party organisation. The same applies on all other levels. The representatives for political work are responsible to their party organisations and at the same time work directly under the military commander.[20]

The function of the politorgans and politworkers — i.e. the heads and personnel of the politorgans, the full-time secretaries of the party and Free German Youth organisations and teachers of Marxism—Leninism in military education institutes, teaching and research establishments and party organisations — is to implement the decisions of the party in the military sphere and ensure that they are adhered to. They are also responsible for the political and ideological education of the members of the People's Army, they organise competitions, initiatives and campaigns on specific occasions to stimulate the troops to particular achievements and they support the work of the Free German Youth organisations in the army. But the politorgans also acquire insight into particular interests and expectations in the military sphere at an early stage so that an assessment can be made of how far these correspond with party decisions or whether new decisions will be required. A party information system has been built up throughout the armed forces to ensure that the central party organs are always supplied with adequate information on the situation in the staff and troop units. A number of factors, such as the role of the individual branches of the armed forces, the importance of the various categories of weapons in the strategic concept, differences in technical standards between branches or units and different conditions of service can lead to the development of particular interests. This need not necessarily lead to conflicts between the party and the army or between sections of the forces, or 'technicians' and 'party politicians'.[21] The constant improvement in officers' training with a consequent increase in political knowledge, together with the fact that the Politbureau and the party apparatus have devoted particular attention to military interests and requirements, have helped to keep the potential for conflict to a minimum. A further factor is that a number of persons in the SED Central Committee Politbureau either have direct functions in military defence or security (the Minister of Defence, H. Hoffmann, the Minister of State Security, E. Mielke) or used to exercise these (Willi Stoph, now Chairman of the Council of Ministers) or are responsible for them in the party (the General Secretary himself, Erich Honecker, and P. Verner, Security Secretary). This ensures an adequate basis for the consideration of matters of military policy in the 25-member Politbureau (17 full members and 8 members without voting rights).

Militarism or militarisation in the GDR?

The military policy of the SED, the presence of military personnel on political bodies, the many measures of Socialist military training and education and the constant protestations of esteem for the military cause many Western observers to believe that militarism is rife in the GDR.[22] They do not attempt to differentiate or ask whether it might not be more correct to speak of a trend to militarisation. This is partly due to the fact that there is no clearly defined concept of militarism in Western sociological research so that writers are inclined to use the two concepts for the one problem.[23]

The German—American historian Alfred Vagts distinguishes between a military and militaristic deployment of the armed forces:

> The distinction is fundamental and fateful. The military way is marked by a primary concentration of men and materials on winning specific objectives of power with the utmost efficiency... It is limited in scope, confined to one function, and scientific in its essential qualities. Militarism, on the other hand, presents a vast array of customs, interests, prestige, actions and thought associated with armies and wars and yet transcending true military purposes... Its influence is unlimited in scope. It may permeate all society and become dominant over all industry and arts.[24]

Vagts' definition enables us to identify a number of criteria of militarisation: the existence of a standing army, a clearly defined relation between the military and society and clearly defined functions for the military within the general policy of the state. The military sphere itself is a separate area within the framework of national policy as a whole and it does not necessarily enjoy priority over the others. Militarisation proceeds further with the appropriate political and social consequences when a policy is adopted which accords the military a special place in society, for example, when political leaders attempt to give special emphasis to the role of the military as a socio-political factor, entrusting major functions to it in the process of political and ideological education; when military norms, principles and customs are transferred to wide areas outside the military sphere where they exercise an influence on behaviour, and society begins to assume more and more of the features of a military organisation. Generally this development goes hand in hand with a policy which gives priority to meeting the requirements of the military both in the economic and other spheres.

The social aspect of militarisation is given special emphasis by the Polish sociologist, J. Wiatr. Wiatr regards militarisation as existing when efforts are made to bind the civilian and military spheres of society together organically so as to transfer military norms, principles and customs to non-military spheres. Wiatr, whose definition of militarisation is what other writers understand by militarism,[25] also suggests a condition which can lead to the change from militarisation to militarism. He takes up what Ritter and others regard as the main criterion of militarism, namely the close relations between the military and politics,[26] and explains that Socialist countries cannot become militaristic. In these countries there cannot be a polarisation of political and military power, since the army is completely integrated into society and cannot threaten the leading role of the party.

Western sociologists do not accept that Socialism and militarism are mutually exclusive. Jahn, for example, goes back to Karl Liebknecht who saw militarism as the result of the extreme need for defence at home and abroad. Jahn accuses the Socialist states of being thoroughly militarised and of having developed a 'defence militarism'.[27] Marxist–Leninist scholars, on the other hand, argue that the ability of a state to mobilise if necessary all the forces in its society for its defence is not necessarily an indicator of militarism.[28]

Senghaas assumes that the traditional concept of militarism is losing more and more of its significance now because the historical reality associated with the concept is dying. In modern societies there is no longer a distinction between civil and military areas. One must proceed from an integration of political, economic, scientific, technological and military spheres, a social complex which is more than a military—industrial complex. If this complex, which tends to be identical with the prevailing social order, becomes dominated by military premises one can say that this is militarism. These developments can be determined by participation in the quantitative and qualitative arms race and by the need for defence against movements to change the system. In such a case the military would be used together with other power apparatuses to protect the existing power structure and enforce loyalty.[29]

These concepts are not accepted by scholars in the GDR. They take the view that the bourgeois historians, sociologists and political scientists are not in a position adequately to grasp the phenomenon of militarism. Here they are assuming that militarism is exclusively a phenomenon in a class society, that it takes on particular features in the Imperialist stage of development of capitalist society and is no longer possible in the stage of Socialism/Communism. Militarism as 'the transfer of prevailing military forms to political and civilian life'[30] is only possible under monopoly capitalism but not in a Socialist society. Modern militarism, moreover, is not only embodied in the Imperialist armies,

> ... it is a system which penetrates almost every sphere of capitalist society. This system is based on the omnipotence of the military, aggression towards other countries and suppression at home, the subjection of all social life to the needs of rearmament, preparation for war and the conduct of war.[31]

Modern militarism has other features, such as the military—industrial complex, which is its economic base and political instrument, the arms race and the ensuing militarisation of the economy, the internationalisation of militarism and the increasing conflict between aggressive aims and the potential developed for this on the one hand and the limited possibilities for expressing this potential in political power on the other.[32]

The many different aspects of the concept of militarism have resulted in its being used in apparently illimitable ways. But this is probably largely because the concept is too vague. It can be narrowed down by 'very precisely defining the character and structure of the order from which it has emerged when discussing the phenomena and functions of militarism'.[33] This cannot be done by declaring that militarism is possible for one form of society but not for another. It is not enough simply to point to the economic structure of a society and not take other factors, such as the form of the political regime, the relation between domestic and foreign policy, economic aims and interests, socio-political strategies etc. into account.

The difference in the concepts used in the discussion also shows that the borders between militarism and militarisation are fluid. Militarisation can precede the transition of a society to militarism. The development from the one to the other would appear to be possible if for example in times of crisis it appears possible to solve political problems with military means and measures of military policy dominate all other policy areas. This then leads to a dominance of military interests and aims in the society and the behaviour of the political leaders becomes oriented to military maxims. The resulting political state could be described as militarism. There are different preconditions for this: socio-economic and political factors as well as socio-political values, domestic and foreign policy aims and the instruments needed to implement them. Militarism can, for example, be furthered by a readiness to solve conflicts in a society with military power. Certainly the economic structure and resulting vested interests will play an important part in the development of militarism. This can be seen from the expansive policies of great capitalist states oriented to economic interests. But power policy aims which are not determined by economic conditions have also brought political action and behaviour which can be described as militaristic. In such cases foreign policy has been reduced to military policy. One example of this is the war between Vietnam and the People's Republic of China, which was not over changes in political or economic conditions. The dominance of security interests and the use of military power to achieve foreign policy ends was also characteristic of the military actions of the Soviet Union and some of its allies in 1968 in Czechoslovakia and the entry of the Soviet Union into Afghanistan in 1979. In this case the Soviet Union acted alone and according to these criteria the action should be qualified as militaristic. However, it cannot be taken as proof that the whole Soviet system is militaristic. The same could be said of the United States and its intervention in the Dominican Republic in 1965 or its engagement in Vietnam. So we can say that there is one form of militarism which has something to do with capitalism, i.e. the economic structure of a society and the resulting interests. But there is apparently another form of militarism for which the stimuli derive from a synthesis between security and power political interests. The Socialist states with their particular economic and social conditions would appear to be immune from the first kind but that cannot be said with the same certainty for the second.

Let us apply these criteria to the GDR and see if we can obtain an answer to the question of whether the East German state can be described as militaristic or not. Certainly over the last few years social and economic efforts to build up the national defence system have been greatly strengthened and the repercussions of this on the economic process cannot be overlooked. Rising costs are also proving an increasing burden on the realisation of socio-political aims.[34] However, decisions on armaments may affect economic policy decisions in some industries but one cannot say that the whole economy of the GDR is militarised or that it is subordinate to military policy. Nor can one say that all political, economic and social processes are determined by military premises or that the military are an instrument of enforcing and maintaining loyalty. The military leadership organs are tied into the decision-making structures for society as a whole and the forms and nature of political control over the military are such that the problem of loyalty between the political and military leaders has never been able to develop into a conflict. Moreover, the political and military potential of the GDR are not such that she can play an independent part in the Warsaw Pact. The main decisions on her military policy depend on the Soviet Union and one of the decisive prerequisites for the development of national as opposed to alliance interests is also lacking, insofar as the military is not a separate interest group in external and security policy nor does it have the institutional autonomy to help it to a special position in the political decision-making process. Finally the role of the military in the GDR is further restricted by the fact that ultimately it is not the National People's Army but the army of the Soviet Union which guarantees the security of the state. Moreover, the GDR is territorially satisfied and has no expansionist interests. She aims to achieve her foreign policy goals primarily with instruments of non-military policy. However, this does not on principle exclude the possibility of the use of instruments of military power. Hence the clause in the SED programme, 'the defence of Socialist achievements', although this certainly does not refer only to defence against external influences. It is a reference to the military components in the GDR's security policy. Nevertheless the use of military instruments as political means or to threaten other countries is not a feature of the system. The militarisation of foreign policy doctrines is usual in other political systems and regions as well. What is specific to the Socialist foreign policy doctrine is the arrogance with which a relation between Socialism and the use of power threats is denied.[35]

The existence of the armed forces, of paramilitary organisations, security apparatuses, structures and attitudes which have military implications or overtones in the civilian spheres of society in the GDR and, last but not least, the broadly-based programme of pre-military education and training suggest that it would be appropriate to examine the social and political consequences of these developments. Every political system tries to win the loyalty of members of its own society. The SED wants more, it wants the active participation of its citizens in the implementation of the political aims of the party. But loyalty and co-operation cannot be achieved solely or even mainly through military and paramilitary organisations or institutions or through mechanisms which are oriented to military premises. If social policy made use only of these means we should have to say that the GDR is a militarised society. But although there are many contradictory features in public life in the GDR we cannot make such a global statement. Military policy is still limited to certain social areas and it does not cover all of social life. That there is nevertheless a clearly recognisable trend to greater militarisation is closely bound up with the development of the political situation in which the GDR finds herself: she is not only caught up in the general conflict between hostile political systems but also exposed to the specific problems of the German question.

The SED leaders base their policy on the assumption that it is the aim of the West in the present political, economic and ideological battle to weaken the political and social systems of the Socialist countries and hence of the GDR as well. In order to reduce the danger of a military confrontation and improve conditions for foreign policy measures the GDR is interested in concluding agreements with Western states, including the Federal Republic of Germany, in areas of mutual interest and in continuing the policy of detente.[36] She attempts to overcome the dilemma between foreign policy and economic interests on the one hand and ideological and propaganda interpretations of the international situation on the other by maintaining that she is threatened by 'abrupt changes in policy' in the Imperialist states and that this necessitates further defence efforts. The domestic political situation is also made more difficult by the fact that there are signs of a growing divergence between the interests and expectations of the people and the policy of the party leaders. Progress in social policy is often slowed down by shortages in supplies and in some areas the exercise of individual and collective rights and liberties and participation in the formation of political objectives is unsatisfactory. The SED tries to achieve greater social and political stability not only by continuing the socio-political strategy but also by devoting more resources to political and ideological work. This is also designed to prepare the people for the event of war. Within the framework of this policy the military has been given the function of an instrument for the social and political education of the people.

These factors suggest a tendency to militarisation in the GDR as a result of the synthesis between political and military requirements which derives from the excessive need for security. It is characterised by the expansion of security ideology with little tolerance of divergent political attitudes and efforts to give military principles and values a high standing in civilian areas as well. But this does not dominate internal developments. Military policy and propaganda activities are certainly not inconsiderable and they have been successful in developing the NVA into a modern army. But a number of problems still remain in the implementation of the SED military programme. Even if the leaders' aim were to militarise their society they are very far from achieving this. The GDR in its present state cannot be described as a militaristic system, unless one aspect is considered in isolation from all the others. But interpretations of this kind run the danger of seeing developments in one system as only the reaction to behaviour in the other and they take insufficient account of differences in inherent conditions. They tend to overlook the causes of the domestic problems in the GDR as well as her specific security needs and to destroy any chance of a real contribution to the peaceful settlement of the conflicts which do exist within each of the societies as well as between them.

Notes

1 *Protokoll des IX. Parteitages der SED*, Berlin (GDR), Dietz Verlag, 1976, vol.2, p.220.
2 Hoffmann, H., *Sozialistische Landesverteidigung. Reden und Aufsätze 1974–Juni 1976*, Berlin (GDR), Militärverlag, 1979, p.540.
3 'Gegen Aggression- für Unterstützung der Sowjetarmee', in *Neues Deutschland (B)*, 2 March 1949, no.51, p.1.
4 On integration cf. Tiedtke, St., *Die Warschauer Vertragsorganisation*, Munich, Vienna, Oldenburg, 1978, pp. 61–7.
5 As an example cf. Grümmert, J., 'Die Waffenbrüderschaftsbeziehungen eines Panzerverbandes der NVA zu seinem Partnerverband der GSSD 1970–1976', in *Militärgeschichte 2/1980*, pp. 169–76; and Greese, K., Schramm, P. and Voerster, A., 'Die Waffenbrüderschaftsbeziehungen der NVA zur polnischen Armee in den siebziger Jahren' in *Militärgeschichte 3/1980*, pp. 279–89.
6 *The Military Balance 1979–1980*, The International Institute for Strategic Studies, London 1979, p.15. Forster, Th. (for a group of authors), *Die NVA*, 5th completely revised edition, Markus, 1979, p.150, gives 50,000.
7 Forster, op.cit., p.172 and *The Military Balance*, loc.cit.
8 Nawrocki, J., *Bewaffnete Organe in der DDR*, Berlin (West), Holzapfel, 1979, p.155. *The Military Balance*, loc.cit.
9 *Gesetz über die Zivilverteidigung der DDR*, GB1. I, 1970, no.20. *Dienstlaufbahnordnung der Zivilverteidigung*, GB1. I, 1977, no.34.
10 'Gemeinsam den Sozialismus verteidigen', in *Neues Deutschland*, 23 November 1968, no.325, p.5.

11 Cf. Rodejohann-Recke, H., 'Sozialistische Wehrerziehung in der DDR', in Studiengruppe Militärpolitik, *Die nationale Volksarmee*, Hamburg, Rowohlt, 1976, pp. 100–33. Henrich, W. (ed.), *Wehrkunde in der DDR*, Bonn, Hohwacht, 1978. Hübner, W., 'Zur führenden Rolle der Partei bei der sozialistischen Wehrerziehung nach dem VIII. Parteitag der SED', in *Militärgeschichte I/1979*, pp. 5–16.

12 Schiel, W., 'Das brüderliche Bündnis der Armeen der Länder des Sozialismus — eine grosse Errungenschaft der Oktoberrevolution', in *Militärwesen, Beilage 2 zu No. 6/1957*, p.9.

13 Hoffmann, H., *Sozialistische Landesverteidigung. Aus Reden und Aufsätzen 1970–1974*, Berlin (GDR), Militärverlag 1974, p.194.

14 Teller, G., 'Mit ganzer Kraft für die Erfüllung des gesellschaftlichen Auftrages der GST', in *Militärwesen 4/1979*, pp. 3–8.

15 Cf. Erbe, G., et al., *Politik, Wirtschaft und Gesellschaft in der DDR*. 2nd edition, Opladen, Westdeutscher Verlag, 1980, pp. 340–42 and 184–7. For the success rate see Schmitt, K., *Politische Erziehung in der DDR*, Paderborn, Schöningh, 1979, pp. 200–2.

16 On conscientious objectors see Studiengruppe Militärpolitik, op. cit., pp. 155–76.

17 Hoffmann has been a member of the SED Central Committee Politbureau since 1973.

18 Cf. Blanke, B.M., *Die politisch-ideologische Bildung und Erziehung in der Nationalen Volksarmee. Zum Verhältnis von Militär, Partei und Gesellschaft in der DDR*, Bonn, 1975, pp. 246–56.

19 *Percentage of Officers from the Working Class*

1963	1965	1971	1975
82.7	82.2	79.0 (80)	70.0

Percentage of Officers who are Members and Candidates of the SED

1963	1965	1971	1975
96.3	95.0	98.0	99.0

Source for the first table: Blanke, B.M., op.cit., p.243. The figure 80 per cent for 1971 is given by Hager, K., *Die entwickelte sozialistische Gesellschaft*, Berlin (GDR), Dietz, 1976, p.17. 1975: *Ostseezeitung*, 28/29 February 1976, supplement.

Source for second table: Blanke, op.cit., p.244.

20 *Militärlexikon*, Berlin (GDR), Militärverlag, 1974 edition, p.297.

21 The argument put forward by R. Kolkowicz is examined by D. Herspring, *East German Civil–Military Relations. The Impact of Technology 1949–1972* (New York, Praeger, 1973) in relation to the People's Army.

22 For example, Nawrocki, J., op.cit., p.11 or K.W. Fricke, 'DDR-Verteidigungsgesetz neu kodifiziert', in *Deutschland-Archiv* 12/1978, p.1238. For a different view see Th. Forster, op.cit., p.10.

23   This is clear from the group of essays in Berghahn, V.R. (ed.), *Militarismus*, Cologne, Kiepenheuer und Witsch, 1975.
24   Vagts, A., *A History of Militarism, Civilian and Military*, London, Hollis and Carter, 1959, p.13.
25   Wiatr, J., 'Sozio-politische Besonderheiten und Funktionen von Streitkräften in sozialistischen Ländern', in *Beiträge zur Militärsoziologie, Kölner Zeitschrift für Soziologie und Sozialpsychologie*, Sonderheft 12/1968, Cologne, Westdeutscher Verlag, p.109.
26   Ritter, G., 'Das Problem des Militarismus in Deutschland' in Berghahn, V.R., op.cit., p.196.
27   Jahn, E., *Kommunismus – und was dann? Zur Bürokratisierung und Nationalisierung des Systems der Nationalstaaten*, Hamburg, Rowohlt, 1974, p.138.
28   Giertz, H. and Küttler, W., 'Zur Inhaltsbestimmung und historischen Dimension des Militarismusbegriffs', in *Militärgeschichte 4/1976*, p.417.
29   Senghaas, D., 'Überlegungen zur gegenwärtigen Militarismus-Problematik', in Berghahn, V.R. (ed.), op.cit., p.159.
30   Rau, G., Schulze, H. and Stubner, E., 'Das Problem des Militarismus und die Armeen der beiden deutschen Staaten', in Schulz, R. and Steiner, H., *Soziologie und Wirklichkeit, Beiträge zum 6. Weltkongress für Soziologie in Evian, 1966*, Berlin (GDR), Deutscher Verlag der Wissenschaften, 1966, p.120.
31   Hoppe, G., *Kritik der imperialistischen deutschen Wehrsoziologie* Berlin (GDR), Militärverlag, 1965, p.131.
32   Autorenkollektiv, *Militarismus heute*, Berlin (GDR), Militärverlag, 1979, p.27.
33   Berghahn, V.R. (ed.), op.cit., p.31.
34   The economist J. Kuczynski argues that without the expenditure on armaments in the GDR a 4-day or 35-hour week would be possible, that gas, electricity, city transport and telephone calls would be free and a progressive reduction in rents could be undertaken. (For some data on the relations between armaments and unemployment see *Horizont 47/1977*, p.24.) R. Rompe, member of the Academy of Science of the GDR, complained that on the one hand some disciplines are being overstrained by the arms race and others, such as medicine, food, environment protection and education, are being neglected ('Standpunkte und Streitpunkte' in *Spektrum 3/1973*, p.11).
35   Cf. Hoffmann, H., 'Sozialismus und Frieden werden sicher verteidigt', in *Neuer Weg 2/1979*, p.53. Hoffmann commented elsewhere that he would be glad if he could say: 'The last battle has been fought with the enemy of peace'. 'Was ist Sache?' in *Armeerundschau 2/1977*, p.3.
36   Cf. Axen, H., 'Der Aufbau des Sozialismus in der DDR und die Entwicklung in der Welt' in *Einheit 3/1979*, p.264.

5 The education system and society

Gert-Joachim Glaessner, Free University, Berlin

Introduction

In every Soviet-type system the education sector has been a key part of the 'new social order'. This applies to the GDR as well. In the words of the East German educationalist, Helmut Klein, education policy was and still is intended to 'create constantly improving conditions for our people to develop their abilities to the full and develop in harmony'. This, according to Klein, is by no means only a pedagogical question, nor is it a matter of the appropriate organisation of education facilities, teaching and learning methods and so on. On the contrary, education policy is 'part of overall policy in the Socialist countries'.[1]

Changes in the education sector in the GDR have always been both part of and a reaction to development trends in other social areas and they have been intended to develop or correct the political, economic, social and cultural processes which have been planned, initiated or developed in these sectors. So education policy has always been an integral part of the political and social aims announced by the ruling party. Its targets are not established autonomously. Education policy measures in the GDR can only be understood if they are seen in the context of the general development of the social system and as an essential element in social policy. This was made very clear at the beginning of the 1960s, when necessary economic reforms (initiated in 1963 as 'The new economic system of planning and direction of the national economy', – NÖS) brought changes in society as a whole which did not stop at the education system. The Law on a Uniform Socialist Education System of 1965[2] can be seen as the expression of the concept that all areas of society, not only the economy, must be formed and developed according to a plan.

To make this relation clear I shall first describe the role played by the education sector in the general organisational and institutional structure of the GDR and then subject its most important functions to a closer analysis. First, however, it is necessary to give a brief outline of the present structure of the education system in the GDR.

Structure and development of the Education System

The system is comprised firstly of the formal institutions and facilities which form the 'uniform Socialist education system'. They are:

(a) day nurseries, kindergarten, 'learn and play' afternoons: these are not obligatory but they carry out carefully defined pedagogical work and as institutions of pre-school education they form part of state education planning;

(b) polytechnic general schools, which have ten classes (years) ('Allgemeinbildende polytechnische Oberschulen');

(c) the vocational training institutions;

(d) the institutions which provide university entrance qualifications, mainly the 'higher polytechnic general schools' ('Erweiterte Oberschulen' – EOS);

(e) professional schools ('Fachschulen');

(f) universities and colleges;

(g) adult education institutes.

(see figure 5.1).

In accordance with the 1965 Education Act the formal structure of the education system covers all stages from pre-schooling through the ten-year general schools, the higher general schools, vocational training, professional schools and universities to adult education institutes. An essential structural element is mobility between the various stages, i.e. generally there are several ways of acquiring a particular qualification, each designed for different age groups and phases of development.

The basic decision to allow as much mobility as possible between the various stages of education can be seen most clearly in those institutions which provide formal university entrance qualifications (Abitur):

(a) The higher general schools (about 10 per cent of pupils from the last year at general school are admitted to the EOS at present);

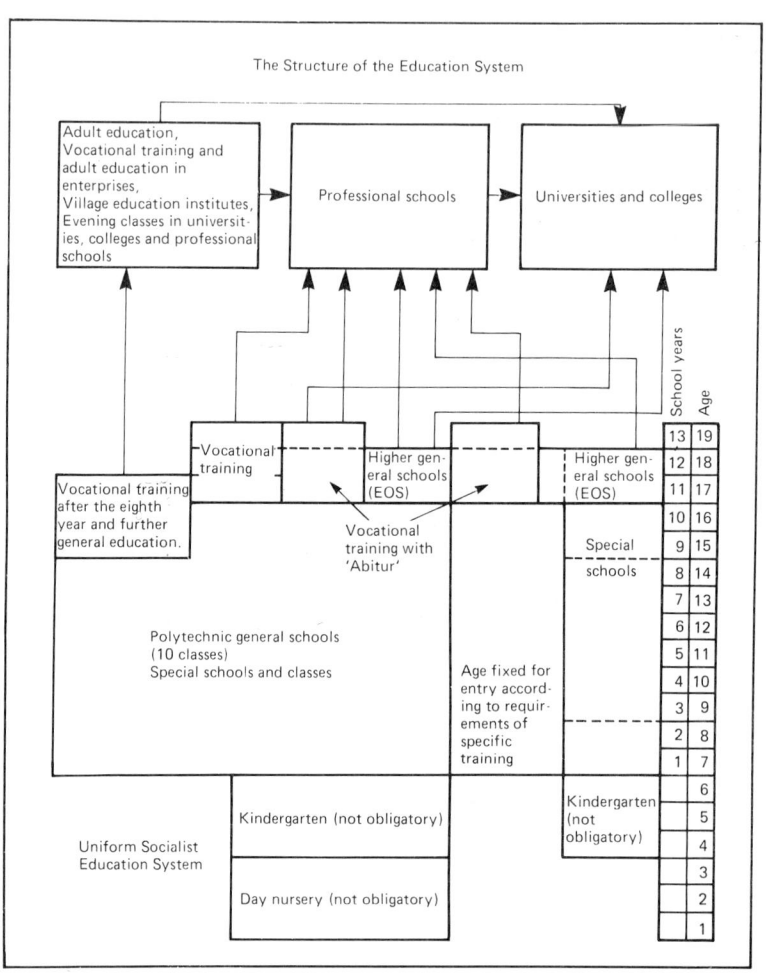

Figure 5.1   The structure of the education system[3]

Further training measures	Further training institutes			
	SED	State	Economic	Others
1 Training for leading positions (mainly Category I)	Academy of the Social Sciences; Party University; Central Committee special schools.	Academy of Constitutional Law.	Central Institute of Socialist Economic Planning.	Trade Union College.
2 Training for middle positions (largely Category II and some Category III)	Regional[1] party schools; special schools run by regional party leaders.	School of Constitutional Law.	Institute of Socialist Economic Planning; Industrial branch colleges.	Youth College run by FDJ[3]; Trade union regional schools; Industrial union schools; Union one-year courses.
3 General further education for 'cadres'	Marxist–Leninist district[2] schools	Enterprise academies run by district councils and regional councils; Central Enterprise Academy of the Council of Ministers.	Industrial branch academies; Enterprise academies in nationally-owned plants and 'combinates' (Trusts).	FDJ regional youth schools; Trade union district training centres.

1 regional = 'Bezirk'
2 district = 'Kreis'
3 FDJ = Free German Youth

Figure 5.2 Institutes of training and further training for 'cadres'

(b) Special schools and classes (mainly for language teaching, science and mathematics);

(c) 'Abitur' classes in vocational training institutes;

(d) Adult education institutes and vocational schools in Socialist enterprises (these offer courses for the examinations held at the end of the 8th, 10th and 12th year at school and special crash courses for certain faculties);

(e) The professional schools which are a potential preparatory stage for university entrance;

(f) Workers' and Agricultural Workers' Faculties (there are now only two, in the University of Halle and the Mining Academy in Freiberg).

In addition, however, there are a large number of educational institutions which are not regarded as part of the uniform education system but which play a decisive part in the social system of the GDR. They are organised by various bodies, the party, the state, economic organisations and mass organisations and they train people specially chosen for leading positions in various sectors of political, economic and social life, to be cadres. Access to these institutions is not open to anyone, it is determined by 'cadre' policy, which is beyond the scope of this essay.[4]

Table 5.1
The development of the education sector[5]

Number of pupils (10th year)		Entrants for university entrance qualification (Abitur)		Skilled worker qualification examinations		Leavers of vocational schools		University graduates	
1955	–	1955	19,678	1955	–	1955	–	1955	7,617
1960	64,108	1960	18,282	1960	125,877	1960	24,544	1960	15,005
1965	–	1965	19,332	1965	197,756	1965	33,633	1965	20,878
1970	184,800	1970	25,709	1970	260,495	1970	36,265	1970	22,312
1971	190,900	1971	25,233	1971	222,802	1971	37,924	1971	23,300
1972	194,400	1972	27,797	1972	223,574	1972	41,847	1972	27,821
1973	197,100	1973	27,940	1973	229,586	1973	46,638	1973	32,846
1974	207,800	1974	25,527	1974	247,562	1974	50,975	1974	36,256
1975	226,400	1975	24,490	1975	257,261	1975	43,030	1975	36,521
1976	237,000	1976	23,095	1976	243,793	1976	38,982	1976	32,629
1977	241,200	1977	23,196	1977	238,697	1977	42,234	1977	27,115
1978	244,200	1978	22,938	1978	246,284	1978	41,179	1978	28,927

Table 5.2
Expenditure for education purposes from the state budget [6]

Year	Total (in Marks)	of which:		
		general schools	vocational training, adult education	vocational schools, universities, colleges
1971	6,369,366	2,493,132	640,892	1,455,154
1972	6,836,657	2,648,523	676,547	1,541,354
1973	7,274,550	2,971,093	706,275	1,590,486
1974	7,833,446	3,192,702	638,302	1,647,554
1975	8,275,353	3,394,587	694,852	1,720,577
1976	8,907,051	3,461,151	746,867	1,816,901
1977	9,273,262	3,564,538	804,928	1,873,180
1978	9,538,582	3,566,896	867,829	1,925,388

Table 5.3
Education funds: development according to economic sectors [7]

	Funds used		Increase 1975 over 1962	
	1962	1971	Total increase in %	Average annual increase in %
	in millions M			
Economy as a whole	66,465	150,881	227.0	6.5
Industry and production crafts	24,066	58,899	244.7	7.1
Building	3,658	10,284	281.2	8.3
Agriculture and forestry	11,544	17,193	148.9	3.1
Transport, post, telecommunications	4,815	10,956	226.4	6.5
Trade	6,682	13,624	203.9	5.6
Other production and non-production sectors	15,657	40,325	257.1	7.5

However, the available statistical data only permit reliable statements on the quantitative development of the institutions of the uniform Socialist education system.

The same applies to the data on the funds committed for education purposes from the state budget or the 'education funds' of the various sectors of the economy.

The position of the education sector in GDR society

In the organisational and institutional structure of Soviet-type societies we can distinguish between four sectors from the educational sociological point of view: the education system, the political and administrative system, the employment sector and the 'cadre' sector. To examine education policy only with regard to the function of the education system itself would be to take a one-dimensional view, and neither the socio-political goals nor their results would be properly assessed. But in no highly industrialised society can education policy aims be understood without a consideration of the requirements and expectations of the political and administrative system.[8]

In this context the term 'political and administrative system' means the differentiated organisational structure of government in Soviet Socialist societies, which they themselves call 'the system of class dictatorship'. The term covers all the state organs and social organisations with which the 'ruling class' exercises its power and secures its interests. Hence class dictatorship consists of the 'Marxist–Leninist party', its 'main instrument', the state apparatus in the narrower sense (the government, administrative apparatus, the armed forces and other security organs, the judiciary and representative bodies), and the 'transmission instruments', the unions and other mass organisations. The political and administrative system is characterised by the specific linking of the avant-garde claims of the Leninist party with state forms of the exercise of power. This has led to a de facto 'instrumentalisation' of the state for the aims of the party, but at the same time made the party dependent on the functioning of the state governing apparatus.[9]

The use of the rather vague term 'employment sector' is justified by the need to determine education requirements not only with regard to those of industry but those of all areas and sectors in society. Only in this way would it appear possible to recognise changes in requirements and possible shifts within and between the primary, secondary and tertiary sectors (agriculture or mining; manufacturing; services). The main problem of all empirical studies so far on the development of the occupational and qualification structure is that — for whatever reason — they concentrate more or less exclusively on the production sector but derive general statements from it. A wider perspective — especially since empirical field work is not possible in the GDR — would appear to be needed if we are to keep in view the special conditions to which the various areas and sectors are subject and avoid over-hasty generalisations.

Studies of these problems so far have largely disregarded the specific conditions of the political system in the GDR: the inter-dependence between the education system, the political and administrative system

Performance \ Expectations	Political and administrative system	Employment sector	Education system	Cadre sector
Political and administrative system		Securing the political, legal and institutional framework. Provision of data for social and economic planning, socio-structural developments	Securing the political, legal and institutional framework. Planning aims (1 normative – for the high general education of Socialist people; 2 contribution to the realisation of the WTR[1] concept.)	Securing the 'reproduction' of the cadre sector through co-option mechanisms
Employment sector	Provision of manpower to secure the social reproduction process		Provision of material. Establishment of requirements. Determining future occupational and qualification structure. Establishment of characteristic requirements and occupations	Provision of recruits to the cadre sector
Education system	Social education and political socialisation. Creation of normative loyalty (deontic function). Influence on socio-structural processes	Quantitative and qualitative satisfaction of the qualification requirements. Provision of qualifications for specific occupations and jobs. Provision of 'flexibility-potential'/cognitive ability		Provision of qualifications enabling holder to take cadre position
Cadre sector	Securing the avant-garde claim of the SED. Ideology. Development of social aims. Planning and social leadership	Provision of qualified leaders to meet the quantitative and qualitative requirements of the employment sector	Provision of teaching personnel	

1 WTR = see p. 199

Figure 5.3 The relation between the education system, the political and administrative system, the employment sector and the cadre sector in the GDR

and the employment sector are very largely formed and influenced by the political requirements of the 'cadre sector'. To the extent to which traditional cadre selection, which was solely concerned with political reliability, has been supplemented by criteria designed to ensure that persons in leading positions hold high occupational qualifications the general education system has been involved as well. The setting up of formalised training courses, the establishment of specific qualifications for people in leading positions and the differentiation of the methods of cadre need planning and administration have had decisive repercussions on the education sector. Only against the background of the cadre question is the education policy pursued by the SED in the 1960s understandable.[10] For these purposes the 'cadre sector' is defined pragmatically: it includes those positions and functions which the party regards as 'strategically' important and which it includes in specific categories. Persons who hold positions on the various levels of the governing apparatus are assigned to categories which determine the level of their position in the overall hierarchy.

The relations between the four sectors of society in the GDR can be shown schematically as in figure 5.3. Let us examine these relations in more detail in four functional areas of the education system: its education and socialisation, its socio-structural, its economic and its political functions.

Education and socialisation

The labour movement's concept of education differed and still does differ from that of 'bourgeois' educationalists. The latter saw and frequently still see education as a comprehensive (if possible 'humanist') general education but the labour movement has operated with a concept of education oriented to occupational and social practice in a society reorganised on democratic lines. This is the concept of education which is always cited in the GDR but it has largely lost its democratic impetus, being subordinated both in theory and in practice to the axioms of Marxist–Leninist theory.

Statements of political programmes at party congresses, education conferences and similar functions always declare the comprehensively educated Socialist personality — more recently the 'Communist personality' — to be the primary aim of all practical and theoretical work in education. There is unanimous agreement among educationalists and policy-makers, as well as sociologists and economists, that the education system functions as a means of securing greater social equality and as an instrument of a long-term process of social homogenisation.[11] But despite such optimistic statements it cannot be denied that the education system prepares young people for a society in which not only different qualifications but also differing social behaviour are required. Despite all the proclamations of unity parts of the education system only prepare young people for less highly qualified jobs, while others prepare for academic training and hence for the subsequent exercise of leadership functions.

The concept of general education as used in the GDR does tend to minimise the dichotomy between vocational qualification and general education; nevertheless there is tension between the aim of providing education (in the sense of general ability to think, understand and act) and providing qualifications (in the sense of ability to do a particular job of work). It cannot be denied that all too often education in the GDR is reduced to the mechanistic view of a 'variable which is dependent on other social processes and their requirements and conditions'[12] and seen only in its function as provider of qualifications.

Nor can it be denied that the requirements of a world of work which is hierarchically structured and dominated by authority relationships are not in keeping with the ideal image of an individual who has enjoyed a high level of general education and hence is capable of participation in political decision-making on an equal basis. Moreover, such a high degree of general culture and education could not, or only to a very limited extent, be incorporated into the main function of this world of work. These political and social conditions make the reduction of the concept of education to that of qualification more understandable.

In the late 1950s and early 1960s it was believed that the scientific and technical revolution (referred to as the WTR — wissenschaftlich-technische Revolution) would within a relatively short space of time change the existing structures of the world of work and hence remove the present restrictions on the individual, and as long as this seemed likely the emphasis on qualification may have appeared justified. After all, it could be assumed that a comprehensive education would be the natural consequence of further scientific and technical development. It was expected that the share of intellectual and creative work would rise very quickly while the percentage of heavy physical work would be reduced, so that not only higher skill qualifications but even more creative ability would be needed. Greater flexibility and mobility would be possible, indeed they would be necessary and they should largely be provided by the education system. The 1965 Education Act was intended to provide the structural and material prerequisites for this. But these expectations have not been fulfilled. The education system is still faced — indeed to an even greater degree — with the task of preparing young people for a society in which quite different qualifications, knowledge, skills and behaviour are required.

In contrast to the view widely held in the GDR that the existing structures and forms of division of labour are the expression of social 'legitimacies' and that the task of the education system must be to prepare young people for existing social conditions, the educational sociologist Artur Meier argues that this is too narrow a view, reducing the socialisation achievements of the education system to mere adjustment:

> Socialist education always serves to provide an active adjustment to given social conditions and provides at the same time the means to overcome them. It is a dialectical process of introduction to social reality and preparation for social possibility. It is a dialectical unity of tradition (the heritage of the past) and innovation (renewal). Like the reproduction process of society itself, to which it is related, it serves the constant restoration of social conditions and at the same time their expansion and renewal. Hence education always has a dual dialectical social role, the preservation and handing on of the past and the anticipation of the future.[13]

But in this dual aim the education system reaches its limits, limits which are not set by itself but formulated and controlled by the political system. It is not only on the lower levels that the political and ideological reservations of the party leadership against too much individuality in thought and ideas can have a counter-productive effect. One of the most renowned sociologists in the GDR, Jürgen Kuczynski, recently pointed this out in connection with technical and university education: in his view neither present nor — even more emphatically — future needs will be met by a system which produces ill-educated, passive Socialists, even if they have a high degree of occupational skills (Kuczynski explicitly uses the term *'Fachidioten'* — specialised idiots). Such persons will for that very reason be incapable of solving the many different problems they will be confronted with in the world of work.[14]

The education system and social structure

All existing education systems are more or less selective. An education policy which is bound to an emancipatory aim is therefore always faced with the problem of how to reconcile the selection function — which decides on social and occupational opportunities for the individual — with the postulate of equality of opportunity. This conflict, which has characterised discussion on education reform in the Western systems, appears in a different form in the GDR: equality of opportunity is not exclusively or even mainly a matter concerning the individual; on the contrary, the main concern is equality of opportunity for social groups, strata and classes. Hence there is a highly important historical component. In the early years the SED were aiming to 'redistribute opportunities'. They were prepared to deny opportunities to gifted individuals if they came from social classes who had up to then kept the majority of the population out of the institutes of higher education, and so open up for the first time higher education to industrial and agricultural workers. But even now that a new 'Socialist' intelligentsia has been created through this practice, elements of individual inequality of opportunity remain. The selection principles still contain the question of 'social background', together with the criteria of ability in the chosen field and socio-political activity in line with SED aims.

The task which was originally thought to be temporary, providing all social groups, strata and classes with education opportunities corresponding to their share in the population as a whole, has become a permanent obligation. But now that nearly 80 per cent of the population is regarded as belonging either to the working class or to the co-operative farmers, it is increasingly difficult to operate with such general terms as 'working class' in education policy. Within such a huge group living and working conditions vary considerably. If real 'social equality of opportunity' is to be created precisely these differences should play a part in the selection process. Hence it is not surprising that individual social classes and strata, and groups which have so far been disadvantaged, such as women, are represented in higher education courses in proportion to their share of the total population. But it is hardly possible to make statements on whether and how different social conditions, e.g. the difference between children of skilled workers or white collar workers and unskilled workers, regional differences resulting from the gap which still exists between urban and rural areas, or other factors, play a part in the selection decisions.

But however just the selection procedure in the education system may be it does not automatically create equality of opportunity in the employment system. The politically motivated selection mechanisms in the choice of persons for strategically important positions in the administration, mass organisations and so on speak as clearly here as does the small percentage of women in these positions.[15]

With the need for replacement and new personnel which lasted until the 1960s — and was intensified by the stream of refugees into the Federal Republic, in which university graduates and skilled workers were disproportionately represented — capacity in the education system was considerably expanded, as table 5.1 shows. This was especially the case in higher education, i.e. universities, colleges and professional schools. In two decades the qualification level of workers in the GDR was raised considerably, the qualification structure fundamentally changed and individual opportunities for education and vocational training greatly improved.

Table 5.4
Qualification structure of all persons employed in the GDR (in percentage)[16]

	1962	1971	1975	1980	1990 (estimate)
Unskilled and semi-skilled	59.7	42.3	32.9	26	20
Skilled workers/master craftsmen	33.6	46.0	53.0	58	60
Professional schools cadres	4.3	7.4	8.6	10	12
University cadres	2.4	4.3	5.5	6	8

Education policy-makers and planners in the GDR have always known that they must consider not only present but also future requirements if they were to make realistic prognoses of the need for capacity expansion in their system. But at the beginning of the 1970s it became clear that the ideas of growth based on the old 'WTR' concept no longer applied and that the expansion of the education system had produced a level of qualification (and appropriate social expectations) beyond what might be expected to be the requirements of the employment system within the near future.

Economic function

These problems point to the third function of the education system, its economic function. The postulate of equality, which found its structural equivalent in the 1950s in the uniform general school, was no longer sufficient for the education sector as a whole, with its vocational training, professional schools, universities and large areas of adult education, when a new role for education had to be determined in the context of economic and political reforms which marked the end of the socio-economic transformation period of the GDR system and introduced a phase of 'letting things become routine', or consolidation of what had been achieved. If progress was to be secured over the longer term it was essential to provide exact information on the relations between technical and economic developments and the functions of the education sector. Hence here as in other sectors (the adaptation of cybernetics, for example, and of systems theory and conduction approaches) an obvious solution was to make use of a discipline which was also being developed in Western capitalist countries and had already produced some effects: education economics.[17] But the GDR found itself faced with the same problem as Western education planners: there were and still are neither reliable methods of forecasting nor exact knowledge of what the concrete effects of education processes are on social development and especially economic growth. Nevertheless, for most education economists the decision as to what material resources should be provided for the education sector is only an optimisation problem.[18] Such a telescoped procedure makes the postulate of equality and the comprehensively educated Socialist personality which is always declared the primary aim of education policy in the GDR, a dependent variable of economic rationality and optimal economic growth. In the final analysis the aim of creating a comprehensively educated Socialist personality is only taken into account as long as it does not conflict with economic aims. The usual argument that 'social and individual educational needs within the framework of existing economic possibilities' are the basis for education planning in the GDR[19] cannot disguise this shift in emphasis, especially since it has so far been restricted to the development of need-oriented planning models. But these have been oriented to the expected future demands on the individual's power to work and not his educational requirements. It is only recently that there has been some indication of a move away from this economic telescoping. Although the importance of the economic function of the education sector is not denied, it is admitted that education processes should not only be assessed and planned according to economic criteria: 'while the need for general and special education is in principle unlimited, the social need for specific occupational qualifications depends on the concrete state and speed of development in the technical, economic and organisational conditions of the reproduction process'.[20] It is emphasised that both aspects have to be taken into account in planning if the 'sign-post function' of the education sector is to be ensured. The recent decisions by the Council of Ministers and the General Board of the Free German Trade Union Federation on further education and a decision by the SED Politbureau on questions of university policy show that these arguments have also found their way into the political decision-making process.[21]

According to the latest estimates no noticeable expansion of the higher qualification sector is planned for the coming decade and attention will focus on consolidation of what has been achieved. This means that the education system will in all probability concentrate on changing the proportions between individual training sectors and subjects, which do not adequately meet the needs of industry, the administration and so on, and achieving a more balanced development. This will make the effect of the education system on its 'products', those who leave its institutions and enter the world of work, calculable over the longer term. This kind of consolidation work will also affect the system itself: its transformatory function within the framework of the development of the social structure (towards an elimination of the social division of labour and more social and political equality) will remain largely reduced. What remains for education economics and policy is fine tuning and the correction of sectoral and regional discrepancies.

The political function

The political function of the education sector can be characterised with three concepts: uniformity, differentiation and the creation and maintenance of hierarchies. We have already pointed out that education policy-makers in the GDR use the concept of uniformity de facto only for those parts of the education system which belong to the 'uniform Socialist education system'. Even if one accepts this limitation, developments in education policy over the last decade necessitate a review of the problem of uniformity and differentiation in the education system. The uniform general school, for decades a guarantee of a socially just and politically desirable distribution of education opportunities, is undergoing increasing structural differentiation. But education policy, and even more so decisions in education planning in favour of differentiation of the education system in the secondary sphere, has brought the GDR face to face with the problem of how a balanced and ideologically legitimate relation can be achieved between special encouragement of ability on the one hand and equality of opportunity for all on the other. A particularly clear expression of these efforts at differentiation are the 'special classes' in the general schools, or the 'special schools', which 'take a limited number of pupils of high ability to meet the special requirements of the economy, science, sport and culture and further this ability in a specific way'.[22]

The assurance of equal educational opportunities for all and a rising level of general education for all is hard to reconcile with this kind of differentiation of the education system or individual stages in it. Differentiation means recognising special ability at an early stage and encouraging it. This may satisfy the postulate that the education system provides 'unhindered access to education graded according to the standard of ability' but if the social determinants of ability are neglected, it can all too easily lead to a de facto favouring of certain social groups to the disadvantage of others (e.g. the children of unskilled workers and agricultural workers).

The decision as to what degree of uniformity can be maintained in the education system in view of the increasing degree of social differentiation and diversification remains a political question. The institution of special education and training courses (e.g. the special schools), the adjustment of selection criteria to current political and planning requirements, the reduction or expansion of training courses or changes in their content, and especially changes in the relation between general education and special education, can therefore ultimately be shown as due to temporary development trends and politically legitimated, but they can easily acquire an impetus of their own and obliterate the original education aims.

That changes of this nature can have far-reaching consequences for educational aims can be seen from the developments of the last decade which has been characterised by economic restrictions: the structural decision in favour of a uniform and hence first and foremost penetrable education system has not been formally revoked but its implications are increasingly coming under pressure. A more critical selection of entrants to institutions of higher education is matched by a clear restriction on 'compensatory' education measures. Opportunities for acquiring qualifications in any other than the 'normal' way have steadily deteriorated. This is clear from the numbers of participants at the appropriate courses at adult education institutes.

Table 5.5
Numbers of participants at courses in adult education institutions for the examinations at the end of the 8th, 10th and 12th school years and in preparation for college or university entrance[23]

Year	Participants
1955	—
1960	85,761
1965	57,510
1971	73,224
1972	60,169
1973	44,647
1974	36,446
1975	31,252
1976	26,530
1977	21,605
1978	18,841

Evening classes and correspondence courses in universities, colleges and professional schools which for nearly twenty years offered large numbers of adults good opportunities of acquiring higher qualifications have been very much restricted.

At present expansion is only going on in further training measures related to the occupation of people at work, especially for skilled workers in industry.

Table 5.6
New entrants to evening and correspondence courses[24]

	Professional schools	Universities
1955	–	4,404
1960	25,828	8,702
1965	20,623	7,083
1970	32,148	10,082
1971	31,897	9,939
1972	24,245	8,174
1973	19,769	5,375
1974	16,374	4,679
1975	17,644	4,318
1976	16,107	3,451
1977	17,336	3,404
1978	16,978	3,400

Table 5.7
Qualification measures in industry

	1971	1973	1975	1977	1978
Training as:					
Skilled worker	39,495	54,288	49,257	57,571	57,270
Master	20,411	19,923	17,002	17,472	18,014
University entrance	9,752	11,249	8,202	6,972	6,015
Further training:					
Skilled workers	51,168	65,232	77,949	147,759	265,189
Masters	17,140	23,608	28,380	55,935	59,994
University cadres	3,490	3,112	2,651	42,802	44,455

These — selected — data, if they are seen in the context of the overall numbers of pupils and students, show that the real chances of the individual acquiring higher education in various ways have deteriorated. Particularly for socio-culturally disadvantaged groups, and especially for women, this is a serious reduction in the range of occupational (and hence social) opportunities, which have so far been very much greater than those in Western societies. In view of these trends it cannot be said that the education system of the GDR is characterised by a high degree of mobility or that it enables people to reach a particular educational aim in many different ways, especially by combining work and study.

But the uniformity and mobility of the system are even more strongly affected by the fact that parts are designed for the education and training of cadres for the various organisations of state control.

This can be seen firstly in the existence and expansion of educational institutions for the SED organisation and the control apparatuses of the state and the economy, agriculture or the mass organisations, and also in the greater use made of institutions of the uniform education system, especially the professional schools and universities, for the further education and training of future leaders.

The central institutions for the education and training of cadres differ in their structure and teaching material from those of the uniform education system. All their students are specially selected on the grounds of political suitability as well as their ability in their chosen subject. The cadre requirements of the organisation concerned and the views of the competent department of the SED are also taken into account. Hence the various apparatuses perpetuate their assessment and selection criteria in the training and education process itself.[25] The fact that academic training is generally a prerequisite for a leading position has also meant that cadre policy is having an increasing effect on the uniform education system itself. Success or failure at university (there are few failures in the higher general schools, so university entrance is practically assured by acceptance in this sector) is the decisive factor for a future career in the cadre hierarchy, and as all university graduates are regarded as potential cadres the appropriate criteria will certainly affect the selection process of the general education institutes.

The growing importance of cadre policy in the various stages of the education hierarchy is particularly apparent in the different selection criteria and mechanisms. In the various stages of the general education system, and especially upon admission to university or technical college and the subsequent placing of graduates, three main criteria, as we have said, are used in assessment: ability in the subject area, political and ideological reliability and 'social balance'. The order of priority of these considerations and repeated attempts to put them into operation, are conditioned by prevailing politico-economic and education policy concepts and possibilities. Again different emphasis is placed on subject ability and political criteria in the various forms of application (individual or secondment from an enterprise, administration office, etc.). As secondment for a course of study brings various benefits (job security for personal attendance and part-release for correspondence courses among others) people at work are largely dependent on this route. That means that they are subject to two selection processes: firstly (like school-leavers and other applicants) the decision by the university or college selection committee, and then approval by the competent cadre departments of the place which is to second them.

Despite the unity of qualification in subject matter and political and ideological considerations, which is postulated at all education and training stages and in vocational practice, friction can arise in the selection process, as this is at the same time an instrument of co-option and self-recruitment for the political leadership. This friction has its origin in different assessment criteria which may under certain circumstances prove difficult to reconcile. The principles of cadre policy offer little guarantee that at least the two main selection criteria — ability in the chosen subject and political and ideological reliability — can be given equal weight. While subject ability is of considerable importance in the applications from the 'EOS' leavers, the secondment practice of the cadre departments in industry or administration will generally be guided more by political considerations. But even where subject ability is the main concern, the choice will largely depend on whether the person seconded is expected to be able to cope with the demands of the leading position he is to take after completing his course, which is largely financed by the office or enterprise seconding him. The selection process also contains informal elements which can be of considerable importance. There is great opposition to a formalisation of these, such as is provided for in the appropriate legislation. They include relatively good acquaintance with the candidate and a multiplicity of personal loyalties, likes and dislikes which apparently have considerable influence on the actual selection process.

The educational institutions which serve only the education and training of future leaders are quite outside the general admission principles and regulations. The lack of statutory norms to cover them within the framework of the general admission regulations for all universities and similar institutions is not accidental: there are many aspects of selection criteria in the general education system which cannot apply in the cadre sector.

Apart from the education and training given in the universities and colleges we can say that cadre qualification takes place exclusively in the educational institutions of the organisations concerned, graded according to the hierarchy of their leadership functions. If the requirements of cadre policy have shut these institutions off from the general education system, there is relatively close co-operation between the educational institutions of the party, the state and the economic apparatus. The cadres for the state and the economy are almost all trained in special institutions. The SED institutions are of particular importance: progress through the various stages of party schooling is still an essential prerequisite for any position on any of the levels of this hierarchy. The leading function of the Central Committee apparatus on the central level and of the subordination of the other cadre training institutions to their central institutions as far as subject matter is concerned (the Party University, the Academy of Constitutional Law, the Central Institute of Socialist Economic Planning) is to prevent divergences developing in the party and in the apparatus of the state and the economy, and to keep open the possibility of placing Category cadres in various parts of the apparatus, ensuring politically desirable and administratively efficient horizontal flexibility. This community of aim also determines the relation of these institutions to the other institutions in the education system. While, at least in the economy, there are still relatively close ties and contractual relations between the institutions of the uniform Socialist education system on the middle level, these do not exist on the central level. The Party University, the Central Institute for Socialist Economic Planning of the SED Central Committee and the Academy of Constitutional Law were created to train cadres for the highest levels of organisations of state control apparatus and ensure an adequate succession. They are almost exclusively concerned with leadership techniques and specialised knowledge (insofar as this is not acquired through experience) in the organisation concerned and hence they cannot form part of the general education system.

Summary

The picture which emerges from an analysis of education policy in the GDR differs according to whether one puts the main emphasis on structural conditions or social and political effects. But an analysis only of the structure of the education system is not enough: the restrictions to which the sector was subject after the VIIIth SED Party Congress may not have affected the 'uniform Socialist education system' but they have changed its real function. The original aim of ensuring as much equality of opportunity as possible has at least been modified; the selection function has acquired disproportionate significance.

However, the consolidation of the education system and the shift in aims should not be seen in isolation: they are part of the attempt to preserve the social and political structures in the GDR, as in other 'real Socialist' countries, as far as possible unchanged. What changes there are are kept within the close legal and ideological bounds of the system. Even the 'calculated experiment' in the 1960s which was part of the economic reforms is now possible only in a few cases. As in general socio-policy, this has led to a more pragmatic approach in education policy as well, which has moved away from the Utopian and idealistic aim of 'equality', adopting an 'opportunistic' stance with regard to prevailing social conditions and problems. Certainly over the longer term this may mean that the education sector, which has always been held up as an example, and was regarded as having achieved equality earlier than the world of work or the political sphere, will lose its legitimation function for the system as a whole. In view of the close ties between the education system and the functional conditions of the dominant bureaucracy it is hardly likely that the education system will succeed in freeing itself even partially from the crude requirements of the economy and the direct interests of the party and giving the different social interests and needs a chance to formulate and implement their education requirements.

Notes

1   Helmut Klein, *Bildung in der DDR. Grundlagen, Entwicklungen, Probleme*, Reinbek b. Hamburg, 1974.
2   'Gesetz über das einheitliche, sozialistische Bildungssystem vom 25. Februar, 1965', in *GB1 I*, no.6, p.83 ff.
3   Günther, K.-H. and Uhlig, G., *Geschichte der Schule in der Deutschen Demokratischen Republik 1945–1971*, Berlin (DDR), 1974, p.246.
4   In more detail see Glaessner, G.-J., *Herrschaft durch Kader. Leitung der Gesellschaft und Kaderpolitik in der DDR am Beispiel des Staatsapparates*, Opladen, 1977.
5   Compiled from the *Statistische Jahrbücher der DDR*, 1960 to 1979.
6   *Statistisches Jahrbuch der DDR*, 1978, p.249; 1979, p.251.
7   *Ökonomie und Bildung im Sozialismus. Aktuelle Probleme der Bildungsökonomie*, Berlin (DDR), 1977, p.35.
8   Cf. Hurrelmann, K., *Erziehungssystem und Gesellschaft*, Reinbek b. Hamburg, 1975.
9   Cf. Neugebauer, G., *Partei und Staatsapparat in der DDR. Aspekte der Instrumentalisierung des Staatsapparates durch die SED*, Opladen, 1978.
10   Cf. Glaessner, G.-J. and Rudolph, I., *Macht durch Wissen. Zum Zusammenhang von Bildungspolitik, Bildungssystem und Kaderqualifizierung in der DDR. Eine politisch-soziologische Untersuchung*, Opladen, 1978.
11   Cf. Meier, A., 'Schule und Dialektik der Sozialstruktur in der sozialistischen Gesellschaft', in *Deutsche Zeitschrift für Philosophie*, 23rd year (1975), no.10, p.1332.
12   Op.cit., p.1331.
13   Meier, A., *Soziologie des Bildungswesens. Eine Einführung*, Berlin (DDR), 1974, p.31 f.
14   Kuczynski, J., 'Fachstudium kontra Allgemeinbildung? Spezialisierung und interdisziplinäres Verhalten', in *Forum*, 34th year (1980), no.4, p.8 f.

15 Cf. Gast, G., *Die politische Rolle der Frau in der DDR*, Düsseldorf, 1973.
16 Langen, E.-M., *Technisierungsgrad der Arbeit und Qualifikation der Produktionsarbeiter. Ein Beitrag zu Fragen der Vervollkomnung des sozialistischen Charakters der Arbeit*, Berlin (DDR), 1979, p.48.
17 Cf. Glaessner, G.-J., 'Bildungsökonomie und Bildungsplanung. Vorüberlegungen zu einer Analyse der gesellschaftlichen und politischen Funktion von Bildungsprozessen in der DDR', in *Deutschland Archiv*, Year 11 (1978), no.9, p.937 ff.
18 Cf. Maier, H., 'Bildungsökonomie als Problem und Aufgabe', in *Bildungsökonomie. Aufgaben — Probleme — Lösungen*, Berlin (DDR), 1968, p.32 ff.
19 *Gesetzmässigkeiten der intensiv erweiterten Reproduktion bei der weiteren Gestaltung der entwickelten sozialistischen Gesellschaft*, Berlin (DDR) (1976), vol.1, p.335.
20 Cf. *Ökonomie und Bildung im Sozialismus*, op.cit., p.138.
21 'Für eine weitere Erhöhung des Niveaus der Erwachsenenbildung. Gemeinsamer Beschluss des Ministerrates der DDR und des Bundesvorstandes des FDGB', in *Neues Deutschland*, no.160, 10th July 1979, p.3 ff; 'Aufgaben der Universitäten und Hochschulen in der entwikkelten sozialistischen Gesellschaft. Beschluss des Politbüros des ZK der SED vom 18. März, 1980', in *Neues Deutschland*, no.68, 20th March 1980, p.3 f.
22 Akademie der Pädagogischen Wissenschaften (ed.), *Das Bildungswesen der Deutschen Demokratischen Republik*, Berlin (DDR), 1979, p.63.
23 *Statistisches Jahrbuch der DDR*, 1966, p.470; 1979, p.295.
24 *Statistisches Jahrbuch der DDR*, 1979, p.296 ff.
25 Cf. in more detail Glaessner, G.-J. and Rudolph, I., op.cit.

6 Continuity and change: cultural policy in the German Democratic Republic since the VIIIth SED Party Congress in 1971

Irma Hanke, Technical University, Munich

Introduction

The all-round development of every member of society is part of the Utopian core of Marxist—Leninist ideology. In all the Socialist countries, therefore, cultural policy is intended to help create conditions which enable the abilities of all to unfold fully. As this is seen as a long-term process, cultural policy is an important instrument of social transformation. Termed 'the Socialist cultural revolution' it is to work on the consciousness and day-to-day behaviour of the individual and bring to full fruition what began as a political and economic revolution.

This broad conception also means that cultural policy is an important instrument to help secure power. In its Marxist—Leninist form a Socialist society is always conceived as an organised socio-political system. It can only develop and be transformed in accordance with prognoses if the party's leading role remains assured in every social sphere. Art and culture can help to achieve a more effective and lasting influence on the thought and feelings of society than political or ideological argument could achieve alone, partly because art and culture work through the emotions to establish new values and desired patterns of social behaviour.

Cultural policy therefore helps to integrate the people into the socio-political system. It also creates a means of self-representation abroad, as the common or national cultural heritage is represented. Cultural policy furthers the identification of the people with their state. That is of particular importance in a divided country and particularly the GDR, which did not come into being as the expression of the will of the people and still suffers from this lack of legitimation today. Efforts to provide cultural legitimation form a major area of rivalry with the system in the Federal Republic.

In the Marxist view culture is a materialist category; it is therefore not an isolated social phenomenon but the result and at the same time a prerequisite for the struggle with nature in the work process, a component of all social relations and conditions. It has both material and intellectual components, 'whether these consist of the universal productive forces of society and the individual which emerge from the social reproduction process or unique creative achievements by special individuals'.[1]

In the everyday and political vocabulary of the GDR a 'narrower' concept has survived beside this broader view, often described as 'intellectual' culture. This is, among other things, a result of traditional bourgeois elements which still have some influence in the GDR today. They have certainly helped to define the names and tasks of political institutions: the Ministry of Culture, for example, was originally only responsible for art and literature.

It is in this narrower sense that we will first examine the cultural policy of the SED although we will bear in mind its greater claim and ideological significance: as a Leninist party the SED assumes that the process of the emergence of culture can be taken under comprehensive direction and integrated into the overall policy of the party.[2]

We may therefore expect to find a cultural policy which corresponds to each specific stage in the development of the GDR and meets the objective requirements of the various situations as defined by the party. Changes in direction in cultural policy are not spontaneous, they are the result of the party's political assessment of the situation and prospects for development. Apparent contradictions can be explained by general requirements. Against the background of the SED's cultural policy up to the VIIIth Party Congress (in 1971) we therefore ask how far the party leaders have succeeded in achieving their political aims and what resistance they have met with. As decisive steps were taken in the years before 1971 we shall, by way of introduction, see what the developments in cultural policy were up to that time, what fluctuations this policy was subject to and with what heritage it began.

The tradition

Cultural policy in the GDR in 1971 after a quarter of a century of post-war history was a strange mixture of progressive, extremely conservative and restrictive elements. It was the result of the implementation of the aims outlined above in a post-Fascist society.

Anti-fascism

In 1945 East Germany found itself with a cultural life whose bourgeois forms had for the most part survived but whose intellectual substance was largely destroyed. The traditional German view of culture, in which greater value is placed on 'intellectual' elements than on a 'materialist' civilisation, had (as a result of the bourgeois intelligentsia's distaste for politics) not proved capable of withstanding the National Socialist movement. The bourgeoisie had either capitulated or cut themselves off. The labour movement had been destroyed. The cultural élite had emigrated. Compensating for the 'destruction of the German spirit' was indeed the most immediate and overriding task. A concept was carefully worked out by the Soviet Occupation Forces together with the Communist Party (later the SED) and entailed 're-schooling' to anti-fascism on the basis of the alliance policy developed in the 1930s by the United Front, supported ideologically by an aggressive humanism. It needed a policy of national reunification, which remained the primary aim up to 1955 but was never abandoned as a claim until 1970, and a careful organisation policy to create an increasing number of key positions and ensure that cultural life was steered in the right direction.

The main institutions of bourgeois culture were restored: the theatre, orchestras, museums, libraries — only the press was immediately centralised. New publishing houses and a film company were founded and the intelligentsia were offered their own means of organisation and representation.[3] Indeed, altogether this policy was extremely favourable to the bourgeois intelligentsia, showing marked respect for 'those who work with their minds'. Of considerable importance for the relation to the past was the focus on a democratic tradition in German history, in which resistance and emigration were seen as manifestations of anti-fascism. It was in the GDR — and not in the Federal Republic — that the state made efforts to persuade the emigrants to come back.

This policy of a 'new beginning' has left unmistakeable marks and it created determinant factors in the cultural life of the GDR which are still having an impact today. Greater emphasis has been laid on national elements, there is much greater respect for tradition and for the progressive elements in the cultural heritage as represented by the emigrants. The GDR has continued to lay great stress on anti-fascism and — last but not least — academics and artists enjoy a very privileged material position, which is underlined by the extensive system of art prizes and state scholarships.

Socialist realism

Nevertheless, political conformism has been expected of the artistic intelligentsia and it has been enforced since 1950 through the establishment of an official doctrine in art: artists are under an obligation to support Socialist realism and hence to engage in the battle against 'formalism' — elements characteristic of the Shdanov era in the Soviet Union. Artists were expected to be 'volkstümlich' (of the people), later 'volksgebunden' (bound to the people). A partial, optimistic presentation of present and everyday material with positively conceived central characters who were to be typical of the Socialist future was required. The insistence on partiality excluded a critical or pessimistic view of contemporary society. The 'formal' experiments of the Western modernists, who saw themselves as the product of a breach with traditional forms in literature and art, were rejected — they were described as 'dehumanising', accused of denying the 'revolutionary subject' (the working class and the Communist party) and of putting an apolitical 'cosmopolitanism', which stabilised existing power structures, in the place of a revolutionary internationalism. The propagation of the rigid canons of Socialist realism cut the GDR off in a very short time from artistic developments in the West, although during the years immediately after the war artistic contact with the West had been most eagerly sought after.

However much has been written on the reasons for the aesthetic theory of Socialist realism, insistence on it has always had a political function and it has remained one of the party's cultural policy steering instruments. Observance of the rules has been enforced by a number of state control organs founded during a second phase. They were only replaced in 1954 by the Ministry of Culture after a series of bitter controversies over cultural policy. The new ministry was to be more appropriate to the particular conditions of literary and artistic production. It still directs most of the cultural activities in the GDR; it is responsible among other things for licensing publishing plans and so it controls book production; the Ministry also controls theatre repertoires, musical life and the various forms of entertainment.

The official cultural policy has always been only partially accepted by practitioners of the arts, but it has been extremely difficult to oppose. In 1953, after the revolt of 17 June, and again in 1956, as a result of the XXth Congress of the Soviet Communist Party, manifest opposition broke out — for the last time to such an extent — among the intellectuals. It ended with long prison sentences for the dissidents. Other intellectuals and writers who were critical of the dominant party line left the GDR in the following years and moved to the Federal Republic.

The Socialist cultural revolution

At the same time, in 1956, the party began to insist on more concern with problems of ideology and the 'formation of consciousness', and the term 'Socialist cultural revolution' gradually came into use for this.[4] Since 1955 the Federal Republic and the GDR had been incorporated into hostile power blocks and the party leaders were trying to step up the development of an independent Socialist society. The 'Socialist revolution in ideology and culture'[5] served several aims at once: firstly it was to check the intelligentsia, who were inclined to 'revisionist' back-sliding, by giving them a concrete task. They were to contribute to the better integration of the new society whose revolution had so far been largely achieved from above and post facto create a mass basis for the new state by establishing closer ties between the working class and the intelligentsia. The Vth party congress in 1958, at which the '10 Socialist Moral Commandments' were announced, the development of 'Socialist Brigades' as a new form of community life and work and the 1st Bitterfeld Conference in 1958, in which writers and artists were instructed to co-operate closely with workers,[6] were all in the same way the expression of an attempt to activate hope and enthusiasm for the new society. Workers were to show artists the way — artists to help the workers to storm 'the heights of culture'. But what was to be reckoned as culture was still prescribed by the party. So there was no spontaneous co-operation, which might have led to the development of new art forms. The return to the revolutionary traditions of the proletarian art of the 1920s, hitherto neglected and in some cases rejected as 'sectarian', could therefore hardly have had an effect, even if these have since become part of the accepted tradition of the cultural past.

The slogan of the Bitterfeld movement, 'Reach for a pen, pal, the Socialist national culture needs you!', was soon withdrawn. The expectation it expressed that there could be a nation not only of reading but also of writing workers, the old Marxist hope that the division between mental and physical work could be overcome, proved an illusion.[7]

Nevertheless this phase had important after-effects. The programme of the 'Bitterfeld Route' survived, as did its demand that the arts and especially literature should be oriented to questions of the plant and production (even if in the 1960s attention was to concentrate not on the worker but on the planner and leader); it was only after the VIIIth party congress that the extraordinary restriction on the range of subjects for art which the programme imposed was lifted. What remained was the memory of the atmosphere of a new beginning, together with the belief in the moral power of art and its power to change the world. This was the formative experience of that generation of artists and writers who were to form the protest group of 1976.

What remained above all was a considerable widening of the cultural interests of broad sections of the population and the growth in lay art. This was supported by very active cultural work in the plants by the unions, who continued the educational concern and efforts of the old labour movement: books were given as premiums to workers, works' visits organised to theatres and concerts, a union library set up in plants with a wide range of specialist books and literature, authors came to plants to read from their own works, commissions were given in the visual arts, and 'cultural achievements' were included in the economic and cultural competition between Socialist brigades.[8] These included the establishment of plant orchestras, lay choirs and workers' theatre groups. These measures certainly helped to strengthen the awareness that participation in cultural life was part of the obligation of the Socialist worker and that cultural life was something that concerned him. But the need for entertainment tended to be suppressed, especially efforts to orient to Western rock and pop culture, influences which were bitterly opposed.

The German Socialist national culture

The term 'Socialist cultural revolution' remained in use in the 1960s — in contrast to the practice in other Socialist states,[9] but the underlying meaning changed. The term now, especially in connection with the theory of the scientific and technological revolution, was used to mean the 'unity of the technical and cultural revolution'[10] in which the all-round personality was to be created and the level of production of a surplus society achieved through planned increases in the standard of knowledge. In the process of the Socialist cultural revolution a German Socialist national culture was to emerge. In building up its Socialist state the GDR wanted to show itself as 'the better Germany' and cultural achievements were to compensate for its lack of external and internal recognition. At the end of the 1960s, in the new society which was called 'the Socialist community of people', art and culture were to provide the certainty of harmony established. So there was demonstrative concern for the cultural heritage and an art which represented 'humanist values'; representation of conflict, as far as this did not result from the (victorious) struggle of the new against the old, was prohibited. Tendencies to greater independence in art and literature which did not meet these criteria, a more critical approach or attempts at greater realism were blocked on several occasions and most effectively at the 11th Plenary of the SED Central Committee in 1965. A number of distinguished writers and dramatists had works forbidden and performances stopped, films had to be withdrawn and directors had to indulge in self-criticism in public.

As a result of this policy writers imposed a harsher self-censorship. State control of publication practice was also stepped up through the expansion of a system of approval bodies before any publication was allowed. The political impact of the invasion of Czechoslovakia in 1968 also strengthened resistance to any form of innovation in cultural activities.

On the other hand public hearings, which meant that detailed comments on individual works of art and literature were on the agenda at party congresses and Central Committee plenaries, assured writers and artists of a highly attentive audience, sensitive to the slightest nuance of criticism, at least from the intelligentsia. The need on the part of the general public to see its experiences expressed in literature and art as they could not be expressed in public, in the centrally steered mass media, greatly contributed to creating an awareness among artists that they were a moral element in society, and this in turn increased the weight of their utterances: a dilemma which the party struggled with in vain in the 1970s.

From Ulbricht to Honecker

The sterile atmosphere of public culture, the over-emphasis on the claim to represent the German nation, the propagation of the concept of the 'cultured nation', whose educational diet, however, was prescribed, the lack of international contact which resulted from the 'official aesthetic', were increasingly felt to be a burden during the last years of Ulbricht's regime.

It was against these encrustations that Erich Honecker, who had himself been a mouthpiece of party criticism at the 11th Plenary and was now First Secretary of the SED, directed the statement which was addressed to the artistic intelligentsia: 'If one proceeds from the firm position of Socialism there can in my view be no taboos'.[11]

This made three things clear: firstly, that there had been taboos; secondly, that the Socialist standpoint, 'partiality', was taken for granted; there could be no discussion and certainly no concessions over that; and thirdly that the scope allowed to artists and writers, and the possibilities for formal, aesthetic and material experiments, would in future be greater.

Artists and writers were now seen as valid partners of the party, and the people now deemed capable of enjoying even art which had hitherto been forbidden. This was not only an indication of the specific concern for cultural policy but an attempt to reduce alienation between the party leaders and the artists, and between the party leaders and the general population. But Honecker certainly did not suggest that there might be an autonomous art. That would never be possible under Marxism–Leninism. So there was no change of attitude, but there would be a change in method; this was to be brought more into line with the general concept of Honecker's policy, the need to concentrate on the 'here and now'.

The political and ideological preconditions for Honecker's cultural policy

Indeed the change in the general line of the SED which the transfer of power from Ulbricht to Honecker brought was bound to have an effect on cultural policy. The party's aim was now to eliminate the contradictions of the Ulbricht approach and win the intelligentsia over to the new direction.

It became apparent at the VIIIth SED Party Congress and from subsequent statements by leading state and party functionaries that the changes envisaged were considerable. The GDR abandoned its ideological special role with regard to the doctrine of the Soviet Communist party (Socialism as a relatively independent formation of society, the thesis of the Socialist Community of People and so on) and the expectations this entailed. It moved away from its orientation to the achievement of a united Socialist Germany, so softening the incessant rivalry with the system in the Federal Republic. Only on the basis of a consistent delimitation of its own system — from the point of view of the GDR — was a regulation of relations between the two Germanies possible. This was achieved at the beginning of the 1970s and it opened the way to the wave of diplomatic recognition of the GDR and its membership of the United Nations.

Both the loss of the old national identity and the new 'world status' required the development of a new national consciousness. The task appeared all the more difficult as it was not possible to isolate the people from the constant effects of the media and the growing stream of visitors from the Federal Republic. Immunisation through a 'Socialist consciousness' and Socialist patriotism was vital. This could only come from pride in national achievements and it required greater concern for the traditions of the GDR: cultural policy was expected to play its part.

In domestic policy the leading role of the party was stressed through emphasis on the class nature of society (and the party's claim to represent the working class). This diminished the superior role which had been allocated to the intelligentsia in the 'Socialist Community of People' under Ulbricht and focused more attention on the existence of social conflict, which had been rather underplayed up to then. The focus on the problems of 'real Socialism' proved pragmatic; it brought a considerable reduction in the great plans of the Ulbricht era and greater preoccupation with the everyday problems of the population in general. The recognition of economic contingencies and the lack of scope for development in the current world situation had a dampening effect, but changes in attitude were unmistakeable. After the dynamic restructuring of the first decades the tempo of development naturally slowed down and there was greater need to concentrate on the present. But where up to then the hope of removing injustices in the near or attainable future had made it possible for people to bear the faults of the present, as society crystallised sensitivity to these injustices grew because they could no longer be regarded as temporary. This greater sensitivity made it more difficult to mobilise society for long-term aims if they did not at the same time bring an immediate improvement in the existing situation.

To this extent the 1970s were years in which policy was carefully dosed to satisfy different groups in society. At the same time the party tried to achieve greater politicisation to counteract the growing awareness of stagnation and the necessity for restriction to what was really possible: greater concern was shown for the 'subjective factor', efforts were made to win the personal commitment of the individual to official aims, to encourage a more intense 'Socialist awareness', in other words to ensure conscious and rational behaviour in line with Socialism and increase participation in 'Socialist democracy'. This culminated in the attempt, following discussions in the Soviet Union, to develop a national life style, a 'Socialist way of life', as the expression of changed patterns of behaviour, to create an indigenous culture with Socialist means of production which could be defended ideologically.

In face of the threats from a crisis-prone capitalist world the main emphasis was no longer on the hopes of what the technological revolution would bring, but on security, the safety and order of society (the classical paternalist tradition of the petty German states), although these values were now oriented to the Socialist world system. But expectations of a future Communist society, as expressed in the SED party programme of 1976, remained rather vague.

Cultural policy was to help this adjustment to present-day GDR society by highlighting the many possibilities for development offered by 'real' Socialism and furthering the process of ideological reorientation which was to lead to the adaptation of the Socialist way of life. The question that remained unsolved was how to handle artists who attempted to use the scope allowed to them in other than the expected way.

The main elements of the new cultural policy

At the VIIIth SED Party Congress little attention was at first focused on cultural policy, apart from the statement that the 'further increase in the material and cultural standard of living of our people', i.e. a close relation between cultural and economic factors, was a main task for future policy.[12] In his report to the congress Erich Honecker only touched on questions of cultural policy. However, he did emphasise the obligation of those who create culture with regard to the expectations and claims of the public and the aim for 'clearer and clearer alignment between artistic and ideological responsibility', the need to represent everyday life and 'themes of benefit to Socialist society'. Finally he expressed the party's willingness to accept 'the creative search for new forms', stressing, however, that the defensive nature of art, its 'important contribution in the battle against the attempts at ideological diversification by the Imperialists', should be taken for granted.[13]

This was in fact an outline of future cultural policy, but the basic statement from the party came only a year later, at the VIth Plenary of the Central Committee in 1972. The speaker was Kurt Hager, Central Committee Secretary for Science and Culture since 1955, who had also been responsible for earlier key formulations.

The theses put forward by Hager on this occasion[14] were included in the party programme for 1976,[15] underlining their fundamental and long-term significance. Since that date there have been shifts in emphasis but no fundamental changes in the theoretical statements from the party on cultural policy. We can summarise and outline five points fundamental to cultural policy in the 1970s:

(a) a 'broad' concept of culture to replace the narrower concept;

(b) greater attention to the planning and control of cultural processes and greater encouragement of social participation;

(c) a re-definition of the contents of Socialist (national) culture, and furtherance of cultural integration in the Socialist Community of States;

(d) retention of the doctrine of Socialist Realism in art, but a widening of its formal means of expression;

(e) emphasis on the ideological function of art and intensification of the Socialist cultural revolution.

A new concept of culture

The results of the 6th Plenary of 1972 were summarised by Alexander Abusch, a leading cultural functionary:

> As we are working for the planned and proportional development of the people's economy our consultations are concerned with the planned and proportional development of our Socialist society as a whole. We shall combine adherence to our principles, a broad range and differentiation with concretisation of the targets to be achieved over the coming years for the new culture and way of life of Socialism. The procedure will underline the real nature of Socialism in that the material concern of our society for its working people will necessarily also mean an improvement of cultural life, the renovation of human relations, ethics and morals, indeed of the whole way of life.[16]

This is a comprehensive concept of culture, comprising not only intellectual culture but all the conditions of life of all the people as expressed in a wide range of requirements. There was to be corresponding differentiation in meeting these requirements. In view of the theories held up to then this was an extraordinary step. People who expressed needs were no longer to be regarded as people to be educated, to be led up to pre-defined targets, but as people who were to be satisfied. This view, which is clearly determined by efforts to secure mass loyalty, corresponds to the 'realism' of the Honecker era. It has its parallels in education, social and wage policy, where the recognition that only a few can rise strengthens efforts to make the lower rungs of the Socialist ladder more attractive or at least more bearable.

The impact of the new 'broad' view of cultural policy in turn had considerable repercussions on the development of a Marxist aesthetic, which we can only touch on here. The canon of what was declared binding for the Socialist realist concept of the aesthetic was widened and the breadth and variety of literary styles and art forms given a theoretical basis.

The questions of which classes in society reacted to what art and literature, and what living and working conditions were necessary for the acquisition of culture were examined in a number of cultural and sociological studies.[17] The intensity with which the possibility of the working class experience of culture was discussed may certainly command admiration. But the results of the studies were disappointing. Until then the belief had been held that cultural policy was being increasingly effective in that ever widening circles were participating in cultural life, but it now became apparent that there were still broad sections of society who had not been touched by this at all. There was also criticism of the critical and appreciative faculty in the audience for the arts. Other leisure activities were crowding out cultural interests in the narrower sense. In the hope of achieving better results the existing range of instruments was refined and new approaches were tried. Greater efforts were made to involve workers in the organisation of cultural activities, for example through the formation of programme advisory committees for the theatre; there was more concentration on cultural work in the plant and the possibilities for active participation were widened (there are now about 7,000 amateur choirs and more than 2,000 amateur theatre groups in the GDR).[18] The range of children's literature and children's theatre was extended in the hope of creating interest in culture at an early age.

But finally it was also recognised that more attention should be paid to the need of broad sections of the people for entertainment. East German facilities were to be developed to counteract the influence of the more attractive range on offer from the West in the form of films, television and rock music.

So the party hoped to be able to launch an offensive against one of the main sources of attack from Western ideology. In fact the recognition of the need for the right type of culture, especially for young people, has brought remarkable results: beat groups have been permitted, discotheques opened and youth fashions — the jeans cult — accepted. The more relaxed style has made a great deal of difference to the quality of life. More club houses have also been opened in rural areas to serve as 'centres with facilities for dancing and proper social contact'.[19]

The leisure society has been gaining ground in the GDR as well, and its needs have to be met. The range of hobby activities has been widened and better recreation facilities are now available. These range from a 'pub cult' to juke boxes and slot machines.[20] The acknowledgement of needs which were once denied is a recognition that the 'Socialist way of life' also requires the variety of supply characteristic of a highly industrialised society. However, again there are considerable economic difficulties. It is always being pointed out that few funds are available for the expansion of the cultural infrastructure, particularly in rural areas and the new residential districts, and that basic economic needs must come first. In fact expenditure on culture, e.g. for the maintenance of culture centres,[21] has been very much stepped up in comparison with the 1960s but it is not yet sufficient to make up for the neglect of the past. A further difficulty is that the expansion of cultural facilities cannot, in the dominant view, be left to the initiative of individual or spontaneous groups, it always has to be put into the hands of social organisations such as the Free German Youth or the Free German Trade Unions.

But the theoretical discussion is concentrated not on the world of leisure but, in accordance with the views of Marxism—Leninism, on the 'culture of labour', for labour is the keystone of the Socialist way of life. However, the concept of what is needed in the way of culture in the world of work seldom goes beyond what has been attempted in Western industrial enterprises to 'improve human relations' and create a more aesthetic, in other words, a better working environment. These efforts may well make a great deal of difference to the individual worker but it is evident that in the official view they will always remain subordinate to the aim of increasing productivity. At any rate they are intended to compensate for working conditions which are felt to be inadequate.[22]

The planning and control of culture

A decision to satisfy various cultural requirements does not mean that these can develop spontaneously and certainly not that they can be organised independently. In the party's view cultural needs have to be directed, they need ideological control and further developments must be planned. Manifestations such as action art, street theatres or any unconventional mass art are regarded as direct and self-determined intervention in social processes and they are virtually impossible. Any cultural activity has to go through a ponderous apparatus: even the production of 'polit-posters', eagerly sought after by young people in the GDR, is hardly possible without going through a cumbersome academic process.[23] As with books, each project needs the approval of official bodies, whose regulations and procedures have to be taken into account. Needs are only recognised when they can be fitted into what has already been planned.

The greater importance attached to culture in the party's overall concept can be seen from its inclusion in control and planning processes. This brings both greater ideological control by the party and greater differentiation of the cultural bureaucratic apparatus and at the same time greater participation by social organisations in advisory bodies.[24] SED district and regional secretaries are instructed to intervene more frequently in cultural policy decisions to ensure that there are no unforeseen developments.

In 1973 Hans-Joachim Hoffman was appointed Minister of Culture and for the first time a man from the central party apparatus (and not, as hitherto, a specialist on culture), held the post. Hoffmann has given special emphasis to long-term concepts in all areas of culture and the 'meaningful application of the principles of democratic centralism in the planning and control of cultural processes'.[25]

Since 1975 there has been long-term planning for major cultural events. These are carefully staged to ensure 'coordination of their aims, prerequisites and proportions' and 'cooperation between all the social forces'.[26] Honecker, SED General Secretary and Chairman of the Council of State, himself took the chair in the preparation committee for the celebrations to mark the 500th birthday of Martin Luther in 1983, a demonstrative gesture which undercut and warded off criticism from the church and was intended to show the breadth of national interest and tradition.

In keeping with the targets of the economic plan, cultural planning is intended to ensure the 'proportionate' development of culture as a social sphere, i.e. its development proportionate to socio-political planning as a whole. Hence the 'development trends of the cultural needs of the people' have been laid down up to the year 1990 in co-operation with stage planning bodies. For the Socialist countries as a whole there has even been talk of planning up to the year 2000.[27]

Cultural planning also includes training functionaries to work on all levels in the appropriate institutions of education and training.[28]

Cultural questions are playing an increasing part in political discussion and they are an item in the performance ratings of enterprises and districts. The inclusion of cultural planning in an overall politico-ideological, artistic and economic concept has also brought institutional changes and in some cases expansion. The Ministry of Culture, for example, now has a 'General Directive for Entertainment'.[29] There are also provisions for 'regular consultations between the First Secretaries of districts or regions and writers and artists'.[30]

The need for activation through ideological and political influence is partly the result of the cumbersome nature of the cultural administrative apparatus itself. This is always inclined to favour an institutionalised, long-term and calculable programme and shows a natural tendency to perpetuate what already exists. These conservative elements favour the traditional heritage, theatres, concerts and so on, and in the visual arts, historical preservation, but these are in any case well-established elements in the plans.

The socialist national culture

The renunciation of the concept of one German nation and the acceptance of the need to establish an independent Socialist nation in the GDR was bound to have repercussions on cultural policy. The main cultural institutions and organs still used the term 'Deutsch' in their names; it was part of their image. Acceptance of the fact that the GDR constituted a separate entity entailed a reinterpretation of the German past and this had to be integrated in a way which strengthened the identity of the GDR. The Federal Republic of Germany and the German Democratic Republic are 'states of the German nation'. As the difference between them lies in their social systems, a new image of the GDR, which was to be built up into a new national consciousness, could only be developed through the ideological fixation of this difference.[31] Hence the defensive battle was stepped up and Socialist elements were stressed, while the affinity of the state with other Socialist countries was underlined. A natural consequence was acceptance of the fact that the GDR was integrated into the Socialist community of states, culturally as well. However, the efforts to achieve community with countries which have a very marked sense of national pride again brought the GDR face to face with the fact that its own identity was very weak.

It would appear that the efforts to strengthen this identity had an effect on cultural policy in practice. Simply renaming the cultural institutions was not enough.[32] Difficulties would appear to have arisen in determining what the 'national character' of the GDR should be. For a time the term 'national culture' was dropped. Then after the mid-1970s it came back into use again, now in the sense of the process of the formation and development of the Socialist nation, in which the development of an independent culture, especially in literature and the arts, plays a major part.[33] Writing on the emergence and history of the GDR has been stepped up and the accounts are supposed to follow the development scheme of other Socialist countries. Political history has its counterpart in histories of literature and art, in which GDR culture is seen as the natural consequence and continuance of progressive German culture, and at the same time a constituent of the new cultural heritage.[34] The big anniversaries of the foundation of the GDR have offered welcome occasions for self-affirmation.

Research into local history and the revival of elements in the tradition which had been ignored, for instance the Prussian character and achievements, or Expressionism, served the same purpose. A comprehensive range of memoirs and the repeated demand that writers should give expression to the process of 'growing into the new society' were further attempts to create a lasting legitimation base through building up traditions.

In literature the painful subject of delimitation appeared with particular harshness. It brought into discussion the question of what remained or was lacking in the way of common German features. In the phase of preparations for the Basic Treaties the concept which had been developed in the 1968 GDR constitution that there were 'two states of one German nation' was taken up in the Federal Republic. The continuing unity of the nation was then seen in the West as no longer dependent on the union of states but on the 'continuing sense of the people that they belong to one nation', this being 'the result of a common language, innumerable family ties and a common history and literature'.[35] Hence cultural unity transcended the differences in the political systems. It was an old theory, and had already been put forward by the Austrian poet, Hofmannsthal, in his reference to 'literature as the intellectual arena of the nation'.[36]

The GDR has always taken a vigorous stand against the thesis of cultural unity, in recent times with increasing vehemence. The thesis is regarded as the 'cultural reflex of keeping the German question open',[37] ignoring as it does the class basis of the arts, their partiality and the ideological function which they fulfil. The Socialist national culture of the GDR is developing as a new historical type, it is determined by the culture of the working classes and in its social features has nothing in common with the Imperialist culture of the FRG. A common language and tradition are seen as only of ethnic value; in the new society they are acquiring a new quality through integration with Socialism.[38] The formation of a Socialist nation is an 'inevitable component of the Socialist revolution',[39] in other words, it is itself the expression of the historical transformation process. This argument stresses the fundamental division. Special emphasis is given to the revolutionary components of the cultural tradition to show how different the Socialist nation is, and to illustrate how the traditions of German culture are being adapted and absorbed into the new system. Attempts are being made, by publishing only literature which is held to be desirable, and through exhibitions, films and television drama, to make Socialist realist culture the basis of a common understanding of the values of Socialist society. To this extent mass participation in cultural life is a means of political stabilisation. Literature and art criticism are expected to direct discussion to the great questions of philosophy and ethics and so stimulate commitment and the will to participate.[40]

The culture of the FRG, on the other hand, is seen as the culture of Imperialism, corresponding to the interests of the ruling class. Where it contains elements of a 'second culture' with democratic, Socialist components these could be selectively included in the national and progressive cultural life of the GDR.[41]

In fact, however, and despite all the efforts at seclusion, literary relations between the two states have strengthened at an unofficial level. There has been especial interest in this on the part of the FRG. Where the West Germans' attitude to the culture of their Eastern neighbour used to be one of disinterest, if not arrogance, the negotiations between the two states aroused more interest in the literature and art of the GDR, while the book and art market in the West offered East German writers and artists a wider public, with a common language and origin, but oriented to the standards of the Western modernists. It became possible for them to break away from the provinciality of their own society, the result of the many years of cultural isolation under Ulbricht.

The literature of the FRG also offered access to the literature and ideas of the European Left — and this had been considerable since the student protest movement of 1968. This increased interest among the GDR intelligentsia in the discussion on 'one German literature' (which of course includes Swiss and Austrian writers), however much they felt themselves to be representatives of the German Democratic Republic and might have, in the past, contributed to the formation of the new national consciousness.

Integration into the international culture of Socialist realism did not offer a real substitute for this. But it did form an important aspect of cultural policy in the GDR, and it will certainly gain in importance. Since 1973 there have been regular meetings between the Secretaries for Ideology of the Socialist states, as well as meetings at ministerial level and between representatives of national writers' associations. There are a large number of personal meetings between GDR writers and artists and their colleagues in other Socialist countries and some close personal ties have developed. A strong network of cultural agreements with all the Socialist countries underlines and characterises cultural relations. Co-operation with Soviet institutions (e.g. publishers) is particularly important. The number of works from other Socialist countries in GDR publishing programmes, theatre repertoires etc. has grown appreciably in the 1970s. Efforts are still being made to further integration, as is frequently stressed by the party and its functionaries.

The ties between the Socialist cultures are largely bilateral. However, they run up against language problems, and further difficulties arise from the very different national structures and interests, with correspondingly different cultural policies, in the various Socialist states. Declarations of intent and what is really achieved are often far apart.

The breadth and range of Socialist realism

The question of how much scope should be allowed for experiment in art has been and apparently still is a subject of controversy even among the party leaders. This can be deduced from the at times contradictory statements which have come from leading functionaries. It was not until the 6th Plenary of the SED Central Committee that Kurt Hager formulated the key principles — Socialist realism, a firm Socialist standpoint, partiality and proximity to the people. He added:

> Our cultural policy is directed to the furtherance of a living, rich and varied art . . . Socialist realist art is called upon to express and give artistic form to all that the Socialist personality needs for its full development. This orientation is an organic part of the general policy of our party. It is not a 'temporary variant' but a long-term perspective.[42]

What was rejected, however, was identification with 'modernist' movements in art, whose avant-gardism was seen as the product of an Imperialist society and regarded as having a 'dehumanising' effect.[43]

There were other indications at the plenary that the SED has always been concerned with the political aims of art and that this is what the term 'Socialist realism' really stands for. Greater freedom to experiment with form may have been granted but the general tendency and statement are still under control.

The Minister for Culture re-emphasised this at the IXth SED Party Congress: 'We say quite openly that culture and art are and will remain weapons in the great battle of our time and in future too we shall ensure that they are used as sharply and effectively as possible'.[44]

But the climate has really changed in the intervening years; this is apparent not so much in programmatic statements as from the actual behaviour of the cultural bureaucracy. Access to Western literature has been made easier and the circle of those who can now be included in general discussion because they are 'yesterday's avant-garde' has been widened. A number of controversial books by leading GDR writers have now been published, art exhibitions have included items which, clearly created before 1971, have been banned from public showing until the new direction began to operate. Some plays which had been forbidden have been produced despite criticism from party functionaries. It is even more astonishing to see with what intensity the new works have been discussed in public and how questions of literature and art have gained in weight and importance. Patterns of identification have developed and found expression in widespread discussion. It was no doubt the recognition that the processes of self-expression would facilitate integration into the existing structures which caused the party not to restrain so much as to lead the movement itself, and accept even critical writers. Thus the heads of party and government took part in the opening of the VIIth writers' congress in the autumn of 1973, and *Neues Deutschland*, the official party newspaper, featured reports on the congress, which was characterised by free and open discussion on a number of issues, on its front page for several editions.[45]

Society generally seemed to be enjoying success, not only in cultural but in economic and foreign policy as well. This has made it easier for the party to accept criticism as long as this helped the process of inner consolidation or appeared acceptable in view of the expected improvement in the standard of living. The party leaders gave the impression that they were capable of countering conflict with discussion. The mood concealed the fact that there were a considerable number of problems still unsolved, not least among them the fact that a well-known singer, Wolf Biermann, had been forbidden to perform or publish since 1965, and a tacit taboo was still maintained on any real criticism of the party, its policies and leadership. Any literature which was political in the narrower sense fell victim to this.

In the autumn of 1976 the course of cultural policy changed yet again. Pressure against individual artists and writers was stepped up but this only became generally known when Biermann, invited to make a public appearance in the FRG, had his East German citizenship taken from him 'for serious infringement of the rights of citizenship'.[46] He was refused permission to return to the GDR. He had publicly criticised the regime although he stressed his solidarity with it.

Deprivation of citizenship had been a notorious weapon of the National Socialists and among its victims were many leading Communists. Use of this method was not expected from the state which had always placed great weight on anti-fascism, and the move deeply shocked all those who had grown up with a belief in the superior moral quality of Socialism. Many writers believed with some justification that they had played a considerable part in the difficult job of building up the international reputation of the GDR and that this had now been undermined at one stroke. The act was also an act of aggression against artistic freedom; it hit the professional interests of all of them, an issue over which so many battles had been fought in the past.

In an open letter to the press 12 leading writers asked for reconsideration of the action against Biermann and registered a protest against his banishment. In the next few days about a hundred other writers and artists joined them. The letter was not printed in the GDR press, which called for declarations of solidarity with the party. The detailed discussion was in the West German press, but this exposed the writers of the letter to criticism within the GDR that they had put ammunition into the hands of the class enemies in the West, although the letter had contained a declaration of loyalty to the state of the German Democratic Republic.[47]

The climate deteriorated to such an extent that during the following months a number of writers, actors and producers left the GDR, never to return. Some younger writers were arrested and Robert Havemann, a critic of the regime, was placed under house arrest.

That action against Biermann was taken to force critics in the arts back on to the party line became clear from a number of statements. Kurt Hager, for instance, stated a few weeks after the event:

> I think Biermann's banishment cleared the air like a thunderstorm and clarified the fronts. It showed how closely related art and politics are and that it is necessary to ensure in our theoretical and ideological work that there is absolute clarity on the relations and phenomena of the class war between Socialism and Imperialism. We must always combine the elucidation of our theories and policies with ideological dissemination, with the destruction of anti-Communism, revisionism and ultra-Left 'theories'. In this respect we need a different tone, a different tune, namely a partial and aggressive note to help strengthen the position of Socialism and further consolidate peace; this will contribute to the annihilation of our foes.[48]

The viciousness with which the party reacted to the growing crisis no doubt stemmed from a lack of security. The signs of opposition among intellectuals who were true to Socialism but critical of the regime were to be smashed before they could take proper form.

The human rights movement, which had brought a wave of applications to leave the country in the wake of the European Security Conference, the beginnings of Euro-Communism, which were under discussion everywhere, and the 'leftist' ideas penetrating from the FRG had given rise to unorganised and still largely divergent sympathy movements. These were strengthened by the growing disillusionment with 'real' Socialism, the deterioration in the economic situation and the general tendency to stagnation. Clearly the party leaders were hoping to squash these tendencies by banishing Biermann, who was later accused of having been the ringleader of a 'third route'.[49]

In August 1977 Rudolf Bahro, another critic of the regime, was arrested. His book *Die Alternative. Zur Kritik des real existierenden Sozialismus* (The Alternative: A Criticism of the Socialism that Really Exists) had been published in the FRG.[50] In January 1978 a 'Manifest des BDKD' (Manifesto of the Association of Democratic German Communists) appeared in the West German news magazine *Der Spiegel*. The authorship was never really clarified but the article certainly dealt with subjects which were under discussion in the GDR.[51]

All this was bound to unsettle the party and the means it used were on principle those used by the Soviet Union and Czechoslovakia to get rid of dissidents. As those who had been deprived of their citizenship were regarded in the West as citizens of the FRG the measure actually made things easier for them. It is also possible that personal and political differences between the party leaders escalated the problems.

The party and the artistic intelligentsia after the banishments

Since then it has been hard to tell what course the party is really pursuing. In January 1977 a decision was taken by the Politbureau on 'political leadership in the cultural sphere' but only certain sections were published.[52] According to this two principles are still valid: the party's claim to ideological leadership is to be strengthened and the particularity of artistic production, with which the ideological contents are inseparably linked, will be respected. Confrontation with the refractory artists is no longer frontal, but is being fought out through professional associations and party groups. The utilisation of the practices of 'Socialist democracy' to discipline those who meet with displeasure has often put considerable strain on group relations within the small number of artists' associations. Enforced disputes with colleagues have harmed personal relations and destroyed old friendships, and this has often been harder to bear than the public ostracism of former times.

A number of writers have been excluded from the association and so lost much professional security. They have also lost easier access to Western literature and information and to the mass media of the GDR. Anyone who expressed criticism was forced into political and sometimes social isolation. His works would no longer be published or they only appeared in very small editions; they would be rejected on the grounds that the quality was inadequate, or they would be tacitly ignored. If books then appeared in the FRG the author would be punished for currency offences.[53] In the face of tactics such as these solidarity was of little avail.

On the other hand the artistic associations and institutions continued to receive preferential treatment from the party. Their congresses and jubilees[54] were taken as occasions for a particularly forceful demonstration of the relationship of trust and confidence which existed between 'power and intellect'.

Erich Honecker, for example, made time for a four-hour discussion with the board of the Writers' Association. Its chairman, Hermann Kant, said later: 'It was an exchange of views, and what is understood by party leadership, leadership by the party . . . was given expression'.[55]

The breadth and variety of artistic forms has, however, been respected in recent years, and the choice of artistic means has widened. (This has actually amounted to a separation between content and form which should have been anathema to Marxists.) The visual arts have benefited particularly from this. Apparently there are no longer any objections to including abstract painters in the cultural heritage or of giving the commission to design a national monument to the Peasants'

Wars of the 16th century to a prominent Mannerist such as Werner Tübke.[56]

Critical works on drama and literature have also been accepted[57] but anything which could have formed a crystallisation point for dissatisfaction has remained unperformed or unpublished. The more evident it became that the demand for an increase in Socialist awareness was to compensate for the collapse of the expectations of the years of building the 'New Society', the more sensitively did the party react to any expression of pessimism. The loss of activist hopes for the future was regarded as the expression of the crisis of Imperialism. Expression of the fact that reality could not be measured against abstract ideals and the present would have to be seen in the light of the future, that Socialism needed an active attitude to life, was the minimum required of artists.[58] Kurt Hager gave expression to this in a speech in which he almost seemed to be wooing commitment.

There have recently been a number of cautious course corrections in practice but never a basic change in policy. Some well-known critical writers have received public recognition and some controversial books have been reprinted. Recently a number of authors who wanted to travel abroad have been given visas which are valid for several years and still allow them to return. Some of their earlier work is still on sale in the GDR. The house arrest on Havemann, a scientist and critical Communist, has been lifted (Havemann died in 1982). Other critics, such as Bahro, who had been imprisoned, have been amnestied and, like others, allowed at their own request to move to the FRG. Writers living in the GDR have fought out their cultural policy controversies in the West German media and published in the West works which would not have been accepted in the GDR; only after a long silence was one exemplary case taken up and a prominent writer pubished for currency offences. These regulations and the harsher criminal legislation against 'libel on the GDR'[59] are available as instruments and used against rebels as seems opportune.

At present the leaders seem mainly concerned to stimulate an impression of moderate satisfaction: to create a climate with no major conflicts from which more far-reaching protests could develop. In any case protests by writers remain isolated. Artists and writers are a highly respected but very small group and their privileged position prevents any real solidarity with other social groups. On the other hand the role of intellectual leadership, which the intellectual opposition aspires to in other East European states, has never been a concern of theirs.

Conclusion

It is difficult to estimate what the consequences of the present situation are likely to be in terms of future development. Writers and artists who moved to the Federal Republic, and those who remained in the GDR but made use of the opportunity to publish in the West, have proved that they are strong enough to get their views accepted, but the price has been high. There is no group cohesion. Their political dependence has been amply demonstrated.[60] But even the party can only use pressure to a certain extent if it does not want to lose all its credibility. It needs the writers.

Generally those involved describe the climate as oppressive. Young artists are certainly encouraged and large quantities of literature on relatively banal subjects are being published, but the dominant mood in the cultural sphere is one of caution, while the protagonists wait or manoeuvre very carefully. It is not coincidence that keeping silent has been one of the central themes of recent literature.

The situation is not unlike that during the last years of Ulbricht's regime — the party may have greater tactical flexibility but the old hopes of a speedy and inevitable change have gone. Cultural policy under 'real' Socialism may have been able to overcome the rigidity of the Ulbricht regime but over decisive issues, such as the establishment of a basis of trust between the party and the intelligentsia, it has so far failed. The often repeated desire for reconciliation between power and intellect shows that the old conflict in German culture is still going on, though in a different form — not so much lack of concern for the intellect (as we find in the FRG) — but as an attempt to make this subservient, to politicise it. Fear in the party, which led to the elimination of any room for individual interpretation of what is meant by Socialism has also destroyed precisely that excess of imagination which could lead to innovation.

Almost all the GDR writers who expressed themselves in public in the FRG did so as advocates of a Socialist society.[61] Scarcely any of them was in basic opposition to the party or the government of the GDR. If the party leaders are not capable of making better use of such loyalty their sense of insecurity must be great indeed. No doubt they felt they were acting under pressure. But in banishing writers the party damaged its own anti-fascist tradition and had to see its doctrine called in question all over the world. Some of the major representatives of cultural life in the GDR have gone into voluntary exile and the Federal Republic has become a buffer zone for GDR writers. In acting as they did the SED leaders denied themselves the opportunity to practise an active cultural policy which would have documented to the world the strength of 'real' Socialism.[62] They moved contrary to the line they had themselves so often proclaimed.

Moreover, in acting out of the compulsion to self-preservation the party apparatus destroyed its chance to further what should have been its main aim: the sense of identification with 'real' socialism.

Nevertheless, if we take a look back at the list of functions outlined at the beginning of this chapter we can see that the SED has been able to use the classical method of a Marxist–Leninist party organisation policy, and build up a very considerable cultural infrastructure. In doing so it has shown a great deal of effort and zeal. It has opened the gates of culture to all its citizens. The 'realistic' cultural policy of the 1970s did liberate cultural life from the dogmatism of traditional concepts and modernise through differentiation. At the same time, however, the consistent widening of the concept of 'the culture of the people as a whole', with its greater realism, encouraged the process of assimilation to the more private life styles of Western industrial societies. The attempt to compensate for this with greater ideological leadership seems to have been only partially successful. The controversies over individual writers and the doctrine of 'the art of Socialist realism' have shown that loyalty to the political order may be enforced but that a credible representation of the hope of a liberated Communist society cannot be made to order. It has proved very difficult to use cultural policy as a means to secure the leadership through delimitation and exclusion. Its contribution to the transformation of society, measured by its Utopian goals, has remained limited.

There can be no doubt, however, that cultural policy has made an important contribution to the integration of GDR society. Whether a national identity will develop from this may be doubted. The main problem for cultural policy in the GDR is still that it may be able to organise the 'participation of all' but it can hardly enforce the 'full development of all'. This needs freedom and space, political freedom as well, and bureaucratic Socialism has always destroyed any attempt at this. Whether the lack of ability to come to terms with the intelligentsia by acknowledging conflict is a result of the system in the GDR, or whether it is of historical origin and hence may one day become obsolete, only the future will tell.

Notes

1   'Kultur', in Berger, Hanke, Hentschel et al. (eds), *Kulturpolitisches Wörterbuch*, Dietz Verlag, Berlin, 2nd edition 1978.

2   According to party policy cultural policy is defined as 'the totality of the principles, aims, tasks and measures for the deliberate and planned furtherance of Socialist culture and its mutual relations with the political, economic, social, ideological and other tasks of the development of society as a whole'. 'Kulturpolitik', in *Kulturpolitisches Wörterbuch*, op.cit.

3   In the 'Kulturbund zur demokratischen Erneuerung Deutschlands', founded in 1945, in the 'Akademie der Künste', founded in 1950 and the artists' associations founded in 1950 as part of the 'Kulturbund' and which became independent in 1952.
4   *Erklärung der Beratung von Vertretern der Kommunistischen und Arbeiterparteien der sozialistischen Länder*, Berlin 1957, p.14.
5   Ibid.
6   Material on the Bitterfeld Conference is to be found in Schubbe, E. (ed.), *Dokumente zur Kunst-, Literatur- und Kulturpolitik der SED*, Seewald Verlag, Stuttgart, 1972, pp. 552—62.
7   See Schlenker, W., *Das kulturelle Erbe in der DDR. Gesellschaftliche Entwicklung und Kulturpolitik 1945—1965*, J.B. Metzlersche Verlagsbuchhandlung, Stuttgart, 1977, p.137 ff; and Schmitt, H.J., *Einführung in Theorie, Geschichte und Funktion der DDR-Literatur*, J.B. Metzlersche Verlagsbuchhandlung, Stuttgart, 1975, with contributions from Struwe, M., Villwock, J., Scharfschwerdt, J., Wollf, L.W. and Trommler, F. on this phase.
8   Socialist brigades are workers' collectives and they are supposed to act according to the slogan 'work, learn and live in the Socialist way'. They are obliged both to fulfil economic targets and develop cultural activities and these are then compared with the work of other brigades with which they compete. On the development of cultural activities see the statistics at the end.
9   He was regarded as a dupe of Maoist ideas and the GDR continued to follow the Leninist interpretation of this concept.
10   Kessler, H. and Staufenbiel, F. (eds), *Kultur in unserer Zeit. Zur Theorie und Praxis der sozialistischen Kulturrevolution in der DDR*, Dietz Verlag, Berlin, 1965, p.168 ff.
11   *Neues Deutschland*, 18 December 1971, quoted from Rüss, G. (ed.), *Dokumente zur Kunst-, Literatur- und Kulturpolitik der SED, 1971—1974*, Seewald Verlag, Stuttgart, 1976, p.287.
12   *Minutes of the discussions at the VIIIth SED Party Congress of 15.—19.6.1971*, Dietz Verlag, Berlin, 1971, vol.1, p.61 ff.
13   Ibid., pp. 94—6.
14   'Zu Fragen der Kulturpolitik der SED', speech by Kurt Hager at the 6th SED Central Committee Congress, printed in Rüss, op.cit., p.493 ff.
15   See *Protokoll der Verhandlungen des IX. Parteitages der SED, 18.—22.5.1976*, Dietz Verlag, Berlin, 1976, vol.2, p.246.
16   Contribution to the discussion from A. Abusch at the 6th Plenary of the SED Central Committee 1972, in Rüss, op.cit., p.533. Abusch, former Minister of Culture (from 1958—1961), was at this time a member of the Cultural Committee of the People's Chamber.

17   See inter alia, John, E. and collective of authors, *Beiträge zur Entwicklung sozialistischer Kulturbedürfnisse*, Dietz Verlag, Berlin, 1975; *Lebensweise, Kultur, Persönlichkeit. Materialien vom II. Kongress der marxistisch—leninistischen Soziologie in der DDR 1974*, Deitz Verlag, Berlin, 1975; Strützel, D., et al., 'Soziologische Untersuchungen zur Kulturentwicklung im Sozialismus', in *Wissenschaftliche Zeitschrift der Karl-Marx Universität Leipzig, Gesellschafts- und Sprachwissenschaftliche Reihe, 1976*, Heft 3, p.243—7; Staufenbiel, E. and collective of authors, *Kulturelle Bedürfnisse der Arbeiterklasse. Die Entwicklung kultureller Bedürfnisse und ihre Wirkung im ökonomischen Reproduktionsprozess*, Dietz Verlag, Berlin, 1975. For a summary: Jäger, M., 'Die Kulturpolitik in der DDR nach dem VIII. Parteitag der SED', in *Deutschland Archiv, Sonderheft 1975*, pp. 124—37.
18   *Deutsche Demokratische Republik — Handbuch*, VEB Verlag Enzyklopädie Leipzig, 1979, pp. 633 and 643.
19   SED programme, op.cit., p.246.
20   'Fliessband, Bier und etwas Brecht', Gespräch mit Helmut Hanke über Fragen der sozialistischen Lebensweise', in *Sonntag*, vol.34, no.9 of 2 March 1980, p.8.
21   State expenditure on culture from *Statistisches Jahrbuch der Deutschen Demokratischen Republik*, Staatsverlag der Deutschen Demokratischen Republik, 1979. (After 1975 including concerts and guest appearances and cinemas):

1960	649 million Marks
1965	802 million Marks
1970	1,082 million Marks
1975	1,953 million Marks
1978	2,175 million Marks

A comparison with produced national income is even more interesting. This is taken from Koch, H., 'Über den kulturhistorischen Platz der entwickelten sozialistischen Gesellschaft', in *Weimarer Beiträge*, vol.26, issue 1, 1980, p.12:

Key data for increases in the material standard of living (Index 1950 = 100)

	1960	1970	1977
Produced national income	262	401	568
Average monthly income from work	178	243	305
Individual consumption	250	347	478
Payments and subsidies from the state from social funds for cultural organisations (including radio and television)	208	347	683

22   The innovation movements are to fulfil the same compensation function and are hence often quoted in this connection. On the culture of labour see Gillen, E., 'Kultur und "subjektiver Faktor" in der DDR — Zur Debatte um das Konzept der "Arbeitskultur" in den 70er Jahren', in Gassner, H. and Gillen, E., *Kultur und Kunst in der DDR seit 1970*, Lahn-Giessen Anabas Verlag, 1977, pp. 9—39.
23   On the production of posters in the GDR since the VIIIth Party Congress see 'Interview mit R. Grüttner', in Gassner and Gillen, op.cit., p.232.
24   This includes for instance programme advisory committees for theatres, advisory councils to the ministries and so on. The final programmes for publishers and the allocation of paper is agreed with the board of the writers' association.
25   *Protokoll der Verhandlungen des IV. Parteitages*, op.cit., Band 1, p.365.
26   'Pläne für das Kulturleben, Interview mit Hans-Joachim Hoffmann', *Neues Deutschland*, 16 September 1973, in Rüss, op.cit., p.835. Like all the other data festivals, memorial days and special concert weeks are included in the report by the statistical office in the GDR.
27   Hoffmann, H.-J. and Kühn, W., 'Kulturpolitik im Interesse des arbeitenden Menschen', in *Einheit*, H. 7/8, 1978, p.787. See also Marten, J., 'Theoretische Probleme der Planung künftiger Kulturentwicklung', in *Weimarer Beiträge*, H. 10/1979, pp. 5—22.
28   The establishment of the special school 'Hans Marchwitza' for cultural functionaries in 1973 and the 'Akademie für Weiterbildung beim Ministerium für Kultur', 1973.
29   *Anordnung über die Bildung der Generaldirektion beim Komitee für Unterhaltungskunst*, cf. Rüss, op.cit., p.782 ff.
30   Hager, op.cit., p.524.
31   See Zimmermann, H., 'The GDR in the 1970s', in *Problems of Communism*, vol.XXVII, March—April 1978, p.13; and 'Zu einigen Aspekten der innenpolitischen Situation der DDR', in Erbe, G. et al., *Politik, Wirtschaft und Gesellschaft in der DDR*, Westdeutscher Verlag, Opladen, 1979, p.33.
32   Together with the constitutional change in 1974 the name of the 'Deutscher Kulturbund' was changed to 'Kulturbund der DDR', and that of the 'Deutscher Schriftstellerverband' into 'Schriftstellerverband der DDR' (1973). There were similar changes in the names of other cultural associations.
33   See Rüss, op.cit., p.20.
34   Haase, H. and collective, *Geschichte der deutschen Literatur, vol.11; Literatur der Deutschen Demokratischen Republik*; Volk und Wissen VEB Berlin, 1976; Gärtner, H. and collective, *Die Künste in der*

Deutschen Demokratischen Republik. Henschel Verlag Kunst und Gesellschaft, Berlin, 1979.
35 Brandt, W., 'Bericht zur Lage der Nation, 23.2.1972', in *Bericht der Bundesregierung und Materialien zur Lage der Nation, 1972*, edited by Bundesministerium für innerdeutsche Beziehungen, p.VIII.
36 von Hofmannsthal, H., 'Das Schrifttum als geistiger Raum der Nation', in Steiner, H. (ed.), *Prosa IV. Gesammelte Werke in Einzelausgaben*, S. Fischer Verlag, Frankfurt, 1977.
37 Hoffmann, H.-J., 'Kultur und Kunst in den geistigen Kämpfen unserer Zeit', in *Weimarer Beiträge 2/1980*, p.13.
38 'New morals will emerge, new customs and traditions rooted in the needs of Socialist life. Old traditions will receive a new, Socialist impetus . . . So changes in certain ethnic qualities, features and characteristics will come about and this will enrich the German ethnic. The concept "German" will acquire a Socialist significance in our new society.' Kosing, A. and Schmidt, W., 'Geburt und Gedeihen der sozialistischen deutschen Nation', in *Einheit* no. 9/10, 1979, pp. 1068–1075, here p.1074.
39 See *Programm der SED*, op.cit., p.247.
40 'Beschluss des Politbüros des ZK der SED zu Aufgaben der Literatur- und Kunstkritik', in *Sonntag*, 48, 1977, p.2. The steering function of literature and the theatre is helped by the fact that the number of new titles which are published each year (not including new editions) in imaginative literature (belles lettres) is not very high (about 450 to 500). This has not greatly increased in recent years. But the average edition is considerable, being about 15,000 to 20,000 even for a first edition and 40,000 to 50,000 for a paperback. Books that prove successful and are regarded as desirable run into many editions, but figures on these are rarely published. The 'echo effect' of the media is important: almost all the better known book titles are adapted for the theatre, film or television and so reach a wider audience.
The official GDR statistics (*Statistisches Jahrbuch der DDR*) for 1979 (p.308) contain figures on book production under various headings. For 'belles lettres', which includes re-issues but not children's or young people's literature, there are 1,176 titles (covering 49 pages) with editions totalling 27,224,000.
On mass culture see also Koch, H., 'Über den kulturhistorischen Platz der entwickelten sozialistischen Gesellschaft', in *Weimarer Beiträge*, Heft 1, 1980, p.15 f.: 'For every 1,000 of the population in all age groups there were in 1978: 302 registered users of public libraries, 634 visits to theatres, 4,795 visits to cinemas, 3,467 visits to cultural centres and clubs, 189 visits to concerts, 1,920 to museums, 840 to zoos, 755 trips abroad.' (Trips abroad include visits to the Federal Republic by old-age pensioners for whom there are no travel restrictions.)

41   According to Lenin there are elements of such a culture, forming in contrast to the culture of the ruling class, in every national culture, Lenin, W.I., 'Kritische Bemerkungen zur nationalen Frage', in *Werke*, vol.20, Berlin 1968.
42   Hager, op.cit., p.507.
43   Ibid., p.507 f.
44   *Protokoll des IX. Parteitags*, op.cit., vol.1, p.362.
45   *Neues Deutschland*, 15, 16, 17, 18, November 1973.
46   On the Biermann case see the documentation in *Deutschland Archiv*, vol.10, H. 1, 1977, pp. 69–105; here p.72.
All the major cultural policy events have been commented on in the *Deutschland Archiv*. See also the essays by Jäger, M., Kleinschmidt, H., Sander, H., Rossade, W., Rühle, J. and the special issue 1977 *Kultur und Gesellschaft in der DDR*.
47   Ibid., p.75.
48   Hager, K., 'Der IX. Parteitag der SED und die Gesellschaftswissenschaften', in Akademie für Gesellschaftswissenschaften beim ZK der SED (ed.), *Der IX. Parteitag und die Gesellschaftswissenschaften*, Dietz Verlag Berlin, 1977, p.53. On the fear of ultra-left ideologies see also the resolution on literary and art criticism, op.cit. (Note 40).
49   Hager, K., op.cit. (Note 48), p.52.
50   Bahro, R., *Die Alternative. Zur Kritik des real existierenden Sozialismus*, Europäische Verlagsanstalt Cologne, Frankfurt/M., 1977.
51   *Der Spiegel*, issues 1 and 2, 1978 of 2 January and 9 January 1978. The manifesto of what claimed to be organised opposition within the SED was signed by a 'Central Coordination Group of the BDKD' (Association of Democratic German Communists).
52   From the report by the Politbüro to the 35th Central Committee meeting. The reporter was Erich Honecker. *Neues Deutschland* 18 March 1977, reprinted in *Deutschland Archiv*, H. 5, 1977, p.542 ff. resolution mentioned on p.553 f.
53   These tactics, which were also designed to direct social envy on to the writers, were used, for instance, against Stefan Heym, who had been a critic of the national cultural policy for many years and was able to maintain his independence precisely because he had a reputation and an income in the West, and against the philosopher Robert Havemann (verdicts of 22 May 1979 and 25 May 1979).
54   For example the VIIIth writers' congress in 1978, at which several prominent writers were not present, the 30th anniversary of the GDR Academy of Arts 1980 and Erich Honecker's meeting with the board of the Cultural Association and the presidents of the Artists' Association and the Academy of Arts in 1979; see the speech by the General Secretary: 'Die Kulturpolitik unserer Partei wird erfolgreich verwirklicht' in *Neues Deutschland* 23/24 June 1979 only one month after the events mentioned above (Note 53).

55   Opening speech by Hermann Kant, President of the Writers' Association, at the congress in *Neue Deutsche Literatur*, H. 7, 1978, p.11. Recognition of the honour accorded in these meetings, at which artists and writers were able to talk to the great men in the party and the state on equal terms is also manifest in comments by other participants.
56   The upswing in the visual arts in the 1970s met with extraordinary public interest. The VIIth GDR Art Exhibition 1972/73 had 656,000 visitors and the VIIIth in 1977/76 over a million. Obviously it had proved possible to encourage people who were not traditionally interested in the arts to go.
57   Inevitably in a small state like the GDR personal or group relations will play a considerable part; these have varying degrees of success for writers and artists, i.e. the principles of patronage apply. The different degrees to which the local party functionaries intervene in cultural activities also play a major part. In 1977/78, for example, the Mitteldeutscher Verlag in Leipzig was able to publish critical books and only re-issues were prevented (due to the interest the books had aroused): Heiduczek, W., *Tod am Meer*; Loest, E., *Es geht seinen Gang*. Heiduczek's book caused the Ministry of Education (Volksbildungsministerium) to lodge an official protest with the Soviet Embassy.
58   Hager, K., 'Die Akademie der Künste und die sozialistische Kultur' in *Sonntag* 14, 6 April 1980, pp. 2 and 3, here p.3.
59   The third amendment to the criminal code of 28 June 1979 widened the scope of section 219, 'Illegal contacts', to make even the attempt to send 'manuscripts, writing or other material which might damage the interests of the German Democratic Republic abroad' illegal. *Gesetzblatt der Deutschen Demokratischen Republik*, Part 1, no.17, 2 July 1979.
60   In view of the social or state control of commissions and publication political dependence is always economic dependence as well.
61   In this they differ from most East European emigrants. Of course these writers were concerned not to let themselves be marketed in the media in the FRG as opponents of the GDR regime. At any rate the public in the FRG were forced to recognise that their state is not regarded by East German dissidents as a longed-for alternative but only as the lesser of two evils.
62   Foreign cultural policy, although it played a major part in this period after the wave of international recognition, has not been considered here, for reasons of space. See Jacobsen, H.A., 'Auswärtige Kulturpolitik' in Jacobsen, H.A. (ed.), *Drei Jahrzehnte Aussenpolitik der DDR*, Oldenbourg-Verlag, Munich, Vienna, 1980, pp. 235–60.

7 Social policy and the transformation of society
Helga Michalsky, University of Heidelberg

The rediscovery of social policy

The VIIIth SED Party Congress in 1971 brought a new orientation in social policy. At last the party appeared to be ready to acknowledge the long-accumulated consumer needs of the population and its new 'Main Task' was proclaimed as being designed 'to increase the material and cultural standard of living'. Great emphasis was laid on social policy, which the leaders appear to have regarded as a suitable means of keeping implementation of the new policy within materially defensible limits. The slogan of 'the unity of economic and social policy' was a useful formulation. It was capable of flexible interpretation and it tied any promise that might be made to economic preconditions.

The new policy was given concrete expression in the first social policy programme to follow the congress. This emphasised the general obligation on the part of the leaders to 'do everything possible for the well-being of the people' and named the measures which were to be adopted immediately or in the course of the coming five-year plan for the period from 1971 to 1975. There were three main items:

1. The solution of the housing problem: this was declared to be the 'core' of the programme. By 1990 sufficient new accommodation was to have been provided and enough old property modernised to ensure adequate supply.

2   A rise in real incomes: this was to increase and improve individual consumption and it entailed a number of measures:

(a) an increase in wages and performance bonuses in conjunction with increases in productivity;
(b) an increase in minimum wages and pensions;
(c) the introduction of voluntary supplementary insurance (FZR);
(d) general applicability of the new pension laws (introduced for new pensions in 1968);
(e) an increase in all pensions and social security benefits.

3   An increase in the production of consumer goods and in the services sector:[1] this was to ensure that the higher real incomes were used to satisfy individual needs.

In all these areas undeniable successes were achieved during the following five-year planning period.[2] The IXth Party Congress in 1976 confirmed the new policy and fixed further aims:

(a) a graded increase in holiday entitlements;
(b) a gradual transition to the 40-hour week;
(c) more help for families with two and more children;
(d) a better standard of living for old-age pensioners, particularly through the creation of suitable jobs for older workers.

A week after the congress further expensive measures were announced. The main emphasis was on demographic policy and a reduction in working time for shift workers[3] but there were also further increases in the level of social security (minimum wages, pensions and social aid).

However, the general economic conditions under which the GDR has had to pursue her growth aims in recent years have brought a modification in the practice of the concept of the 'unity of economic and social policy'. The prices of imported raw materials have risen everywhere and the GDR has to pay more for capital goods from the West as fuel costs here have risen. In the years immediately after 1971 the dominant theme was the promise that better economic performance would bring a direct improvement in living conditions, but since 1976 the people have been urged to do their utmost at work in view of what has already been achieved and the targets set in the social policy programme.[4]

The title of this section, 'The rediscovery of social policy', is a reference to two aspects of recent developments: the very great improvement in social benefits after 1971, and the upgrading of social policy in GDR political rhetoric, making it one of the 'integration factors' for the new Socialist society. There has also been a striking increase in the tendency to equate social policy with domestic policy. This is taken by Western observers as a sign that there are growing problems in both areas.[5]

Of course the GDR has always had a social policy. However, for many years the benefits remained on the very low initial level and so they became increasingly unsatisfactory. The policy covered the traditional areas of social insurance, job security and job protection. During the occupation period a reform of social insurance was initiated. This followed concepts put forward by the trade unions and the Social Democrats during the Weimar Republic. The Communists, whose ideology had prevented them from developing concepts of their own, adopted these ideas. Tactical considerations may also have played a part. The 'Social Policy Guidelines' published by the SED in 1946 were certainly a concession to the Social Democrats in the new party.[6]

As all the social policy measures of the following decades were clearly determined by economic considerations the SED leaders soon came under criticism outside the GDR for orienting their policy to growth or production. This is still the case; indeed there is more integration of social and economic policy now that social policy is no longer regarded by all GDR theorists as an infringement of Socialist principles.[7] GDR authors are now claiming that only in the Socialist society can the relation between social and economic policy be free of contradictions.[8]

Many observers have wondered why social insurance was not given a more prominent place in the political programme after 1971. The area has played only a minor part in propaganda, but the measures actually implemented show that a considerable part of expenditure on social policy is concentrated in this field, especially on pensions.

During the 1950s the ideologists who were working to justify the differences in welfare between the FRG and the GDR discredited social policy, arguing that it was an 'instrument of capitalist myth-building' and representing it as diametrically opposed to the aims of Socialism. For a long time the term 'social policy' was avoided altogether and the less invidious phrase 'social security' was used instead. It covered first and foremost social insurance, the right to work, occupational safety and health. However, the traditionally close attention paid to this area by the trade unions gradually brought the term back into use, as the unions used it before the general discussion on the aims and contents of a 'Socialist social policy' began.[9] The theoretical justification of a 'Socialist social policy' which began in the mid-1960s had to take account of this heritage.[10]

During this period, in keeping with the strong orientation of social life in the GDR to the world of work, it was proposed to develop social policy at enterprise level. Even the SED Secretary-General, Walter Ulbricht, stressed the significance of social policy at local and enterprise level at the VIIth SED Party Congress in 1967. The idea lived on in enterprise planning of living and working conditions but it did not produce any noticeable successes.[11] In retrospect it is hard to avoid the impression that in failing to give this concept concrete form the GDR lost an opportunity to develop a social policy to suit the specific needs of its own system. What it has done is to follow the path of Western social policy.

But for the later priorities it was certainly significant that social policy did not have to start at zero: the new programme after 1971 could build on a foundation which had been laid at an early date. It was only under such conditions that an area such as housing policy could become the core of the new approach.

Although there was certainly continuity in this policy area in the GDR the sudden increase in political interest needs clarification. GDR authors simply point to the achievements in social development, which now make higher social benefits possible. But this is not enough to explain the 1971 watershed. Outside the GDR three explanations are usually put forward in conjunction: they cover the historical, political and ideological significance of the change.

Firstly, for decades the GDR polemicised against the concept of social policy as pursued in capitalist states, although in practice it had proved highly efficient and flexible and this should have offered a legitimation base. On a comparison of systems the GDR was dropping further behind and it needed to act to secure the loyalty of its citizens. Moreover, the policy of material stimulation during the 1960s had brought more social differentiation than could possibly be politically desirable. Secondly, it was easier for the political leaders to concede that the level of demands by the population had risen since the economic situation appeared good and promised well for coming years. Finally, there was a change in the ideological framework conditions. This is generally held to be the most important and far-reaching of the preconditions for the 1971 change. It was recognised that the transition phase to the completion of the Communist society would last longer than had at first been assumed. It was therefore concluded that further specific measures would be needed to co-ordinate the general aim with the particular interests of certain social groups.[12]

GDR authors are vehement in their reaction to any suggestion that the SED might have undertaken 'ideological corrections'. Considerable attention has been paid to a West German study which gives a brief outline of current social policy aims in the GDR and a very convincing account of the importance of the Socialist theory of economic growth for the purpose of recognising and satisfying social needs. Since the political leaders had pledged themselves to an interpretation of this theory in terms of unity of social and economic policy, which by definition eliminates conflict, the problems which result are not seriously discussed. Instead GDR socio-political literature repeatedly rejects the suggestion that there is no basic difference between the aims and conditions of social policy under Socialism and under capitalism. To do otherwise would, of course, undermine the claim that Socialism is the superior doctrine. The controversy reveals the fundamental difficulties inherent in any attempt to formulate general socio-political principles and apply these to specific areas of responsibility while at the same time giving convincing proof of the conjunction of theory and practice.[13]

The present state of development and its effect on social policy aims and measures

There are two characteristic points of reference for discussion on social policy in the GDR: the broad perspective, in which social policy is the expression and instrument of the formation of an advanced Socialist society, and the micro-sphere, the formulation of its concrete tasks in the present phase of the development of the Socialist society. Regarding the change introduced with the VIIIth Party Congress there is, on the one hand, stress on continuity but at the same time emphasis on what is new. It would appear that to the extent that Western interpretations of the change encounter resistance the desire in the GDR grows for a smooth transition and a sense of tradition.

A central question is the position of social policy in the overall strategy of the Communist party. It is stressed that social policy is a 'component of the uniform policy of the working class', a 'comprehensive policy for society', but not that it is an autonomous sphere. It takes effect 'throughout the process of the formation of social relations and the material and ideal conditions which underlie these'. What matters is active influence on the social structure. The long-term aim is the classless society; social structural analysis and policy become instruments of social development.[14]

The basis and aim of social policy as pursued by the SED and the Socialist state is therefore the transformation of GDR society.[15] Analysis of the present structure of society is a vital precondition for its 'planned, long-term development'. Shaping the social structure is the most comprehensive function social policy has to fulfil in the Socialist state. It includes demographic policy, the gradual elimination of differences between classes and groups, the creation of a 'Socialist way of life' and the satisfaction of needs; it also includes patterns of working time and leisure, social aspects of incomes policy and the supply of consumer goods and services. Stress is laid on the fact, however, that Socialist development cannot come from individual measures of social policy alone; changes in material conditions and the development of patterns of behaviour and thought must form one uniform whole.[16]

It is claimed that social policy principles are inherent in Marxism—Leninism, and that these differ fundamentally from all other theories and practices in this field. These principles are:

(a) both partiality and a scientific approach;
(b) a combination of scientific—technological developments with social developments;
(c) both uniformity and differentiation;
(d) an organic combination of distribution according to the principle of performance and social need;
(e) solidarity as class-determined behaviour;
(f) rationality and efficiency;
(g) central state planning and control on basic issues and an increase in personal responsibility.[17]

This is hardly more than a collection of platitudes. The principles contain analogies with the principles of Socialist political economy and echoes of the general principles of Marxism—Leninism. But the principles are of little relevance for the problems of social policy in practice. Nor will they give us any information on the real priorities which are set in this field, and which appear to be determined according to the patterns of decision-making familiar in Socialist states. As developments which affect social policy are on the one hand regarded as part of an inevitable process, while the determination of the concrete measures and tasks is a matter for the central organs of the state, the decisions taken by the leaders are held to be beyond criticism and the lower levels, i.e. enterprises, are to take a responsible part in the implementation of the general aims.[18] Without rational aids to making a decision on the need for one or the other measure 'uniformity and differentiation' becomes an objective category for decisions on social developments. There are three principles which are supposed to direct the implementation of this in measures of social policy: social homogenisation as the overall aim, the reduction of social differences as a shorter-term aim, and the need for a more differentiated acknowledgement of performance to stimulate further development.[19] The contradictory effects which these principles can produce are explained by reference to the transitional nature of Socialist society, while the ambivalent relation between performance and need is interpreted positively as a stimulus to development. It is in keeping with the ideology that the two conflicting elements are justified so as not to jeopardise the unity of social policy.

As this concept of social policy can give rise to conflicting interpretations and measures which may have very different effects, it is hardly surprising that it has been very differently evaluated. Assessments range from a readiness to accept the egalitarian dimension[20] to the view that the inclusion of this concept of social policy in the theoretical and ideological apparatus of Marxism—Leninism is the 'announcement and prior legitimation of further socio-political steps in the direction of an authoritarian society, described as egalitarian but with growing social inequalities'.[21]

Even those who concede that the concept has a credible sociopolitical dimension hold that insufficient funds and information are available and that inadequate concrete targets and intermediary goals have been set.[22] To what extent the principles and measures of social policy will take effect to the advantage of the general aims can only be examined in specific cases. Studies which have been made show that there is a great discrepancy between the claim and the reality, even if the policy has certainly had some successes.

In comparison with the elevated socio-political aims which have been proclaimed for the new social policy its actual fields of operation are all too familiar. The main attention focuses on housing policy, health and social security, with social insurance, holidays and recuperation facilities, environment policy and finally family policy forming important areas. The three which we will consider in more detail would appear to be best suited to give an impression of the general relation between the principles of social policy and its individual measures.

Social insurance Apart from certain regulations to afford greater safety at work, in most countries social insurance was the beginning of state social policy. As social insurance can take very different forms and be oriented to very different concepts, it would appear to offer a good field for a closer examination of whether what has been attempted and achieved in the GDR is really an implementation of the principles of Marxism—Leninism. The issue of old-age pensions, in particular, will enable us to see how the principle of 'uniformity and differentiation' has been applied and with what success.

Housing policy This is the showcase of GDR social policy. Here, if anywhere, the specific features of the policy should be apparent. It is also interesting to find out why housing policy in particular should come to be at the top of the priority list.

Family policy This has been the focal point of various trends and it has caused considerable problems in the GDR. The problem structure contains elements which are characteristic of this society but it includes some which occur in other societies too. Hence the solutions deserve closer analysis with regard both to their effects within the GDR social system and the possibility of transfer to other systems.

Social Insurance: from minimum security to differentiated benefits for pensioners

In the post-war years the political forces in the Soviet Occupied Zone made a daring and rigorous break with the traditional German system of social insurance. Instead of a pensions system graded according to types of insurance (old-age, sickness, death, accident, unemployment), groups insured (public servants, war veterans and war widows, white collar workers and blue collar workers) and level of benefits, they introduced one global insurance. Claims were made uniform and the insurance was extended to cover those groups in the population who had not so far been obliged to contribute. The level of benefits, the definition of the type of benefit and the mode of calculating this were oriented — with slight modifications — to the old system. Although some groups lost some of their claims and were dissatisfied, the then provisional state actually brought upon itself an extremely heavy financial burden.

Since 1956 social insurance has been divided into two categories. Eighty-five per cent of the population are in the blue and white collar workers' insurance system run by the Free German Trade Unions, and more than 14 per cent are self-employed (farmers, craftsmen, other self-employed persons and professionals) and are in the state social insurance system. Altogether, therefore, more than 99 per cent of the working population is insured. The conditions for payment of benefit have been levelled out and made very much more difficult. The members of the old white collar workers' insurance and their dependents in particular have had to take cuts as benefits were levelled down to the old blue collar insurance level. Even at this early stage the political leaders made it clear that in the new society employment or work was to be regarded as the social norm for all persons who were capable of working. It is still assumed in the legislation on social insurance that on principle all people of working age (men up to 65, women up to 60) will earn their living by working. Pensions for widows or other dependents are therefore all dependent on conditions which prevent a person working (old age, small children — one under three, two under eight). In cases where a person qualifies for two or more pensions of the same kind only the higher is paid. When people qualify for different kinds of pension (widows with pensions of their own) the whole of the higher is paid and 25 per cent of the lower.

Not only did the introduction of obligatory insurance greatly widen the circle of those insured, but the number entitled to benefits also rose rapidly in the following years. As the minimum pension was at first also granted to persons who had paid less than 15 years' contributions the unfavourable demographic structure of the GDR had a direct effect on the social insurance bill. A large number of pensioners had not paid in enough to cover what they were drawing out and altogether the share of persons of pensionable age in the total population rose. In relation to the workforce it increased between 1950 and 1974 from 21.6 per cent to 33.7 per cent.[23] As the contribution rates remained unchanged while wage increases only had an effect up to the threshold of 600 Marks (the contribution threshold which remained in force), the revenues of the social insurance institutions (pensions and health) had already dropped below their disbursements by 1951–55. The supplement paid by the state, which was 625 million Marks during this period, rose rapidly in the following years, as can be seen from the following table. The cost development of the pensions system must be seen as one of the main reasons why there were only marginal increases in benefits until the pension reform of 1968. Hence a pensions system which was very laudable when introduced (bearing in mind the economic situation in Germany at the time) dropped to a lower and lower level of performance, so that subsequent developments blotted out the initial achievement of introducing minimum pensions at this level. In the 1960s particularly, as the dynamic system operated in the FRG began to work increasingly to the advantage of pensioners, old-age pensions in the GDR began to lag more and more behind.

Table 7.1
Revenue and expenditure of the Free German Trade Union Federation (FDGB) Social Insurance System
(in billions of Marks)[24]

	Revenue	Expenditure	State supplement
1951–55	26,453	27,078	0,625
1956–60	31,088	34,803	3,715
1961–65	34,335	44,280	9,945
1966–70	37,639	54,432	16,793
1971–75	46,541	77,953	31,412

However, criticism was directed not only at the minimum pensions but also and indeed mainly at the differential between the average pension and the average income. The level of pensions fluctuated until very recently between a good quarter and just on 30 per cent of earned income.[25] Even without the voluntary supplementary insurance which is now possible (see below) the relation was still only 30 per cent in 1978 despite the pension reform.[26]

In the reform of 1 July 1968 the political leadership simply adjusted pensions to the higher level of incomes but only with effect for new pensions. New methods of calculation raised benefits by one third on average. It was not until 1972 that this new method of calculation was applied to pre-1968 pensions as well. The measure was long overdue but apparently the leaders felt that they were in a position to do this only after the economic situation had improved. Table 7.2 shows the development of average pensions in the GDR.

Table 7.2
Pensions of blue and white collar workers (FDGB) and members of the State Insurance Scheme
(in Marks per month)[27]

Type of pension	1960	1965	1970	1975
Old age	146	163	188	248
Invalidity	142	154	207	264
Widows	120	131	157	210
Orphans	66	66	75	108

A few further improvements have been made, the most important of which is the voluntary supplementary pension insurance (Freiwillige Zusatzrentenversicherung) introduced in 1971. This initially offered the possibility of taking out an insurance for those parts of income which exceeded 600 Marks, up to a threshold of 1,200 Marks. Since 1977 the upper threshold has been abolished. The supplementary insurance provided an alternative to raising the obligatory insurance threshold of 600 Marks. This had proved the most persistent obstacle to a closer relationship between (individual) income from work and the later pension, as it only entitled to a maximum pension of 410 Marks (after 50 years' contributions). In contrast to the pension from the obligatory insurance, which is calculated from a combination of a fixed amount (110 Marks) and rising amounts per year insured in relation to the income during the last 20 years at work and hence favours lower incomes, contributions and pensions in the voluntary supplementary category show a linear rise. As this supplementary insurance is not available to those who were already drawing a pension when it was introduced, at present revenue is rising very much faster than payments. Apart from the fact that it will differentiate the income situation of future pensioners the supplementary insurance, which is similar to an obligatory pension (in that it also affects the amount of sick pay and other benefits), is easing the strain on the state purse (see table 7.1 on p.250) which has to make up the ever widening gap between the revenue and expenditure of the obligatory schemes (in 1978 the expenditure of the FDGB scheme was 22,351.6 million Marks and the state subsidy 9,853.6 million = 44.1 per cent; expenditure on the state scheme was 3,204.0 million Marks and the state subsidy 1,675.0 million = 52.3 per cent). For social insurance as a whole the state contribution rose from 38.2 per cent in 1971 to 48.3 per cent in 1977.[28]

But use has always been made of the possibility of running special benefit schemes. A large number of these now exist and together with the supplementary pension scheme for members of the 'intelligentsia' introduced in 1950 and 1951 they are now available for employees of the post and railways (1956), the police, the military, the customs and excise and major selected industries. They expressly serve to create greater differentiation and privilege. Other similar schemes are the honorary pensions granted since 1952 to state functionaries and the pensions paid since 1965 to the victims of fascism and the fighters against fascism. New types of scheme have been introduced during the last ten years which follow the traditional patterns of pension rights in the German public service, securing for their members pension rights up to as much as 90 per cent of their final net earnings. These schemes benefit leading and specialised staff in the ministries (since 1969/70), those employed in health and social work (1974) and teachers (1976). While the increases in pensions during recent years mainly benefited persons with low pensions and so have been regarded as an expression of the protective function of social policy, the special schemes would appear to be an expression of the stimulation and steering function which social policy is also supposed to exercise.[29] These additional pension schemes are handled very discreetly and this is no doubt due to the fact that in the majority of cases it is very difficult to prove any particular achievement to justify the higher benefits. The political leaders must be well aware that in the view of the majority of the population these schemes are rather an infringement of the principle on which the obligatory schemes are supposed to operate. Moreover, the difference between these pensions and those of the general schemes must provoke resentment.

The development of pension schemes in the GDR shows that the basic principles have been modified over the course of time. After a long phase of equalisation for by far the greater majority of pensioners the voluntary supplementary scheme has established a tendency to differentiation. On a lower level the development is now similar to what has occurred in the Federal Republic. Pensioners are no longer disadvantaged as a group, instead the social differentiation of the working population continues into retirement. So the development of differentiated pensions is a result of increasing wage differentials.

But although one can recognise certain parallels between the GDR and the Federal Republic considerable differences still remain. However, these cannot necessarily be regarded as the characteristics of Socialist states.

Clearly for cost reasons the GDR is limiting herself to only gradually bringing pensions into line with incomes from work. This is being done only out of the contributions received from the insured.

As general pensions are not automatically adjusted to incomes from work, the actual level of pensions is directly dependent on the aims of the economic plan. So the equal treatment of pensioners is a political decision which can be revoked.

In view of the volume of expenditure on pensions in the 1950s and 1960s the decision in favour of largely equal pensions was the most social form of distribution. In fact during these two decades people at work have very greatly improved their standard of living to the disadvantage of pensioners more than would have been possible if, for instance, the level of contributions had been raised. In the Federal Republic it was only after the pension reform of 1957 that pensions improved steadily together with incomes. Before that date only people at work benefited from the economic growth. In both states economic reconstruction took priority. In the East in reforming social insurance in 1947 the state laid upon itself an obligation from which the Western Allies recoiled.[30]

Even if pensions do come to be a more accurate reflection of incomes in future the concept of a pension according to need will still have great political value. Thus if minimum pensions are increased disproportionately in the future as well, minimum insurance could on comparison be more satisfactory.[31] However, the differentiation of need-oriented incomes shows that the principle of performance is being applied here too (on a comparison of social assistance, minimum pensions and minimum wages).[32]

The expansion of the special pension schemes is a highly critical point in view of the official interest in equal pensions and the principle of performance. These schemes have always made it possible for the political leaders to keep the level of social insurance lower than would otherwise have been possible.

The argument that in Socialist states the principle of state security takes precedence over the principle of insurance applies only with considerable reservations to the GDR. The maintenance of social insurance contributions despite the growing subsidy which the state has to provide has maintained the conviction on the part of the population that this is an insurance. The insurance principle has now de facto been strengthened through the application of the principle of equivalents (equal contributions give equal entitlements) in the supplementary insurance scheme.[33]

Housing policy: from neglect to priority

No modern state now leaves the provision of housing solely to market forces. The scope and direction of state intervention can be said to range from a 'comprehensive' to a 'supplementary' housing policy.[34] Socialist states have always pursued a comprehensive housing policy, i.e. the state has always determined the quantitative and qualitative development of the range of housing on offer, its distribution and cost (rents) — how much the individual has to pay directly out of his earned income for his accommodation. We shall briefly discuss with regard to the GDR the issues of comprehensive planning and control of housing, guarantees of low and stable rents, and planning for housing within the general economic plan.

Housing is to be distributed according to need and the principle of performance. Workers, shift workers and families with several children are to be given preference. Housing is also allocated according to economic considerations (e.g. in industrial estates) and in acknowledgement of special service to the state.

The right to accommodation is laid down in the constitution and it is assessed 'according to economic possibilities and local conditions'. There is a shortage of housing and strict criteria are applied. The rules of 23 square metres per person and one room per member of a household show the state of development. People have to apply for housing, and there are housing commissions to process and approve the applications; approval is needed for an exchange of apartments and all housing is subject to general control. These are the institutional consequences of the principles of comprehensive housing policy. Complaints that arrangements are inflexible and bureaucratic and that decisions, especially the extent to which persons or groups are favoured, are inscrutable are the norm.

Low rents are the ideological cornerstone of housing policy in the GDR. Rent subsidies, which covered more than half the real cost of accommodation, amounted to 1.4 billion Marks in 1978. That is just on a quarter of the expenditure out of the fund for the housing programme and the administration of the existing stock (1978: 6 billion Marks; 1971: 2.1 billion).[35]

In 1966 rents which were supposed to cover costs were introduced for new apartments but these have now been reduced for all households whose net income is less than 2,000 Marks. The purpose of this is to achieve a representative distribution of these apartments. As in 1978 only 12.2 per cent of households had a net income of over 2,000 Marks[36] it would appear that for a long time new apartments remained a prerogative of this small minority. The new rents, which have been reduced by about a third, are not to exceed between 3 and 5 per cent of the household's net income. At a rent of 104 Marks (132 in Berlin) for a three-room apartment, however, the allocation of accommodation according to the size of the family is an absolute essential (see table 7.3).[37]

Table 7.3
Average rents for new apartments
(for households with a net income of up to 2,000 Marks)

	Berlin	Other districts
2-room apartment	82	75
3-room apartment	107	85
4-room apartment	132	104

Unlike a market economy, where a shortage of cheap accommodation is ascribed to market forces, in the GDR the supply of housing is a matter of political decision-making. Within the framework of the overall economic plan decisions are taken on the quantity and quality of housing. The number and size of new apartments, the volume of repair and modernisation work which is to be carried out, and the number of old buildings which are to be replaced all form part of the target data as do norms such as the amount of space available to each person, the equipment and fittings in (larger) new projects.

Immediately after the war the housing situation in what is now the GDR was not bad but deliberate postponement of new building and neglect of what housing was available, for which the state must largely be held responsible, turned a relatively satisfactory situation into the reverse. By 1971, when a decision was taken gradually to introduce changes into housing policy, the existing housing stock was too old and in a very bad state of repair, with modernisation and rebuilding urgently needed. Change was indicated at the VIIIth Party Congress but it is only since the IXth Party Congress in 1976 that the improvement of the housing situation has enjoyed the highest social priority. The housing construction programme is the core of the social policy programme for 1976: by 1990 the housing shortage is to be overcome. By that date 10 million inhabitants, i.e. almost two thirds of the present population, are to be living in new or modernised apartments. The main aim is to achieve a uniform level of fittings and amenities for every family. In figures this means that between 1976 and 1990 altogether 2.8 to 3.0 million apartments will have to be built or modernised. Between 1945 and 1979 2.4 million apartments were provided, nearly 2 million of them new[38] and almost the same number are to be provided during the decade from 1981 to 1990 — 2.1 million, one third of these modernisations, at a cost altogether of 145 billion Marks. As 94 billion has already been spent on housing construction between 1971 and 1980 this means a considerable increase in expenditure. If economic growth does not proceed as planned — and there is much to suggest this — it would appear likely that the percentage of modernisations will be increased so that the overall target can be met.[39]

Statistics on the amenities of the total housing stock and new apartments show firstly how low the level is in the housing stock as a whole, and at the same time how great the differences are between the new and old buildings and the difference between urban and rural areas (see table 7.4).[40]

Table 7.4
The amenities of the total housing stock

	1971	1979
Number of apartments	6,057,000	6,713,900
Apartments per 1,000 persons	355	401
of which (in percentage)		
with central heating	11	22
bath/shower	39	)
inside toilet	42	) 50
running water	82	89
of which (in percentage) (1980)	in urban districts total	in rural districts total
with central heating	35.4	17.8
warm water	55.6	33.6
bath/shower	66.4	44.7
inside toilet	76.5	44.8
running water	100	84.9

Sources: GDR official statistics (*Statistische Jahrbücher*); DIW.

The GDR has achieved considerable success with its accelerated housing construction programme. In new building the number of apartments completed has risen, as planned, year by year, and after modest beginnings the improvement of fittings has also made good progress (see table 7.5).[41]

Table 7.5
The amenities of new apartments (in percentage)

	1960	1965	1970	1975	1978
Warm water	17.5	77.3	98.8	99.2	100.0
Central heating	8.9	42.1	73.8	89.5	94.8
Bath/shower	99.1	99.6	99.3	100.0	100.0
Balcony/loggia	39.0	52.0	69.0	72.0	–

Source: GDR official statistics (*Statistisches Jahrbuch der DDR 1979*), Berlin 1979, p.145.

The present level of amenities only corresponds to that in the Federal Republic in 1960.[42] Comparative figures for other Socialist states are not available but would presumably be more favourable to the GDR. But even if all the present plans are realised by 1990 the GDR will only have reached the standard the Federal Republic had attained in 1968.[43] But this would entail greater current expenditure on repairs, without which the condition of the new apartments would deteriorate too rapidly.

The picture is hardly more favourable on a comparison of the size of apartments and the space available per person. The average size of modern apartments is 60 sq.m per apartment in the GDR as compared with 105 sq.m in the FRG. However, this does not reflect the very considerable social differentiation in housing construction in the Federal Republic.

An obstacle in the way of equal distribution of housing in keeping with the targets of social policy is the very great differences in standards between old and new apartments. As new building is disproportionately concentrated in urban districts and there are also great differences between districts in the provision of new housing which does not reflect the general quantity available the housing programme is not likely to produce more regional equality.[44] This is not likely to be achieved with the new modernisation measures either, as these are not distributed with an aim to equalising supply. They are graded into three categories, the simplest of which, the provision of running water, an inside toilet and sewerage merely goes to show that the GDR is obviously forced to go on using housing which is really obsolete.[45] Moreover, it appears that a change in orientation is taking place.

The energy shortage has already given rise to discussion on how to insulate buildings better. A further problem, which will also affect the quality of the living environment, is the increasing desire to limit the amount of land available for building. Greater density in building is being demanded together with a reduction in the size of plots for owner-occupier built houses from the present 500 sq.m to 250/300 sq.m.[46]

Private housing construction has been encouraged and expanded in recent years in the GDR. Since 1974 it has accounted for just on 10 per cent of new housing construction. The advantages are openly discussed: it is held to improve the general stock of housing, create living accommodation in areas which have been neglected by state planning, save the state money because of the amount of private capital which is contributed and at the same time reduce purchasing power for other consumer expenditure. It mobilises labour and can create living accommodation for groups which are to have preferential treatment (large families need contribute only 10 per cent instead of 25 per cent of the capital). Co-operative housing construction offers similar advantages to the state. Its share fluctuates but up to 1976 was generally above that of individual construction (accounting for 36.3 per cent of new building in 1976). Here expenditure norms replace the criterion of one room per person and building approvals are allocated like apartments.[47]

Critics of the 'building and modernisation boom' object both to the urban results of the new housing programme and the concepts which are being realised. They recall the almost forgotten discussion on Socialist living patterns, which are now virtually only to be found in some aspects of the concept of 'residential complexes'. In the designing of residential areas according to the criterion of proximity to the workplace they see their argument confirmed that the time and nature of the change in the housing construction programme are not due to need but to production requirements (e.g. industrial sites).[48] There are signs that by no means all the people in the GDR want to live in a new apartment[49] but this can hardly be interpreted as criticism of individualistic living environments such as are to be found in capitalist societies.

Family policy: women at work and a large family

The situation of the family in the GDR is largely characterised by the fact that most women work. In 1978 86.7 per cent of women of working age were employed part or full time. The number of women on shift work is also rising. This development has been enforced by the political leaders both for economic and ideological reasons. In view of the real requirements (the desperate shortage of labour) the economic argument has taken precedence. The main ideological argument is that women can only achieve equal status with men if they are economically independent. Full employment for women is therefore represented as one of the progressive social norms.[50]

The aim of full employment for women has certainly not been achieved. A second concept has been propounded roughly over the last ten years: that the two- or three-child family is the best combination of social and personal interests. The social interest is held to be the reproduction of the population, and personal interests to lie in 'the happy family circle'. The advantages of brothers and sisters for personal development are stressed.

It is, of course, hard to co-ordinate the two.[51] Certainly they impose a heavy burden on mothers who work, as they have to bring up their children, do the housework and cope with their job, and outside the GDR the two aims are generally seen as a source of conflict which works to the disadvantage of women and quite often of children as well. Inside the GDR the problems and difficulties are often admitted, but attempts are being made at least at ideological harmonisation. The heavy demands on women are claimed to be particular opportunities which the system offers, and the chance to do shift work is a recognition of their equal status.[52]

The propagation of the large family as the social norm is in considerable contrast to the real trend in the GDR, which has been towards the one-child family or childless marriage, at least up to the mid-1970s. Indeed, agitation in favour of the large family is largely due to the decline in the birth-rate. In 1972 demographic policy was made the main focus of social policy. The immediate occasion for the first group of measures was the legalisation of abortion up to the 12th week of pregnancy. The improvement of maternity leave (among other measures, an extension from 8 to 12 weeks and an increase in the lump sum payable for each birth to 1,000 Marks), the introduction of easier working conditions for mothers in full-time jobs and with several children (introduction of the 40-hour week instead of 43¾ for women on shift work with at least two children and for others with at least three, and additional holidays) and financial aid if places in crèches are not available and the mother would otherwise have to stop work — none of these measures had the desired effect. The fertility rate (live births per 1,000 women of child-bearing age), which had in any case been dropping for years, plummeted from 69.0 to 58.0 between 1971 and 1972. The trend continued, although more slowly, until 1974

(51.9), but since then it has been rising again. In 1977 it stood at 63.1. However, what is known as the net reproduction rate is now only 90 per cent, as demographers stress, i.e. only 90 per cent of the present generation of women will be replaced by their children. The figures for the birth-rate are more favourable, because they do not reflect changing demographic conditions. Here again the low was in 1973 and 1974 (10.6 in each year), but by 1978 the 1970 rate had been regained (13.9 as compared with 9.4 in the FRG).[53]

This rise could not have been achieved through the 1972 measures alone. Following the IXth Party Congress (in 1976) very much better measures were introduced. Maternity leave was extended again, this time to 20 weeks and in exceptional cases 22; together with pregnancy leave, which remained unchanged at 6 weeks this gave women 6 months off work, and brought the GDR to the head on an international comparison. The working week is now reduced to 40 hours for all women in full-time employment who have two or more children. The most important and — from the point of view of the economy the most expensive — of the new measures is known as the 'baby year'. After their second child mothers can claim release from work with pay for one full year. They then receive a maternity allowance in lieu of wages. This corresponds to sick pay but has a minimum threshold. Women remain within the social insurance scheme during this year and afterwards can claim their old job back. They can also claim release from work with job guarantee for their first child, but in that case they lose both their social insurance and their maternity pay. Moreover all women also acquire one extra year's credit in the pension insurance scheme for every child, regardless of whether they worked during the year or not. Women who have borne and brought up five and more children acquire the right to a minimum pension even if they have never worked. Women also have the right to stay at home with pay (sick pay) if the child is ill. Mothers who cannot find a place in a crèche and therefore have to stay at home receive financial aid even for the first child. This is raised to the level of normal maternity pay if a second child is born before the end of the year.

As expected it was mainly the number of second and more children which rose (1977: 23.5 per cent), but the number of first children also showed an absolute increase (1977: 7 per cent over the previous year). The rising birth-rate is generally ascribed to the 'baby year'. The measure proved an immediate success; 90 per cent of all women entitled to do so leave work for one year after the birth of their second child (1977 figure), i.e. only 10 per cent make do with the statutory 6 months maternity leave. If the GDR leaders had in fact hoped that more women would be content with the statutory maternity leave once this was extended their hopes were dashed.[54]

The 1972 measures went to the core of the conflict between the aims of family policy. In 1976 the demographic policy measures were further improved. The concessions in the economic sphere are obvious, as are the costs. The costs for the overall programme to help women and the family rose between 1970 and 1977 from 3.5 billion Marks to 5.9 billion, i.e. by around 70 per cent.[55]

Although the literature gives the impression of planned development, family policy as it is now being pursued is clearly the result of modifications to the original concept. The problems have not really been solved; in some respects they have worsened. At a very early stage in its development the GDR took a decision in favour of the general employment of women. The 1949 constitution states the unrestricted right of every woman to work, while the Basic Law of the Federal Republic of Germany only grants women the right to work where this is reconcilable with family obligations or where these require that they should do so. The decision reflects both the Marxist conviction that women can only be liberated through economic independence and the need for labour by the economy. Marriage and the family were not rejected but changes were expected both in family relations and in the relation between the family and society. Many Communists and Socialists saw in the bourgeois family and its basis, the distribution of roles between the sexes, an institution to suppress women and reproduce bourgeois ideas. They were therefore convinced that family duties could be and should be transferred to social institutions for the benefit of women and children. A beginning was made by giving preference to the construction of crèches, kindergartens and day nurseries. The hope that this would accelerate belief in and acceptance of the new social order played a major part in this policy. But this aspect in particular met with vehement resistance from a society which by no means shared the prevailing political view on the function of the family. So the basic concept of sexual equality came under ideological pressure from two sources: it was suspect both as a means simply to sugar the pill of economic pressure and as an attack on the right of parents to bring up their own children. As the implementation of the policy rather strengthened these fears it did not prove possible over the coming decades to modify these views to any noticeable extent.

In the 1960s, however, the role of the family as an educational institution received rather more recognition. The revision came from the acknowledgement that the family exercised the strongest influence on the rising generation and that it was not possible to train children against their parents' wishes to conform to the Socialist society. As a logical consequence, therefore, the parents were to be given a greater share in the educational process, the aim of which was, in the SED interpretation, prescribed by Marxism—Leninism. As in many other areas the official view on the education of children and young people is that there are no longer any fundamental differences between family and social interests. This is to assume that Socialist family relationships have developed in the GDR and that there is a family of the Socialist type.[56] The new attitude to the role of the family also had an effect on education outside the family: child centres and homes became increasingly oriented to family structures and more attention was concentrated on co-operation with the parents in youth work.[57] The consequences of this change for an uncompromising policy of sexual equality, however, remained almost entirely at the stage of declamatory principles.

A bridge has been built between recognition of the family as an indispensable educational institution and the demand for equal treatment of women in Socialist society by interpreting employment as necessary for the development of the personality, not only of the mother herself, but of all the members of the family as well. The equality of women (a process which is not yet concluded) is defined as a characteristic element in Socialist family relations. The family legislation of 1965 officially eliminated the functional distribution of roles within the family and for the first time declared the up-bringing of children and work in the household to be the joint responsibility of both partners, but apart from appeals there have been no attempts to influence the actual practice in families. The concept of equal partnership also entails a recognition of equal claims to education and to occupational and professional advancement. The successes in the field of general schooling and occupational qualification are among the visible signs of social change in connection with the high percentage of women at work. However, in the world of work the women and girls are by no means keeping up with the men; they are not even doing work which their qualifications would entitle them to. A very much larger percentage of women than men are working below their qualification level. Even special programmes to help women have so far done little more than marginally improve the situation. Although the desire on the part of women for a distribution of functions within the family on partnership principles may well be very real, traditional behaviour patterns in both sexes mean that even in education the old clichés on the different roles of the sexes are handed on. The fact that they still have to do between 70 per cent and 80 per cent of the housework and carry other family obligations makes it very much more difficult for women to take part in political or public life or to acquire higher qualifications. The high divorce rate (2.6 per 1,000 inhabitants in 1978) and the fact that in more than 60 per cent of cases it was the wife who asked for the divorce are an expression of the many tensions which exist and in which — according to statements by women seeking a divorce — the unequal distribution of roles at home plays a part. But even if many women, faced with a choice between family and a career, put the family first, it would be wrong to conclude that the desire for a life at home with the family is widespread in the GDR. The high percentage of part-time work, although this is officially frowned on (35 per cent in 1973 — no figures have been published since), however, shows how difficult it is in many cases to maintain a full-time job. But the general shortage of labour means that it is much easier for women to find a part-time job in the GDR than in the FRG.[58]

There is still a big gap between the ideals of Socialist family life and the reality, and demographic policy has been adjusted to take better account of this. But this has been done in such a way that the traditional patterns of behaviour have been rather strengthened and given material support. There has not been pressure to new patterns of behaviour. What criticism there is of this policy in the GDR is directed to the possible jeopardising of the principle of equality as the social policy measures take effect, especially the 'baby year' and the reduction in working time. Clearly many men see these measures as a welcome opportunity to leave family duties and housework even more to their wives. This is the only feasible explanation for the statement by a distinguished woman family lawyer in the GDR that the special support given to mothers in the new social policy measures 'neither restricts nor removes the obligation laid upon both partners in the family legislation to care for their children and their household'.[59] The argument can also be seen as defensive. It is argued that it is unjustifiable to criticise the measures in this way, since their success can in any case only be expected in 'the unity of political and ideological work and in the realisation of certain social policy measures'.[60] This is a good illustration of the way in which reality, ideological claims and current policy are placed in a 'meaningful' context. But this practice means that even developments which can basically be seen as positive achievements, such as the level of schooling and occupational qualifications among younger women, are not presented in a way which corresponds with reality.

Altogether the handling of ideology is probably the crucial point both in family policy and the interpretation of family relationships. We have already indicated the ideological evaluation of shift and part-time work. Reproductive behaviour is also seen in a political and ideological context. In contrast to Western states, where with a comparable demographic development family policy has become a bone of contention between the political parties, there has been no discussion in the GDR on the legitimation of demographic policy. On the contrary, the political leaders simply declared this an indispensable instrument of the formation of a Socialist society and no doubt they had in mind the importance of the labour potential for economic development. But as the effect of these social policy measures requires decisions on the part of individuals, individuals are held to have particular obligations. One of the political and ideological tasks of the state is to convince citizens of the value of stable marital relations and educate them to the view that 'children are a necessary and desirable prerequisite for a harmonious marriage'.[61] At the same time divorce procedure is being made more difficult. Less directly, but in a way that is ideologically more compelling, it is also concluded that: 'On the other hand objectively there is the responsibility on the part of the citizens themselves, every man and every woman, to use their freedom to the full and make use of every objective possibility for developing their potential in the interests of a stable and happy community; this will have a noticeable effect on the development of its members to full Socialist personalities'.[62] The new demographic policy is seen as the end of a family policy which was specific to certain groups, for the policy which is now being pursued will generally create favourable conditions for starting a family.[63]

'Socialist Social Policy': its achievements, limits and ideology

The areas we have been able to consider here are only a small section of the programme of social policy tasks and aims in the GDR and we must ask whether they are representative enough to enable general conclusions to be drawn on the policy as a whole and its present implementation. Of course we cannot simply generalise from statements on the level of benefits. But since both housing construction and family benefits are among the priority areas in the programme, what has been done here can be taken as a sign of the general intention and of what is possible in the field as a whole. The policy on pensions is a programmatic part of the general aim of raising real incomes. In fact pensions occupy a specific place in the hierarchy of incomes in the GDR and during the last decade they have benefited from a general and considerable increase. The range of benefits and the increase in pensions are therefore a part and consequence of the increase in real incomes which has also been an aspect of social policy in the last ten years. The improvements in the fields we have examined have, however, had very different results.

Pensions from social insurance have risen roughly proportionally to incomes over the last ten years. But without the benefits of the voluntary supplementary insurance, which is only gradually beginning to raise the level of new pensions and hence also create greater differentiation between recipients of pensions, the great differential between average earnings and average pensions and the relatively low gap between minimum and average pensions are likely to remain. This general relationship, however, is not necessarily reflected in the annual increases, which are continuous in the case of incomes while pensions move upwards in jumps, as the rates are not adjusted every year. This means that old people in the GDR (19 per cent of the population), unless they enjoy the privilege of special pension schemes (the percentage who do is not known) or are still employed, live in much more modest circumstances than the working population, although they are not needy.

The average pensioner lives roughly on the same level as the lower income groups. But the two groups draw from different social funds. Some pensioners — although the percentage is very low — live in highly subsidised old people's homes and care centres. The difference between the rates they pay in these homes and the minimum pension leaves them financially much better off than many a person at work. Free public transport saves pensioners a lot of money, especially in towns. However, those who do not work are cut off from a wide range of attractive services, including popular holiday resorts (although not visits to the West!) and the comforts of modern apartments. With regard to the housing programme we can say that the correspondence between the age of the accommodation and that of its inhabitants is growing even closer than it already is. The differentiation in pensions which the voluntary supplements will bring is bound over the longer term to affect what pensioners derive from the social fund. The levelling of pensions below the level of the average income, which has been the case up to now, has justified extra-income benefits for all pensioners but these will increasingly be called in question as pensions become more differentiated. Pensions policy seems to be motivated not so much by a comparison with other Socialist states as by the pressure to compete with the Federal Republic.

In discussing the housing construction programme I pointed out that the accelerated modernisation of the existing stock and the construction of new housing had become urgently needed after years of neglect of this sphere. This programme too derives its standards of comparison rather from the non-Socialist neighbour to the west than from other Socialist states. Although the expectations of the people can be taken as a spur to action the need to improve the infrastructure in industrial growth areas is certainly a major factor. The social policy aim of improving housing is directly related to economic development. The negative side of this is that the very great regional discrepancies which already exist are unlikely to be eliminated. In this programme, as in pension policy, the political leaders would appear to be going to the limits of what is possible so that no further improvements can be expected beyond what has been achieved and planned so far, i.e. any real approach to the standards in the West will remain a matter for a distant future.

Unlike pensions and housing policy, in which the dominant aim is to improve the general standard of living, family policy has still an important political and ideological dimension. Demographic policy justifies an economic requirement in terms of politics and ideology but needs material incentives for its implementation. GDR social scientists attempt to counter criticism of their social policy measures by pointing out that there is unity between material and ideological processes. In their view this is a characteristic of Socialist social policy, but the way in which the political and ideological dimension is used to justify family policy rather speaks for the instrumental character both of ideology and of social policy.

The theoreticians avoid the test of whether their social policy measures will each contribute to bring the classes and levels of society closer together by arguing that short-term measures cannot be taken as indicators of long-term aims. But this is a questionable argument, especially if we see that various measures, such as the differentiation of pensions, are working directly contrary to this aim. Social policy has brought very considerable improvements and easing of their living conditions for the inhabitants of the GDR generally and certain groups in particular. But the original free trade union or Socialist concept of social egalitarianism, which is rejected in the GDR as 'levelling out', has not been replaced by any clear alternative. On the other hand the concept of growth-oriented social policy which plays an important part in the interpretation of GDR social policy does not explain adequately sectoral priorities and instruments. This means that social policy in the GDR does not greatly differ from that in non-Socialist states. What does mark it off is the unresolved claim that the conflict between economic and social policy can be eliminated.

Notes

1   Schmunk, G. and Collective, *Marxistisch—leninistische Sozialpolitik*, Berlin (GDR), Verlag Tribüne, 1975, pp. 19—20.
2   Honecker, E., *Bericht des ZK der Sozialistischen Einheitspartei Deutschlands an den IX. Parteitag der SED (18.—22.5.1976)*, Berlin (GDR), Dietz Verlag, 1976, pp. 32—9.
3   Programm der Sozialistischen Einheitspartei Deutschlands; cf. Schneider, E., *Die SED der 80er Jahre. Das neue Programm und Statut der Partei*, Berichte des Bundesinstituts für ostwissenschaftliche und

internationale Studien 23/77, pp. 82—4. According to GDR statements the costs of the social policy programme vary between 10 billion Marks (*Radio DDR*, July 1976) and 14.3 billion (Hermann Axen in his report at the 2nd plenary of the SED Central Committee in September 1976). Western estimates are actually around 17 billion (Winters, P.J. in *Deutschland Archiv*, 12/77, pp. 1233 ff.).
4 On the development of the economic situation in the GDR see the half-yearly reports by the Deutsches Institut für Wirtschaftsforschung, Berlin, *DIW-Wochenberichte*. In 1977 alone the prices for raw materials climbed by 10 to 15 per cent (*DIW-Wochenbericht* 6/78, p.66).
5   Ludz, P. Ch., *Mechanismen der Herrschaftssicherung*, Munich, Carl Hanser Verlag, 1980, pp. 141—2.
6   See Hockerts, H.G., *Sozialpolitische Entscheidungen im Nachkriegsdeutschland*, Stuttgart, Klett-Cotta, 1980, pp. 21 ff., especially p.25; 'Sozialpolitische Richtlinien der SED' in *Dokumente der Sozialistischen Einheitspartei Deutschlands*, vol.I, Berlin (GDR), Dietz Verlag, 1951, pp. 139—48.
7   Leenen, W.-R., *Zur Frage der Wachstumsorientierung der marxistisch—leninistischen Sozialpolitik in der DDR*, Berlin, Duncker and Humblot, 1977, sets new accents, especially pp. 62—71.
8   See Winkler, G., *Soziale Sicherheit — sozialer Fortschritt*, Berlin (GDR), Verlag Tribüne (1978), pp. 13—14; Manz, G. and Winkler, G. in Institut für Soziologie und Sozialpolitik der Akademie der Wissenschaften der DDR (ed.), *Theorie und Praxis der Sozialpolitik in der DDR*, Berlin (GDR), Akademie Verlag, 1979, pp. 20—6.
9   Representative of this position is Thude, G., *Soziale Sicherheit-Sozialpolitik in beiden deutschen Staaten*, Berlin (GDR), Verlag Tribüne, 1965.
10 The basic work is in an unpublished 'Habilitation' thesis: Ulbricht, H., *Aufgaben der sozialistischen Sozialpolitik bei der Gestaltung der sozialen Sicherheit in der DDR*, Leipzig, 1965.
11 For an attempt at a theoretical base: Winkler, G. and Collective, *Sozialpolitik-Betrieb-Gewerkschaften*, Berlin (GDR), Verlag Tribüne, 1972.
12 See Leenen, W.-R., op.cit., especially pp. 27—30 and 188—9; Ludz, P. Ch., *Die DDR zwischen Ost und West. Politische Analysen 1961—1976*, 3rd unrevised edition. Munich, Verlag C.H. Beck, 1977, pp. 22—3; Mitzscherling, P., *Zweimal deutsche Sozialpolitik*, Berlin, Duncker and Humblot, 1978, p.109.
13 Most recently, Winkler, G., 'Sozialpolitik und Lebensweise', in *Deutsche Zeitschrift für Philosophie*, Berlin (GDR), 1/80, pp. 38—46.
14 Institut für Soziologie und Sozialpolitik der Akademie der Wissenschaften der DDR (ed.), op.cit., especially pp. 12—26; see also the predecessor of this handbook: Schmunk, G. and Collective, op.cit; and Winkler, G., op.cit., pp. 38—41.

15   Institut für Soziologie und Sozialpolitik der Akademie der Wissenschaften der DDR (ed.), op.cit., p.134.
16   Op.cit., p.144.
17   Op.cit., pp. 26–35.
18   Op.cit., pp. 33–35.
19   Op.cit., pp. 28–30.
20   Zimmermann, H., 'Sozialpolitik als Gesellschaftspolitik?' in *DDR-Report*, Bonn, Verlag Neue Gesellschaft, 12/76, pp. 749–53; id. 'Die DDR in den 70er Jahren', in Erbe, G., et al., *Politik, Wirtschaft und Gesellschaft in der DDR*, Opladen, Westdeutscher Verlag, 1979, pp. 13–82, especially pp. 52–7 (revised version of an article which first appeared in English: 'The GDR in the 1970s' in *Problems of Communism*, March–April 1978, pp. 1–40); see also Himmelmann, G., 'Sozialpolitik in sozialistischen Systemen?' in *Politische Bildung*, Stuttgart, Ernst Klett Verlag, 2/78 pp. 57–69, especially pp. 65–8.
21   Ludz, P. Ch., op.cit., p.137.
22   See the titles in Note 20, especially Zimmermann, H. in Erbe G., et al., op.cit., p.53.
23   Leenen, W.-R., op.cit., p.194; Rühl, H. and Weisse, H., *Sozialpolitische Massnahmen – konkret für jeden*, Berlin (GDR), Staatsverlag der DDR, 1978, p.98.
The account of pensions is based on: Leenen, W.-R. op.cit., pp. 116–44, pp. 182–88, tables p.191 ff.; Mitzscherling, P., op.cit.; Institut für Soziologie und Sozialpolitik der Akademie der Wissenschaften der DDR (ed.), op.cit., pp. 346–74; Renneberg, G. and Türschmann, G., *Die Sachleistungen und die Geldleistungen der Sozialversicherung der Arbeiter und Angestellten,* 2nd revised edition, Berlin (GDR), Verlag Tribüne, 1979.
24   Rühl, H. and Weiss, H., op.cit., p.63.
25   Leenen, W.-R., op.cit., p.182.
26   *Statistisches Jahrbuch der DDR*, Berlin (GDR), Staatsverlag 1979, pp. 106, 340 and 341.
27   Mitzscherling, P., op.cit., p.98.
28   Institut fur Soziologie und Sozialpolitik der Akademie der Wissenschaften der DDR (ed.), op.cit., p.363; and Haase, H.E., 'Wachsende finanzielle Belastungen der DDR-Wirtschaft und ihr Ausweis im Staatshaushalt', in *Deutschland Archiv*, Cologne, Verlag Wissenschaft und Politik, 8/79, pp. 818–38, p.833.
29   Faude, M., 'Strukturelemente sozialistischen Sozialrechts am Beispiel des Altersrentenrechts der DDR und der UdSSR' in *Jahrbuch für Ostrecht*, 1/79, pp. 106–44, p.115.
30   For example, Hockerts, H.-G., op.cit., pp. 79–80 for the British.
31   Minimum pensions were last increased on 1 December 1979 (*Gesetzblatt der DDR*, Part 1, p.331). Since then they have varied according to the number of years worked between 270 and 340 Marks.

32   Leenen, W.-R., op.cit., pp. 182—3; see also *Statistisches Jahrbuch der DDR 1979*, op.cit., p.106; Institut fur Soziologie und Sozialpolitik der Akademie der Wissenschaften der DDR (ed.), op.cit., p.242; on 1 December 1979 (for a single person) social assistance was 230 Marks, minimum pension for less than 15 years insured 270 Marks, minimum pension for 15 or more years insured 280—340 Marks.
33   On the relation between the principle of insurance and that of state security see Beyme, K. von, *Sozialismus oder Wohlfahrtsstaat?*, Munich, Piper, 1977, pp. 72—7.
34   Teich Adams, C., 'Interests, Parties and the Public Role in Housing', in Heidenheimer, A., Heclo, H. and Teich Adams, C., *Comparative Public Policy*, New York, Macmillan, 1975, pp. 69—96, especially pp. 70—4.
35   Winkler, G., 'Sozialpolitik zum Wohle des Volkes', in *Einheit*, Berlin (GDR), Dietz Verlag 7/8—80, pp. 854—6.
36   Ibid.
37   Ibid.
38   Melzer, M., 'Qualitative Aspekte der regionalen Wohnungsversorgung in der DDR', in *Die DDR im Entspannungsprozess. Lebensweise im realen Sozialismus*, Cologne, Verlag Wissenschaft und Politik, 1980, pp. 148—62, 150.
39   Melzer, M., 'Regionale Unterschiede der Wohnungsqualität in der DDR' in *DIW-Wochenbericht*, Berlin. Duncker and Humblot, 32-33/79, 16 August 1979, pp. 343—50; cf. Schmiechen, K., 'Wachsende Ansprüche an den Wohnungsbau', in *Die Wirtschaft*, Berlin (GDR), 4, April 1980, pp. 6—7.
40   Melzer, M., op.cit. (Note 39), p.347.
41   Institut für Soziologie und Sozialpolitik der Akademie der Wissenschaften der DDR (ed.), op.cit. p.308.
42   Melzer, M., op.cit. (Note 39), p.347.
43   Melzer, M., op.cit. (Note 38), p.162; cf. articles in *Architektur der DDR*, 8/79, pp. 466—73; 7/79, p.386.
44   Melzer, M., op.cit. (Note 38), pp. 159—60; cf. Melzer, M., op.cit. (Note 39), p.348.
45   *Statistisches Jahrbuch*, op.cit., p.144; *Architektur der DDR* 2/80, pp. 68—73.
46   Cf. the articles in *Architektur der DDR* in Note 43; also *Architektur der DDR* 3/80, pp. 132—6.
47   Langhof, M., 'Zum Bedeutungswandel der Wohnungspolitik in der DDR' in *Deutschland Archiv*, Cologne, Verlag Wissenschaft und Politik, 4/79, pp. 390—405, especially pp. 396—9.
48   Langhof, M., 'Sozialistische Lebensweise — ideologischer Kampfbegriff oder sozialökonomische Planungskategorie?' in *Die DDR im Entspannungsprozess*, op.cit., pp. 18—28.

49 Staemmler, G., 'Wohnungswünsche von DDR-Bürgern', in *Die DDR im Entspannungsprozess*, op.cit., pp. 163—72.
50 Grandtke, A., 'Zur Entwicklung von Ehe und Familie', in *Zur gesellschaftlichen Stellung der Frau in der DDR*. Ed. Wissenschaftlicher Beirat 'Die Frau in der sozialistischen Gesellschaft', Akademie der Wissenschaften der DDR under the direction of Prof. H. Kuhrig and Dr sc. W. Speigner. Leipzig, Verlag für die Frau, 1978, pp. 229—53; cf. Walther, R., 'Familienbeziehungen und Erziehung der Kinder', in *Einheit* 11/79, pp. 1157—65; for a critical view: Helwig, G., 'Zum Stellenwert der Familienerziehung in der DDR', in *Deutschland Archiv*, 12/79, pp. 1311—5.
51 Helwig, G., 'Frauenförderung und Familienpolitik in der DDR unter besonderer Berücksichtigung der Bevölkerungs- und arbeitsmarktpolitischen Ziele', in *Deutschland Archiv*, Sonderheft 1975, pp. 46—57; Schultze, H., 'Wesentliche Einflüsse auf das reproduktive Verhalten der Menschen und ihre Bedeutung für die demografische Entwicklung', in *Wirtschaftswissenschaft*, 1978, pp. 546—64. This is representative of the discussion in the GDR.
52 Dunskus, P., et al., 'Zur Verwirklichung des Rechtes auf Arbeit für Frauen', in *Zur gesellschaftlichen Stellung der Frau in der DDR*, op.cit., pp. 86—144, pp. 130—31.
53 A good account with cost calculations is in Vortmann, H., 'Geburtenzunahme in der DDR — Folge des "Babyjahrs', in *Vierteljahreshefte zur Wirtschaftsforschung*, 3/78, pp. 210—32; id. 'Anhaltend hohe Geburtsraten in der DDR', in *DIW-Wochenbericht* 30/79, pp. 315—21; see also *Statistisches Jahrbuch der DDR 1979*, op.cit., p.366.
54 Vortmann, H., op.cit., p.318 (table); see also Dunskus, et al., op. cit., p.107.
55 Vortmann, H., op.cit., 1978, p.219.
56 Grandtke, A., op.cit., pp. 231—3.
57 Cf. Bauer, R. and Bösenberg, C., *Heimerziehung in der DDR*. Frankfurt/New York, Campus Verlag, 1979, pp. 48—52; Busch, F.W., *Familienerziehung in der sozialistischen Pädagogik der DDR*, Ullstein Materialien. Frankfurt am Main, Ullstein Verlag, 1980 (1st edition 1972).
58 Kuhrig, H. and Speigner, W., 'Gleichberechtigung der Frau — Aufgaben und ihre Realisierung in der DDR', in *Zur gesellschaftlichen Stellung der Frau in der DDR*, op.cit., pp. 65—73; Dunskus, P. et al., op.cit., pp. 113—26.
59 Grandtke, A., op.cit., p.249.
60 Institut für Soziologie und Sozialpolitik der Akademie der Wissenschaften der DDR (ed.), op.cit., p.426.

61 Schultze, H., op.cit., p.562.
62 Grandtke, A., op.cit., p.251.
63 Ibid., p.248.

8 Relations between the two German states
Gerhard Wettig, Federal Institute for East European and International Studies, Cologne

The basic situation

The division of Germany into two states incorporated into two hostile systems and power blocks is a new phenomenon in more than a thousand years of German history. It can be seen, moreover, as the arbitrary result of external circumstances — largely the fact that the armies of the Western powers and the Soviet Union occupied certain areas in 1945. The dividing line does not follow any indigenous, cultural or religious borders within Germany, for all the country's multitude of contrasts. No act of will by the people brought the division about or confirmed it — on the contrary until well into the 1950s there was even official agreement in both parts of Germany that the separation should be ended as soon as possible.

The two German states emerged as fragments in 1949, each requiring completion through the addition of the other. Neither, as it existed, could be fitted into the traditional scheme of European nation states. As only a part of the German nation, each lacked the usual national identity and legitimation. The Federal Republic of Germany and the German Democratic Republic were oriented to a concept of Germany as a whole, the political and state organisation of which had been destroyed and should be reinstated.

But as the division of Germany became established and as it actually came to form the basis of peace in Europe, the two German states increasingly felt the burden of the 'temporary arrangement'. Neither, as long as it was oriented to a national goal outside itself, and a goal which was rapidly becoming less and less attainable, could offer a national identity to its people. Theoretically, every German could, as a German, feel equally bound to the other state or at least regard his own as an unsatisfactory and merely provisional affair. On what loyalty could the leaders count, especially in the by no means improbable case that the latent conflict might break out openly? Would, indeed should, Germans shoot at Germans?

Taken logically, the concept of one Germany meant that the people could relativise their obligation to their own state. In the last resort it would be conceivable for them to turn against their leaders in order to achieve unity with the other state. In each the leaders could on principle meet this challenge either by themselves taking the offensive in demanding reunification or by seeking to establish an identity and legitimation base other than that of the German nation. The first could conflict with the world political situation, while the second would constitute a psychological anomaly in a Europe still dominated by the concept of the nation state. In such a dilemma half-hearted, contradictory and evasive statements were the most likely reaction.

The — at least rhetorical — intensity of the early years of the East—West conflict which broke out openly in 1947—48 has long evaporated. Despite the continuance of political hostilities the two world powers are clearly making every effort to avoid direct military conflict and ensure that their allies do not undertake any potentially dangerous steps. Her European neighbours see in the division of Germany — still generally regarded as too strong — a guarantee of balance and stability. For the two alliances in the East and in the West the two German states are of crucial value. They are a decisive element in securing political cohesion and creating the advanced position which each side regards as necessary. The Federal Republic is the military factor which makes the continental defence system possible. Its presence in the GDR enables the Soviet Union to exercise particularly effective control of political developments in Eastern Central Europe, offering as it does the possibility of a two-pronged military attack.[1] For all these reasons it has since the 1950s and 1960s been less and less possible for either German state to query the status quo — even symbolically.

The phase of non-relations between the two German states

The political division of Germany is the result of the Cold War which broke out openly in mid-1947. As Europe split apart the division became formalised along the borders reached by the hostile occupying powers in Germany. By the following autumn the political confrontation between East and West was fully apparent on German soil. In 1948 the East put an end to co-operation in the bodies responsible for the whole of Germany — the Allied Control Council, the Berlin Military Command and the Berlin civic administration.

In the German capital the Soviet Union attempted to blockade the Western sectors and exercise pressure on the non-Communist deputies to gain control of the city. If this had succeeded, and especially if the simultaneous campaign for national unity in Germany had had greater political effect in the Western zones, the Moscow-controlled SED (Sozialistische Einheitspartei Deutschlands — Socialist Unity Party of Germany, the ruling party in East Germany) would have gained considerable influence throughout the country; at the very least the formation of a West German state would have been greatly delayed or hindered.

But the strong resistance put up by the Germans to the Soviet occupying forces and their Communist supporters foiled these efforts. In September 1949 the Federal Republic of Germany was founded. The German Democratic Republic, proclaimed a month later, could only claim power over the territory under Soviet domination.

The Basic Law of the Federal Republic of Germany was formulated by elected representatives of the people — even if not entirely without Allied influence. The parliament and government were chosen in free elections. The constitution and organs of the state of the GDR on the other hand had no such legitimation. Hence the Federal Republic claimed to be the only German state which was the result of the will of the people; she therefore had the right to speak and act for those Germans who had been denied the right of self-determination.

According to this argument the Federal Republic of Germany was only a provisional arrangement and should acquire her proper form as the state representing the whole of Germany as soon as political circumstances permitted. From this it followed that only the Federal Republic could represent the national interests of the Germans abroad. When the two German states acquired sovereign rights in foreign policy in the 1950s the Federal Republic insisted that other countries were to recognise her as the only legal German state: they should maintain diplomatic relations with her and not with the GDR.[2]

The GDR also declared that she was the only German state which had the right to exist, arguing that the Federal Republic had been imposed on the German people in the Western zones against their will by the 'American Imperialists and their abettors'. The legitimacy of the GDR was derived from two 'People's Congresses' organised and controlled by the SED leaders. Some West German sympathisers also took part in these congresses, the second of which passed the formal resolutions accepting the constitution and government of the GDR, whose leaders accordingly proclaimed that the entire German people had constituted this as their national state. The GDR was held to be the national home of all the Germans, the only step necessary for her completion being the extension of her sovereignty to West German territory.[3]

So each claimed that they were in fact the only German state. But their proper status could only be established by the absorption of one into the other. In the Federal Republic the desire for national representation took on legal form. Various aspects of international law were cited to justify the claim and the demand for reunification. Politically emphasis was laid on the argument that in accordance with the people's right to self-determination national unity must be based on free elections. This hit the GDR on a vulnerable spot as her people had been given no opportunity to express their will and were in fact very largely in opposition to the SED regime.

The SED leaders relied mainly on ideological arguments. They maintained that the GDR was 'the state of the workers and peasants', while only the 'upper bourgeoisie' had had a say in the creation of the Federal Republic. In their eyes the two German states represented, in social terms, the people and their enemies. From this it followed that the West German workers, as soon as they could really express their will, would naturally opt for the GDR. At the same time, however, the SED leaders made every effort to prevent any such expression of will: their suggestions for reunification were that the power relations governing the whole of Germany should be established first. Only after that could the other questions, including the possibility of elections, be considered.[4]

As the standpoints were irreconcilable and the major powers in any case jealously guarded their positions in Germany, these pronouncements on national unity were in practice largely polemical. Each side accused the other of sabotaging its efforts to re-establish unity in Germany. This led to the claim that the other state had caused the division. The Federal Republic clung to the view that the Soviet Union had destroyed co-operation between the Four Powers in Germany after 1945, rendering the consensus of the German people impossible by the separation of the Soviet zone.

The GDR on the other hand officially justified her existence by maintaining that she was the German state established by the anti-Hitler powers in 1945. The USSR had fulfilled the Potsdam agreement 'to the letter', while the Western powers had disregarded it. In this interpretation the GDR was the German state which had been designed and decided upon at the Three Power Conference in Potsdam and the Western powers had arbitrarily and unilaterally split West Germany off.

This was mainly to convince the East Germans, who did largely hold their state to blame for the division of Germany, that they should identify themselves with the GDR as the force for German unity.

In fact, efforts for unity largely amounted to an attempt on the part of each of the states to overpower the other. The representatives of the GDR hoped that they would achieve their ends after the Americans moved out of Europe. The West Germans, on the other hand, placed their trust in the political and economic attractiveness of their system, believing that the internal difficulties in the GDR (the dissatisfaction of the people, the numbers moving to the Federal Republic, the inefficiency of the economic system) would undermine the state or at least render it a growing burden to the Soviet Union. Then, many thought, the moment would come in which negotiations with the Soviets on the release of the territory might prove possible. These expectations led the West Germans — in contrast to the SED — to adopt a rather passive and defensive role in practice, although the fact that little more than verbal support for the demand for national unity was forthcoming from the Western powers will certainly have played a part.

However, West German hopes that national unity would be easier to achieve as time went on proved vain. The interest displayed by the Soviet Union at the end of the 1940s and in the early 1950s in re-establishing one German state was only short-lived and could not later serve as a point of departure for efforts to achieve a mutually acceptable arrangement. The Soviet interest in reunification was based on the assumption that the USSR had achieved a sufficiently strong position in the GDR and among the mass of the population in the West to be sure of acquiring overall influence in a reunited Germany. But the conditions named by Moscow suggest that it was improbable that any agreement could have been reached in 1952 between East and West,[5] apart from the pressure to compromise resulting from the imminent rearmament of Western Germany.

There is little evidence that a compromise might have been possible in 1953.[6] Also, the relaxation of political pressure inside the GDR released the hostility to the regime, which had hitherto been suppressed. The rioting on 17 June 1953 revealed to the Soviet leaders how weak their position was. Since then any political development which might lead to rapprochement or reunification of the two parts of Germany has been regarded by the Soviet leaders as dangerous and quickly suppressed. The Soviet leaders switched to a two-state policy in Germany and followed this in 1954 by the development of a two-state theory in international law.

But even before June 1953 it was recognised by the Russians that attempts to gain political influence in Germany by promising reunification were not without risk. The hermetic sealing of the borders to West Germany and Berlin in May 1952 was a clear indication of this. The shock of 1953 showed the extent of rejection of the Soviet Communist system and the extent to which the controls which were supposed to guarantee the political conformity of the East Germans had failed.

During the rest of the 1950s the leaders in the USSR and the GDR were repeatedly confronted with the problem that the possibility of flight to West Berlin and thence into the Federal Republic offered the East Germans a constant and real alternative to adjustment to the Communist regime which had been forced upon them. The collectivisation of the farms in 1959/60 marked the beginning of a crisis. Emigration reached such proportions that economic planning became virtually impossible; the state itself would have been in danger had the exodus continued. The leaders in Moscow and Berlin decided to seal the borders to the Western sectors in Berlin as from 13 August 1961 by building a wall.[7]

This changed the situation in Germany totally. Deprived of the possibility of fleeing to the West the inhabitants of the GDR had to come to terms with their regime as best they might. West German hopes that the GDR would one day find itself close to collapse and the Soviet leaders be persuaded to open negotiations on releasing their zone were dashed. The international political situation also changed. As early as the mid-fifties Soviet campaigns for détente (which were always followed by further confrontation at the vulnerable focal point, Berlin) had made the Western countries less inclined to display solidarity with the hard line against Moscow. The Federal Republic found that her allies were less and less willing to see the satisfaction of the West German claim to reunification as a precondition of any attempt at reconciliation between East and West.[8] When President Kennedy came to power in 1961 it was made clear that the USA was no longer prepared to let consideration for West German sensitivity prevent her from seeking ways of easing confrontation with the Soviet Union. It was taken for granted in Washington that a prerequisite for this was acceptance, if not actually acknowledgement, of the status quo.

At the time no West German politician saw this so clearly as Egon Bahr. He realised that the West Germans could no longer pursue the national issue through confrontation with the GDR. As there would be no possibility of overcoming East Germany national unity could only be achieved by co-operation. A policy of this nature seemed all the more essential as the virtual prohibition on any human or social contact between the two parts of the country threatened over the longer term to erode all the ties across the dividing line which had so far kept the Germans' sense of unity alive. The aim in the East was clearly to enforce such a physical division of the two parts of Germany that the people would gradually grow away from each other, albeit against their will, and ultimately lose any common basis for communication. To prevent this Bahr strove to reach agreement between the two states on personal contacts, opening up prospects of 'change through rapprochement'.[9] This was the conceptual basis of the policy pursued by the SPD/FDP government in Bonn after 1969/70.

The GDR government was concerned to compensate as far as possible for the catastrophic effect of sealing the frontier. After 1963 the leaders therefore repeatedly acceded to proposals from Willy Brandt (then Mayor of West Berlin) to allow passes to West Berliners, who were totally cut off from their surroundings, to visit relatives and friends in the Eastern part of the city.[10] At the same time the GDR stepped up her national propaganda. A 'National Document' was promulgated in East Berlin, presenting the GDR as the defender of the concept of national unity against the 'West German separatists'.[11]

Proclamations of national unity involved the GDR in no risk as long as the West Germans continued to take a hesitant and rather passive line. The situation changed when the SPD leaders in 1966 unexpectedly took up a routine proposal from the SED leaders for a dialogue between the two parties. The East at first went some way towards accepting the counter proposal, but as it became clear that events could not be steered in the way they desired the initial agreement was withdrawn. Apprehension lest an initiative in the 'bourgeois' sense should develop over the German question appears to have been the motive. Many of the SED top functionaries were not prepared to make any contact with the 'class enemy in the West' and Soviet anxiety to prevent any uncontrolled initiative on the German issue will have been a further motivating force.[12]

The breakdown of the SED–SPD dialogue ushered in a new phase in relations between the two German states. The SPD recognised that it was heading in the right direction with its active policy. When it formed a new government in December 1966 together with the CDU/CSU, the SPD began to take the GDR leaders up on their professions to unity much more frequently and more insistently. West German efforts were directed to increasing the possibilities for human contact between the two states and preserving what common ground and ties remained.

The GDR leaders reacted by stepping up their policy of seclusion and eliminating the symbols of German unity. They were helped by the fact that the SPD could not, on account of its coalition with the CDU/CSU, work towards any discussions on government level. It was therefore officially proclaimed in the GDR that the Federal Republic of Germany was using subversive means to gain influence. Were the

Federal Republic really interested in good relations she would recognise the GDR as an equal and sovereign state and enter into negotiations with her on the normalisation of relations on this basis.[13]

But it was not only the situation in Germany which made it appear to leading members of the FDP and SPD that a change in policy towards the GDR was needed. Developments in Europe and in the world generally also indicated this. After the mid-1960s Bonn's Western allies increasingly came to regard the Federal Republic as a country which, on account of her legal reservations towards the division of Germany and the Oder-Neisse line, should be regarded as territorially unsatisfied and hence an obstacle to the relaxation on the basis of the status quo which was beginning to seem possible between East and West. There was a danger that the solidarity of the NATO countries with Bonn might be lost. The USSR attempted to exploit the situation by proclaiming that all Europeans were united in condemnation of the 'revanchist' West Germans and putting increasing physical pressure on Federal rights in West Berlin.

In the spring of 1969 the Federal Republic was challenged by both world powers to accept the concept of détente. In Washington President Nixon and his security adviser Kissinger began energetic efforts to end the Cold War with the Soviet Union, which had become linked with the American involvement in Vietnam, and attempted to reach agreement with Moscow on a wide range of questions. The Soviet leaders indicated to Bonn that they were interested in certain aspects of economic and political co-operation. After the shock to their own sphere of influence through the events in Czechoslovakia in 1968 the Soviet leaders were attempting to consolidate their position through talks and co-operation with Western governments. The proposal for a European Security Conference was held to be a major issue but there was no hope of the West agreeing to this without West German participation.

Negotiations on relations between the two German states

In October 1969 an SPD/FDP government was formed in Bonn. Brandt was the new Federal Chancellor and he stated that he would proceed upon the assumption of the existence of two German states. This was the expression of his readiness to enter into treaty arrangements between the Federal Republic and the GDR. However, the Federal government made it clear that it did not regard the GDR as foreign territory and could therefore not recognise the state under international law. Only a 'special intra-German relationship' would be possible. This concept evolved from the intention to maintain the overall concept of one German nation. The two German states were to take up relations with each other on an equal basis but at the same time they were to reaffirm their joint responsibility for safeguarding the common issues which still remained. In practice the Federal government was mainly concerned to achieve 'better human conditions in divided Germany', and improve the channels of contact and communication between the people on each side of the dividing line.

The West German offer seemed to its initiators attractive enough to bring the SED leaders to the negotiating table. The prospect of world-wide recognition, together with equal rights and partnership with the other state should, in their view, prove a temptation which the GDR, so far virtually ignored on the international stage, would find it hard to resist. But their hopes proved in vain. The functionaries in East Berlin reacted with maximal demands and a refusal to make any concessions at all. Between the GDR and the Federal Republic there must be full diplomatic relations. Any common national ground was denied. Certainly the concept of common nationality could not be used to suggest that the 'sovereign state of the German Democratic Republic' was under any obligation to accept 'better human conditions'. The reaction was designed to provoke a refusal from Bonn. Again it seemed that the primary motivating factor in East Berlin was fear of any real contact.

But the Federal Republic had other means of influencing policy. She had taken up the Soviet proposal for a Security Conference right at the start and utilised this for her own ends. She declared that she would exert her influence with her — very sceptical — NATO partners in favour of the conference if the necessary conditions were created to ensure a satisfactory result. By this the Federal Republic meant first and foremost a prior settlement of the conflict in Germany, i.e. the question of Berlin and relations with the GDR. Otherwise, the Federal Republic explained, the security conference would be overshadowed by unresolved tension and doomed to failure. Bonn also declared its readiness for negotiations on the normalisation of relations with the Soviet Union. Here the Russians were mainly concerned to achieve recognition of their territorial influence in Eastern and Central Europe; this question was of major importance to the Soviet leaders. The two points were a strong incentive to them to accede to the wishes of the West Germans, as was soon to be seen.[14]

In talks with the West German Chancellor's envoy, Bahr, in Moscow between February and May 1970 the Soviet Foreign Minister Gromyko accepted the idea of continued four-power responsibility on certain issues. This offered the Russians an important legal basis to justify intervention in the event of any national German dynamic. The West Germans, on the other hand, were anxious to establish four-power responsibility as this presupposed the existence of one legal territory. This also meant however, that the GDR and the Federal Republic of Germany were subject to four-power agreement regarding their mutual negotiations. The West Germans interpreted this as meaning that the GDR would have to accept responsibilities resulting from the existence of the four-power territory of Germany and the four-power city of Berlin. The result of the negotiations was the Moscow Agreement of 12 August 1970 which laid down the 'inviolability of frontiers'.

The first steps initiated by the USSR in East Berlin over relations between the two German states during the winter and spring of 1969/70 were followed by a long period of stagnation. The East German rejection of the West German initiative could only be overcome by a third party. The breakthrough came in the four-power negotiations on Berlin. The Soviet Union had been confronted by the West German government with the indication that it could only obtain a parliamentary majority for the Moscow Agreement if a satisfactory arrangement would be made over Berlin. The Western powers added that they would only participate in the Security Conference, which the Federal Republic supported, if the Soviet Union showed goodwill over the Berlin issue. That was the test of Soviet desire for détente and only that would render the conference meaningful.

Under these circumstances the Soviet Union in 1971 declared herself ready to ease the situation with regard to transit traffic from West Berlin to the Federal Republic by ensuring that the GDR entered into an obligation to deal with this quickly and give vehicles a clear passage. In the autumn of 1971 representatives of the two German states worked out the practical details on the basis of this assurance.[15] The Quadripartite Agreement opened the way to further negotiations on Germany. The Soviet leaders urged the GDR government not to reject the Bonn proposals for negotiations on the basis for inter-German relations. After the Moscow Agreement and the Quadripartite Agreement came into force in May and June 1972 the governments of the two German states began initial discussions. Two months later the stage of official negotiations was reached.

The two standpoints were as far away from each other as ever. The Federal Republic held to her concept of a special intra-German relationship. But the GDR insisted that the other German state was 'Imperialist foreign territory' with which she had nothing either socially or nationally in common. The GDR was the 'Socialist nation', and could have nothing to do with the 'capitalist nation' in the West. The East German regime expressed particular anger at the fact that Bonn regarded the German question as 'open'. History had decided this matter once and for all. The people of the GDR had made an irrevocable choice and created their own national state.

So the representatives of the GDR demanded that their West German negotiation partners should formally confirm the political and national division of the former Germany in a treaty. Only on this basis could there be any normal relations between the two states. A practical consequence of this demand was that the Federal Republic should change her citizenship laws. Up to 1967 both parts of Germany recognised only one German citizenship. After that date the GDR established her own. Now the Federal Republic was to be required to establish independent citizenship as well.

But that would have meant that inhabitants of the GDR could no longer be treated by the West German authorities as citizens of the Federal Republic if they wished. Moreover, the special relationship between West Berlin and the West German state would have been called in question. As confirmed in the Quadripartite Agreement, the Western sectors in Berlin are not a constituent part of the Federal Republic of Germany, they are 'tied' to it in many ways. This means that the inhabitants of the Western sectors of Berlin have largely the same status as West Germans but they cannot claim citizenship of the Federal Republic. If Bonn had abandoned the concept of one German citizenship, an independent citizenship would also have been needed for West Berliners, and this would have been to concede that the city had a separate status, similar to that of an independent foreign state. It would have been tantamount to acceptance of the East German demand for full separation between West Berlin and the Federal Republic of Germany.

The West German negotiators pointed out that the GDR would have to acknowledge the four-power status of Germany and draw the logical conclusion from this that a special intra-German relationship should be established. If the Western powers and the Soviet Union still exercised joint powers throughout Germany, an agreement which would seal the division and at the same time be of the nature of a peace treaty was legally impossible. On the contrary, the two sides should emphasise that they were acting in awareness of the continued unity of Germany. In the West German view this laid upon both states the obligation in practice to further contact and communication between the people on each side of the dividing line and to reach agreement on the appropriate steps as part of the treaty.

The GDR representatives, on the other hand, demanded that the West German negotiators should leave these questions aside as it would not be possible to reach agreement on them. Attention should concentrate rather on those points where agreement could be reached. This amounted to a suggestion that only those questions which the GDR desired should be discussed. The West German delegation rightly objected that the treaty would not be in conformity with the Basic

Law if it held no reference to the continuance of a German nation. It would not be politically acceptable in the Federal Republic and doomed to failure right from the start. The West German side also insisted that the Federal Republic must be able to point to 'an easing of the human situation' as a result of the treaty if they were to present it in parliament with any prospect of success — especially as they were in a difficult situation with a precarious majority.

The Treaty on the Basis of Relations between the Two German States, which was initialled on 8 November 1972, is a compromise. The preamble stated that the two states emerged from 'historical conditions' and left 'the different views of the Federal Republic of Germany and the German Democratic Republic on basic questions, including the national question' out of consideration. The specific reference to the 'national question' (in the singular) was for the West Germans a sufficiently clear indication that the German problem continued to exist.

The text of the treaty itself stated that the two sides had not reached agreement on the question of citizenship. In practice the GDR had accepted the continuance of West German citizenship law. It was difficult to find a formula to bridge the differences of opinion on whether relations between the two states were 'intra-German' or foreign. The West Germans succeeded in preventing the usual exchange of ambassadors between the two states. Instead 'Permanent Representatives' were to be appointed. To the West Germans this certainly expressed the special nature of the relationship. The East German side took cognizance of this but did not adopt the view.

So the treaty is a *modus vivendi*. This is typical of East—West détente agreements: the two sides cannot solve the principal conflicts and leave each other scope for different interpretations of jointly agreed formulations. The conflict, which still exists, is softened by 'practical regulations', i.e. jointly agreed procedures for potential conflict situations. In carrying out these procedures each side can maintain its own views and interpretations.

The question of human concessions was regulated in agreements which form part of the treaty. The GDR after long opposition finally agreed to improve conditions for travel. West Germans could in general visit their friends and relatives in the GDR. For the people in the borderline territories in the Federal Republic there was some easing of the border traffic. The GDR also reaffirmed that as hitherto persons past retirement age could visit the Federal Republic. All other inhabitants of the GDR would only be permitted to leave the country in exceptional cases (on 'urgent family business', such as the death or marriage of brothers and sisters, children and parents). This was because the authorities still feared an exodus to the West. The treaty also provided for improved telephone connections between the two German states, which had been severely restricted since the beginning of the 1950s. The many and in some cases repressive postal conditions and prohibitions imposed by the GDR for cross-border mail were eased. Finally the two German states agreed to exchange accredited journalists and permit them the free exercise of their profession.[16]

The GDR's policy of seclusion from the West

Together with the regulations on visits by West Berliners to the East laid down in the Quadripartite Agreement[17] the treaty agreements of the autumn of 1972 laid upon the GDR obligations which clearly weakened the seclusion policy she had so far pursued against the West. Certainly there was no longer any real ground to fear a large-scale exodus of people of working age to the West but the SED leaders apparently also feared that their own citizens would be ideologically and politically affected by the millions of West Germans who would now pour into the country. How strong this fear was can be seen from the fact that the SED Politbureau, when initialling the treaty, launched an appeal to its citizens to avoid any contact with the 'class enemies' who would now enter the country, and designed a programme to make the appeal more convincing. This had little effect, so the SED leaders had recourse to force.

As far as possible internal counter-measures were introduced to reduce the scope for contact created by the treaty. Young men before, during and after their military service were declared 'carriers of secret information' and forbidden contact with visitors from 'Imperialist foreign countries'. People who worked in the party and state apparatus (the latter included the local authorities and cultural institutions) were placed in the same category. Workers in large plants had in many cases to pass 'voluntary resolutions' that they would avoid contact with Western visitors, even contact by letter or telephone. Checks and controls were introduced to ensure that the prohibitions were maintained and the resolutions kept. There was, for instance, an obligation to keep a 'visitors' book' for 'foreign' visitors. However, as time went on it became apparent that on the lower level the prohibitions were not being enforced with the same severity all over the GDR.

These measures caused internal problems. A two-tier society began to form with regard to contacts with the West, which were eagerly sought after in the GDR: some persons could maintain contact with the West but others could not. Particular difficulties arose as those groups and classes who were of the greatest importance to the regime and whom it therefore sought particularly to protect were most disadvantaged:

young people, workers, party functionaries and civil servants. The reaction among these groups was one of dissatisfaction. The regime was less concerned about old people and the sick or the remaining members of the bourgeoisie and made little effort to protect them from contact with the West. They were regarded as fringe groups who in any case could hardly be won to the Communist regime. The tolerance practised here made these groups relatively satisfied.

The discrimination problem was made worse by economic circumstances. In her foreign trade relations the GDR had long suffered from not having sufficient Western currency to meet her needs. The normalisation of relations with the Federal Republic opened up ways of acquiring further D-Marks. One was to allow presents of money to be given by West Germans to their relatives and friends in the East. All over the GDR 'Intershops' were opened in which Western visitors and inhabitants of the GDR who had been given Western currency could buy goods which were otherwise not available at all, or only available in inferior quality or at horrendous prices.

So Western currency became a second currency in the GDR. But only those who were allowed contact with the West could obtain it. As time went on the D-Mark began to acquire more and more significance: goods and services were shifted from the state distribution network into the Western currency sector and became scarcer for the general public. Private suppliers such as craftsmen and workmen increasingly began to demand payment in D-Marks. This devalued the work done by the East Germans for their own currency and relations with 'Aunt Emma' in the West became the optimal source of income.

The two-tier hierarchy in shopping facilities again discriminated against precisely those classes and groups which the regime wished to keep particularly 'pure'. Tensions in society and discontent with the regime, even penetrating far into the SED itself, were the result. The government attempted to rectify this by introducing a regulation in March 1979 that the D-Marks had to be exchanged for coupons before being spent. But this only caused general anger: those who had the currency became afraid that questions might be asked about where they got it from, while those who could not get it were still envious of the continued privileges others enjoyed and felt they had access to only a second-rate currency.

The East German seclusion policy encountered further difficulties in the media. For many years most of the inhabitants of the GDR had been able to tune into West German television and radio programmes. More than two thirds of the country made use of this possibility. Official attempts to prevent this had failed during the 1950s and 1960s and the SED leaders had eventually come to terms with the existence of Western television. In concluding the Basic Treaty they assumed that the admission of accredited West German journalists would not fundamentally alter the situation. To protect themselves against any unforeseen difficulties they passed a ruling in February 1973 providing for reprisals against undesirable reporting.

But over the course of years the presence of Western journalists had a considerable effect on the impact of the West German media in the GDR. The West German correspondents sent back much faster and fuller reports than had formerly been available to their editors at home and could provide information on events the SED leaders would have preferred to hide or problems which were officially taboo. Moreover, the inhabitants of the GDR co-operated actively with the journalists: not only dissidents but, to an even greater extent, ordinary people turned to them with their fears and worries. The resultant news items and pictures were beamed back into East German living rooms. The substantiation of information in television pictures was particularly effective. News items which the SED leaders were anxious to keep from their people formed the main topic of conversation at breakfast tables and at work. The West German media were, so to speak, a substitute for the lack of free speech in the GDR.

The SED leaders tried to stop this. Accredited Western journalists were an obvious point for pressure; they were the weak link in the news chain from the GDR to the Federal Republic and back again. The Communist functionaries were concerned to discipline not only individual correspondents but their editors in the West as well. First they tried reprisals against individual persons and media. Again and again journalists working in East Berlin have had to pay the penalty for apparent infringements which not they, but their editorial departments, have committed. In April 1979 came a comprehensive ruling forbidding any contact or news collection which was not officially sanctioned and controlled. Since then journalists have not been able to take pictures on the street or approach private individuals without express permission. In June 1979 inhabitants of the GDR who came into contact with Western journalists were threatened with severe penalties. Since then any information given to 'foreigners' can be regarded as a 'treasonable act' and carries a heavy penalty.[18]

Despite all the restrictions imposed by the GDR authorities considerable improvements have been achieved in contact and communication between the two German states. Where formerly about 2.5 million West Germans went into the GDR every year on a visit, the figure is now between 7 and 8 million. In addition to visits to relatives contact with friends and tourism are permitted. Every year from the GDR, 1.3 million old age pensioners visit the Federal Republic. But the number of persons in the GDR of working age who obtain permission to travel to the West on 'urgent family business' is pitiably small, barely 40,000.

One factor which has helped to swell the stream of visitors from the West to the East is the amnesty granted to several million persons who 'fled the Republic', i.e. moved to the West, and who under citizenship legislation passed in the GDR in 1967 were officially regarded in the East as GDR citizens. An agreement reached in the autumn of 1972 freed them of their East German citizenship and pardoned them for infringements of GDR laws, including 'flight from the Republic'. For the older generation, who account for a large percentage of visitors from the West as well, the arrangements under the Health Agreement ensuring them free medical treatment in either country upon presentation of their sickness insurance certificate is a major factor.

Finally the GDR government has repeatedly granted further concessions in negotiations with Bonn which were not provided for in the treaty. The first and a very important step in this direction came in December 1974, when the GDR government agreed to allow West Germans generally to use their cars when visiting the East. Up until then this had only been allowed in special cases. In view of the inadequate public transport facilities in the GDR this made the visitors much more mobile and enabled them to make more intensive use of their time. The GDR also lifted the restriction which had limited visitors to the area for which they had received a permit. From then on every person who was entitled to visit the GDR was free to travel anywhere in the country. However, this only benefits people with friends and relatives in the GDR because tourists are still tied to the routes where they have hotel bookings, which must be made in advance.[19]

Nevertheless considerable difficulties still remain. The GDR imposes heavy road taxes on visitors who bring their cars. This ruling was extended in 1977 to the visits by West Berliners to the Eastern part of the city, which had until then been exempt. The complicated visa formalities and the price charged for a visa (paid for West Berliners by the state) still make traffic across the frontier difficult and expensive. In addition the GDR insists that every person who visits the GDR or East Berlin should exchange a certain sum of money into East Marks at the frontier for every day the visit is to last. For those who are going to stay with friends or relatives and are bringing them presents of goods or money this is often a quite useless expenditure. Pensioners have so far been exempt from this ruling. In November 1973 the GDR government, acting against an agreement made in December 1971, imposed double, and in some cases, four times this sum in compulsory exchange on West Berliners and extended the ruling to pensioners.[20] It took a year of patient negotiation before the West German government succeeded in inducing the GDR to revoke part of the compulsory exchange rate increase and re-establish the exemption for old-age pensioners. The concessions had to be paid for by a number of long-term financial benefits to the GDR.

The East German representatives managed to prevent the deal from being publicised. However, when in the autumn of 1980 the destabilising events in Poland took place, causing renewed fear in the GDR, the leaders appear to have felt that another increase could be imposed without making them appear to be breaking an inter-state agreement. In the October of that year the East German government increased the compulsory exchange rate from 13 or 6.50 D-Marks per day to 25 D-Marks, at the same time cancelling the exemption for old-age pensioners and children under 16. The measure hit particularly those Germans from the West who came to see friends and relatives in the GDR. They have few expenses, since they do not need hotels or restaurants, while their hosts expect presents in the form of goods which are not available in East Germany or money to spend in the 'Intershops'. The compulsory purchase of East German Marks is for them a needless expense. They therefore see the compulsory exchange rate as an 'entrance fee' imposed by the East German authorities. Many find the measure so stringent that they have virtually given up visiting the GDR. The number of visitors from the West has dropped to less than 50 per cent.

Since 1972/73 the material concerns of the GDR have in fact been very apparent whenever the two states have been involved in trying to cope with difficulties which have arisen or achieving further 'human concessions'. The Federal Republic grants East Germany a large number of economic and financial advantages. Some of these derive from the fact that trade between the two states is regarded by West Germany as 'intra-German' trade — a special status the GDR is prepared to accept in this field but not in politics or on state questions. The fact that trade between the two states is treated on an internal and not external basis brings great advantages to the GDR. The Federal Republic does not impose customs or excise duties on imports from East Germany and refrains on principle from imposing quantitative or qualitative import restrictions. It also grants the GDR an interest-free credit line.[21]

The readiness of the West German government to extend this to DM 825 million in November and December 1974 was a major incentive to the GDR government to reduce somewhat the compulsory currency exchange imposed in 1973 and grant some relaxation of the entry conditions. Concessions by the GDR to the Federal Republic in the sphere of human relations are regularly bought by the West with economic or financial concessions. Even when Bonn is concerned to eliminate difficulties which have arisen over transit traffic to West Berlin material generosity to the East plays a crucial role in settling the issues. It can be said that relations between the two German states have become largely economic: political conflicts of a minor kind emerge now and then and are often subsequently settled with economic means.

This has, however, not prevented the GDR leaders from raising the compulsory currency exchange rates to proportions so far unheard of in October 1980.

In much the same way, the Federal Republic has not succeeded in persuading the East German authorities to lower the age threshold for visits to the West. At first this seems hard to understand. If East Germans were allowed to visit the Federal Republic five years before they retired they would hardly be able to build up a new career and hence be encouraged to flee from the East. But the GDR sees this differently: if some of the working population were able to visit the West, thus enjoying privileges which were denied to the rest, there might again be the risk of a two-tier society, and that is exactly what they want to avoid.

Co-operation and conflict between the two German states

On the basis of the Quadripartite Agreement the existence of West Berlin has stabilised. Nevertheless, conflicts have remained. The clauses in the Agreement in which the three Western powers confirm the ties between the city of Berlin and the Federal Republic have been the cause of fundamental dissent. With the approval of Moscow the GDR will only accept that 'connections' (Verbindungen) exist: any form of special relationship between West Berlin and West Germany is denied. With the support of the Soviets the GDR claims that there are specific ties between Berlin and the East German and other East European states. Bonn, however, maintains that there are special ties between West Berlin and the Federal Republic. The question assumes practical significance whenever the West German side represents West Berlin interests, through its diplomatic representations or in concluding treaties. As the Basic Treaty only contains a regulation stating that this 'can' happen the GDR government has a certain scope for action which it utilises in its dealings with Bonn within the relatively narrow limits imposed by Moscow. But in questions where her principal interests are not affected the GDR has been guided to a greater extent than the Soviets ever have by economic considerations. As the West German side has considerable economic and material advantages to offer the GDR government has generally been prepared to accede to the inclusion of West Berlin when requested by the Federal Republic of Germany on specific occasions as a particular concession.

Transit traffic between West Germany and West Berlin is also subject to detailed procedural regulations laid down in the Quadripartite Agreement and the ensuing intra-German agreements despite the fundamental dissent over the basic issue. The East German government regards the obligations laid upon it in the Quadripartite Agreement not as resulting from the inter-Allied agreements of 1944/45 and then specified in detail in 1971 but as a voluntary concession. Accordingly it argues that it has the right to modify these obligations in cases where its vital or security interests are affected. On some occasions temporary restrictions which appeared totally unjustified to the West have been imposed on transit traffic, the pretext being that there was risk of infection or a police search was necessary. Of politically greater importance was the prohibition on group travel through the GDR to West Berlin imposed by the border authorities in the GDR in the summers of 1976 and 1978. The reason given was that the groups might misuse the traffic routes. In the Western view this was hardly likely. In each case however, the groups were travelling to take part in events in West Berlin which the GDR regarded as undesirable and it was assumed that this was the 'misuse' of the traffic routes (although there was nothing in the relevant clause in the treaty to justify this action). Difficulties during the visit to West Berlin by President Carter and Federal Chancellor Schmidt in the summer of 1978, which was attacked by the GDR, were also counter to the agreements. However, in this case the Soviets appear to have induced the GDR to back down fairly quickly.

It would appear to be one of the basic facts in Soviet—East German relations that the GDR has to keep within the limits imposed by the Soviet Union over the Berlin question, especially as regards transit traffic. The Moscow line is clear: the Soviet Union would be responsible for any engagement which might result from a confrontation with the Western powers (especially the USA) in a conflict over Berlin. Hence the Soviets regard it as essential to control any developments which might lead in this direction.

The traditionally greater militancy of the GDR was fully unleashed for a time when the USSR in the summer of 1974 regarded reprisals as necessary over the establishment of the Federal Office for Environment Protection in West Berlin, which it opposed. Acting unilaterally and in contravention of the arrangements laid down in the treaty the GDR excluded all members of the institute from transit travel to West Berlin. Further restrictions were threatened if the Federal Republic were to establish more offices in the city. After extreme Western pressure the GDR, after practising the prohibition once, did not enforce it again. But the Soviets, acting through diplomatic channels in the Western capitals, secured a tacit assent that no further Federal institutions would be established in Berlin.

The visit to Bonn by Leonid Brezhnev at the beginning of May 1978 brought a basic clarification of Soviet—West German relations. The Federal Government agreed to exercise restraint in the use of its rights in West Berlin while the Soviets gave an assurance that further reprisals would not be taken. From then on the GDR no longer had Soviet backing for disruptive or restrictive measures affecting the transit routes.[22]

The quality of the routes linking West Berlin and the Federal Republic is of vital importance for the development of Berlin. Despite the high transit fees charged the GDR made little effort to keep the motorways and roads serving West Berlin in good condition. The surfaces deteriorated steadily, especially after the agreements on transit travel brought a considerable increase in the volume of traffic between the Federal Republic and West Berlin. The railway connections between the city and the West were also in bad condition. Goods traffic on the internal waterways was hampered by technical deficiencies in harbour and other facilities. Eventually the West German government decided to take action to try to improve matters.

After lengthy preliminaries the East German government finally agreed on 9 December 1974 to open negotiations on the extension of the transit routes leading across its territory from the Federal Republic to West Berlin. The authorities in the East appeared to feel that it would be advantageous to have roads and other communication links across their territory, which would greatly serve their interests as well, renovated at West German expense. The two governments proceeded upon the assumption that negotiations would start at the beginning of January 1975.

However, unforeseen difficulties arose. The GDR leaders had only given the Soviets a general outline of their intentions. After the announcement of 9 December 1974 the Soviet ambassador in East Berlin objected that the matter should first have been clarified in consultations with the USSR. The Soviet objection amounted to insistence that the GDR, before taking any steps towards an agreement with the other German state, should inform Moscow of all the details. This was done during the early months of 1975. Only when the Soviets were convinced that the East German plans would not contravene their interests in any way and had been assured that the economic advantages resulting from this co-operation between the Federal Republic of Germany and the German Democratic Republic would not only benefit the GDR, was the way free for negotiations between the two German states to start.

Behind the Soviet pressure lay considerable distrust. The main concern was apparently to prevent too strong an economic orientation of the GDR to the West and gain some advantage for the USSR from economic co-operation between the two German states. The restrictions which the USSR had long been imposing on East German engagement in 'inner-German' trade were not to be evaded by any other kind of economic agreement. But beyond this there was a further consideration. For two decades Soviet policy had been designed to prevent anything which might open up prospects of development of German unity. If the two German states entered into economic co-operation this might lead to rapprochement in other spheres as well. Strict control was necessary to exclude any possibility of this.

On 19 December 1975 the negotiations between the two German states were concluded. It was agreed that the stretch of motorway between Marienborn and West Berlin, which was just on 180 km in length, should be thoroughly renovated and that two short stretches should be given a third lane in each direction. The Federal Republic agreed to pay 90 per cent of the costs of the work. Further construction work, which was of no interest to the East Germans, was paid for in full by Bonn. Altogether the West German government thus incurred costs of DM 262.23 million. It was also agreed that rail connections between the Federal Republic and West Berlin should be improved by increasing the speed at which trains could travel, opening a new crossing over the border to shorten the journey, enlarging the service and using better and more comfortable trains. For these improvements the West German government provided another DM 44.6 million.[23]

In June 1978 after previous consultations between East Berlin and Moscow representatives of the two German states again began negotiations on extending traffic facilities between the Federal Republic and West Berlin. Agreement was reached on 16 November 1978. The GDR agreed to build a branch of the Berlin—Rostock motorway in the direction of Hamburg and open this to transit traffic instead of the old main road no.5. The West Germans were to contribute DM 1.2 billion to the cost. Repairs were to be carried out to the canals used in transit traffic in the GDR and Bonn promised DM 120 million towards the cost of this. The Federal government allocated another DM 70 million for the opening and extension of the Teltow canal, which shortened the link to the south of West Berlin. At the same time the total annual sum payable to the GDR of DM 400 million, from which according to the existing agreement 12.5 per cent should have been deducted as the volume of traffic was less than had been expected, was increased to DM 525 million. The Federal government also declared itself willing to discuss payment of a further sum up to DM 500 million should agreement be reached on expanding the border crossing at Herleshausen/Wartha.[24]

As tension grew in the world after the NATO armament decision and the Soviet military intervention in Afghanistan the East Germans grew concerned that this could have a negative effect on relations between the two German states. The GDR government showed interest in concluding the agreement on the extension of the crossing at Herleshausen/Wartha and the two-lane extension to the one-way stretch of the motorway between Marienborn and Berlin as soon as possible. After some delay due to the situation in Bonn the agreement was concluded on 30 April 1980.

The East German government appeared to be interested in taking co-operation further than had been possible up to then. There was talk not only of electrifying the railway lines between the East German border and West Berlin but, even more important, energy supply proposals were put forward. In 1974/75 negotiations had taken place between the Federal Republic of Germany and the Soviet Union on the construction of a nuclear power station near Königsberg (Kaliningrad). The plant was to be built and financed by the West German side. The repayments would be in the form of electricity supplies to West Berlin and West Germany. The West Germans were interested in the creation of a link which would enable electricity to be supplied from West Germany to West Berlin at any time should the need arise. The arrangement did not materialise because both Poland and the GDR in particular, were not prepared to have the supply lines built over their territory, as they did not see any advantage to themselves from the project.

At the beginning of 1980 the GDR government gave Bonn to understand that it was prepared in principle to accept such a link. There was discussion about the construction of a lignite power station by West German firms, repayments again to be in the form of electricity supplies from East Germany to the Federal Republic and West Berlin. These considerations came to an end, at least temporarily, in the autumn of the same year, when the SED leaders decided to give priority to seclusion measures and disregard West German interests. The decision was not against the interests of the East German government, since the co-operation agreements already concluded in addition to the financial and commercial benefits enjoyed by the GDR in relations with West Germany provided sufficient material support for some time to come.

There is co-operation between the two German states in the technical as well as the economic sphere. The agreements on health and veterinary matters of 1974 and 1979 could be taken as typical of these areas, where political problems hardly arise. The communication between courts and state lawyers which has now been achieved has done much to reduce the enormous difficulties of settling the many complex personal relationships inside Germany, as have the channels for non-commercial payments transactions across the border, although these are still very limited.

A border commission has been appointed and its work has created a legal basis for territorial settlements along the border, apart from the controversial stretch along the Elbe. Co-operation has also been reached in cases of damage and on water supplies across the border and on the working of a lignite seam which stretches into both territories.[25]

In other areas, however, enormous difficulties still remain. The problems start with environment protection, where the Federal Republic is exposed to large-scale pollution of the rivers Werra and Elbe which flow from the GDR. But the main problems are in the field of contact and encounters on the social level. Sports meetings have been largely normalised but exchanges in the fields of culture, science and education are under-developed even in comparison with relations to other East European countries.

The East German policy of societal seclusion finds expression in resistance to cultural agreements. Mutual arrangements are envisaged in this sphere in the Basic Treaties but the GDR leaders have hindered them by their insistence that all cultural items and objects formerly in Prussian ownership are the rightful property of the GDR and should be handed over to it. According to this theory the cultural heritage which the Prussian state built up largely with the finances of its Western territories belongs to the GDR. As the old museum quarter is in the Eastern part of the city, West Berlin would, according to this argument, lose virtually all its art treasures. As there is no likelihood of the Federal Government accepting this argument there is little risk to East German seclusion policy from any comprehensive cultural exchange programme. As a counter measure the West German government blocks scientific and technical exchanges between the two German states, which the competent authorities in East Germany would be very glad to have.[26]

Relations between the two German states have constantly been hampered by the regressive East German policy in the human and social sphere. Again and again West Germans and West Berliners have been prevented from entering East Berlin and the GDR although no real reasons could be produced for this. Since 1976/77 (especially during the early months), for example, the GDR authorities have reacted to the growing desire of their people to travel abroad by preventing the relations and friends of persons living in the GDR who seemed untrustworthy from entering the country and doing the same to all people who have been legally entitled to move to West Germany since 1972. In the mid-1970s the East Berlin police sealed off the entrance to the offices of the West German Permanent Representative to prevent any advice being given to would-be emigrants.

At about the same time news that small children whose parents had fled to the West were being forcibly adopted and obliged to give up their identity caused strong feelings in the West. The East German government for its part accused the West German government of doing nothing about or even secretly abetting commercially organised escapes.

In the summer of 1975 for a time West Germans who accidentally crossed the badly signposted border in front of the East German barriers were shot at by East German border patrols and taken away. It was only after the shooting of an Italian communist had aroused international protest that the border guards were instructed not to fire in such cases.

In the spring and summer of 1979 the reprisals which the East German government took against foreign journalists and its own citizens to prevent undesirable news from reaching the West German media caused a six months' break in relations on the political level. Hence the envisaged co-operation agreement on the extension of the Herleshausen/Wartha crossing point was still under discussion when the general situation between East and West deteriorated drastically in December 1979.

But the efforts of the West German government to reunite families have brought many successes over the years. Since 1963 it has also been West German practice to buy out political prisoners from the GDR, although the price has now risen from originally on average DM 40,000 per person to nearly DM 60,000. Altogether so far nearly DM 1 billion has been paid to the GDR for this purpose.[27] Generally old-age pensioners are allowed to move to the Federal Republic if they wish, as the West German state then takes over responsibility for their pensions.

Conclusion

The Federal Republic pursues a policy towards the GDR which brings considerable financial advantages to East Germany. The payments which Bonn makes in the co-operation projects are greater than the resultant economic advantage to the West. The motive is therefore political. The needs of West Berlin of course play a crucial role in these decisions. Basic conditions for the economic and social development of the city can only be secured and improved beyond the provisions of the Four Power Agreement, which is a subject of controversy on both sides, so far as the government of the GDR is willing to allow. But as interest in this on the East German side is rather negative the West German government has to purchase the good-will of the East Berlin regime with financial concessions. The payments which the West German side makes in the co-operation agreements always contain a political fee.

There is a further consideration in Bonn. The social–liberal policy towards the GDR devised by Egon Bahr in the 1960s was based on the recognition that neither the dominance of the Soviet Union nor the Communist regime could be eliminated in the GDR. East Germany may often have proved crisis-prone in the past and may have considerable internal difficulties to cope with in future too, but an attempt to exploit that situation would be fruitless. In an emergency the Soviet Union would resort to armed force and 'normalise' the situation as she did in Czechoslovakia. That would serve no-one — on the contrary it would presumably spark off a dangerous East—West crisis in Central Europe.

The West German government is concerned to create conditions of external and internal stability in West Germany. It therefore regards unrest in the GDR as undesirable. At the same time, however, the Federal government would like to see the usual repressive practices of a Communist regime reduced as far as possible. The East German government is to be encouraged wherever feasible to do this. Bonn is therefore inclined to support any policy in East Germany which is designed to satisfy the consumer wishes of the people in the GDR and compensate in this way for the regime's lack of national and ideological legitimacy. To Bonn there would appear to be a hope that the SED leaders might increasingly seek to cement their hold with material temptations rather than political force. This should be encouraged in order to consolidate peace in Central Europe and ease human conditions in the GDR. The East German government makes use of the West German willingness to make financial concessions but on principle it denies that there is any connection between domestic policy and policy on Germany. As regards the other German state it insists on a strict 'national separation' and this permits of no real common ground.

The advantages which the GDR derives from relations with the Federal Republic of Germany have wrought a fundamental change in GDR interests. When in 1969/70 the West German government began to normalise relations with the other Warsaw Pact states the East Berlin regime felt threatened. There appear to have been fears that East Germany might be 'undermined' by 'subversive manoeuvres'. Continued pressure was needed from the Soviet side before East Berlin was ready to enter into serious negotiations with Bonn.

Now the situation is exactly the reverse. It is the leading men in the GDR who most value relations with the other German state. The inner-German confrontation which Ulbricht tried with might and main to maintain in 1970 appears, ten years later, as a danger which his successor Honecker is making every effort to avert. The Soviets, on the other hand, who in the early 1970s forced their East German allies onto a course of reconciliation with Bonn, now appear as a potential threat to relations between the two German states, largely through the deterioration in the world situation which they have brought about. Since the Afghanistan crisis the SED leaders have realised more clearly than ever that the interests of Central European states can be badly damaged by the ambitions of the Soviet Union in other areas.

The change in the East German attitude has been further facilitated by a policy on the part of the Federal Republic which is designed to acknowledge the existence of two German states but at the same time apply the facts of national unity to relations with the East. This both conforms to the requirements of the international political situation and takes into account the needs of the people in a divided Germany. It justifies the co-operative relation which Bonn is seeking with the other German state and for which it is prepared to pay a considerable price. The attitude of the East German government to this is ambivalent. The leaders would like to take every possible advantage of the economic advantages offered but at the same time they fear that any rapprochement between the two German states in the political and especially the social or human sphere could undermine control of the population and lead to greater ideological and political communion with the West. They therefore waver in their relations with Bonn between acceptance of the economic co-operation offered and a policy of seclusion from the West.

No doubt the SED leaders would prefer to have at the same time and without concessions on their part both the material advantages of co-operation with the West and the inner security of hermetic seclusion. This conflict of interests is at the root of the basic difficulties which still characterise relations between the two German states: for the West German government the hope of being able to achieve further relaxation in the GDR is of course the main motivating factor.

Notes

1 Cf. Gasteyger, C., *Die beiden deutschen Staaten in der Weltpolitik*, Munich, Piper Verlag 1976, pp. 58–83.
2 The problems of GDR recognition and its role in world politics are thoroughly analysed by End, H., *Zweimal deutsche Aussenpolitik. Internationale Dimensionen des inner-deutschen Konflikts 1949–1972*, Cologne, Verlag Wissenschaft und Politik 1973.
3 Cf. Kopp, F., *Kurs auf ganz Deutschland? Die Deutschlandpolitik der SED*, Stuttgart, Seewald Verlag 1965, passim.
4 Sühlo, W., *Der Zusammenhang von nationaler und gesellschaftlicher Spaltung der deutschen Nation in seiner Bedeutung für die Deutschlandpolitik der DDR*, Stiftung Wissenschaft und Politik, Ebenhausen/Isartal, SWP-S170, June 1970; Scheuner, U., 'Das Problem der Nation und des Verhältnisses zur Bundesrepublik Deutschland', in Jacobsen, H.-A., Leptin, G., Scheuner, U. and Schutz, E. (eds), *Drei Jahrzehnte Aussenpolitik der DDR*, Munich–Vienna, Oldenburg 1979, p.92.

5   Cf. Meyer, G., *Die sowjetische Deutschland-Politik im Jahre 1952*, ed. by Arbeitsgemeinschaft für Osteuropaforschung (sold by Böhlau Verlag, Cologne/Graz) 1970; Graml, H., 'Die Legende von der verpassten Gelegenheit', in *Vierteljahreshefte für Zeitgeschichte*, vol.29 (1981), pp. 301—41; Wettig, G., 'Die sowjetische Deutschland-Note', in *Deutschland Archiv*, vol.15 (1982), pp. 130—48.
6   Cf. Wettig, G., 'Die sowjetische Deutschland-Politik am Vorabend des 17. Juni', in *17. Juni 1953*, ed. I. Spittmann/K.W. Fricke, Cologne, Verlag Wissenschaft und Politik 1982, pp. 56—69.
7   Cf. Kuppe, J., 'Phasen', in *Drei Jahrzehnte Aussenpolitik der DDR*, op.cit., pp. 182—91; Kupper, S., 'Politische Beziehungen zur Bundesrepublik Deutschland 1955—1977', in *Drei Jahrzehnte Aussenpolitik der DDR*, op.cit., pp. 406—24; Catudal, H.M., *Kennedy and the Berlin Wall Crisis*, Berlin (West), Berlin-Verlag, 1980.
8   Cf. Planck, C.R., *Sicherheit in Europa. Die Vorschläge für Rüstungsbeschränkung und Abrüstung*, with a Foreword by Helmut Schmidt, Munich, Oldenburg Verlag 1968.
9   Cf. Egon Bahr's statement at Evangelische Akademie Tutzing on 15 July 1963 in Meissner, B. (ed.), *Die deutsche Ostpolitik 1961— 1970. Kontinuität und Wandel. Dokumentation*, Cologne Verlag Wissenschaft und Politik 1971, pp. 45—8.
10 Kupper, S., loc.cit., pp. 424—7.
11 Cf. Riklin, A. and Westen, K., *Selbstzeugnisse des SED-Regimes. Das 'nationale Dokument'. Das erste Programm der SED. Das vierte Statut der SED*, Cologne, Verlag Wissenschaft und Politik 1963.
12 Cf. Wettig, G., *Community and Conflict in the Socialist Camp. The Soviet Union, East Germany and the German Problem 1965—1972*, translated by Moreton, E. and Adomeit, H., London, Hurst and New York, St Martin's Press 1975, pp. 20—32.
13 For inter-German relations during the second half of the 1960s see Wettig, G., op.cit., pp. 33—47; Kuppe, J., op.cit., pp. 192—197; Croan, M., 'Entwicklung der politischen Beziehungen zur Sowjetunion seit 1955', in *Drei Jahrzehnte Aussenpolitik der DDR*, op.cit., pp. 361— 6; Kupper, S., loc.cit., pp. 427—34.
14 Moreton, N.E., *East Germany and the Warsaw Alliance. The Politics of Détente*, Boulder/Colorado, Westview Press (Replica edition) 1978, pp. 105—48; Wettig, G., op.cit., pp. 64—73.
15 Moreton, N.E., op.cit., pp. 182—200; Wettig, G., Community and Conflict, op.cit., pp. 104—17; Wettig, G., *Das Vier-Mächte-Abkommen in der Bewährungsprobe*, Berlin (West), Berlin-Verlag 1982 (2nd edition).
16 Kupper, S., loc.cit., pp. 438—42; Wettig, G., Community and Conflict, op.cit., pp. 118—35. The text of the Basic Treaty is contained in Bundesministerium für innerdeutsche Beziehungen (ed.), *Zehn Jahre Deutschlandpolitik. Die Entwicklung der Beziehungen zwischen der*

Bundesrepublik Deutschland und der Deutschen Demokratischen Republik 1969—1979. Bericht und Dokumentation, Bonn, February 1980, pp. 202—11; Bundesministerium für innerdeutsche Beziehungen (ed.), *Texte zur Deutschlandpolitik*, vol.11, Bonn, January 1973, pp. 268—301. See also Zündorf, B., *Die Ostverträge, Moskau/Warschau/ Prag/Das Berlin-Abkommen/Die Verträge mit der DDR*, Munich, Verlag C.H. Beck 1979, pp. 211—319.

17 The text of the agreement is contained in *Zehn Jahre Deutschlandpolitik*, op.cit., pp. 175—8; *Texte zur Deutschlandpolitik*, op.cit., vol.9, Bonn, February 1972, pp. 351—62. For a juridical evaluation see Zündorf, B., op.cit., pp. 176—87, 197—201; Zivier, E.R., *Der Rechtsstatus des Landes Berlin. Eine Untersuchung nach dem Viermächte-Abkommen vom 3. September 1971*, Berlin (West), Berlin-Verlag 1974 (2nd edition), pp. 155—60.

18 Kupper, S., loc.cit., pp. 446—52; Wettig, G., 'Die Strategie der Annäherung und die Abgrenzung in der Westpolitik der UdSSR und der DDR (1966—1975)', in Deutsche Gesellschaft für Friedens- und Konfliktforschung (Gerda Zellentin) (ed.), *Annäherung, Abgrenzung und friedlicher Wandel in Europa*, Boppard/Rhein, Boldt Verlag 1976, pp. 328—34, 342—50; Oldenburg, F., and Wettig, G., 'The Special Status of the GDR in East—West Relations' in *East-Central Europe* (University of Pittsburgh), vol.6, no.2 (Fall 1979), pp. 181—4; Wettig, G., 'Can Economic Aid Bring About Relaxation in the GDR?' in *Aussenpolitik*, German Foreign Affairs Review (Hamburg), 1979, no.4, pp. 388—92; McCauley, M., 'East Germany: The Dilemmas of Division', in *Conflict Studies* (London), no.119, June 1980, pp. 1—19; Wettig, G., 'Seclusion in the GDR's Westpolitik', in *Aussenpolitik*, 1981, no.2, pp. 121—9.

19 *Zehn Jahre Deutschlandpolitik*, op.cit., pp. 14—15, 280—1. General overviews of the developments in the relationship between the two German states in the 1970s are provided by Gasteyger, C., op.cit., pp. 107—23.

20 *Zehn Jahre Deutschlandpolitik*, op.cit., pp. 13—14; Presse- und Informationsamt des Landes Berlin (ed.), *Dokumentation zur Anordnung der Regierung der DDR über die Durchführung des verbindlichen Mindestumtauschs von Zahlungsmitteln vom 5. November 1973*, January 1974; Wettig, G., 'Das Funktionieren der Besuchsregelung für West-Berliner', in *Deutschland Archiv* (Cologne), 5/1980, pp. 509—17.

21 Lambrecht, H., 'Die Entwicklung der Wirtschaftsbeziehungen zur Bundesrepublik Deutschland' in *Drei Jahrzehnte Aussenpolitik der DDR*, op.cit., pp. 453—72; Ehrmann, C.-D., Kupper, S., Lambrecht, H. and Ollig, G., *Handelspartner DDR. Innerdeutsche Wirtschaftsbeziehungen*, Baden-Baden, Nomos 1975.

22 Cf. Kupper, S., loc.cit., pp. 443—6; Wettig, G., 'Das Problem des

Zugangs nach West-Berlin seit dem Vier-Mächte-Abkommen' in *Beiträge zur Konfliktforschung* (Cologne), vol.8, no.3, summer 1978, pp. 28–41; Wettig, G., 'Die Bindungen West-Berlins bei der Anwendung des Viermächte-abkommens', in *Deutschland Archiv* (Cologne), vol.12, no.9, September 1979, pp. 920–37; Gasteyger, C., op.cit., pp. 124–9; Catudal, H.M., *A Balance Sheet of the Quadripartite Agreement on Berlin. Evaluation and Documentation*, with a Foreword by Kenneth Rush, Berlin (West), Berlin-Verlag 1978.

23 Cf. *Zehn Jahre Deutschlandpolitik*, op.cit., pp. 15, 47, 325–7; Oldenburg, F. and Wettig, G., 'The Special Status of the GDR in East–West Relations', in *East-Central Europe*, vol.6, no.2, pp. 173–86.

24 Cf. *Zehn Jahre Deutschlandpolitik*, op.cit., pp. 15–16, 47–8, 341–53.

25 *Zehn Jahre Deutschlandpolitik*, op.cit., pp. 16–17, 25–7, 30–40, 49–50, 51–6, 275–6.

26 Cf. *Zehn Jahre Deutschlandpolitik*, op.cit., pp. 50–1, 58–66.

27 Meyer, M., *Freikauf – Menschenhandel in Deutschland*, Vienna–Hamburg, Paul Zsolnay Verlag 1978.

9 Output policy in the GDR in comparative perspective
Klaus von Beyme

The GDR has been neglected in studies of comparative Communism. East Germany has frequently been seen as a part of the 'German problem' rather than as an independent member of the Soviet Bloc.[1] The East German élite has been considered second only to Bulgaria in obedience to the Soviet will. But motives have been less respected than in the case of Bulgaria: 'It would seem that the Bulgarians follow a strict party line because they have little to lose and something to gain, . . . the East German élite conforms, however, because of insecurity and dependence'.[2] The GDR has been looked upon as the archetypal satellite echoing the USSR. This has discouraged most Western researchers from examining independent sources of domestic policy in the GDR,[3] whilst West German researchers have normally been more limited in their outlook and have concentrated — sometimes simply from lack of knowledge of Slav languages — exclusively on various domestic German problems. Only German specialists on the Soviet Union have sometimes made comparisons, but these have usually been limited to the Soviet Union and East Germany. Emphasis on the German problem predominates in West German comparative social sciences. Starting with the impetus which came from the 'Report on the State of the Nation' under Peter Ludz, comparisons have been limited to the two German states.[4] These comparisons have tried to avoid a normative bias by imposing Western values on the GDR, though such efforts have been hardly recognised by critics who have sided with the official standpoint of East Berlin.[5]

Foreign observers who have not stuck to a comparison of institutions but have included social and political culture, have generally seen more convergent features in the two German societies than have the majority of West German observers.[6] Comparisons of Socialist countries by scholars living in these systems have been even more restricted in outlook, concentrating either on the model of Socialism in its mature state and arguing against the 'fetishism of particular features' imputed to Western scholars who classify sub-models of Socialism,[7] or starting to delineate the model and continuing to fragment it in country-by-country studies; rarely has the overall concept been kept in mind.[8]

Most Western typologies of Socialist systems suffer from the fact that the types apply only to one country: Chinese, Soviet or Cuban developments are compared with 'the East European countries'. Most typologies are based on highly selective criteria, frequently concentrating on the political sphere or on economic development. The author of this chapter is committed to the idea that indicators of output policy are the best means of arriving at more comprehensive but still differentiated typologies.[9]

Socialist systems are output oriented. Socialist policies serve the realisation of ideological goals which are ranked according to a relatively consistent system of ideological pronouncements and postulates and which are translated into material policy guidelines by Communist parties and planning élites. Like the above attempts at typologies, comparative research into Socialism cannot simply stop at the 'inputism' of most earlier theories, especially those theories based on totalitarianism. Only the search for indicators of the translation of policy goals in Socialist countries will avoid premature normative judgements. Measuring the achievement of goals does not necessarily imply approval or disapproval of the goals declared to be relevant in given planning periods. Moreover, the comparison of achievements in terms of indicators actually facilitates comparison with Western countries, if the figures are carefully interpreted in the light of the differences between the Socialist and capitalist systems. Comparisons based on indicators are sometimes criticised both in Socialist countries and among those Western scholars who look sympathetically on the Socialist countries.[10]

The argument that the 'Kennziffern' used in the GDR or the 'pokazately' in the USSR are both fundamentally and qualitatively different from Western indicators is hardly convincing. A country like Rumania, living in the tradition of Latin languages, has always called its 'Kennziffern' 'indicatori'. After ten years of criticism of Western social indicator theory and after so many attempts to discredit research on the 'quality of life' as another dirty trick of the Imperialist bourgeoisie', the leading Soviet sociological journal was recently even allowed to discuss the problem of qualitative indicators on the same terms as they are debated in the West.[11]

The GDR like other output oriented systems is prolific in its publication of data. For a fair comparison it is better to use the statistical yearbooks of COMECON from Moscow, if data are available. Only in a few areas does the GDR refrain from publishing figures (such as growth of wages, cf. table 9.1, line 7). In the field of social stratification the GDR has been ranked together with Albania among those countries which have not produced sufficient data to be included in a comparative analysis,[12] but this is hardly justified. Even though indicators do not lead to a quantifiable performance model, nevertheless they still help us to escape the traditional exchange of statements of ideological superiority into the field of a more modest sectoral comparison.

Comparing the figures, we note that in spite of the high cost of redistribution campaigns in human terms, the GDR was slower in nationalising industries (lines 1 and 2) and collectivising trade and agriculture than most other East European countries. Yet over the longer term the GDR has emphasised the 'Socialist sector' to a greater degree than have some of its East European neighbours (line 5). The concomitant concentration process in manufacturing and agriculture is the lowest for the Soviet Bloc (line 3). A great number of smaller and medium-sized enterprises were allowed to continue whilst the concentration of agriculture into the huge 'super-kolkhozy' of the Soviet Union was not imitated in the GDR. In 1976 East Germany had still the smallest agricultural units in the Socialist camp.[13]

In spite of having the lowest ratio of agricultural workers (line 4), food production was — with some exceptions relating to regional or temporary difficulties — more satisfactory than in bigger agrarian countries such as Poland, Rumania and the USSR. The GDR is among the leaders in mechanisation if we accept the indicator 'number of tractors per 1,000 hectares' (line 6). The figures for Poland, which are superior to the GDR, perhaps indicate a private sector over endowed with tractors rather than pointing to a high mechanical efficiency in the agricultural sector as a whole.

Industrial output in the GDR is considerable; the country ranks second in the Socialist camp and about 9th or 10th in the world. In spite of the many shortcomings of the East German production process, such as adopting the vices of the Soviet 'ideology of tons' — a gross-output orientation of the planning system, energy waste, and losses through investments in gigantic and prestigious but not very useful projects — the GDR on the whole is too modern to have copied the entire economic system of the Soviet Union. Yet real hegemony in the Eastern bloc certainly does not lie with the economically most

Table 9.1
Indicators on systems performance

	GDR	Bulgaria	Czechoslovakia	Hungary	Poland	Rumania	USSR
Production sphere							
1 Proportion accounted for by the Socialist sector (in percentage) gross industrial production in 1950	77.6	97.5	96.0		96.7	92.4	76.0 (1924)
2 Retail trade turnover	47.2	94.3	91.7		83.0	88.5	47.3 (1924)
3 Industrial enterprises up to 500 and over 10,000 workers (1965)	42.7 2.5	31.8 3.8	7.2 12.6	9.7 14.5	21.2 3.2	13.6 5.5	
4 Percentage of workers employed in agriculture (1979)	10.5	24.9	14.3	21.8	26.9	31.1	20.6
5 Socialist sector in agriculture (1978) (coll. and state agr.)	94.8	99.9	91.6 (1971)	98.3	24.2	90.6	100.0
6 Number of tractors per 1,000 hectares	21.9	10.5	20.1	9.7	24.4	9.3	4.5
7 Increase of real wages for factory and office workers (1960=100) 1968 (1970=100) 1978	125 n.d.	131 118	121 125	118 126	116 146	133 146	123 128
8 Importance of bonuses in the wage structure (in percentage) Pieceworker (1972) Timeworker (1972)	42.7 46.0	11.9 21.5	20.7 20.9	9.5 9.5	n.d. n.d.	n.d. n.d.	17.9 (1974) 19.1 (1974)
9 Gross investment as a percentage of GNP 1955–1966 1979	20.7 20.1	34.0 22.8	25.2 24.6	23.9 25.6	25.5 25.1	n.d. n.d.	26.6 24.9
10 Energy consumption 1976 per capita in kilograms	6,789	4,710	7,397	3,553	5,253	4,036	5,259
11 Share of labour productivity in the growth of national income (in percentage) 1966–70 projected 1971–75	70 100	51 70	78 95	48 68	48 75	n.d. n.d.	68 80–85
12 Computers in use per million inhabitants (1970)	21	5	16	8	6	2	23
13 Share of intra-COMECON trade (1979) turnover	68.8	78.4	68.5	52.1	54.7	39.7	55.7

Distribution sphere

14 Personal taxes (in percentage)	4.6	27.1	12.4	5.3	1.0	9.7	8.4
15 Inflationary trends according to consumer price indices (1970=100) 1978	99.7	104.7	104.1	132.1	136.1	108.1	101.9
16 Life expectancy (1977)							
Men	69.0	68.7	66.9	66.5	66.9	67.5	64
Women	74.9	73.9	73.7	72.4	74.5	72.1	74
17 Population growth per 1,000 (1977)	−0.1	5.4	7.2	4.3	10.1	10.0	8.5
18 Divorce rate (1977)	2.6	1.5	2.1	2.6	1.3	1.2	3.5
19 Physicians per 10,000 (1978)	24.6	28.3	30.1	26.6	n.d.	16.8	35.4
Population per physician (1976)	523	453	404	439	615	750	299
20 Hospital beds per 10,000 (1979)	105	90.3	77.7	82.1	72.2	89.5	123
21 Number of apartments constructed per 10,000 population (1979)	97.2	75	81.1	82.4	80.5	87.1	73
22 Occupants per apartment (1977)	2.5	3.4	3.0	2.9	3.6	n.d.	n.d.
23 Housing conditions							
running water indoors	82.1	28.2	49.1	n.d.	47.3	12.3	n.d.
WC (about 1965)	56.6 (1971)	11.8	39.5	n.d.	33.4	12.2	n.d.
24 Urbanisation							
Percentage of urban population (1978)	76	61.2	67.5	n.d.	57.5	49.0	62.0
25 Education							
Percentage of school-age population receiving education (about 1975)							
2nd level (14–17/18 years)	90	87	n.d.	62	53	57	71
3rd level (20–24 years)	24.5	18.7	11.2	11.2	15.7	8.7	21.7
26 Students per 10,000 population (1978/79)	76.0	108.0	121.0	99.0	138.0	87.0	195.0
27 Children of pre-school age attending pre-school establishments (in percentage) 1979	78.3	50.5	46.3	56.8	27.2	41.8	43.2
28 Proportion of state budget allocated to education and social welfare (1976/77)	34.6	31.3	44.7	26.8	18.7	20.9	35.6
29 Communication 1978: yearly number of copies per person	177	98	93.4	98	76	58	148
30 Radio and TV per 1,000 of population (1978)	330	183	266	246	213	156	237
31 Telephones per 1,000 of population (1978)	97	34	105.3	55.8	41.1	24.9	13.3
32 Letter mail per 100 of population (1978)	7.4	3.2	8.3	8.2	4.2	3.8	3.6

Table 9.1 (cont.)

	GDR	Bulgaria	Czechoslovakia	Hungary	Poland	Rumania	USSR
Political sphere							
33 Membership of Communist parties							
Number (in mill.)	1.9	0.78	1.3	0.75	2.3	2.5	15.6
Percentage of population	11.3	7.5	4.6	6.6	6.5	11.3	5.9
34 Proportion of							
Workers	56.9	41.1	45.2	58.3	40.9	50	42
Peasants	5.6	23.6	5.0	14.2	9.3	20.6	13.6
Intelligentsia	31.1	30	31	27.5	22.3	22	44
as a percentage of Communist party membership (about 1975/76)	(1980)						(1977)
35 Comparative measures of freedom (scale 1–7, 1=highest level of rights)							
Political rights	7	n.d.	7	6	6	7	7
Civil liberties	7	n.d.	6	5	5	6	6
36 Anomic participation (1948–1967) Death from domestic political violence	140	1	74	40,000	553	n.d.	399
37 Military expenditure in billion dollars	4.7	1.1	3.5	1.0	4.6	1.4	124.0
per capita (in dollars)	285	128	229	101	131	66	490
38 Military manpower (in 1,000)	162	149	195	93	317	184	3,568
39 Paramilitary (in 1,000)	571	189	133	75	445	737	460

Sources:

1 K.I. Mikul'skii: *Klassovaya struktura obshchestva v stranakh sotsializma*, Moscow, Nauka, 1976, p.47; V.I. Vanin: *Gosudarstvennyi kapitalizm v KNR*, Moscow, Nauka, 1974, p.16.
2 As Note 1.
3 M.Os'mova: 'Kontsentratsia promyshlennosti v stranakh SEV', *Voprosy ekonomiki*, 1971, no.8, p.99.
4 '*Statisticheski ezhegodnik stran-chlenov SEV*', 1980, Moscow, *Statistika 1980*, pp. 403 ff.
5 Ibid., 1978, p.42.
6 Statistical Surveys, in *Jahrbuch der Wirtschaft Osteuropas/Yearbook of East European Economics*, Munich, Isar, 1979, vol.8, pp. 457 ff.
7 'Institut mirovoi sotsialisticheskoi sistemy AN SSSR: Ekonomika stran sotsializma 1970' g. Moscow, 1971, p.219. Statisticheskii ezhegodnik, op.cit., 1979, p.53.
8 *Oplata truda pri sotsializme*, Moscow, Ekonomika, 1977, p.102 f.

9. Bergson, A., *Productivity and the Social System. The USSR and the West*, Cambridge/Mass., Harvard UP, 1978, p.207 for 1955–56, for 1979: Statisticheskii ezhegodnik, op.cit., 1980, p.46.
10. *UN Statistical Yearbook*, New York 1979, pp. 390 ff.
11. Keck, A., *Leistung, Wachstum, Wohlstand. Unser Nationaleinkommen – Quelle des gesellschaftlichen Reichtums*, Berlin (East) 1972, p.59.
12. Wilczynski, J., 'Cybernetics, Automation and the Transition to Communism', in Mesa-Lago, C. and Beck, C. (eds), *Comparative Socialist Systems*, Pittsburgh UP, 1973 (397–417), p.402.
13. Statisticheskii ezhegodnik, op.cit., 1980, p.373.
14. Statistical surveys, op.cit., p. 458 ff.
15. *ILO Yearbook of Labour Statistics 1979*, Geneva, 1979, pp. 549 ff.
16. *UN Statistical Yearbook 1978*, New York, 1979, pp. 76 ff. Statisticheskii ezhegodnik, op.cit., 1980, p.10.
17. *UN Statistical Yearbook 1979*, pp. 893 ff. Statisticheskii ezhegodnik, op.cit., 1980, p.443.
18. As Note 16.
19. As Note 17.
20. As Note 17.
21. Statisticheskii ezhegodnik, op.cit., 1980, p.185.
22. Statistical Surveys, op.cit., pp. 481 ff.
23. *UN Statistical Yearbook 1973*, New York 1974, pp. 728 ff.
24. Statisticheskii ezhegodnik, 1979, p.14.
25. *UNESCO Staistical Yearbook 1976*, Paris 1977, pp. 161 ff.
26. As Note 25.
27. Statisticheskii ezhegodnik, op.cit., 1980, p.422.
28. Statistical Surveys, op.cit., p.458 ff.
29. Statisticheskii ezhegodnik, op.cit., 1979, p.333.
30. As Note 29.
31. As Note 29.
32. As Note 29.
33. *Kommunisty mira – o svoikh partiyakh*. Prague, Mir i sotsializm, 1976, pp. 92 ff.
34. *Kommunisty mira*, op.cit., pp. 93 ff. *Rocznik statystyczny*, 1978, GUSt 1978, p.22. *Einheit*, 1980, no.10, p.1021. *Partiinoe stroitel'stvo*, Moscow, 1978, 4th edition, p.111.
35. Gastil, R.D. (ed.), *Freedom in the World. Political Rights and Civil Liberties 1978*, Boston, G.K. Hall, 1978, pp. 10 ff.
36. Taylor, C.L. and Hudson, M.C., *World Handbook of Political and Social Indicators*, New Haven, Yale UP, 1972, pp. 110 ff.
37. The International Institute of Strategic Studies (IISS): *The Military Balance 1980–81*, London 1980.
38. As Note 37.
39. As Note 37.

developed countries.[14] Some indicators such as per capita energy consumption, share of labour productivity in the growth of the national income, and computers in use (lines 10–12) show the GDR to be amongst the best of the Socialist countries. On the other hand it was at the bottom of the COMECON list for gross investment as a ratio to GNP[15] – whereas West Germany was nearly at the top of the OECD list (line 9). The precarious loyalty situation in the East German rump state apparently forced the government into investing more in consumption sectors compared with other Socialist countries.

The GDR – more so than even Czechoslovakia and Hungary – has a very weak internal raw material base and there are virtually no reserves of labour in the country. This means that there have been very limited possibilities of compensating for insufficient growth of labour productivity by additional employment.[16] The GDR until 1961 – when the Berlin Wall was built – lost more than 3 million from its labour force. It was hardly possible to compensate for the labour scarcity by importing foreign labour as in West Germany. Only about 50,000 Poles and Hungarians were temporarily employed in the GDR. The mobilisation of women was merely a minor contribution since women were in some cases less well trained than men in spite of the efforts of the educational system to bring about sex equality in the labour market. The GDR ranks second behind the USSR (51.5 per cent) in the Socialist camp in the percentage of women among the total employed population.[17] No other Socialist country has had to experiment so extensively with economic reforms and employ bonuses as an incentive to both pieceworkers and hourly paid workers (line 8) in an effort to compensate for labour scarcity by improving morale among the workforce. West German Neo-Marxists have therefore been more critical of the GDR because of its alleged 'return to capitalism' than of any other Socialist country.[18]

Mobilisation of all labour reserves ultimately contributed to the slow-down in the growth of labour productivity. Though the contribution of labour productivity to the growth in national income is higher than that of other COMECON countries (line 11), it has been calculated at one-third below the corresponding West German rate.[19] Even Walter Ulbricht admitted in 1963 that there was a productivity gap of 25 per cent between the two German states.[20] The GDR – like Czechoslovakia alone – has been highly dependent on foreign trade and its dependence on internal COMECON trade is greater than any other Socialist country except only Bulgaria (line 13). The GDR does not compare with Bulgaria, however, because it benefits from special arrangements between the two German states. The GDR has not always used its privileged position in regard to the EEC countries via West Germany to fill technological gaps and obtain necessary goods from the

West.[21] Again, regard for consumer needs provides part of the explanation.

In the distribution sphere the performance of the GDR is also quite considerable. The standard of living is higher than in the other Socialist countries. The COMECON figures for wage increases are incomplete for the GDR in the 1970s but among the more developed countries — starting from a higher level — the GDR had higher increases in real wages in the 1960s than comparable economic systems (line 7). Personal taxes (line 14) are low and losses from inflationary effects are actually the lowest in the Eastern Bloc (line 15). Population growth — which consumed part of the surplus even in developing Socialist economies (most strikingly in Poland and Rumania) was actually negative by the end of the 1970s — comparable only with West Germany (line 17). In the performance of the health system, measured by indicators such as life expectancy (line 16), physicians per 10,000, population per physician (line 19), and hospital beds per 10,000 (line 20) the COMECON figures show a better result only for the USSR, but this is not in itself an indicator of higher quality medical care. The GDR shows the best performance in housing (lines 21–23), though it is more urbanised than any other country (line 24); this normally lowers performance in housing since in most countries living space — though not necessarily the amenities and comfort of the apartments — is greater in the country. Compared with West Germany the performance is less impressive. Though the Eastern parts of Germany suffered less damage during the war and had to absorb fewer refugees from the Oder-Neisse territories, the GDR did not keep pace with the Western parts of Germany but rather fell back to the standards of Italy.[22]

In education the picture is less clear since data on enrolment in schools at the 2nd and 3rd levels set out in UNESCO and COMECON statistics are not comparable (lines 25 and 26). Measuring educational effort in more sophisticated areas which need high investment such as pre-school institutions (line 27), even the USSR loses its superiority over the GDR, though it still ranks higher in the mobilisation of the female labour force. The proportion of the state budget allocated to education and social welfare is another indicator. In these sectors the GDR is exceeded only by Czechoslovakia and the USSR (line 28). In Socialist countries total resources devoted to education tend, in the early stages of Socialism, to be greater than in most capitalist countries. Proportions of national budget items need, however, careful examination. On the whole, Socialist countries spend less on salaries for teachers yet increase the relative costs of higher education compared with capitalist systems.[23] In some fields of education the performance of the GDR has been even better than that of the Federal Republic. But West Germany caught up part of the way in the late 1960s.[24]

In communication the GDR occupies a leading position in the COMECON statistics (lines 29–32). Only in numbers of telephones per 1,000 of the population and letter mail per 100 did Czechoslovakia have a slight advantage over the GDR. In the social security system the GDR experienced the most unfavourable starting conditions of all the Socialist states apart from Russia because of extremely high human losses during the war and, in contrast with the Soviet Union, an extremely unfavourable age structure of the population since 3 million people had left the country to move to the West. East Germany did not match West Germany, especially in the field of old age pensions, but came close to the level of Austria.[25] Allowances compared with wages seem to be higher in the Soviet Union than in the GDR, but this does not indicate any superiority of the USSR over the GDR, since the general wage level is considerably higher in the GDR.[26] The poor performance of East German social policy is due to the orientation of the economy to production.[27] Social help for deviants and protection against unforeseeable risks are better developed than in most other Socialist countries although below the standards of the Western welfare states. Part of the health system on the other hand, has at times been considered superior to that of West Germany.[28]

The predominantly negative image of the GDR results from its record in the political sphere. Data in this field are still scarcer than in the two other spheres. Comparisons of political rights and civil liberties rank the GDR at the bottom of all the East European countries (line 35). The repressive capacity of the system is considerable, comparing the numbers of paramilitary personnel (line 39), who frequently also have a number of functions in domestic affairs. Only the Soviet Union has higher military per capita expenditure. Comparing the workforce with the total population the GDR is actually above the Soviet level (lines 37 and 38). The proportion of people organised in the party is the highest in the Eastern Bloc. The orthodox insistence on workers remaining the predominant group in the social structure of Communist parties is characterised by more of an 'ouvrierisme' than in other East European countries, including the 'motherland of Socialism' (line 34). Data on refugees, political prisoners and anomic participation (line 36) could complete the picture, but they would hardly be comparable as the data on violence have shown (line 36). There is, however, some evidence that legitimation in the system is achieved predominantly via economic and social performance, another parallel between the two German states.

With the exception of Bulgaria the GDR is frequently classified as the most dependent satellite in the Soviet sphere of influence. If this judgement seems to be correct in foreign policy, this does not mean that domestic institutions and policies are not highly autonomous. The education system is unique in the Socialist camp. The Soviet system of a ten-class school system has not been copied nor did the Soviets impose a completely new educational system on their zone of occupation after 1945.[29] In vocational training the GDR in some respects became a model for other East European countries. Also the social security system is individual, and conserves many features of the older imperial system in Germany, whereas less developed Socialist countries which started to build up social security systems from scratch copied the Soviet system much more closely.[30] The constitutional system was very closely followed by most Socialist countries: even in the GDR constitution of 1974 fewer concessions to German traditions were made. But even institutions which started as Soviet copies, such as the 'Staatsrat' modelled on the Presidum of the Supreme Soviet after Ulbricht, developed into a more formal institution with powers no longer comparable with the Soviet model.[31] Functional change outlives initial imitations.

One of the main problems of a quantitative analysis of the system's performance is our ignorance of the causal links between institutions and the performance of the regime. Even economists have become more sceptical about measuring the comparative effectiveness of an economic system as a whole. Many differences in performance are due less to economic and political institutions than to certain features of political and social culture.[32] Even negative experiences and periodical frustrations with the ups and downs of the cycles of economic reforms have not completely ruined the efficiency of the system. As a Polish economist, comparing Poland with the GDR, put it: 'Our economic reform model is far superior to the East German but the East German performance is far superior to ours'.[33]

When even economic systems with tangible indicators are difficult to rank according to their efficiency, any attempt at classifying the whole social and political system is hopeless. Most typologies of rank-orders are unsatisfactory. In political taxonomies the GDR is classified as 'consultative authoritarianism' together with the Soviet Union, Bulgaria and Rumania and in opposition to the 'quasi-pluralistic authoritarianism' of Hungary, Poland and Czechoslovakia in the mid-sixties.[34] Even classifications which include more socio-economic variables lump the GDR together in one cluster with Bulgaria and the USSR.[35] Again the result is not satisfactory, since although the GDR may have common traits with Bulgaria in the political sphere, the degree of development of the two societies is not comparable. Complex scoring systems summarising the developmental level have allotted sufficient points to the GDR to put it at the head of all the Socialist countries, followed by Czechoslovakia, Hungary, USSR, Bulgaria, Poland and Rumania.[36] In spite of some oddities in the scores (the GDR is said to rank below Bulgaria in the field of education, a hypothesis for which there is little evidence (cf. lines 25–28)), this sequence of ranking is more plausible than the above-mentioned clusters.

Political and social culture explains a good deal of the variance in those fields where quantitative data are not available. We have almost no subjective indicators on Socialist systems. Even if we could generate them, pioneers of the Western social indicators' movement have cautioned us against believing that by studying objective indicators we can come to grips with the analysis of satisfaction.[37] Performance and satisfaction do not coincide, especially in free countries. We have the experience from under-directed capitalist countries. But it becomes more and more true of the Socialist systems that Socialist governments can control all social processes to an ever-smaller degree by over-directing agencies from above.

Notes

1 Cf. Legters, L.H. (ed.), *The German Democratic Republic. A Developed Socialist Society*, Boulder/Co., Westview Press, 1978, p.5.
2 Wesson, R.G., *Communism and Communist Systems*, Englewood Cliffs, Prentice Hall, 1978, p.149.
3 Adomeit, H. and Boardman, R. (eds), *Foreign Policy Making in Communist Countries*, Saxon House, Farnborough, 1979, p.81.
4 Some of the recent comparisons: Behr, W., *Bundesrepublik Deutschland – Deutsche Demokratische Republik. Systemvergleich Politik, Wirtschaft, Gesellschaft*, Stuttgart, Kohlhammer, 1979; Böger, K. and Kremendahl, H., *Bundesrepublik Deutschland – Deutsche Demokratische Republik: Vergleich der politischen Systeme*, Stuttgart, Metzler, 1979, 2 vols; Eckhardt, K.-H., *Die DDR im Systemvergleich. Didaktisches Sachbuch zum Verständnis von Plan und Marktwirtschaft*, Reinbek, Rowohlt, 1978; Hamel, H. (ed.), *BRD-DDR. Die Wirtschaftssysteme*, Munich, Beck, 1977; Jesse, E. (ed.), *Bundesrepublik Deutschland und Deutsche Demokratische Republik. Die beiden deutschen Staaten im Vergleich*, Berlin, Colloquium, 1980; Jung, H. et al., *BRD-DDR. Vergleich der Gesellschaftssysteme*, Cologne, Pahl-Rugenstein, 1971; Ludz, P. Ch., *Deutschlands doppelte Zukunft*, Munich, Hanser, 1974; Mitzscherling, P., *Sozialpolitik im geteilten Deutschland*. Hannover, Niedersächsische Landeszentrale für politische Bildung, 1971; Waterkamp, R., *Herrschaftssysteme und Industriegesellschaft, BRD-DDR*, Stuttgart, Kohlhammer, 1972.
5 Cf. Cless, O., *Sozialismusforschung in der BRD. Das herrschende DDR-Bild und seine Dogmen*, Cologne, Pahl-Rugenstein, 1978, p.209.

For a more balanced view: Gransow, V., *Konzeptuelle Wandlungen der Kommunismusforschung. Vom Totalitarismus zur Immanenz*, Frankfurt, Campus, 1980.
6   Cf. Krejci, J., *Social Structure in Divided Germany*, London, Croom Helm, 1976, pp. 206 ff.
7   *Die entwickelte sozialistische Gesellschaft. Wesen und Kriterien. Kritik revisionistischer Konzeptionen*, Berlin (East), Dietz, 1973, p.344; Syusyukalov, B.I., *Sotsialisticheskoe obshchestvo: problemy dialektiki razvitiya*, Moscow, Mysl', 1973.
8   A catalogue of nine criteria which is widely used was outlined by Topornin, B.N., *Politicheskaya sistema sotsializma*, Moscow, Mezhdunarodnye otnosheniya, 1972, p.12 f. Typical for the a-theoretical country-by-country approach: Ciepielewski, J. (ed.), *Kraje socjalistyczne po drugiej wojnie światowej 1944–1974*, Warsaw, PWN, 1977.
9   von Beyme, K., *Politics and Economics in Socialist Countries. A Comparative and Developmental Approach*, New York, Praeger, 1982.
10 Ende, R., *Sozialindikatoren und Systemvergleich. Zur Analyse intersystemarer Beziehungen*, Frankfurt, Campus, 1979, pp. 100 ff.
11 Connor, W.D., *Socialism, Politics, and Equality. Hierarchy and Change in Eastern Europe and the USSR*, New York, Columbia UP, 1979, p.6.
12 *Ezhegodnik stran- chlenov SEV*. Moscow, Statistika 1980 (and earlier issues).
13 Wädekin, K.-E., *Sozialistische Agrarpolitik in Osteuropa*, Berlin, Duncker and Humblot, 1978, vol.2, p.290.
14 Triska, J.F. and Cooks, P.M. (eds), *Political Development in Eastern Europe*, New York, Praeger, 1977, p.285.
15 Bergson, A., *Productivity and Social System. The USSR and the West*, Cambridge/Mass., Harvard UP, 1978, p.206.
16 Brus, V., *Socialist Ownership and Political Systems*, London, Routledge and Kegan Paul, 1975, p.163.
17 Shishkin, M.M., *Sotsial'no-ekonomicheskie problemy zhenskogo truda*, Moscow, Ekonomika, 1980, p.30 f.
18 Neumann, P., *Zurück zum Profit. Zur Entwicklung des Revisionismus in der DDR*, Berlin (West) VSA, 1973.
19 Schnitzer, M., *East and West Germany. A Comparative Economic Analysis*, New York, Praeger, 1972, p.363.
20 Quoted in Leptin, G., *Die deutsche Wirtschaft nach 1945. Ein Ost-West-Vergleich*, Opladen, Leske, 1971, p.66.
21 Bethkenhagen, J., et al., 'Über den Zusammenhang von aussenwirtschaftlichen Interessen der DDR und Entspannung', in *Die DDR im Entspannungsprozess*, Cologne, edition Deutschland Archiv, 1980 (3–17), p.11; von Beyme, K., 'Détente and East–West Economic

Relations' in *Journal of Politics*, 1981, no.4, pp. 1192—1206.
22 *Bericht der Bundesregierung und Materialien zur Lage der Nation*, 1971, Bonn, 1971, p.119.
23 Pryor, F.L., *Public Expenditures in Communist and Capitalist Nations*, London, Allen and Unwin, 1968, p.216.
24 Hearnden, A., *Bildungspolitik in der BRD und DDR*, Düsseldorf, Schwann, 1973, p.269.
25 Scharf, C.B., 'Correlates of Social Security Policy. East and West Europe', in *International Political Science Review*, 1981 (57—72), p.69.
26 Cf. von Beyme, K., 'Soviet Social Policy in Comparative Perspective', *International Political Science Review*, 1981 (73—94), p.80.
27 Leenen, W.R., *Zur Frage der Wachstumsorientierung der marxistisch—leninistischen Sozialpolitik in der DDR*, Berlin, Duncker and Humblot, 1977.
28 Rolf, H., *Sozialversicherung oder staatlicher Gesundheitsdienst? Ökonomischer Effizienzvergleich der Gesundheitssicherungssysteme der BRD und der DDR*, Berlin, Duncker and Humblot, 1975, p.204.
29 Kuhnert, J., 'Berufliche Bildung als Prüfstein der Bildungspolitik in der SBZ', *Deutschland-Archiv*, 1980, no.7, pp. 736—49.
30 Cf. von Beyme, K., *Sozialismus oder Wohlfahrtsstaat. Sozialpolitik und Sozialstruktur der Sowjetunion im Systemvergleich*, Munich, Piper, 1977, p.25.
31 Erbe, G. et al., *Politik, Wirtschaft und Gesellschaft in der DDR*, Opladen, Westdeutscher Verlag, 1980, 2nd edition, p.132.
32 Brown, A. and Gray, J. (eds), *Political Culture and Political Change in Communist States*, London, Macmillan, 1977.
33 Quoted in Nove, A., *The Soviet Economic System*, London, Allen and Unwin, 1978, p.367.
34 Skilling, H.G., 'Group Conflict and Political Change', in Johnson, C. (ed.), *Change in Communist Systems*, Stanford UP, 1970 (215—34), p.223.
35 Welsh, W.A., 'Toward an Empirical Typology of Socialist Systems' in Mesa-Lago, C. and Beck, C. (eds), *Comparative Socialist Systems. Essays on Politics and Economics*, Pittsburgh, University of Pittsburgh Center for International Studies, 1975 (52—91), p.77.
36 Pirages, D.C., 'Socioeconomic Development and Political Access in the Communist Party-States', in Triska, J.F. (ed.), *Communist Party-States. Comparative and International Studies*, New York, Bobbs-Merrill, 1969 (249—81), p.261.
37 Bauer, R.A. (ed.), *Social Indicators*, Cambridge/Mass., Harvard UP, 1966, p.221.

10 Bibliography
Walter Völkel, Free University, Berlin

This bibliography is based on information from the library and catalogues of the *Zentralinstitut für sozialwissenschaftliche Forschung* of the Free University of Berlin. We have tried to present relatively recent results of research work on the GDR. The bibliography therefore concentrates on literature which has been published after 1970.

Main sections

1   Periodicals, newspapers.
2   Statistical works, comprehensive studies, history.
3   History of the German working class movement from the East German perspective, history of the KPD/SED.
4   SED.
5   Parties in the Democratic Bloc.
6   Social and mass organisations.
7   State and law.
8   The military system.
9   Media and propaganda.
10 Foreign policy, foreign trade.
11 Western industrial countries and the Third World in the literature of the GDR.
12 The German question, relations between the FRG and the GDR. The problem of divided Berlin.

13 The Federal Republic and West Berlin from the East German perspective.
14 Economic history.
15 Political economy, economics.
16 The economic system.
17 Economic policy and economic planning, environmental policy.
18 Industry, transportation.
19 Agriculture.
20 Trade and services.
21 Organisation of industrial plants.
22 Sociology and demography.
23 Social policy.
24 The churches.
25 Arts and culture.
26 Science and education.
27 Psychology.
28 Historical science.
29 Mathematics and natural sciences.
30 Marxism—Leninism.
31 Research.

1   Periodicals, newspapers

West

abg. *Analysen und Berichte aus Gesellschaft und Wissenschaft.* Ed. Institut für Gesellschaft und Wissenschaft (IGW) an der Universität Erlangen-Nürnberg. Erlangen: Deutsche Gesellschaft für zeitgeschichtliche Fragen. Publication dates: occasionally.

DDR Report. (GDR journals and books). Ed. Gesellschaft für Politische Bildung. Bonn: Verl. Neue Gesellschaft. Publication dates: monthly.

Deutschland Archiv (Journal on West German and GDR policy matters). Cologne: Verl. Wissenschaft und Politik. Publication dates: monthly.

Europa-Archiv. Ed. Deutsche Gesellschaft für auswärtige Politik, Bonn. Bonn: Verl. für internationale Politik. Publication dates: semi-monthly.

FS-Analysen. Ed. Research agency for economic and social questions in the two Germanies, Berlin. Publication dates: occasionally.

GDR Bulletin. Newsletter for Literature and Culture in the German Democratic Republic. Washington University. Publication dates: three times a year.

IGW-Referatedienst aus Gesellschaft und Wissenschaft in der DDR. Ed. Institut für Gesellschaft und Wissenschaft (IGW) an der Universität Erlangen-Nürnberg. Publication dates: monthly.

Informationen. Ed. Bundesministerium für innerdeutsche Beziehungen in Zusammenarbeit mit dem Gesamtdeutschen Institut — Bundesanstalt für gesamtdeutsche Aufgaben. Publication dates: bi-weekly.

Jahrbuch für Ostrecht. Ed. Institut für Ostrecht, Munich. Herrenalb: Verlag für internationalen Kulturaustausch. Publication dates: semi-annually.

Osteuropa. (Journal of current questions on East Europe). Ed. Deutsche Gesellschaft für Osteuropakunde, Berlin und Stuttgart. Stuttgart: Deutsche Verlags-Anstalt. Publication dates: monthly.

Sozialistisches Osteuropakomitee. Ed. Sozialistisches Osteuropakomitee, Hamburg. Publication dates: monthly.

Pädagogik und Schule in Ost und West. Ed. Johannes Giesberts, Karl Knoop, Horst E. Wittig. Paderborn: Ferdinand Schöningh Verl. Publication dates: three-monthly.

Politik und Kultur. Ed. Arnulf Baring u.a. Berlin: Colloquium Verl. Publication dates: 6 issues per year.

Pressespiegel. (Taken from GDR newspapers and journals). Ed. Bundesministerium für innerdeutsche Beziehungen. Publication dates: 2 to 3 issues per month.

Recht in Ost und West. (Journal covering the comparison of legal matters and legal problems between the two Germanies). Ed. Arwed Blomeyer, Walther Rosenthal. Berlin: A.W. Haynz's Erben. Publication dates: bi-monthly.

Deutsche Studien. Ed. Karl-Heinz Gehrmann, Walter Hildebrandt, Hans Lades. Bleckede: Verlag Emil Meissner. Publication dates: quarterly.

East

Arbeit und Arbeitsrecht. (Journal for employment and employment law). Berlin: Verl. Die Wirtschaft. Publication dates: monthly.

Sozialistische Arbeitswissenschaft. (Journal on the science of work). Ed. Zentrales Forschungsinstitut für Arbeit beim Staatssekretariat für Arbeit und Löhne. Berlin: Verl. Die Wirtschaft. Publication dates: 6 issues per year.

Architektur der DDR. (Journal on town planning and architecture). Berlin: Verl. für Bauwesen. Publication dates: monthly.

Armee-Rundschau. (Magazine for soldiers). Berlin: Militärverlag der Deutschen Demokratischen Republik. Publication dates: monthly.

Asien, Afrika, Lateinamerika. (Journal of the central council for Asian, African and Latin American studies in the GDR). Berlin: Akademie-Verl. Publication dates: 6 issues per year.

Deutsche Aussenpolitik. Berlin: Deutscher Verl. der Wissenschaften. Publication dates: 12 issues per year.

Beiträge zur Geschichte der Arbeiterbewegung. Berlin: Dietz Verl. Publication dates: 6 issues per year.

Weimarer Beiträge. (Journal for the study of literature, aesthetics and culture theory). Berlin: Aufbau-Verl. Publication dates: monthly.

Berufsbildung. (Journal for the theory and practice of professional training and education). Berlin: Verl. Volk und Wissen. Publication dates: monthly.

DDR-Aussenwirtschaft. Informationen — Dokumente. Berlin: Verl. Die Wirtschaft. Publication dates: weekly.

Neues Deutschland. (Organ of the Central Committee of the SED). Berlin: Verl. Neues Deutschland. Publication dates: 6 issues per week.

Einheit. (Journal for the theory and practice of scientific socialism). Berlin: Dietz Verl. Publication dates: monthly.

FDGB-Review. Berlin: Verl. Tribüne. Publication dates: monthly.

Film und Fernsehen. (Journal on the theory and practice of film and television production). Berlin: Henschelverl. Kunst und Gesellschaft. Publication dates: monthly.

Sozialistische Finanzwirtschaft. (Journal for all financial affairs). Berlin: Verl. Die Wirtschaft. Publication dates: monthly.

Forschung der sozialistischen Berufsbildung. (Scholarly journal of the GDR Central Institute for Vocational Training). Berlin: Zentralinstitut für Berufsbildung der DDR. Publication dates: 6 issues per year.

Forschung, Lehre, Praxis. (Journal of trade union of scientists). Berlin: Verl. Tribüne. Publication dates: monthly.

Forum. (Paper for intellectual problems of the youth). Berlin: Verl. Junge Welt. Publication dates: semi-monthly.

GDR-Export. Berlin: Verl. Die Wirtschaft. Publication dates: occasionally.

GDR-Review. Dresden: Verl. (Illustrated paper). Publication dates: monthly.

Gewerkschaftsleben. Berlin: Verl. Tribüne. Publication dates: monthly.

Der Handel. (Newspaper on the theory and practice of DDR internal business). Berlin: Verl. Die Wirtschaft. Publication dates: 6 issues per year.

Handelswoche. (Newspaper on internal trade and gastronomy). Berlin: Verl. Die Wirtschaft. Publication dates: 26 issues per year.

Das Hochschulwesen. (Newspaper about the DDR higher education system). Berlin: Deutscher Verl. der Wissenschaften. Publication dates: monthly.

Horizont. (A weekly socialist paper about international politics and economics). Berlin: Berliner Verl. Publication dates: weekly.

Informationen zur soziologischen Forschung in der Deutschen Demokratischen Republik. Berlin: Akademie für Gesellschaftswissenschaften beim Zentralkomitee der SED. Publication dates: 6 issues per year.

IPW-Berichte. (Topical information on questions of international politics and economics). Berlin: Staatsverl. der Deutschen Demokratischen Republik. Publication dates: monthly.

IPW-Forschungshefte. (Information on economic, political or ideological questions on state monopoly capitalism). Berlin: Staatsverl. der Deutschen Demokratischen Republik. Publication dates: quarterly.

Neue Justiz. (Journal on law and jurisprudence). Berlin: Staatsverl. der Deutschen Demokratischen Republik. Publication dates: monthly.

Kooperation. (Journal for socialist agriculture and food production). Berlin: Deutscher Landwirtschaftsverl. Publication dates: monthly.

Kultur und Freizeit. (Journal on the theory and practice of intellectual and cultural life). Leipzig: Zentralhaus für Kulturarbeit der DDR. Publication dates: monthly.

Bildende Kunst. Berlin: Henschelverl. Kunst und Gesellschaft. Publication dates: monthly.

Kunst und Literatur. Berlin: Verl. Volk und Welt. Publication dates: monthly.

Law and Legislation in the German Democratic Republic. Ed. Lawyers Association of the GDR. Berlin: Staatsverl. der Deutschen Demokratischen Republik. Publication dates: 2 issues per year.

Deutsche Lehrerzeitung. (Journal of the ministry of education and the central committee of the trade union for education and training). Berlin: Verl. Volk und Wissen. Publication dates: weekly.

Neue Deutsche Literatur. (Monthly journal for literature and criticism). Ed. Schriftstellerverband der Deutschen Demokratischen Republik. Berlin: Aufbau-Verl. Publication dates: monthly.

Militärgeschichte. Berlin: Militärverl. der Deutschen Demokratischen Republik. Publication dates: 6 issues per year.

Der Morgen. (The main publication of the German Liberal-Democratic Party). Berlin: Verl. Der Morgen. Publication dates: 6 issues per week.

National-Zeitung. (The paper of the German National-Democratic party). Berlin: Zeitungsverl. National. Publication dates: 6 issues per week.

News. Dresden: Verl. Zeit im Bild. Publication dates: monthly.

Pädagogik. (Journal on the theory and practice of socialist education). Berlin: Verl. Volk und Wissen. Publication dates: monthly.

Neue Deutsche Presse. (The main publication of the central committee of the GDR journalists union). Berlin: Verband der Journalisten der DDR. Publication dates: monthly.

Prisma. (Topical subjects about the GDR). Dresden: Verl. Zeit im Bild. Publication dates: quarterly.

Probleme des Friedens und des Sozialismus. (Journal of the communist and workers parties on theory and information). Berlin: Dietz Verl. Publication dates: monthly.

Sinn und Form. (Articles on literature). Ed. Akademie der Künste der Deutschen Demokratischen Republik. Berlin: Rütten and Loening. Publication dates: 6 issues per year.

Sonntag. (A cultural political weekly publication). Ed. Kulturbund der DDR. Berlin: Aufbau-Verl. Publication dates: weekly.

Sowjetwissenschaft. (Articles on sociology). Berlin: Verl. Volk und Welt. Publication dates: monthly.

Sports in the GDR. Berlin: Deutscher Turn- und Sportbund. Publication dates: 6 issues per year.

Staat und Recht. Ed. Akademie für Staats- und Rechtswissenschaft der DDR. Berlin: Staatsverl. der Deutschen Demokratischen Republik. Publication dates: monthly.

Theater der Zeit. (Publication of the GDR theatre workers). Berlin: Henschelverl. Kunst und Gesellschaft. Publication dates: monthly.

Tribüne. Organ des Bundesvorstandes des FDGB. Berlin: Verl. Tribune. Publication dates: 5 issues per week.

Volksarmee. Berlin: Militarverl. der Deutschen Demokratischen Republik. Publication dates: weekly.

Neuer Weg. (Main publication of the central committee of the SED on questions of party life). Berlin: Dietz Verl. Publication dates: fortnightly.

Die Weltgewerkschaftsbewegung. Berlin: Verl. Tribüne. Publication dates: monthly.

Die Wirtschaft. (Newspaper on politics, economics and technology). Berlin: Verl. Die Wirtschaft. Publication dates: 14 issues per year.

Wirtschaftsrecht. (Journal on the theory and practice of socialist economic law). Berlin: Staatsverl. der Deutschen Demokratischen Republik. Publication dates: quarterly.

Wirtschaftswissenschaft. Berlin: Verl. Die Wirtschaft. Publication dates: monthly.

Deutsche Zeitschrift für Philosophie. Berlin: Deutscher Verl. der Wissenschaften. Publication dates: monthly.

Zeitschrift für Germanistik. Leipzig: Verl. Enzyklopadie. Publication dates: 4 issues per year.

Zeitschrift für Geschichtswissenschaft. Berlin: Deutscher Verl. der Wissenschaften. Publication dates: monthly.

internationale Zeitschrift der handwirtschaft. (Journal of the standing commission for agriculture of the council for mutual economic assistance distributed in the member countries of the RGW). Berlin: Deutscher Landwirtschaftsverl. Publication dates: 6 issues per year.

Neue Zeit. (Main publication of the German Christian Democrat Union). Berlin: Verl. Neue Zeit. Publication dates: 6 issues per week.

2 Statistical works, comprehensive studies, history

Ash, Timothy Garton: *Und willst du nicht mein Bruder sein . . . .* Reinbek bei Hamburg: Rowohlt 1981.

Auferstanden aus Ruinen, ed. Alexander von Plato, SBZ sur DDR (1945–1949), ein Weg zu Einheit und Sozialismus?, Cologne: Verl. Rote Fahne 1979, (Oktober-Taschenbuch 5.)

Bahro, Rudolf: *Ich werde meinen Weg fortsetzen. Eine Dokumentation* (2nd ed.), Cologne, Frankfurt/Main: Europaïsche Verlags-Anstalt 1979.

Behr, Wolfgang: *Bundesrepublik Deutschland – Deutsche Demokratische Republik. Systemvergleich Politik, Wirtschaft, Gesellschaft,* Stuttgart, Berlin, Cologne, Mainz: Kohlhammer 1979.

Bericht der Bundesregierung und Materialien zur Lage der Nation, ed. Bundesministerium für innerdeutsche Beziehungen, Bonn: Bundesministerium für innerdeutsche Beziehungen, 1971, 1972.

Bibliographie zum öffentlichen Sprachgebrauch in der Bundesrepublik Deutschland und in der DDR, compiled and commented upon by a working party led by Manfred W. Hellmann, Düsseldorf: Pädagogischer Verl. Schwann 1976. (Sprache der Gegenwart 16.)

Bibliographie zur Deutschlandpolitik 1941—1974, ed. Bundesministerium für innerdeutsche Beziehungen, Frankfurt/Main: Metzner 1975 (Dokumente zur Deutschlandpolitik. Beihefte 1.)

Boeck, Walter, *Deutschland: Zwei Staaten, zwei Systeme*, 2nd ed., Freiburg, Würzburg, Ploetz 1978. (Ploetz-Archivmaterialien.)

Böger, Klaus and Kremendahl, Hans: *Bundesrepublik Deutschland — Deutsche Demokratische Republik: Vergleich der politischen Systeme. Unterrichtsmodell für die Sekundarstufe 2*, vol.1, 'Didaktischer Teil', (vol.2) 'Materialien- und Tabellenteil für den Unterrichtsgebrauch', Stuttgart: Metzler 1979. (Schriftenreihe Politische Didaktik.)

Bröll, Werner, Wolfgang Heisenberg and Winfried Sühlo: *Der andere Teil Deutschlands*, 3rd ed. Munich, Vienna: Olzog 1971 (Geschichte und Staat 117/117a.)

Buch, Günther: *Namen und Daten wichtiger Personen der DDR*, 2nd ed., Berlin, Bonn: Dietz 1979.

Bundesrepublik Deutschland und Deutsche Demokratische Republik. Die beiden deutschen Staaten im Vergleich, ed. Eckhard Jesse, Berlin: Colloquium Verl. 1981.

Bussiek, Hendrik: *Notizen aus der DDR. Erlebnisse, Erfahrungen, Erkenntnisse in der unbekannten deutschen Republik*, Frankfurt/Main: Fischer 1979. (Fischer-Taschenbuch 3417.)

DDR-Handbuch, ed. Bundesministerium für innerdeutsche Beziehungen, scientific direction: Peter Christian Ludz und Johannes Kuppe. 2nd ed. Cologne: Verl. Wissenschaft und Politik 1979.

Deutschland, Deutschland: 47 Schriftsteller aus der BRD und der DDR schreiben über ihr Land, Salzburg, Vienna: Residenz Verl. 1979.

East Central and Southeast Europe. A handbook of library and archival resources in North America, ed. Paul L. Horecky, David H. Kraus, Santa Barbara/Calif., Oxford: Clio Press 1976. (The Joint Committee on Eastern Europe Publication Series 3.)

Endlich, Hans: *Die DDR. Eine Einführung in das politische und wirtschaftliche System*, Materialsammlung für die Sekundarstufe I. Hamburg: Verl. Erziehung und Wissenschaft 1978. (Beiträge zur Unterrichtspraxis.)

European Bibliography of Soviet, East European and Slavonic Studies, ed. Thomas Hink, Birmingham: University of Birmingham, vol.1, 1977; vol.2, 1979.

Gellert, Johannes F. and Kramm, Hans-Joachim, *DDR. Land, Volk, Wirtschaft in Stichworten.* Vienna: Hirt 1977 (Hirts Stichwörterbücher.)

Grätz, Frank: *Die DDR*, Munich: Heyne 1979. (Kompaktwissen 92.)

Grosser, Alfred: *Deutschlandbilanz. Geschichte Deutschlands seit 1945.* Munich: Hanser 1970.

Grube, Frank and Richter, Gerhard (eds): *Flucht und Vertreibung. Deutschland zwischen 1944 und 1947.* Hamburg: Hoffmann and Campe 1980.

Gutachten zum Stand der DDR- und vergleichenden Deutschlandforschung. Erstattet vom Arbeitskreis fur Vergleichende Deutschlandforschung unter Vorsitz von Peter C. Ludz, vols 1—4. Bonn: Arbeitskreis für Vergleichende Deutschlandforschung 1978.

Hanhardt, Arthur M.: 'East Germany: From goals to realities', *Political Socialisation in Eastern Europe*, New York: Praeger 1975, pp. 69—91.

Havemann, Robert: 'Die DDR in den zwanzig Jahren nach Stalins Sturz', *Entstalinisierung. Der 20.Parteitag der KPdSU und seine Folgen*, Frankfurt/Main: Suhrkamp 1977, pp. 65—81.

Havemann, Robert: 'Die DDR: Der sozialistische Staat Deutscher Nation', *25 Jahre Bundesrepublik Deutschland*, Vienna, Munich, Zürich: Molden 1974, pp. 333—8.

Hersch, Helga: *A Bibliography of German Studies 1945—1971. Germany under Allied occupation*, Federal Republic of Germany, German Democratic Republic, Bloomington: Indiana University Press 1972.

Hoffmann, Stephan Paul: *National tradition and the development of the German Democratic Republic 1945—1971*, Bucks: University microfilms 1976.

Jaenecke, Heinrich: *30 Jahre und ein Tag. Die Geschichte der deutschen Teilung*, Düsseldorf, Vienna: Pädagogischer Verl. Schwann 1974.

Krisch, Henry: *German Politics under Soviet Occupation*, New York: Columbia University Press 1974.

Lübbe, Peter: *Der staatlich etablierte Sozialismus. Zur Kritik des staatsmonopolistischen Sozialismus*, Hamburg: Hoffmann and Campe 1975. (Kritische Wissenschaft.)

McCauley, Martin: 'East Germany', *Communist Power in Europe 1944—1949*, London: Macmillan 1977, pp. 58—72.

McCauley, Martin: *Marxism—Leninism in the German Democratic Republic. The Socialist Unity Party SED*, London: Macmillan 1979. (Studies in Russian and East European history.)

Materialien zum Bericht der Lage der Nation, ed. Bundesminister für innerdeutsche Beziehungen, Bonn: Heger 1971, 1972, 1974.

Merritt, Anna J. and Merritt, Richard L.: *Politics, economics, and society in the two Germanies, 1945—75* (a bibliography of English works), Urbana: University of Illinois Press 1978.

Nolte, Ernst: *Deutschland und der Kalte Krieg*, Munich, Zürich: Piper 1974.

Erbe, Günter, et al., *Politik, Wirtschaft und Gesellschaft in der DDR. Studientexte für die politische Bildung*, 2nd ed. Opladen: Westdeutscher Verl. 1980.

Reichelt, Paul: *Deutsche Chronik 1945 bis 1970. Daten und Fakten aus beiden Teilen Deutschlands, Freudenstadt:* Eurobuch-Verl. Lutzeyer, vol.1, 1945—57, 1970; vol.2 1958—1970, 1971. (Bonn-Aktuell 4.)

Die DDR vor den Aufgaben der Integration und der Koexistenz. 6. Tagung zum Stand der DDR-Forschung in der Bundesrepublik 13.— 16.6.1973, Referate, Tutzing: Akademie für Politische Bildung 1973. (Deutschland Archiv. vol.6, Sonderheft.)

30 Jahre Deutsche Demokratische Republik, ed. Friedrich-Ebert-Stiftung, Bonn: Verl. Neue Gesellschaft 1979. (Die DDR, Realitäten, Argumente.)

25 Jahre Deutsche Demokratische Republik (DDR), ed. Friedrich-Ebert-Stiftung, Bonn-Bad Godesberg: Verl. Neue Gesellschaft 1974. (Die DDR, Realitäten, Argumente.)

Gleitze, Bruno et al.: *Die DDR nach 25 Jahren*, Berlin: Duncker and Humblot 1975. (Wirtschaft und Gesellschaft in Mitteldeutschland 10.)

DDR. Das politische, wirtschaftliche und soziale System, ed. Heinz Rausch and Theo Stammen, 4th ed., Munich: Bayerische Landeszentrale für politische Bildungsarbeit 1978.

Richert, Ernst: 'Revolutionäre und evolutionäre Tendenzen im DDR-Gesellschaftsprozess', *Sozialstruktur und Sozialplanung in der DDR*, Cologne: Verl. Wissenschaft und Politik, 1975, 19—45.

Rudolph, Hermann: *Die Gesellschaft der DDR — eine deutsche Möglichkeit? Anmerkungen zum Leben im anderen Deutschland*, Munich: Piper 1972. (Serie Piper 30.)

Schneider, Eberhard: *The GDR: The History, Politics, Economy and Society of East Germany*, London: Hurst 1978.

Sontheimer, Kurt and Bleek, Wilhelm: *Die DDR. Politik, Gesellschaft, Wirtschaft*, 5th ed., Hamburg: Hoffmann and Campe 1979. (Kritische Wissenschaft.)

Sozialismus in der DDR. Dokumente und Materialien, ed. Rainer Rilling, 2 vols., Cologne: Pahl-Rugenstein 1979. (Kleine Bibliothek Politik, Wissenschaft, Zukunft 114/I, 114/II.)

Sperling, Walter: *Landeskunde DDR. Eine annotierte Auswahlbibliographie*, Munich: Verl. Dokumentation 1978. (Bibliographien zur regionalen Geographie und Landeskunde 1.)

Staritz, Dietrich: *Sozialismus in einem halben Lande. Zur Programmatik und Politik der KPD/SED in der Phase der antifaschistisch–demokratischen Umwälzung in der DDR*, Berlin: Wagenbach 1976. (Politik 69.)

Starrels, John Murray and Mallinckrodt, Anita M.: *Politics in the German Democratic Republic*, New York: Praeger 1975. (Praeger special studies in international politics and government.)

Steel, Jonathan: *Inside East Germany. The state that came in from the cold*, New York: Urizen Books 1977.

Thurich, Eckart: *Zweimal Deutschland. Lehrbuch für Politik und Zeitgeschichte*. Frankfurt/Main: Diesterweg 1979.

Verzeichnis von Behörden und staatlichen Einrichtungen in der DDR, Berlin: Osteuropa-Institut der FU, Abteilung Recht 1979.

Weber, Hermann: *DDR. Grudriss der Geschichte 1945–1976*, Hanover: Fackelträger-Verl. 1976. (Edition Zeitgeschehen.)

Windmöller, Eva and Höpker, Thomas: *Leben in der DDR*, Hamburg: Gruner und Jahr 1977. (Ein Stern-Buch.)

Zahlenspiegel. Bundesrepublik Deutschland/Deutsche Demokratische Republik – Ein Vergleich (new ed.), Bonn: Bundesministerium für innerdeutsche Beziehungen 1978.

Zimmermann, Hartmut: 'Die DDR in den 70er Jahren. Zu einigen Aspekten der innenpolitischen Situation der DDR', *Politik, Wirtschaft und Gesellschaft in der DDR*, 2nd ed., Opladen: Westdeutscher Verl. 1980, pp. 13–89.

East

Doernberg, Stefan: *Befreiung 1945. Ein Augenzeugenbericht*, Berlin: Dietz 1975.

Einheit — im Kampfe geboren. Beiträge zum 30 Jahrestag der Befreiung vom Faschismus, ed. Karl-Marx-Universität Leipzig, Leipzig: Karl-Marx-Universität 1975.

Wissenschaftliche Entscheidungen — historische Veränderungen — Fundamente der Zukunft. Studien zur Geschichte der DDR in den sechziger Jahren, ed. Institut für Gesellschaftswissenschaften beim ZK der SED, Berlin: Staatsverl. der DDR 1971.

Griebenow, Helmut (leader) et al.: *Entstehung und Entwicklung der DDR*. Collective of authors, Leipzig: Verl. Enzyklopädie 1979. (Landeskunde DDR für Ausländer, Arbeitshefte.)

Geschichte der Deutschen Demokratischen Republik, Collective of authors under the guidance of Rolf Badstübner, ed. Wissenschaftlicher Beirat für Geschichtswissenschaft beim Ministerium für Hoch- und Fachschulwesen, Berlin: Deutscher Verl. der Wissenschaften 1981.

Grundriss der deutschen Geschichte. Von den Anfängen der Geschichte des deutschen Volkes bis zur Gestaltung der entwickelten sozialistischen Gesellschaft in der DDR. Klassenkampf, Tradition, Sozialismus, ed. Ernst Diehl et al., 2nd ed., Berlin: Deutscher Verl. der Wissenschaften 1979.

Heitzer, Heinz: *DDR. Geschichtlicher Überblick*, Berlin: Dietz 1979. (Schriftenreihe Geschichte.)

Statistisches Jahrbuch der Deutschen Demokratischen Republik, vol.1, 1955—vol.24, 1979, ed. Staatliche Zentralverwaltung für Statistik. Berlin: Staatsverl. der DDR 1956—1979.

Die ersten Jahre. Erinnerungen an den Beginn der revolutionären Umgestaltungen, Berlin: Dietz 1979.

Mehls, Hartmut and Mehls, Ellen: *13. August*, ed. Zentralinstitut für Geschichte der Akademie der Wissenschaften der DDR, Berlin: Deutscher Verl. der Wissenschaften 1980. (Illustrierte historische Hefte.)

Mit dem Sozialismus gewachsen. Fünfundzwanzig Jahre DDR, ed. Institut für Gesellschaftswissenschaften beim ZK der SED, Berlin: Verl. Die Wirtschaft 1974.

Mit dem Sozialismus gewachsen. Eine Literaturauswahl aus Anlass des 25. Jahrestages der Gründung der Deutschen Demokratischen Republik, Leipzig: Buchexport 1974.

Neef, Helmut: *Entscheidende Tage im Oktober 1949. Die Gründung der Deutschen Demokratischen Republik*, Berlin: Dietz 1979. (Schriftenreihe Geschichte.)

DDR. Gesellschaft, Staat, Bürger, 3rd ed., Berlin: Staatsverl. der DDR 1979.

Deutsche Demokratische Republik. Handbuch, Leipzig: Verl. Enzyklopädie 1979.

DDR. Werden und Wachsen. Zur Geschichte der Deutschen Demokratischen Republik, Berlin: Dietz 1974.

Die DDR in der Übergangsperiode. Studien zur Vorgeschichte und Geschichte der DDR 1945 bis 1961, ed. Rolf Badstübner and Heinz Heitzer. Berlin: Akademie-Verl. 1979.

Schöneburg, Karl-Heinz: *Von den Anfängen unseres Staates*, Berlin: Staatsverl. der DDR 1975.

Schöneburg, Karl-Heinz: *Staat und Recht in der Geschichte der DDR*, Berlin: Staatsverl. der DDR 1973. (Der sozialistische Staat.)

Streisand, Joachim: *Deutsche Geschichte in einem Band. Ein Überblick*, 4th ed. Berlin: Deutscher Verl. der Wissenschaften 1979.

Statistisches Taschenbuch der Deutschen Demokratischen Republik, vol.1959–vol.1979, ed. Staatliche Zentralverwaltung für Statistik, Berlin: Staatsverl. der DDR 1959–1979.

Kleines politisches Wörterbuch, 3rd ed., Berlin: Dietz 1978.

3 History of the German working class movement from the East German perspective, history of the KPD/SED

West

Zur Aktionseinheitspolitik der KPD 1919–1946, ed. Institut für Marxistische Studien und Forschungen, Frankfurt am Main, Frankfurt/Main: Verl. Marxistische Blätter 1976. (Neudrucke zur sozialistischen Theorie und Gewerkschaftspraxis 8.) (Marxistische Paperbacks 68.)

Angress, Werner T.: *Die Kampfzeit der KPD 1921–1923*, Düsseldorf: Droste Verl. 1973. (Geschichtliche Studien zu Politik und Gesellschaft 2.)

Arbeiterinitiative 1945. Antifaschistische Ausschüsse und Reorganisation der Arbeiterbewegung in Deutschland, ed. Lutz Niethammer, Ulrich Borsdorf and Peter Brandt, Wuppertal: Hammer 1976.

Bahne, Siegfried: *Die KPD und das Ende von Weimar. Das Scheitern einer Politik 1932–1935*, Frankfurt/Main: Campus Verl. 1976. (Campus Studium 515. Sozialgeschichte.)

Die Rote Fahne. Kritik, Theorie, Feuilleton 1918—1933, ed. Brauneck, Manfred, Munich: Wilhelm Fink 1973. (Uni—Taschenbücher 127.)

Duhnke, Horst: *Die KPD von 1933 bis 1945*, Cologne: Kiepenheuer and Witsch 1972.

Eisner, Freya: *Das Verhältnis der KPD zu den Gewerkschaften in der Weimarer Republik*, Cologne, Frankfurt/Main: Europäische Verlagsanstalt 1977. (Schriftenreihe der Otto Brenner Stiftung 8.)

Faschismusanalyse und antifaschistischer Kampf der Kommunistischen Internationale und der KPD 1923—1945, 2nd ed. Heidelberg: Sendler 1974.

Freyberg, Jutta von: *Sozialdemokraten und Kommunisten. Die revolutionären Sozialisten Deutschlands vor dem Problem der Aktionseinheit 1934—1937*, Cologne: Pahl—Rugenstein 1973. (Sammlung Junge Wissenschaft.)

Fricke, Karl Wilhelm: *Warten auf Gerechtigkeit. Kommunistische Säuberungen und Rehabilitierungen. Bericht und Dokumentation*, Cologne: Verl. Wissenschaft und Politik 1971.

Gerhard, Dirk: *Antifaschisten. Proletarischer Widerstand 1933—1945*, Berlin: Klaus Wagenbach 1976. (Politik 64.)

Hauth, Ulrich: *Die Politik von KPD und SED gegenüber der westdeutschen Sozialdemokratie 1945—1948*. Frankfurt/Main: Lang 1978. (Europaïsche Hochschulschriften. Reihe 3. 109.)

Heer, Hannes: *Ernst Thälmann. In Selbstzeugnissen und Bilddokumenten*, Reinbek bei Hamburg: Rowohlt 1975. (Rororo Bildmonographien 230.)

Hemje-Oltmanns, Dirk: *Arbeiterbewegung und Einheitsfront. Zur Diskussion der Einheitsfronttaktik in der KPD 1920/21*, Westberlin: VSA 1973.

Hochmuth, Ursel: *Faschismus und Widerstand 1933—1945. Ein Verzeichnis deutsprachiger Literatur*, Frankfurt/Main: Röderberg 1973.

Kontos, Silvia: *Die Partei kämpft wie ein Mann. Frauenpolitik der KPD in der Weimarer Republik*, Basel: Stroemfeld, Frankfurt/Main: Roter Stern 1979.

Langkau-Alex, Ursula: 'Volksfront für Deutschland?', vol.1, *Vorgeschichte und Gründung des 'Ausschusses zur Vorbereitung einer deutschen Volksfront', 1933—1936*, Frankfurt/Main: Syndikat 1977.

Lehndorff, Steffen: *Wie kam es zur RGO? Probleme der Gewerkschaftsentwicklung in der Weimarer Republik von 1927 bis 1929*, Frankfurt/Main: Verl. Marxistische Blätter 1975. (Marxistische Paperbacks 54.)

Lippmann, Heinz: *Honecker. Porträt eines Nachfolgers*, Cologne: Verl. Wissenschaft und Politik 1971.

Maas, Lieselotte: *Deutsche Exilpresse in Lateinamerika*, Frankfurt/Main: Buchhändler-Vereinigung 1978. (Kleine Schriften der Deutschen Bibliothek 3.)

Mammach, Klaus: *Die KPD und die deutsche antifaschistische Widerstandsbewegung 1933–1939*, ed. Institut für Marxismus–Leninismus beim ZK der SED. Lizenzausgabe, Frankfurt/Main: Röderberg 1974.

Müller, Werner: *Die KPD und die 'Einheit der Arbeiterklasse'*, Frankfurt, New York: Campus Verl. 1979. (Forschung 73.)

Schöck, Eva Cornelia: *Arbeitslosigkeit und Rationalisierung. Die Lage der Arbeiter und die kommunistische Gewerkschaftspolitik 1920–28*, Frankfurt/Main: Campus Verl. 1977. (Campus Studium: Sozialgeschichte.)

Schuster, Kurt, G.P.: *Der Rote Frontkämpferbund 1924–1929. Beiträge zur Geschichte und Organisationsstruktur eines politischen Kampfbundes*, Düsseldorf: Droste Verl. 1975. (Beiträge zur Geschichte des Parlamentarismus und der politischen Parteien 55.)

Staritz, Dietrich: *Sozialismus in einem halben Lande. Zur Programmatik und Politik der KPD/SED in der Phase der antifaschistisch-demokratischen Umwälzung in der DDR*, Berlin: Wagenbach 1976. (Politik 69.)

Sywottek, Arnold: *Deutsche Volksdemokratie. Studien zur politischen Konzeption der KPD 1935–1946*, Düsseldorf: Bertelmann Universitätsverl. 1971. (Studien zur modernen Geschichte 1.)

Thälmann, Ernst: *Zwischen Erinnerung und Erwartung. Autobiographische Aufzeichnungen, geschrieben in faschistischer Haft. Biographische Dokumentation mit einer Thälmann-Chronik*, ed. Kuratorium 'Gedenkstätte Ernst Thälmann', Hamburg, Frankfurt/Main: Röderberg-Verl. 1977.

Vosske, Heinz and Nitsche, Gerhard: *Wilhelm Pieck. Biographischer Abriss*, cop. Berlin: Dietz 1975. Frankfurt/Main: Verl. Marxistische Blätter 1975.

Weber, Hermann: *SED. Chronik einer Partei. 1971–1976*, Cologne: Verl. Wissenschaft und Politik 1976.

Weber, Hermann: *Die Sozialistische Einheitspartei Deutschlands 1946–1971*, Hanover: Verl. für Literatur und Zeitgeschehen 1971. (Edition Zeitgeschehen 16.)

Weber, Hermann: *Die SED nach Ulbricht*, Hanover: Fackelträger-Verl. 1974. (Edition Zeitgeschehen.)

Weber, Hermann: *Von Rosa Luxemburg zu Walter Ulbricht. Wandlungen des Kommunismus in Deutschland*, 4th ed., Hanover: Verl. für Literatur und Zeitgeschehen 1970. (Edition Zeitgeschehen 6.)

Weber, Hermann and Oldenburg, Fred: *25 Jahre SED. Chronik einer Partei*, Cologne: Verl. Wissenschaft und Politik 1971.

Wieszt, Jozsef: *KPD—Politik in der Krise. 1928—1932. Zur Geschichte und Problematik des Versuchs, den Kampf gegen den Faschismus mittels Sozialfaschismusthese und RGO—Politik zu führen*, Frankfurt/Main: Materialismus Verl. 1976. (MOP, Materialismus-Off-Print 1: Koll.: Geschichte und Theorie der deutschen Arbeiterbewegung, Serie 5: 1924—1945.)

East

Dahlem, Franz: *Am Vorabend des zweiten Weltkrieges. 1938 bis August 1939*, 2 vols, Berlin: Dietz 1977.

Geschichte der deutschen Arbeiterbewegung. Biographisches Lexikon, Berlin: Dietz 1970.

Geschichte der Sozialistischen Einheitspartei Deutschlands. Abriss, Berlin: Dietz 1978.

Illustrierte Geschichte der deutschen Novemberrevolution 1918—1919, Berlin: Dietz 1978.

Heider, Paul: *Antifaschistischer Kampf und revolutionäre Militärpolitik. Zur Militärpolitik der KPD von 1933 bis 1939 im Kampf gegen Faschismus und Kriegsvorbereitung, für Frieden, Demokratie und Sozialismus*, Berlin: Militärverl. der DDR 1976. (Militärhistorische Studien 17. NF.)

Erich Honecker. Skizze seines politischen Lebens, Berlin: Dietz 1977.

30 Jahre SED. Protokoll des wissenschaftlichen Colloquiums der Akademie für Staats- und Rechtswissenschaft der DDR am 12. April 1976 zum 30.Jahrestag der Gründung der Sozialistischen Einheitspartei Deutschlands, Potsdam-Babelsberg: Akademie für Staats- und Rechtswissenschaft der DDR 1976. (Aktuelle Beiträge der Staats- und Rechtswissenschaft 152.)

Mewis, Karl: *Im Auftrag der Partei. Erlebnisse im Kampf gegen die faschistische Diktatur*, Berlin: Dietz 1971.

Wilhelm Pieck. 1876—1960. Bilder und Dokumente aus seinem Leben, ed. Heinz Vosske, Berlin: Verl. Neues Leben 1975.

Riedel, Volker: *Freies Deutschland, México 1941—1946. Bibliographie einer Zeitschrift*, Berlin, Weimar: Aufbau-Verl. 1975. (Analytische Bibliographien deutschsprachiger literarischer Zeitschriften 4.)

Sachwörterbuch der Geschichte Deutschlands und der deutschen Arbeiterbewegung, ed. Horst Bartel, Herbert Bartsch et al., Berlin: Dietz, vol.1, A—K, 1969; vol.2, L—Z, 1970.

Seht, welche Kraft! Die SED — Tradition, Gegenwart, Zukunft, ed. Institut für Gesellschaftswissenschaften beim ZK der SED ..., Berlin: Dietz 1971.

Bartel, Horst, et al.: *Das Sozialistengesetz. 1878—1890. Illustrierte Geschichte des Kampfes der Arbeiterklasse gegen das Ausnahmegesetz*, Berlin: Dietz 1980.

Ernst Thälmann. Eine Biographie, Collection of authors under the direction of Günter Hortzschansky, Berlin: Dietz 1980.

Die Vereinigung von KPD und SPD zur Sozialistischen Einheitspartei Deutschlands in Bildern und Dokumenten, Berlin: Dietz 1976.

Vosske, Heinz: *Otto Grotewohl. Biographischer Abriss*, Berlin: Dietz 1979.

Vosske, Heinz: *Wilhelm Pieck*, 3rd ed., Leipzig: Bibliographisches Institut 1979.

Werchan, Inge et al.: *Das Werk von Marx und Engels in der Literatur der deutschen Sozialdemokratie (1869—1895). Bibliographie*, Berlin: Dietz 1979.

Der antifaschistische Widerstandskampf der KPD im Spiegel des Flugblattes 1933—1945, compiled and introduced by Margot Pikarski and Günter Uebel, Berlin: Dietz 1978.

Wohlgemuth, Heinz: *Die Entstehung der Kommunistischen Partei Deutschlands. Überblick*, 2nd ed., Berlin: Dietz 1978.

4   SED

West

Glaessner, Gert-Joachim: *Herrschaft durch Kader. Leitung der Gesellschaft und Kaderpolitik in der DDR*, Opladen: Westdeutscher Verl. 1977. (Schriften des Zentralinstituts für sozialwissenschaftliche Forschung der Freien Universität Berlin 28.)

Grote, Manfred: 'The Socialist Unity Party of Germany', *The Communist Parties in Eastern Europe*, New York: Columbia University Press 1979, 167—200.

Lohmann, Ulrich: *Verfassung und Programm in der DDR*, compiled and introduced by Ulrich Lohmann, Berlin, New York: de Gruyter 1977 (Aktuelle Dokumente.)

Ludz, Peter Christian: *The changing party elite in East Germany*, (Parteielite im Wandel, transl.), Cambridge/Massachusetts, London: The MIT Press 1972.

McCauley, Martin: *Marxism—Leninism in the German Democratic Republic. The Socialist Unity Party SED*, London: Macmillan 1979. (Studies in Russian and East European history.)

Neugebauer, Gero: *Partei und Staatsapparat in der DDR. Aspekte der Instrumentalisierung des Staatsapparats durch die SED*, Opladen: Westdeutscher Verl. 1978. (Schriften des Zentralinstituts für sozialwissenschaftliche Forschung der Freien Universitat Berlin 29.)

Honeckers Parteiprogramm, ed. Friedrich-Ebert-Stiftung, 2nd ed., Bonn: Verl. Neue Gesellschaft 1980. (Die DDR. Realitaten, Argumente.)

Der X. Parteitag der SED. 35 Jahre SED-Politik. Versuch einer Bilanz. *Vierzehnte Tagung zum Stand der DDR—Forschung in der Bundesrepublik Deutschland 9. bis 12. Juni 1981*, Referate. Cologne: Verl. Wissenschaft und Politik 1981. (Edition Deutschland Archiv.)

Programm und Statut der SED ... angenommen auf dem 9. Parteitag der SED ... 1976, Bonn: Gesamtdeutsches Institut 1976. (Seminarmaterial des Gesamtdeutschen Instituts.)

Programm und Statut der SED vom 22. Mai 1976, with introductory comment by Karl Wilhelm Fricke, Cologne: Verl. Wissenschaft und Politik 1976.

Schneider, Eberhard: *Die SED der 80er Jahre. Das neue Programm und Statut der Partei*, Cologne: Bundesinstitut fur ostwissenschaftliche und internationale Studien 1977. (Berichte des Bundesinstituts für ostwissenschaftliche und internationale Studien 1977, 23.)

Schneider, Eberhard: *SED, Programm und Statut von 1976. Text, Kommentar, didaktische Hilfen*, Opladen: Leske and Budrich 1977. (Analysen 21.)

Schwarzenbach, Rudolf: *Die Kaderpolitik der SED in der Staatsverwaltung. Ein Beitrag zur Entiwcklung des Verhältnisses von Partei und Staat in der DDR (1945—1975)*, Cologne: Verl. Wissenschaft und Politik 1976. (Bibliothek Wissenschaft und Politik 17.)

Spanger, Hans-Joachim: *Die SED und der Sozialdemokratismus. Ideologische Abgrenzung in der DDR*, Cologne: Verl. Wissenschaft und Politik 1981.

Starrells, John Murray and Mallinckrodt, Anita M., *Politics in the German Democratic Republic*, New York: Praeger 1975. (Praeger special studies in international politics and government.)

Völkel, Walter: 'Die SED', *Politik, Wirtschaft und Gesellschaft in der DDR*, 2nd ed., Opladen: Westdeutscher Verl. 1980, 90—111.

Waldrich, Hans-Peter: *Der Demokratiebegriff der SED. Ein Vergleich zwischen der älteren deutschen Sozialdemokratie und der sozialistischen Einheitspartei Deutschlands*, with an introduction by Iring Fetscher, Stuttgart: Klett—Cotta 1980.

East

Die weiteren Aufgaben der politischen Massenarbeit der Partei. Konferenz des Zentralkomitees der SED am 25.—26.Mai 1977. Eröffnungsansprache Erich Honecker, Referat Werner Lamberz, Beschluss des Politbüros des ZK der SED vom 18.Mai 1977. Berlin: Dietz 1977.

Badstube, Karl-Heinz: *Partei, Staatsmacht, Staatsvolk*, Berlin: Staatsverl. der DDR 1971.

Honecker, Erich: 'Die nächsten Aufgaben der Partei bei der weiteren Durchführung der Beschlüsse des IX. Parteitages der SED', *Referat des Generalsekretärs des ZK der SED und Vorsitzenden des Staatsrates der DDR auf der Beratung des Sekretariats des ZK der SED mit den 1. Sekretären der Kreisleitungen am 25. Januar 1980 in Berlin*, Berlin: Dietz 1980.

Honecker, Erich: 'Die Aufgaben der Partei bei der weiteren Verwirklichung der Beschlüsse des IX. Parteitages der SED', *Referat des Generalsekretärs des ZK der SED auf der Beratung mit den 1. Sekretären der Kreisleitungen*, with contributions to this speech from *Neuen Deutschland*, Berlin: Dietz 1978.

Honecker, Erich: 'Die sozialistische Revolution in der DDR und ihre Perspektiven', *Rede auf der propagandistischen Grossveranstaltung zur Eröffnung des Parteilehrjahres 1977—78 in Dresden am 26.9.1977*, 2nd ed., Berlin: Dietz 1978. (Vorträge im Parteilehrjahr der SED, 1977—78.)

Ossig, Horst and Gurke, Konrad: *Erfahrungen bei der Anwendung der Leninschen Normen des Parteilebens in den Grundorganisationen der SED*, Berlin: Dietz 1975.

Marxistisch—leninistische Partei und sozialistischer Staat. Berlin, Dietz 1978. (Sozialismus-Erfahrungen, Probleme und Perspektiven.)

Das Prinzip des demokratischen Zentralismus im Aufbau und in der Tätigkeit der kommunistischen Partei, Joint scientific symposium between the Parteihochschule 'Karl Marx' at the ZK of the SED and the Institut für Marxismus—Leninismus at the ZK of the KPdSU, 27.—28.11.1972 in Berlin. Berlin: Dietz 1974.

Schneider, Kurt: *Arbeiterklasse — Partei — Bündnispolitik*, 2nd ed., Berlin: Deutscher Verl. der Wissenschaften 1976. (Probleme des wissenschaftlichen Kommunismus.)

Schüssler, Gerhard and Weichelt, Wolfgang: *Arbeiterklasse, Partei, Staatsmacht*, Berlin: Staatsverl. der DDR 1976.

5   Parties in the Democratic Bloc

West

Kulbach, Roderich and Weber, Helmut in collaboration with Eckart Förtsch: *Parteien im Blocksystem der DDR. Funktion und Aufbau der LDPD und der NDPD*, Cologne: Verl. Wissenschaft und Politik 1969. (Schriftenreihe des Studienkollegs fur zeitgeschichtliche Fragen 3.)

Parteien in beiden deutschen Staaten, ed. Friedrich—Ebert—Stiftung, 3rd ed., Bonn: Verl. Neue Gesellschaft 1979. (Die DDR. Realitäten, Argumente.)

Schmolze, Gerhard: 'Das Elend der Ost-CDU', *Das Elend der Christdemokraten*, Munich: Herder 1977, 74—92.

Staritz, Dietrich: 'Die Entstehung des Parteisystems der DDR', *Das Parteiensystem der Bundesrepublik*, Opladen: Leske Verl. und Budrich 1976, 90—108.

Völkel, Walter: 'Nationale Front, Blockparteien, Gesellschaftliche Organisationen', *Politik, Wirtschaft und Gesellschaft in der DDR*, 2nd ed., Opladen: Westdeutscher Verl. 1980, 112—120.

East

Börner, Rolf: *Für die Souveränität des werktätigen Volkes. Die Mitwirkung der CDU bei der Ausarbeitung der Länderverfassungen und der Verfassung der DDR (1946—1949)*, Berlin: Christlich-Demokratische Union Deutschlands, Sekretariat des Hauptvorstandes 1975. (Beiträge zur Geschichte.)

'Johannes Dieckmann. Beiträge zu seiner politischen Biographie 1945—1969', *Protokoll des Kolloquiums der Kommission zur Erforschung der Parteigeschichte der LDPD . . .* , ed. Sekretariat des Zentralvorstandes der LDPD, Berlin: Buchverl. Der Morgen 1974. (Schriften der LDPD 11.)

Dirksen, Ulrich: *Liberaldemokraten zwischen sozialem Fortschritt und Reaktion. Die LDPD im Kampf um die Entstehung und Festigung des Volkseigentums 1946—1949*, ed. Sekretariat des Zentralvorstandes der Liberal—Demokratischen Partei Deutschlands, Berlin: Buchverl. Der Morgen 1977. (Schriften der LDPD 17.)

Erlebnisse und Erfahrungen christlicher Demokraten aus 3 Jahrzehnten, Berlin: Union Verl. 1975.

Hoyer, Lutz: *Revolution, Kleinbürgertum, Ideologie. Zur Ideologiegeschichte der LDPD in den Jahren 1945—1952*, Berlin: Buchverl. Der Morgen 1978.

Im Bündnis vereint. Beiträge zur Theorie und Praxis der Bündnispolitik, ed. Sekretariat des Zentralvorstandes der LDPD, Berlin: Buchverl. Der Morgen 1971.

'Hans Loch. Beiträge zu seiner politischen Biographie 1945—1960', *Protokoll des Kolloquiums des Wissenschaftlichen Rates der zentralen Parteischule der LDPD . . .*, ed. Sekretariat des Zentralvorstandes der LDPD, Berlin: Buchverl. Der Morgen 1974.

LDPD, Staatsmacht, Landesverteidigung. Referate und Diskussionsbeiträge der Beratungen des Politischen Ausschusses des Zentralvorstandes der LDPD am 19.4. und 10.5.1978, ed. Zentralvorstand der LDPD, Berlin: Buchverl. Der Morgen 1978. (Schriften der LDPD 19.)

30 Jahre LDPD. Reden und Grussadressen, ed. Sekretariat des Zentralvorstandes der LDPD, Berlin: Buchverl. Der Morgen 1975. (Schriften der LDPD 13.)

LDPD auf dem Weg vom 11. zum 12. Parteitag. 1972—1977, Berlin: Buchverl. Der Morgen 1976.

25 Jahre DDR—25 Jahre Mitarbeit der CDU, ed. Sekretariat des Hauptvorstandes der CDU, Berlin: Union Verl. 1974.

Dem Wohle des Volkes verpflichtet. Zeugnisse der Mitarbeit christlicher Demokraten am Werden und Wachsen der DDR, Berlin: Union Verl. 1979.

6 Interest groups and mass organisations

West

Beyme, Klaus von: 'Interessengruppen – Gesellschaftliche Organisationen', *Bundesrepublik Deutschland und Deutsche Demokratische Republik*, ed. Eckhard Jesse, Berlin: Colloquim Verl., 1980, 339–48.

Biermann, Wolfgang: *Demokratisierung in der DDR? Ökonomische Notwendigkeiten, Herrschaftsstrukturen, Rolle der Gewerkschaften 1961–1977*, Cologne: Verl. Wissenschaft und Politik 1978.

Bresslein, Erwin: *Drushba! Freundschaft? Von der Kommunistischen Jugendinternationale zu den Weltjugendfestspielen*, with a foreword by Johano Strasser, Frankfurt/Main: Fischer Taschenbuchverl. 1973. (Fischer Taschenbuch. Informationen zur Zeit 1358.)

Brown, James A.: *The Free German Youth: A functional analysis*, Ann Arbor, Michigan: University microfilms 1975.

Die Nationale Front der DDR – ihre Rolle und Funktion, ed. Friedrich-Ebert-Stiftung, Bonn: Verl. Neue Gesellschaft 1981. (Die DDR. Realitäten, Argumente.)

Der Freie Deutsche Gewerkschaftsbund (FDGB). Geschichte und Organisation, ed. Friedrich-Ebert-Stiftung, 2nd ed., Bonn-Bad Godesberg: Verl. Neue Gesellschaft 1978. (Die DDR. Realitäten, Argumente.)

Glaessner, Gert-Joachim: 'FDJ und Jugendpolitik', *Politik, Wirtschaft und Gesellschaft in der DDR*, 2nd ed., Opladen: Westdeutscher Verl. 1980, 162–173.

Gramatzki, Hans-Erich: 'Die zentralistischen Systeme der UdSSR und DDR', *Gramatzki, Hans-Erich and Gudrun Lemân: Arbeiterselbstverwaltung und Mitbestimmung in den Staaten Osteuropas*, Hanover: Fackelträger 1977, 45–98.

Heyen, Rolf: *Jugend in der DDR. Auf dem Weg zur sozialistischen Leistungsgesellschaft. Jugend in Familie und Organisation, in Schule, Beruf und Freizeit*, Bad Honnef, Darmstadt: Neue Darmstädter Verlagsanstalt 1972.

Freie Deutsche Jugend und Pionierorganisation Ernst Thälmann in der DDR, ed. Friedrich-Ebert-Stiftung, Bonn: Verl. Neue Gesellschaft 1980. (Die DDR. Realitäten, Argumente.)

Mahrad, Christa: 'Jugendpolitik in der DDR', *Jugend im doppelten Deutschland*, Opladen: Westdeutscher Verl. 1977, 195–225.

Organisationen und Verbände in der DDR. Ihre Rolle und Funktion in der Gesellschaft, ed. Friedrich-Ebert-Stiftung, Bonn: Verl. Neue Gesellschaft 1980. (Die DDR. Realitäten, Argumente.)

Rausch, Heinz: 'Massenorganisationen', *DDR*, 2nd ed., Munich: Bayerische Landeszentrale für politische Bildungsarbeit 1974, 224—6.

Simon, Günter: *Ohne sie geht nichts. Gewerkschaften im Alltag der DDR*, Frankfurt/Main: Nachrichten-Verlagsgesellschaft 1979.

Völkel, Walter: 'National Front, Blockparteien, Gesellschaftliche Organisationen', *Politik, Wirtschaft und Gesellschaft in der DDR*, 2nd ed., Opladen: Westdeutscher Verl. 1980, 112—20.

Zimmermann, Hartmut: 'Der Freie Deutsche Gewerkschaftsbund', *Politik, Wirtschaft und Gesellschaft in der DDR*, 2nd ed., Opladen: Westdeutscher Verl. 1980, 149—61.

East

Brzoska, Hans and Röder, Erich: *Gewerkschaftliche Mitwirkung an der betrieblichen Planung*, Berlin: Verl. Tribüne 1976.

Nationale Front des demokratischen Deutschland — sozialistische Volksbewegung. Handbuch, ed. Günther Grosser, Berlin: Dietz 1969.

Gesetz über die Teilnahme der Jugend an der Gestaltung der entwickelten sozialistischen Gesellschaft und über ihre allseitige Förderung in der Deutschen Demokratischen Republik — Jugendgesetz der DDR — vom 24. Januar 1974, Berlin: Staatsverl. der DDR 1975.

Handbuch für den Gewerkschaftsfunktionär. Dokumente, Gesetze, Verordnungen, Beschlüsse, ed. Bundesvorstand des Freien Deutschen Gewerkschaftsbundes, 3rd ed., Berlin: Verl. Tribüne 1974.

Jugend, Weltanschauung, Aktivität. Erkenntnisse und Erfahrungen in der ideologischen Arbeit mit der Jugend, ed. Peter Förster, Berlin: Verl. Neues Leben 1980.

1945 bis 1975. 30 Jahre erfolgreiche Gewerkschaftspolitik. Propagandamaterial zur Unterstutzung der Gewerkschaftsleitungen in Vorbereitung des 30. Jahrestages der Gründung des FDGB, Bernau: 1975. (Gewerkschaftshochschule 'Fritz Heckert' beim Bundesvorstand des FDGB.)

Norden, Albert: *Was die Nationale Front ist und tun sollte*, ed. Nationalrat der Nationalen Front des demokratischen Deutschland, Berlin: Staatsverl. der DDR 1971.

Bickner, Margarete et al.: *Die gesellschaftlichen Organisationen in der DDR. Stellung, Wirkungsrichtungen und Zusammenarbeit mit dem sozialistischen Staat*, Berlin: Staatsverl. der DDR 1980.

Staats- und rechtstheoretische Probleme der Entwicklung gesellschaftlicher Organisationen in der DDR, eds Richard Mand, Dirk Strassenberger et al., Potsdam-Babelsberg: Akademie für Staats- und Rechtswissenschaft der DDR 1978. (Aktuelle Beiträge der Staats- und Rechtswissenschaft 180.)

Roemer, Joachim: *Moralische Verantwortung und sozialistisches Verantwortungsbewusstsein. Gesetzmässigkeiten, Widersprüche und Fragen der gewerkschaftlichen Interessenvertretung bei der Gestaltung der entwickelten sozialistischen Gesellschaft*, Berlin: Verl. Tribüne 1973.

Wörterbuch zur sozialistischen Jugendpolitik, Berlin: Dietz 1975.

7   State and law

West

Balla, Bálint: *Kaderverwaltung. Versuch zur Idealtypisierung der 'Bürokratie' sowjetisch-volksdemokratischen Typs*, Stuttgart: Enke 1972. (Soziologische Gegenwartsfragen NF37.)

Beyme, Klaus von: *Ökonomie und Politik im Sozialismus. Ein Vergleich der Entwicklung in den sozialistischen Ländern*, Munich, Zürich: Piper 1975. (English edition: *Politics and Economics in Socialist Countries. A Comparative and Developmental Approach*, New York, Praeger, 1982.)

Bruhn, Hans-Henning: *Die Rechtsanwaltschaft in der DDR. Stellung und Aufgaben*, Cologne: Verl. Wissenschaft und Politik 1972. (Abhandlungen zum Ostrecht 11.)

Brunner, Georg: *Einführung in das Recht der DDR*, 2nd ed., Munich: C.H. Beck 1979. (Schriftenreihe der Juristischen Schulung 29.)

Brunner, Georg: *Zivilrecht der Deutschen Demokratischen Republik. Zivil- und Familiengesetzbuch mit Nebengesetzen, Urheberrecht, gewerblicher Rechtsschutz, internationales Privat- und Wirtschaftsrecht, Seehandelsrecht*, collection of texts with an introduction and foreword by Georg Brunner, Munich: C.H. Beck 1977.

Fricke, Karl Wilhelm: *Politik und Justiz in der DDR. Zur Geschichte der politischen Verfolgung 1945–1968. Bericht und Dokumentation*, Cologne: Verl. Wissenschaft und Politik 1979.

Glaessner, Gert-Joachim: *Herrschaft durch Kader, Leitung der Gesellschaft und Kaderpolitik in der DDR*, Opladen: Westdeutscher Verl. 1977. (Schriften des Zentralinstituts für sozialwissenschaftliche Forschung der Freien Universität Berlin 28.)

Glaessner, Gert-Joachim and Irmhild, Rudolph: *Macht durch Wissen. Zum Zusammenhang von Bildungspolitik, Bildungssystem und Kaderqualifizierung in der DDR. Eine politisch-soziologische Untersuchung*, Opladen: Westdeutscher Verl. 1978. (Schriften des Zentralinstituts für sozialwissenschaftliche Forschung der Freien Universität Berlin 30.)

Die Grundrechte in beiden deutschen Staaten, ed. Friedrich-Ebert-Stiftung, 3rd ed. Bonn: Verl. Neue Gesellschaft 1979. (Die DDR. Realitäten, Argumente.)

Hanke, Irma: 'Die politische Kultur', *DDR*, 4th ed., Munich: Verl. C.H. Beck 1978, 87—127.

Jesse, Eckhart: *Wahlen im geteilten Deutschland*, Special ed., Berlin: Landeszentrale für politische Bildungsarbeit 1976. (Politik kurz und aktuell 23.)

Lammich, Siegfried: *Grundzüge des sozialistischen Parlamentarismus*, Baden-Baden: Nomos Verlagsgesellschaft 1977.

Lapp, Peter Joachim: *Die Volkskammer der DDR*, Opladen: Westdeutscher Verl. 1975. (Studien zur Sozialwissenschaft 33.)

Lapp, Peter Joachim: *Der Staatsrat im politischen System der DDR (1960—1971)*, Opladen: Westdeutscher Verl. 1972. (Beiträge zur sozialwissenschaftlichen Forschung 9.)

Lohmann, Ulrich: 'Das Rechtswesen', *Politik, Wirtschaft und Gesellschaft in der DDR*, 2nd ed., Opladen: Westdeutscher Verl. 1980, 192—240.

Ludz, Peter Christian: *Mechanismen der Herrschaftssicherung. Eine sprachpolitische Analyse des gesellschaftlichen Wandels in der DDR*, Munich, Vienna: Hanser 1980.

Lüers, Hartwig: *Das Polizeirecht in der DDR. Aufgaben, Befugnisse und Organisation der Deutschen Volkspolizei*, Cologne: Verl. Wissenschaft und Politik 1974. (Abhandlungen zum Ostrecht 12.)

Maier, Herbert: 'Recht', *DDR*, 4th ed. Munich: Verl. C.H. Beck 1978, 262—74.

Maier, Herbert, 'Verwaltung', *DDR*, 4th ed. Munich: Verl. C.H. Beck, 1978, 275—81.

Mampel, Siegfried: *Zu juristischen und sozialen Aspekten des neuen Arbeitsgesetzbuches der DDR*, Berlin: Forschungsstelle für gesamtdeutsche wirtschaftliche und soziale Fragen 1978. (FS-Analysen 1978, 1.)

Neugebauer, Gero: *Partei und Staatsapparat in der DDR. Aspekte der Instrumentalisierung des Staatsapparats durch die SED*, Opladen: Westdeutscher Verl. 1978. (Schriften des Zentralinstituts für sozialwissenschaftliche Forschung der Freien Universität Berlin 29.)

Neugebauer, Gero: 'Der Staatsapparat', *Politik, Wirtschaft und Gesellschaft in der DDR*, 2nd ed. Opladen: Westdeutscher Verl. 1980, 129–36.

Neugebauer, Gero: 'Die Volksvertretungen', *Politik, Wirtschaft und Gesellschaft in der DDR*, 2nd ed. Opladen: Westdeutscher Verl. 1980, 121–8.

Pfarr, Heide M.: *Auslegungstheorie und Auslegungspraxis im Zivil- und Arbeitsrecht der DDR*, Berlin: Duncker and Humblot 1972. (Schriften zur Rechtstheorie 30.)

Reich, Norbert: *Einführung in das sozialistische Recht. Grundlagen, Grundprobleme, System, Quellen, Rechtsbildung, Rechtsverwirklichung*, Munich: Verl. C.H. Beck 1975. (Schriftenreihe der Juristischen Schulung 37.)

Roggemann, Herwig: *Die DDR-Verfassungen eingeleitet und bearbeitet von Herwig Roggemann*, 3rd ed. Berlin: Berlin-Verl. 1980. (Die Gesetzgebung der sozialistischen Staaten, Einzelausgaben 7.) (Quellen zur Rechtsvergleichung aus dem Osteuropa-Institut an der Freien Universität Berlin.)

Roggemann, Herwig: *Strafrechtsanwendung und Rechtshilfe zwischen beiden deutschen Staaten. Grundlagen, Entwicklung und rechtspolitische Aspekte einer Neuordnung des Strafrechtsverkehrs zwischen Bundesrepublik und DDR*, Berlin: Osteuropa-Institut; Baden-Baden: Nomos-Verlagsgesellschaft in Kommission 1975. (Rechtswissenschaftliche Veröffentlichungen 5.)

Sander, Günther: *Abweichendes Verhalten in der DDR. Kriminalitätstheorien in einer sozialistischen Gesellschaft*, Frankfurt/Main: Campus 1979. (Forschung 121.)

Schneider, Eberhard: *Das Menschenrechtsverständnis der UdSSR und der DDR*, Cologne: Bundesinstitut für ostwissenschaftliche und internationale Studien 1977. (Berichte des Bundesinstituts für ostwissenschaftliche und internationale Studien 57/1977.)

Schwindt, Rosemarie: *Demokratie und Zentralismus bei der Mitwirkung der DDR-Bevölkerung in der Strafjustiz*, Meisenheim/Glan: Hain 1979. (Mannheimer sozialwissenschaftliche Studien 16.)

Sieveking, Klaus: *Die Entwicklung des sozialistischen Rechtsstaatsbegriffs in der DDR. Eine Studie zur Auseinandersetzung mit dem Rechtsstaat in der SBZ/DDR zwischen 1945 und 1968*, Berlin: Osteuropa-Institut; Baden-Baden: Nomos-Verlagsgesellschaft in Commission 1975. (Rechtswissenschaftliche Veröffentlichungen 3.)

Stammen, Theo: 'Das zentrale Regierungssystem', *DDR*, 4th ed. Munich: Verl. C.H. Beck 1978, 241—61.

Stammen, Theo, Rausch, Heinz and Maier, Herbert: 'Das politische System', *DDR*, 4th ed. Munich: Verl. C.H. Beck 1978, 185—282.

Stammen, Theo and Rausch, Heinz: 'Der Willensbildungsprozess', *DDR*, 4th ed. Munich: Verl. C.H. Beck 1978, 208—40.

Honeckers Verfassung, ed. Friedrich-Ebert-Stiftung, 3rd ed. Bonn: Verl. Neue Gesellschaft 1981. (Die DDR. Realitäten, Argumente.)

Zivilgesetzbuch und Zivilprozessordnung der DDR mit Nebengesetzen, eingeleitet und bearbeitet von Herwig Roggemann, Berlin: Berlin-Verl. 1976. (Die Gesetzgebung der sozialistischen Staaten. Einzelausgaben 14.) (Quellen zur Rechtsvergleichung.)

Pleyer, Klemens, Lieser, Joachim et al. *Das Zivil- und Wirtschaftsrecht der DDR im Ausklang eines Reformjahrzehnts. Beiträge aus den Jahren 1969—1972*, Stuttgart: Gustav Fischer 1973. (Schriften zum Vergleich von Wirtschaftsordnungen 21.)

East

Arbeitsgesetzbuch und andere Rechtsvorschriften. Textausgabe mit Anmerkungen und Sachregister, ed. Staatssekretariat für Arbeit und Löhne, Berlin: Staatsverl. der DDR 1981.

Aufgaben, Rechte und Pflichten der Abgeordneten. Rechtsvorschriften mit Anmerkungen und Sachregister, Berlin: Staatsverl. der DDR 1975.

Baumgart, Alfred et al.: *Arbeitsrecht. Grundriss*. Berlin: Staatsverl. der DDR 1979.

Demokratie, Entwicklungsgesetze des sozialistischen Staates, ed. Institut für Theorie des Staates und des Rechts der Akademie der Wissenschaften der DDR, Institut für Staat und Recht der Akademie der Wissenschaften der UdSSR, Berlin: Staatsverl. der DDR 1981.

Familienrecht. Lehrbuch, collective of authors under the guidance of Anita Grandke, 2nd ed. Berlin: Staatsverl. der DDR 1976.

Zur Geschichte der Rechtspflege der DDR 1949—1961, collective of authors under the guidance of Hilde Benjamin. Berlin: Staatsverl. der DDR 1980.

Grundfragen des sozialistischen Zivilrechts, collective of authors under the guidance of Joachim Göhring, Berlin: Staatsverl. der DDR 1977. (Grundriss Zivilrecht 1.)

Grundrechte des Bürgers in der sozialistischen Gesellschaft, collective of authors under the guidance of Eberhard Poppe, Berlin: Staatsverl. der DDR 1980.

Kellner, H., Göhring, J. and Kietz, H: *Zivilprozessrecht. Grundriss*, 2nd ed. Berlin: Staatsverl. der DDR 1979.

DDR. Gesellschaft, Staat, Bürger, 2nd ed. Berlin: Staatsverl. der DDR 1978.

Schöneburg, Karl-Heinz: *Staat und Recht in der Geschichte der DDR*, Berlin: Staatsverl. der DDR 1973. (Der sozialistische Staat.)

Sorgenicht, Klaus: *Staat, Recht und Demokratie nach dem IX.Parteitag der SED*, Berlin: Dietz 1976.

Staatsrecht der DDR. Lehrbuch, ed. Akademie für Staats- und Rechtswissenschaft der DDR, Berlin: Staatsverl. der DDR 1977.

Marxistisch—leninistische Staats- und Rechtstheorie. Lehrbuch, ed. Institut für Theorie des Staates und des Rechts der Akademie der Wissenschaften der DDR, 3rd ed. Berlin: Staatsverl. der DDR 1981.

Strafgesetzbuch der Deutschen Demokratischen Republik — StGB — und angrenzende Gesetze und Bestimmungen. Textausgabe mit Anmerkungen, Hinweisen und Sachregister, ed. Ministerium der Justiz, 4th ed. Berlin: Staatsverl. der DDR 1978.

Strafrecht. Allgemeiner Teil. Lehrbuch, ed. Sektion Rechtswissenschaft der Humboldt-Universität zu Berlin, Akademie für Staats- und Rechtswissenschaft der DDR . . . , 2nd ed. Berlin: Staatsverl. der DDR 1978.

Strafrecht. Besonderer Teil. Lehrbuch, ed. Sektion Rechtswissenschaft der Humboldt-Universität zu Berlin, Akademie für Staats- und Rechtswissenschaft der DDR, Berlin: Staatsverl. der DDR 1981.

Strafverfahrensrecht. Lehrbuch, ed. Sektion Rechtswissenschaft der Humboldt-Universität zu Berlin, Berlin: Staatsverl. der DDR 1977.

Verfassung der Deutschen Demokratischen Republik, 3rd ed. Berlin: Staatsverl. der DDR 1975.

Verwaltungsrecht. Lehrbuch, ed. Akademie für Staats- und Rechtswissenschaft der DDR, Berlin: Staatsverl. der DDR 1979.

Wirtschafts- und Aussenwirtschaftsrecht für Ökonomen, ed. Institut für Wirtschaftsrecht der Hochschule für Ökonomie . . . , Berlin: Staatsverl. der DDR 1977.

Zivilgesetzbuch und angrenzende Bestimmungen. Textausgabe, ed. Ministerium der Justiz. Berlin: Staatsverl. der DDR 1980.

Zivilprozessordnung mit Durchführungsbestimmungen. Textausgabe mit Sachregister, ed. Ministerium der Justiz, 5th ed. Berlin: Staatsverl. der DDR 1979.

Zivilrecht. Lehrbuch, 2 vols. Directors and editors: Joachim Göhring and Martin Posch, Berlin: Staatsverl. der DDR 1981.

8 The military system

West

Eisenfeld, Bernd: *Kriegsdienstverweigerung in der DDR — ein Friedensdienst? Genesis, Befragung, Analyse, Dokumente*, Frankfurt/Main: Haag und Herchen Verl. 1978.

Forster, Thomas M.: *Die NVA. Kernstück der Landesverteidigung der DDR*, 5th ed. Cologne: Markus Verl. 1979.

Hartwig, Jürgen and Wimmel, Albert: *Wehrerziehung und vormilitärische Ausbildung der Kinder und Jugendlichen in der DDR*, Stuttgart: Seewald 1979. (Militärpolitische Schriftenreihe 14.)

Herspring, Dale Roy: *East German civil—military relations. The impact of technology, 1949—72.* Foreword by Peter C. Ludz. New York: Praeger 1973. (Praeger special studies in international politics and government.)

Jungermann, Peter: *Die Wehrideologie der SED und das Leitbild der Nationalen Volksarmee vom sozialistischen deutschen Soldaten*, Stuttgart: Seewald 1973.

Marks, Heinz: *GST — vormilitärische Ausbildung in der DDR*, Cologne: Markus Verl. 1970. (Militärsystem der DDR.)

Marks, Heinz: *Die Kampfgruppen der Arbeiterklasse. Ein wichtiges Organ des Militärapparates der DDR*, Cologne: Markus Verl. 1970. (Militärsystem der DDR.)

Nawrocki, Joachim: *Bewaffnete Organe in der DDR. Nationale Volksarmee und andere militärische sowie paramilitärische Verbände. Aufbau, Bewaffnung, Aufgaben, Berichte aus dem Alltag*, Berlin: Holzapfel 1979. (... in der DDR.)

Neugebauer, Gero: 'Militärpolitik und Streitkräfte', *Politik, Wirtschaft und Gesellschaft in der DDR*, 2nd ed. Opladen: Westdeutscher Verl. 1980, 174—91.

Neugebauer, Gero: 'Die sozialistische Wehrerziehung', *Politik, Wirtschaft und Gesellschaft in der DDR*, Opladen: Westdeutscher Verl. 1979, 166–74.

Reservesysteme des Warschauer Paktes. Ein Weissbuch, ed. Rudolf Woller. Munich: Bernard and Graefe 1978.

Tiedtke, Stephan: *Die Warschauer Vertragsorganisation. Zum Verhältnis von Militär- und Entspannungspolitik in Osteuropa*. Foreword by Egbert Jahn, Munich, Vienna: Oldenbourg 1978. (Forschungsergebnisse bei Oldenbourg.)

Die NVA, new ed., (1), Bonn: Bundesministerium der Verteidigung 1978. (Schriftenreihe Innere Führung. Reihe Politische Bildung 20.)

Studiengruppe Militärpolitik. Die Nationale Volksarmee. Ein Anti-Weissbuch zum Militär in der DDR, Reinbek bei Hamburg: Rowohlt 1976. (rororo aktuell 4059.)

Wehrkunde in der DDR. Die neue Regelung ab 1 September 1978, ed. Wolfgang Henrich, Bonn: Hohwacht 1978.

Wehrpflicht, Wehrrecht und Kriegsdienstverweigerung in beiden deutschen Staaten, ed. Friedrich-Ebert-Stiftung, 3rd ed. Bonn: Verl. Neue Gesellschaft 1980. (Die DDR. Realitäten, Argumente.)

Wehrpropaganda und Wehrerziehung in der DDR, ed. Friedrich-Ebert-Stiftung, Bonn: Verl. Neue Gesellschaft 1978. (Die DDR. Realitäten, Argumente.)

Wiener, Friedrich: *Die Armeen der Warschauer-Pakt-Staaten*, ed. Friedrich Wiener, 7th ed., Munich: Bernard and Graefe 1979. (Taschenbuch der Landstreitkräfte 2.)

East

Doehler, Edgar and Falkenberg, Rudolf: *Militärische Traditionen der DDR und der NVA*, Berlin: Militärverl. der DDR 1979. (Serie Politik und Landesverteidigung.)

Handreichung zur sozialistischen Wehrerziehung. (Beiträge zur sozialistischen Wehrerziehung der Schuljugend der DDR), ed. Karl Ilter, Albrecht Herrmann, Helmut Stolz, on the instructions of Ministerium für Volksbildung, Berlin: Volk und Wissen Verl. 1974.

Hoffmann, Heinz: *Sozialistische Landesverteidigung. Aus Reden und Aufsätzen 1974 bis Juni 1978*, Berlin: Militärverl. der DDR 1979.

Honecker, Erich: *Zuverlässiger Schutz des Sozialismus. Ausgewählte Reden und Schriften zur Militärpolitik der SED*, 2nd ed. Berlin: Militärverl. der DDR 1977.

Kiessling, Gottfried: *Krieg und Frieden in unserer Zeit*, Berlin: Militärverl. der DDR 1977. (Serie Politik und Landesverteidigung.)

Militärlexikon, 2nd ed. Berlin: Deutscher Militärverl. 1973.

Militärpolitik für Sozialismus und Frieden. Grundfragen der Politik der SED zum militärischen Schutz der revolutionären Errungenschaften und des Friedens von der Gründung der DDR bis zur Gestaltung der entwickelten sozialistischen Gesellschaft, collection of authors led by Günter Glaser. Berlin: Militärverl. der DDR 1976. (Serie Politik und Landesverteidigung.)

Ökonomie und Landesverteidigung, collection of authors led by Horst Fiedler. Berlin: Militärverl. der DDR 1974. (Serie Politik und Landesverteidigung.)

Scheler, Wolfgang and Kiessling, Gottfried: *Gerechte und ungerechte Kriege in unserer Zeit*, Berlin: Militärverl. der DDR 1981. (Politik und Landesverteidigung.)

Sozialistische Wehrerziehung der Werktätigen. Erfahrungen und Empfehlungen, collection of authors under the direction of H. Thiele, M. Kirchner and R. Neubert, Berlin: Verl. Tribüne 1976.

Zeittafel zur Militärgeschichte der Deutschen Demokratischen Republik 1969 bis 1977, collection of authors from the Militärgeschichtlichen Institut der DDR and led by Toni Nelles. Berlin: Militärverl. der DDR 1979.

9 Media and Propaganda

West

Blaum, Verena: *Journalistikwissenschaft in der DDR*, Institut für Gesellschaft und Wissenschaft an der Universität Erlangen-Nürnberg 1979. (Analysen und Berichte aus Gesellschaft und Wissenschaft 4/1979.)

Blaum, Verena: *Marxismus–Leninismus, Massenkommunikation und Journalismus. Zum Gegenstand der Journalistikwissenschaft in der DDR*, Munich: Minerva-Publikationen 1980. (Minerva–Fachserie Wirtschaftsund Sozialwissenschaften.)

Gruhn, Werner: *Wissenschaft und Technik in deutschen Massenmedien. Ein Vergleich zwischen der Bundesrepublik Deutschland und der DDR*, ed. Institut für Gesellschaft und Wissenschaft Erlangen. Erlangen: Verl. Deutsche Gesellschaft für zeitgeschichtliche Fragen 1979.

Günther, Reinhard: *Feindbild Bundesrepublik aus der Sicht der DDR. Politische Text- und Bildsammlung für Schule und Unterricht.* Bonn-Bad Godesberg: Hohwacht-Verl.(1973).

Marzahn, Barbara: *Der Deutschlandbegriff der DDR. Dargestellt vornehmlich an der Sprache des Neuen Deutschland*, Düsseldorf: Schwann 1979. (Sprache der Gegenwart 48.)

Die Massenmedien der DDR. Presse, Rundfunk, Fernsehen und Literaturbetrieb im Dienste der SED, ed. Friedrich-Ebert-Stiftung. Bonn: Verl. Neue Gesellschaft 1979. (Die DDR. Realitäten, Argumente.)

Otto, Elmar Dieter: *Nachrichten in der DDR. Eine empirische Untersuchung über 'Neues Deutschland'*, Cologne: Verl. Wissenschaft und Politik 1979. (Bibliothek Wissenschaft und Politik 11.)

Picaper, Jean-Paul: *Kommunikation und Propaganda in der DDR*, Stuttgart: Verl. Bonn aktuell 1976. (Bonn aktuell 26.)

Riedel, Heide: *Hörfunk und Fernsehen in der DDR. Funktion, Struktur und Programm des Rundfunks in der DDR*, ed. Deutsches Rundfunkmuseum, Berlin. Cologne: Literarischer Verl. Braun 1979. (Freie Kommunikation.)

Schneider, Beate: *Konflikt, Krise und Kommunikation. Eine quantitative Analyse innerdeutscher Politik*, Munich: Verl. Dokumentation 1976. (Kommunikation und Politik 7.)

Traumann, Gudrun: *Journalistik in der DDR. Sozialistische Journalistik und Journalistenausbildung an der Karl-Marx-Universität Leipzig*, Munich, Berlin: Verl. Dokumentation 1971. (Kommunikation und Politik 2.)

East

Der Anteil der Massenmedien bei der Herausbildung des Bewusstseins in der sich wandelnden Welt, (Wissenschaftliche Beiträge. Protokoll. Internationale wissenschaftliche Konferenz. Sektion Journalistik, VDJ der DDR, AIERI, 9. Generalversammlung der AIERI, Leipzig/DDR, 17.9.–21.9.1974.) (2 vols.) Leipzig: Karl-Marx-Universität 1975.

Bisky, Lothar: *Massenkommunikation und Jugend. Zur Theorie und Praxis der Massenkommunikation und ihren Einflüssen auf die sozialistische Persönlichkeitsbildung und Bewusstseinsentwicklung Jugendlicher*, ed. Zentralinstitut für Jugendforschung, Berlin: Deutscher Verl. der Wissenschaften 1971.

Bisky, Lothar: *Massenmedien und ideologische Erziehung der Jugend*, Berlin: Deutscher Verl. der Wissenschaften 1976.

Harth, Karl-Ludwig: *Reden, informieren, überzeugen*, Berlin: Verl. Tribüne 1974.

Informations- und Öffentlichkeitsarbeit — Erfahrungen aus der Praxis, Berlin: Staatsverl. der DDR 1974. (Der sozialistische Staat.)

Zentralinstitut für Berufsbildung der DDR. *Zur Überzeugungsbildung bei Lehrlingen und Facharbeitern im volkseigenen Betrieb*, Berlin: Verl. Volk und Wissen 1977.

10 Foreign policy, foreign trade

West

Arons, Renée and Tiedtke, Jutta: *Die Entspannungspolitik der UdSSR und der DDR am Beispiel der KSZE—Initiativen*, Frankfurt/Main: Hessische Stiftung Friedens- und Konfliktforschung 1977. (HSFK—Studien 19.)

Drei Jahrzehnte Aussenpolitik der DDR. Bestimmungsfaktoren, Instrumente, Aktionsfelder, ed. Hans-Adolf Jacobsen, Gerd Leptin et al., Munich, Vienna: Oldenbourg 1979. (Schriften des Forschungsinstituts der Deutschen Gesellschaft für Auswärtige Politik 44.)

Bethkenhagen, Jochen and Lambrecht, Horst: *Die Aussenhandelsbeziehungen der DDR vor dem Hintergrund von Produktion und Verbrauch*, Cologne: Bundesinstitut für ostwissenschaftliche und internationale Studien 1979. (Berichte des Bundesinstituts für ostwissenschaftliche und internationale Studien 19/79.)

Bruns, Wilhelm: *Die UNO-Politik der DDR. UNO—DDR*, Stuttgart: Verl. Bonn Aktuell 1978. (Bonn aktuell 41.)

Croan, Melvin: *East Germany: The Soviet Connection*, Beverly Hills; London: Sage Publ. 1976. (The Washington papers 4, 36.)

Dasbach Mallinckrodt, Anita: *Propaganda hinter der Mauer. Die Propaganda der Sowjetunion und der DDR als Werkzeug der Aussenpolitik im Jahre 1961*, foreword by Peter Christian Ludz, Stuttgart: Kohlhammer 1971. (Reihe Kohlhammer.)

Dasbach Mallinckrodt, Anita: *Wer macht die Aussenpolitik der DDR? Apparat, Methoden, Ziele*, with afterword by Hermann Weber, Düsseldorf: Droste Verl. 1972. (Geschichtliche Studien zu Politik und Gesellschaft 4.)

Dietsch, Ulrich: *Aussenwirtschaftliche Aktivitaten der DDR*, Hamburg: Verl. Weltarchiv 1976. (Veröffentlichungen des HWWA—Institut für Wirtschaftsforschung — Hamburg.)

End, Heinrich: *Zweimal deutsche Aussenpolitik. Internationale Dimensionen des innerdeutschen Konflikts 1949—1972*, Cologne: Verl. Wissenschaft und Politik 1973.

Erhöhung der Aussenhandelseffizienz der DDR durch Unternehmenskooperation zwischen Ost und West und Umbau der Aussenhandelsorganisation? Zur Krise der Aussenwirtschaft der DDR, ihren Ursachen und den Möglichkeiten zu ihrer Überwindung, adapted by Hannsjörg Buck, Bonn: Gesamtdeutsches Institut 1979.

Gasteyger, Curt: *Die beiden deutschen Staaten in der Weltpolitik*, Munich: Piper 1976. (Internationale Politik.) (Piper Sozialwissenschaft 37.)

Haendcke-Hoppe, Maria: *Die DDR—Aussenhandelsstatistik und ihr Informationswert*, Berlin: Forschungsstelle für gesamtdeutsche wirtschaftliche und soziale Fragen 1978. (FS-Analysen 3, 1978.)

Die Integration der beiden deutschen Staaten in die Paktsysteme. Hindernis oder Voraussetzung für Entspannung und geregeltes Nebeneinander, ed. Friedrich-Ebert-Stiftung, Bonn-Bad Godesberg: Verl. Neue Gesellschaft 1977. (Die DDR. Realitäten, Argumente.)

Kregel, Bernd: *Aussenpolitik und Systemstabilisierung in der DDR*, Opladen: Leske und Budrich 1979.

Lamm, Hans Siegfried and Kupper, Siegfried: *DDR und Dritte Welt*, Munich, Vienna: Oldenbourg 1976. (Schriften des Forschungsinstituts der Deutschen Gesellschaft für Auswärtige Politik. 39. Reihe: Internationale Politik und Wirtschaft.)

Lentz, Manfred: *Die Wirtschaftsbeziehungen DDR — Sowjetunion 1945—1961. Eine politologische Analyse*, Opladen: Leske und Budrich 1979. (Forschungstexte Wirtschafts- und Sozialwissenschaften.)

Lieser-Triebnigg, Erika: *Das Recht des Aussenhandles in der DDR. Organisation und Arbeitsweise*, Cologne: Verl. Wissenschaft und Politik 1978. (Abhandlungen zum Ostrecht 15.)

Lindemann, Hans and Müller, Kurt: *Auswärtige Kulturpolitik der DDR. Die kulturelle Abgrenzung der DDR von der Bundesrepublik Deutschland*, with foreword by Hans Arnold, Bonn-Bad Godesberg: Verl. Neue Gesellschaft 1974.

Ludz, Peter Christian: *Die DDR zwischen Ost und West. Politische Analysen 1961 bis 1976*, Munich: Beck 1977. (Beck'sche Schwarze Reihe 154.)

Moreton, N. Edwina: *East Germany and the Warsaw alliance. The politics of détente*, Boulder, Colorado: Westview Press 1978.

Radde, Jürgen: *Der Diplomatische Dienst der DDR. Namen und Daten*, Cologne: Verl. Wissenschaft und Politik 1977.

Radde, Jürgen: *Die aussenpolitische Führungselite der DDR. Veränderungen der sozialen Struktur aussenpolitischer Führungsgruppen*, Cologne: Verl. Wissenschaft und Politik 1976. (Bibliothek Wissenschaft und Politik 13.)

The Federal Republic of Germany and the German Democratic Republic in international relations, ed. Günther Doeker and Jens A. Brückner: vol.1 'Confrontation and co-operation'; vol.2 'Organisations'; vol.3 'Organisations' (continued). Dobbs Ferry: Oceana Publications; Alphen aan den Rijn: Sijthoff and Noordhoff 1979.

Schneider, Eberhard: *Die Aussenpolitik der DDR gegenüber Südasien*, Cologne: Bundesinstitut für ostwissenschaftliche und internationale Studien 1978. (Berichte des Bundesinstituts für ostwissenschaftliche und internationale Studien 41/1978.)

Wettig, Gerhard: *Zu den Beziehungen zwischen der Sowjetunion und der DDR in den Jahren 1969—75. Eine zusammenfassende Analyse*, Cologne: Bundesinstitut für ostwissenschaftliche und internationale Studien 1975. (Berichte des Bundesinstituts für ostwissenschaftliche und internationale Studien 23/75.)

East

Aussenhandel DDR. Handbuch, ed. Kammer für Aussenhandel der Deutschen Demokratischen Republik, Berlin: Kammer für Aussenhandel 1977.

Aussenpolitik der DDR. Drei Jahrzehnte sozialistische deutsche Friedenspolitik, ed. Institut für Internationale Beziehungen Potsdam-Babelsberg, collective of authors under the guidance of Stefan Doernberg, Berlin: Staatsverl. der DDR 1979.

Aussenpolitik der DDR — für Sozialismus und Frieden, ed. Institut für Internationale Beziehungen an der Akademie für Staats- und Rechtswissenschaft der DDR, Berlin: Staatsverl. der DDR 1974.

Sozialistische Aussenwirtschaft, collective of authors under the guidance of Eugen Faude, Gerhard Grote and Christa Luft, Berlin: Verl. Die Wirtschaft 1976.

Sozialistische Diplomatie, with foreword by A.A. Gromyko, Berlin: Staatsverl. der DDR 1974.

Effektivität der Aussenwirtschaftsbeziehungen der sozialistischen Volkswirtschaft, collective of authors under the guidance of Helmut Blessing. Berlin: Verl. Die Wirtschaft 1977.

Grosse, Hermann and Puschmann, Manfred: *Wirtschaftsbeziehungen im Zeichen der friedlichen Koexistenz*, Berlin: Dietz 1976. (Schriftenreihe zur sozialistischen Wirtschaftsführung.)

Hänisch, Werner: *Aussenpolitik und internationale Beziehungen der DDR*; vol.1, 1949—1955, Berlin: Staatsverl. der DDR 1972.

Hofmann, Otto and Scharschmidt, Gerhard: *DDR—Aussenhandel gestern und heute*, Berlin: Verl. Die Wirtschaft 1975.

Die Organisation des Warschauer Vertrages. Dokumente und Materialien 1955—1980, ed. Ministerium für Auswärtige Angelegenheiten der DDR, 2nd ed., Berlin: Staatsverl. der DDR 1980.

Sozialismus und Entspannung, ed. Institut für Internationale Beziehungen an der Akademie für Staats- und Rechtswissenschaft der DDR, Institut für Internationale Politik und Wirtschaft, Berlin: Staatsverl. der DDR.

Völkerrecht. Lehrbuch, vol.1, ed. Arbeitsgemeinschaft für Völkerrecht beim Institut für Internationale Beziehungen an der Akademie für Staats- und Rechtswissenschaft der DDR, 2nd ed., Berlin: Staatsverl. der DDR 1981.

11 Western industrial countries and the Third World in the literature of the GDR

West

Güttler, Herbert: 'Imperialismusforschung in der DDR. Anmerkungen zu Gegenstand und theoretischen Grundlagen', *Kultur und Gesellschaft in der DDR. Sonderthema: BRD- und Imperialismusforschung in der DDR. 10 Tagung zum Stand der DDR—Forschung in der Bundesrepublik 31.5—3.6.1977*, Referate. Cologne: Verl. Wissenschaft und Politik 1977. Deutschland Archiv. Sonderheft; vol.10, 11—17.

East

Afrika im antiimperialistischen Kampf. Probleme eines Kontinents, collective of authors under the guidance of Hans Kramer. Berlin: Akademie-Verl. 1978. (Studien über Asien, Afrika und Lateinamerika 23.)

Breetzmann, Martin and Stier, Peter: *Ökonomische Probleme des anti-imperialistischen Kampfes der Entwicklungsländer*, Berlin: Dietz 1976. (Lehrhefte Politische Ökonomie des Kapitalismus.)

Charisius, Albrecht and Lambrecht, Rainer: *Imperialistische Militärblockpolitik. Krisen und neue Varianten in den 70er Jahren*, Berlin: Staatsverl. der DDR 1979. (Blickpunkt Weltpolitik.)

Engelhardt, Klaus and Heise, Karl-Heinz: *Militär-Industrie-Komplex im staatsmonopolistischen Herrschaftssystem*, ed. Institut für Internationale Politik und Wirtschaft, Berlin, Berlin: Staatsverl. der DDR 1974.

Für ein Europa des Friedens und des Fortschritts. Die Kommunisten, die neue Lage in Europa und die Probleme des politisch-ideologischen Kampfes, Berlin: Staatsverl. der DDR 1978. (Arbeiterklasse und revolutionärer Weltprozess.)

Henseke, Hans; Fuchs, Günther and Sonnet, Hans-Erich: *Zu einigen aktuellen Problemen der Politik des französischen Imperialismus*, Potsdam: Pädagogische Hochschule 'Karl Liebknecht' 1975. (Potsdamer Forschungen der Pädagogischen Hochschule 'Karl Liebknecht' Potsdam. Reihe A.14.)

Hexelschneider, Erhard; Kleinwächter, Wolfgang and Raaz, Falko: *Kulturaustausch, Koexistenz, Klassenkampf*, Berlin: Staatsverl. der DDR 1980. (Blickpunkt Weltpolitik.)

Industrialisierung in Entwicklungslandern. Bedingungen, Konzeptionen, Tendenzen, collective of authors under the guidance of Horst Grienig, Gert Kück and Manfred Voigt, Berlin: Akademie-Verl. 1975. (Studien über Asien, Afrika und Lateinamerika 7.)

Die westeuropäische Integration und die Weltwirtschaft, Berlin: Dietz 1979.

Staatsmonopolistischer Kapitalismus und Opportunismus. Ursachen, Wirkungen, Gegenkräfte, collective of authors under the guidance of Werner Paff and Heinz Petrak, Berlin: Dietz 1979.

Kück, Gerd and Kroske, Heinz: *Wirtschaftliche Zusammenarbeit und Integration von Entwicklungsländern. Eine Studie zur theoretischen Problematik und zum praktischen Verlauf*, Berlin: Akademie-Verl. 1976. (Studien über Asien, Afrika und Lateinamerika 14.)

Mährdel, Christian: *Afrikanische Parteien im revolutionären Befreiungskampf. Ein Beitrag zur Analyse und Theorie der nationalen Befreiungsrevolution der Gegenwart*, Berlin: Staatsverl. der DDR 1977.

Internationale Monopole, ed. collectively by Christos Fundulis, Horst Heininger et al., Berlin: Dietz 1978.

Fritsch, Wolfgang, et al: *Nordeuropa — Positionen zur Entspannung*, Berlin: Staatsverl. der DDR 1979. (Blickpunkt Weltpolitik.)

Dankert, Jochen, et al: *Zur Politik des französischen Imperialismus in der Gegenwart*, Potsdam: Pädagogische Hochschule 'Karl Liebknecht' 1978. (Potsdamer Forschungen der Pädagogischen Hochschule 'Karl Liebknecht' Potsdam. Reihe A.30.)

Brehme, Gerhard, et al: *Der nationaldemokratische Staat in Asien und Afrika. Eine staatstheoretische und staatsrechtliche Studie*, Berlin: Staatsverl. der DDR 1976.

Das politische System der USA. Geschichte und Gegenwart, ed. Karl-Heinz Röder, Berlin: Staatsverl. der DDR 1980. (Studien zum politischen System des Imperialismus 1.)

Roder, Karl-Heinz, et al: *Aufstieg und Verfall bürgerlicher Demokratie. USA*, ed. Akademie der Wissenschaften der DDR . . . Berlin, Berlin: Staatsverl. der DDR 1976.

Uschner, Manfred: *Lateinamerika. Schauplatz revolutionärer Kämpfe*, Berlin: Staatsverl. der DDR 1975.

Reinhold, Otto and Timofejew, Timur: *Verschärfung der allgemeinen Krise des Kapitalismus und Arbeiterklass. Ökonomische, politische und ideologische Probleme in West-europa*, Berlin: Dietz 1980.

Westeuropa. Politische und militärische Integration, ed. Institut für Internationale Beziehungen an der Akademie für Staats- und Rechtswissenschaft der DDR, Potsdam-Babelsberg. Militärgeschichtliches Institut der DDR, Potsdam, Berlin: Staatsverl. der DDR 1980.

Westeuropa in der heutigen Welt (Institut für Internationale Politik und Wirtschaft der DDR, Institut für Weltwirtschaft und Internationale Beziehungen der Akademie der Wissenschaften der UdSSR.) Scientific leader: Lutz Maier et al., Berlin: Dietz 1979.

12 The German question relations between the FRG and the GDR. The problem of divided Berlin

West

Berschin, Helmut: *Deutschland — eine Name im Wandel. Die deutsche Frage im Spiegel der Sprache*, Munich, Vienna: Olzog 1979. (Geschichte und Staat. Sonderreihe: Analysen und Perspektiven 1.)

Birnbaum, Karl E., *East and West Germany. A modus vivendi*, Farnborough: Saxon House; Lexington Mass: Lexington Books 1973.

Bowers, Stephen Reed: *The West Berlin Issue in the era of superpower détente. East Germany and the politics of West Berlin, 1968—1974*, Ann Arbor, Mich: Univ. Microfilms International 1978.

Catudal, Honoré Marc: *A balance sheet of the quadripartite agreement on Berlin. Evaluation and documentation*, foreword by Kenneth Rush, Berlin: Berlin Verl. 1978. (Political Studies 13.)

Catudal, Honoré Marc, Jr.: *The Diplomacy of the quadripartite agreement on Berlin. A new era in East—West politics*, foreword by Kenneth Rush, Berlin: Berlin Verl. 1978. (Political Studies 12.)

Cieslar, Eve; Hampel, Johannes and Teitler, Franz-Christoph: *Der Streit um den Grundvertrag. Eine Dokumentation*, Munich, Vienna: Olzog 1973. (Berichte und Studien der Hanns-Seidel-Stiftung 4.)

Fischer, Alexander: *Sowjetische Deutschlandpolitik im Zweiten Weltkrieg: 1941—1945*, Stuttgart: Deutsche Verlagsanstalt 1975. (Studien zur Zeitgeschichte.)

Griffith, William E., *The Ostpolitik of the Federal Republic of Germany*, Cambridge, Mass., London: The MIT Pr. 1978. (Studies in communism, revisionism and revolution 24.)

Haupt, Michael: *Die Berliner Mauer. Vorgeschichte, Bau, Folgen. Literaturbericht und Bibliographie zum 20 Jahrestag des 13. August 1961*, Munich: Bernard and Graefe 1981.

Hennig, Ottfried: *Die Bundespräsenz in West-Berlin. Entwicklung und Rechtscharakter*, Cologne: Verl. Wissenschaft und Politik 1976. (Bibliothek Wissenschaft und Politik 16.)

Hoebink, Hein: *Westdeutsche Widervereinigungspolitik 1949—1961*, Meisenheim am Glan: Hain 1978.

Jaenecke, Heinrich: *Die deutsche Teilung. Von der Potsdamer Konferenz bis zum Grundvertrag*, Frankfurt/Main, Berlin, Vienna: Ullstein 1979. (Ullstein-Bücher 33 051: Zeitgeschichte.)

Lehmann, Hans Georg: *Der Oder-Neisse-Konflikt*, Munich: Beck 1979.

Die Linke und die nationale Frage. Dokumente zur deutschen Einheit seit 1945, ed. Peter Brandt and Herbert Ammon, Reinbek bei Hamburg: Rowohlt 1981.

Mahncke, Dieter: *Berlin im geteilten Deutschland*, Munich, Vienna: Oldenbourg 1973. (Schriften des Forschungsinstituts der Deutschen Gesellschaft für Auswärtige Politik 34.)

Matthey, Ferdinand: *Entwicklung der Berlinfrage (1944–1971)*, Berlin, New York: De Gruyter 1972. (Aktuelle Dokumente.)

Meyer, Michel: *Freikauf. Menschenhandel in Deutschland*, Vienna, Hamburg: Zsolnay 1977.

Motschmann, Klaus: *Sozialismus und Nation. Wie deutsch ist die 'DDR'*, Munich: Wirtschaftsverl. Langen-Müller; Herbig 1979.

Oldenburg, Fred and Wettig, Gerhard: *Der Sonderstatus der DDR in den europäischen Ost–West–Beziehungen*, Cologne: Bundesinstitut für ostwissenschaftliche und internationale Studien 1979. (Berichte des Bundesinstituts für ostwissenschaftliche und internationale Studien.)

Rühle, Jürgen and Holzweissig, Gunter: *13. August 1961. Die Mauer von Berlin*, Cologne: Verl. Wissenschaft und Politik 1981.

Schmid, Karin: *Die deutsche Frage im Staats- und Völkerrecht*, Baden-Baden: Nomos Verl. 1980.

Schweigler, Gebhard: *Nationalbewusstsein in der BRD und der DDR*, Düsseldorf: Bertelsmann Universitätsverl. 1973. (Studien zur Sozialwissenschaft 8.)

Sowden, J.K., *The German question 1945–1973. Continuity in change*, London: Bradford University Press 1975.

Das Viermächteabkommen über Berlin vom 3. September 1971, ed. Presse- und Informationsamt der Bundesregierung, Hamburg: Hoffmann and Campe 1971.

Weber, Werner and Jahn, Werner: *Synopse zur Deutschlandpolitik 1941 bis 1973*, Göttingen: Schwartz 1973. (Schriften des Königsteiner Kreises.)

Wettig, Gerhard: *Community and conflict in the socialist camp. The Soviet Union, East Germany and the German problem 1965–1972*, transl. by Edwina Moreton and Hannes Adomeit, New York: St Martin's Press 1975.

Wettig, Gerhard: *Das Problem des Transits nach West-Berlin*, Cologne: Bundesinstitut für ostwissenschaftliche und internationale Studien 1978. (Berichte des Bundesinstituts für ostwissenschaftliche und internationale Studien 20/1978.)

Wettig, Gerhard: *Die Sowjetunion, die DDR und die Deutschland-Frage 1965–1976. Einvernehmen und Konflikt im sozialistischen Lager*, Stuttgart: Verl. Bonn aktuell 1976. (Bonn aktuell 28.)

Wettig, Gerhard: *Die Berliner Zugangsproblematik vor dem Vier-Mächte-Abkommen von 1971*, Cologne: Bundesinstitut für ostwissenschaftliche und internationale Studien 1978. (Berichte des Bundesinstituts für ostwissenschaftliche und internationale Studien. 1978, 1.)

Wilke, Kay-Michael: *Bundesrepublik Deutschland und Deutsche Demokratische Republik. Grundlagen und ausgewählte Probleme des gegenseitigen Verhältnisses der beiden deutschen Staaten*, Berlin: Duncker and Humblot 1976. (Tübinger Schriften zum internationalen und europäischen Recht 4.)

Zivier, Ernst, R., *Der Rechtsstatus des Landes Berlin. Eine Untersuchung nach dem Viermächte-Abkommen vom 3.9.1971*, 3rd ed., Berlin: Berlin-Verl. 1977. (Völkerrecht und Politik 8.)

East

Das Potsdamer Abkommen. Dokumentensammlung, ed. Historische Gedenkstätte des Potsdamer Abkommens, Cecilienhof, Potsdam, 3rd ed., Berlin: Staatsverl. der DDR 1980.

Kosing, Alfred: *Nation in Geschichte und Gegenwart. Studie zur historisch-materialistischen Theorie der Nation*, Berlin: Dietz 1976. (Grundfragen der marxistisch—leninistischen Philosophie.)

Mehls, Hartmut and Mehls, Ellen: *13.August*, Berlin: Deutscher Verl. der Wissenschaften 1979. (Illustrierte historische Hefte 17.)

Verträge im Dienste der europaischen Sicherheit. Vom Moskauer bis zum Berliner Vertrag, ed. Ministerium für Auswärtige Angelegenheiten der Deutschen Demokratischen Republik, Berlin: Staatsverl. der DDR 1973.

Wyssozki, V.N., *Westberlin (deutsch)*, Moskau: Verl. Progress; Westberlin: Das Europäische Buch (in Kommission), 1974.

Wer gewinnt durch das Westberlin-Abkommen?, Berlin: Redaktion 'aktuell' 1971. (Die aktuelle Antwort.)

13 The Federal Republic and West Berlin from the East German perspective

West

Menzel, Jörg Peter and Pfeiler, Wolfgang: *Deutschlandbilder. Die Bundesrepublik aus der Sicht der DDR und der Sowjetunion*, Düsseldorf: Droste Verl. 1972. (Bonner Schriften zur Politik und Zeitgeschichte 6/7.)

Arbeiterklasse im Kapitalismus. Klassenkampf und Klassenstruktur, ed. Institut für Internationale Politik und Wirtschaft, Berlin, collection of authors led by Hellmuth Kolbe, Berlin: Staatsverl. der DDR 1976.

Arbeiterbewegung im Kapitalismus der Gegenwart. Revolutionstheoretische Grundfragen des Kampfes der Arbeiterklasse um Demokratie und Sozialismus unter den heutigen Bedingungen des staatsmonopolistischen Kapitalismus, collection of authors under the guidance of Rolf Reissig, Berlin: Deutscher Verl. der Wissenschaften 1980.

Gottschling, Ernst: *Demokratie im Zerrspiegel. Zur Kritik bürgerlicher Demokratietheorien*, Berlin: Deutscher Verl. der Wissenschaften 1978. (Weltanschauung heute 21.)

Der Imperialismus der BRD, ed. Otto Reinhold et al., Berlin: Dietz 1971.

Keiderling, Gerhard and Stulz, Percy: *Berlin 1945–1968. Zur Geschichte der Hauptstadt der DDR und der selbständigen politischen Einheit Westberlin*, ed. R. Bauer, Berlin: Dietz 1970.

Konservatismus als politische Strömung und politische Ideologie, responsibility: Manfred Buhr, Berlin: Akademie-Verl. 1978. (Abhandlungen der Akademie der Wissenschaften der DDR, Abteilung Veröffentlichungen der Wissenschaftlichen Räte, vol.1978. W4.)

Kreuzzug gegen die Koexistenz. Psychologische Kriegsführung heute, ed. Institut für Internationale Politik und Wirtschaft, Berlin: Staatsverl. der DDR 1975.

Polizei der BRD. Polizei der Monopole. Entstehung, Aufgaben und Struktur des Polizeiapparats der BRD, seine Rolle im Herrschaftsmechanismus des staatsmonopolistischen Kapitalismus und das Zusammenwirken mit den Geheimdiensten bei der Unterdrückung der demokratischen Kräfte, collection of authors under the guidance of P. Köhler, Berlin: Deutscher Militärverl. 1972.

Schuster, Jürgen: *Parlamentarismus in der BRD. Rolle und Funktionen des Bundestages bei der politischen Machtausübung des Imperialismus*, Berlin: Dietz 1976.

Widersprüche und Tendenzen im Herrschaftssystem der BRD. Zu Problemen imperialistischer Herrschaftskonzeptionen und -praktiken, Berlin: Staatsverl. der DDR 1973. (Politik aktuell.)

14   Economic history

West

Henning, Friedrich-Wilhelm: *Das industrialisierte Deutschland 1914 bis 1972*, Paderborn: Schöningh 1974. (Uni-Taschenbücher 337.)

Obst, Werner: *25 Jahre DDR – Kapitalverschwendung trotz zentraler Planung*, 2nd ed., Cologne: Deutscher Instituts–Verl. 1975. (Sozialistische Modelle.)

Sandford, Gregory William: *The economic and social transformation of the Soviet occupation zone of Germany 1945–46*. A thesis, Madison: Univ. of Wisconsin 1975.

East

Barthel, Horst: *Die wirtschaftlichen Ausgangsbedingungen der DDR. Zur Wirtschaftsentwicklung auf dem Gebiet der DDR 1945–1949/50*, Berlin: Akademie-Verl. 1979. (Forschungen zur Wirtschaftsgeschichte 14.)

Keller, Dietmar: *Lebendige Demokratie. Der Übergang von der antifaschistischen zur sozialistischen Demokratie in der volkseigenen Industrie der DDR 1948 bis 1952*, Berlin: Verl. Tribüne 1971.

RGW–DDR. 25 Jahre Zusammenarbeit, collection of authors under the guidance of Gunther Kohlmey, Berlin: Akademie-Verl. 1974. (Akademie der Wissenschaften der DDR. Schriften des Zentralinstituts für Wirtschaftswissenschaften 9.)

Roesler, Jörg: *Die Herausbildung der sozialistischen Planwirtschaft in der DDR. Aufgaben, Methoden und Ergebnisse der Volkswirtschaftsplanung in der zentral geleiteten volkseigenen Industrie während der Übergangsperiode vom Kapitalismus zum Sozialismus*, Berlin: Akademie-Verl. 1978. (Forschungen zur Wirtschaftsgeschichte 11.)

15   Political economy, economics

West

Bahro, Rudolf: *Die Alternative. Zur Kritik des real existierenden Sozialismus*, Cologne, Frankfurt/Main: Europäische Verlagsanstalt 1977.

Beyer, Achim: *Neue Anforderungen an die wirtschaftswissenschaftliche Forschung nach dem 9. Parteitag der SED*, Erlangen: Institut für Gesellschaft und Wissenschaft an der Univ. Erlangen-Nürnberg 1977. (IGW-Informationen zur Wirtschaftsentwicklung und -politik in der DDR 2/1977.)

Bust-Bartels, Axel and Stamatis, Georg: *Zur Produktionsweise und Theorie der Übergangsgesellschaft.* 2 Beiträge, Giessen, Lollar: Achenbach 1975. (poloek 2000.)

Dietz, Raimund: *Sowjetökonomie: Warenwirtschaft oder Sachverwaltung. Ein Beitrag zur Begründung einer alternativen Theorie des Sozialismus, Studie zur Werttheorie*, Achberg: Achberger Verlagsanstalt 1976.

Haller, Frank: *Sozialistische Akkumulations- und Wachstumstheorie. Zur Kritik der politischen Ökonomie des Sozialismus in der DDR*, Berlin: Duncker and Humblot (in Commission) 1974. (Osteuropa-Institut an der Freien Univ. Berlin. Wirtschaftswissenschaftliche Veröffentlichungen 35.)

Lieber, Paul and Freier, Udo: *Politische Ökonomie des Sozialismus in der DDR*, Frankfurt/Main: Makol Verl. 1972. (Makol Bibliothek 30.)

Neumann, Philipp: *Zurück zum Profit. Zur Entwicklung des Revisionismus in der DDR*, 2nd ed., Berlin: Oberbaumverl. 1974. (Materialistische Wissenschaft 12.)

Wirth, Margareth: *Kapitalismustheorie in der DDR. Entstehung und Entwicklung der Theorie des staatsmonopolistischen Kapitalismus*, Frankfurt/Main: Suhrkamp 1972. (Edition Suhrkamp 562.)

East

Altmann, Eva: *Zur politischen Ökonomie der Arbeiterklasse. Blickpunkt Sozialismus. Herausbildung, Gegenstand, Probleme*, Berlin: Dietz 1974.

Beiträge zur Geschichte der politischen Ökonomie des Sozialismus, ed. Herbert Meissner and Gertraud Wittenburg, Berlin: Dietz 1975.

Friedrich, Horst; Schliesser, Walfried and Schulz, Gerhard: *Gegenstand, Aufgaben und Methode der politischen Ökonomie des Sozialismus*, Berlin: Dietz 1976. (Lehrhefte Politische Ökonomie des Sozialismus.)

Geschichte der politischen Ökonomie. Grundriss, ed. Herbert Meissner, Berlin: Dietz 1978.

Zur Geschichte der politischen Ökonomie des Sozialismus. Von Marx, Engels und Lenin bis zum Sieg des Sozialismus in der UdSSR, collective of authors under the guidance of H. Seifert, Berlin: Verl. Die Wirtschaft 1978.

Heinrichs, Wolfgang and Kratsch, Ottomar: *Die sozialistischen Produktionsverhältnisse*, Berlin: Dietz 1978. (Lehrhefte Politische Ökonomie des Sozialismus.)

Ökonomisches Lexikon, 3rd ed., Berlin: Verl. Die Wirtschaft. Vol. 1, A—G 1978; vol.2, H—P 1979.

60 Jahre politische Ökonomie des Sozialismus, Berlin: Akademie-Verl. 1979. (Forschungsberichte Zentralinstitut für Wirtschaftswissenschaften der Akademie der Wissenschaften der DDR 30.)

Politische Ökonomie des Kapitalismus und des Sozialismus. Lehrbuch für das marxistisch—leninistische Grundlagenstudium, 5th ed. Berlin: Dietz 1979.

Politische Ökonomie und Wirtschaftsleitung, ed. Akademie für Gesellschaftswissenschaften beim ZK der KPdSU, Institut für Gesellschaftswissenschaften beim ZK der SED, Berlin: Dietz 1974.

Theoretische und methodologische Probleme der politischen Ökonomie, ed. Peter Hofmann, Horst Richter et al., Berlin: Verl. Die Wirtschaft 1979.

Reinhold, Otto and Stiermerling, Karl-Heinz: *Politische Ökonomie. Geschrieben für die Jugend*, Berlin: Dietz 1978.

Viertel, Klaus: *Der sozialistische Produktionsprozess*, Berlin: Dietz 1979. (Lehrhefte Politische Ökonomie des Sozialismus.)

Wertgesetz und Wertkategorien in der sozialistischen Planwirtschaft. Eine politökonomische Studie, ed. Waldfried Schliesser, Berlin: Dietz 1979.

Wörterbuch der Ökonomie des Sozialismus, ed. Willi Ehlert, Heinz Joswig et al., 3rd ed., Berlin: Dietz 1973.

16 The economic system

West

Beyme, Klaus von: *Ökonomie und Politik im Sozialismus. Ein Vergleich der Entwicklung in den sozialistischen Ländern*, Munich, Zürich: Piper 1975.

Bahro, Rudolf: *Plädoyer für eine schöpferische Initiative. Zur Kritik von Arbeitsbedingungen im real existierenden Sozialismus*, Cologne: Bund-Verl. 1980.

Biermann, Wolfgang: *Demokratisierung in der DDR? Ökonomische Notwendigkeiten, Herrschaftsstrukturen, Rolle der Gewerkschaften 1961—1977*, Cologne: Verl. Wissenschaft und Politik 1978.

Bing, Wilhelm: *Investitionsfinanzierung in der Zentralverwaltungswirtschaft. Analyse des Prinzips der Eigenerwirtschaftung von Investitionsmitteln in der DDR*, Stuttgart: Gustav Fischer 1970. (Schriften zum Vergleich von Wirtschaftsordnungen 15.)

BRD—DDR. Die Wirtschaftssysteme. Soziale Marktwirtschaft und sozialistische Planwirtschaft im Systemvergleich, ed. Hannelore Hamel, Munich: Beck 1977. (Beck'sche Schwarze Reihe 153.)

Damus, Renate: *Entscheidungsstrukturen und Funktionsprobleme in der DDR—Wirtschaft*, Frankfurt/Main: Suhrkamp 1973. (Edition Suhrkamp 649.)

DDR-Reformbemühungen in Theorie und Praxis. 6. Symposium der Forschungsstelle. Referate am 21. November 1980, Berlin: Forschungsstelle für gesamtdeutsche wirtschaftliche und soziale Fragen 1980. (FS-Analysen 6/1980.)

Deutsches Institut für Wirtschaftsforschung. DDR-Wirtschaft. Eine Bestandsaufnahme von Peter Mitzscherling et al., Frankfurt/Main: Fischer Taschenbuch Verl. 1974. (Fischer Handbücher 6259.)

Cornelsen, Doris et al.: *Handbuch DDR-Wirtschaft*, Reinbek bei Hamburg: Rowohlt 1977. (rororo 6217.)

Eckhardt, Karl-Heinz: *Die DDR im Systemvergleich. Didaktisches Sachbuch zum Verständnis von Plan- und Marktwirtschaft. Erläuterungen — Materialien — Arbeitsvorschläge*, Reinbek bei Hamburg: Rowohlt 1978. (rororo-Sachbuch 7161.)

Heidt, Ulrich: *Arbeit und Herrschaft im 'realen Sozialismus'*, Frankfurt/Main, New York: Campus Verl. 1979. (Forschung 101.)

Hensel, K. Paul; Wessely, Kurt and Wagner, Ulrich: *Das Profitprinzip — seine ordnungspolitischen Alternativen in sozialistischen Wirtschaftssystemen*, Stuttgart: G. Fischer 1972. (Schriften zum Vergleich von Wirtschaftsordnungen 19.)

Hoffmann, Manfred: *Das Volkseigentum an Grund und Boden in der DDR. Ziele, Instrumente und Ergebnisse seiner Bewirtschaftung*, Cologne: Bundesinstitut für ostwissenschaftliche und internationale Studien 1978. (Berichte des Bundesinstituts für ostwissenschaftliche und internationale Studien 29/1978.)

Leipold, Helmut: *Wirtschafts- und Gesellschaftssysteme im Vergleich, Grundzüge einer Theorie der Wirtschaftssysteme*, Stuttgart: Gustav Fischer 1976. (Uni-Taschenbücher 481.)

Obst, Werner: *DDR-Wirtschaft. Modell und Wirklichkeit*, Hamburg: Hoffmann and Campe 1973.

Osers, Jan: *Sozialistische Wirtschaftsmodelle. Unterschiedliche Konzeptionen ökonomischer Koordination, betrieblicher Lenkung und Interaktion sozioökonomischer Bereiche*, Frankfurt/Main, New York: Campus Verl. 1980.

Mitzscherling, Peter et al.: *System und Entwicklung der DDR-Wirtschaft*, Berlin: Duncker and Humblot 1974. (Deutsches Institut für Wirtschaftsforschung. Sonderheft 98.)

Strassburger, Jürgen: 'Das Wirtschaftssystem', *Politik, Wirtschaft und Gesellschaft in der DDR*, 2nd ed., Opladen: Westdeutscher Verl. 1980, 241–98.

East

Arnold, Karl-Heinz: *Volkswirtschaft unter sozialistischen Bedingungen. Ziele und Ergebnisse in der DDR*, Berlin: Panorama DDR 1974. (Aus erster Hand.)

Die Volkswirtschaft der DDR, collective of authors, Berlin: Verl. Die Wirtschaft 1979.

Wölfling, Manfred: *Ein ökonometrisches Modell der Volkswirtschaft der DDR*, Berlin: Akademie-Verl. 1977. (Forschungsberichte, Zentralinstitut für Wirtschaftswissenschaften der Akademie der Wissenschaften der DDR 21.)

17 Economic policy and economic planning, environmental policy

West

Adam, Jan: *Wage control and inflation in the Soviet bloc countries*, London, Basingstoke: The Macmillan Press 1979.

Erdmann, Kurt et al.: *Zu ökonomischen und sozialpolitischen Aspekten des IX. Parteitages der SED*, Berlin: Forschungsstelle für gesamtdeutsche wirtschaftliche und soziale Fragen 1976. (FS-Analysen 5/1976.)

Bryson, Phillip J., *Scarcity and control in socialism. Essays on East European planning*, Lexington, Mass., Heath 1976.

Damus, Renate: *Wertkategorien als Mittel der Planung. Zur Widersprüchlichkeit der Planung gesamtgesellschaftlicher Prozesse in der DDR*, Erlangen: Politladen 1973. (Probleme des Klassenkampfs. Sonderheft 5.)

Dietz, Raimund: *Die Wirtschaft der DDR 1950–1974*, Vienna: Wiener Institut für Internationale Wirtschaftsvergleiche . . . 1976. (Forschungsberichte Wiener Institut für Internationale Wirtschaftsvergleich . . . 37.)

DDR-Wirtschaft unter Effektivitätszwang. 3. Symposion der Forschungsstelle. Referate zur gegenwärtigen Lage und Problematik der DDR-Wirtschaft, Berlin: Forschungsstelle für gesamtdeutsche wirtschaftliche und soziale Fragen 1977. (FS-Analysen 4/1977.)

Die DDR-Wirtschaft zur Halbzeit des Fünfjahrplanes. 4. Symposion der Forschungsstelle. Referate am 23. Nov. 1978, Berlin: Forschungsstelle für Gesamtdeutsche wirtschaftliche und soziale Fragen 1978. (FS-Analysen 1978, 5.)

Erdmann, Kurt: *Intensivierungshemmnisse und Effizienzverbesserungen zur Halbzeit des Fünfjahrplans in der DDR. Aspekte zur Produktionsorganisation und Kombinatsumbildung*, Berlin: Forschungsstelle für Gesamtdeutsche wirtschaftliche und soziale Fragen 1978. (FS-Analysen 4/1978.)

Erdmann, Kurt: *Zur Rolle der Industrieministerien im Organisationsumbau der DDR*, Berlin: Forschungsstelle für gesamtdeutsche wirtschaftliche und soziale Fragen 1979. (FS-Analysen 1979, 5.)

Füllenbach, Josef: *Umweltschutz zwischen Ost und West. Umweltpolitik in Osteuropa und gesamteuropäische Zusammenarbeit*, Bonn: Europa Union 1977. (Schriften des Forschungsinstituts der Deutschen Gesellschaft für Auswärtige Politik.)

Gohl, Dietmar: 'Deutsche Demokratische Republik. Eine Wirtschaftsgeographie', *Harms Handbuch der Geographie*, vol. 'Deutschland', Munich: List 1975, 322–80.

Haendcke-Hoppe, Maria: *Handwerkspolitik der SED 1976 – ökonomische und ideologische Aspekte der Förderungsmassnahmen*, Berlin: Forschungsstelle für gesamtdeutsche wirtschaftliche und soziale Fragen 1976. (FS-Analysen 9/1976.)

Haffner, Friedrich; Laski, Kazimierz and Thieme, Jörg: *Lenkungsprobleme und Inflation in Planwirtschaften*, ed. Karl-Ernst Schenk. Berlin: Duncker and Humblot 1980. (Schriften des Vereins für Sozialpolitik, NF 106.)

Harich, Wolfgang: *Kommunismus ohne Wachstum? Babeuf und der 'Club of Rome'*, 6 Interviews mit Freimut Duve und Briefe an ihn, Reinbek bei Hamburg: Rowohlt 1975.

Himber, Günter: *Westliches Management aus DDR-Sicht. Die Auseinandersetzung mit westlichen Führungsmethoden und Management-Techniken in der DDR*, Erlangen: Institut für Gesellschaft und Wissenschaft an der Univ. Erlangen-Nürnberg 1980. (Analysen und Berichte aus Gesellschaft und Wissenschaft 3/1980.)

Kiera, Hans-Georg: *Partei und Staat im Planungssystem der DDR. Die Planung in der Ära Ulbricht*, Düsseldorf: Droste Verl. 1975. (Geschichtliche Studien zu Politik und Gesellschaft 8.)

Klein, Werner: *Prozesspolitische Hauptinstrumente der Wirtschaftspolitik in der DDR. Eine betriebliche Wirkungsanalyse*, Stuttgart: Gustav Fischer 1975. (Schriften zum Vergleich von Wirtschaftsordnungen 24.)

Kruppa, Adolf: *Wirtschafts- und Bildungsplanung in der DDR. Theorie und Praxis der Plankoordination*, Hamburg: Hoffmann and Campe 1976. (Kritische Wissenschaft.)

Mellor, Roy Egerton Henderson: *The two Germanies. A modern geography*, New York: Barnes and Noble 1978.

Planung und Strukturpolitik in beiden deutschen Staaten, ed. Friedrich-Ebert-Stiftung, Bonn-Bad Godesberg: Verl. Neue Gesellschaft 1976. (Die DDR. Realitäten, Argumente.)

Scherzinger, Angela and Wilkens, Herbert: *Regionalplanung und regionale Wirtschaftsstruktur in der Deutschen Demokratischen Republik*, Berlin: Duncker and Humblot 1979. (Deutsches Institut für Wirtschaftsforschung. Sonderheft 128.)

Thalheim, Karl C., *Die wirtschaftliche Entwicklung der beiden Staaten in Deutschland. Tatsachen und Zahlen*, Berlin: Landeszentrale für politische Bildungsarbeit 1978.

Thalheim, Karl C., *Die Wirtschaftspolitik der DDR im Schatten Moskaus*, Hannover: Niedersächsische Landeszentrale für politische Bildung 1979.

Umweltschutz in beiden deutschen Staaten, ed. Friedrich-Ebert-Stiftung, Bonn: Verl. Neue Gesellschaft 1980. (Die DDR. Realitäten, Argumente.)

Wilkens, Herbert: *Sozialproduktvergleich zwischen der Bundesrepublik Deutschland und der DDR*, Cologne: Berichte des Bundesinstituts für ostwissenschaftliche und internationale Studien 1978. (Berichte des Bundesinstituts für ostwissenschaftliche und internationale Studien 1978, 21.)

Willke, Helmut: *Leitungswissenschaft in der DDR. Eine Fallstudie zu Problemen der Planung und Steuerung in einer entwickelten sozialistischen Gesellschaft*, Berlin: Duncker and Humblot 1979. (Schriften zum öffentlichen Recht 355.)

Die Wirtschaft der DDR am Beginn der achtziger Jahre. 6. Symposium der Forschungsstelle. Referate am 20. November 1980, Berlin: Forschungsstelle für gesamtdeutsche wirtschaftliche und soziale Fragen 1980. (FS-Analysen 5/1980.)

East

Dehmel, Hans-Henning and Fiedler, Maximilian: *Landschaftsschutz in der DDR. Das sozialistische Landeskulturgesetz in der täglichen Praxis*, Berlin: Verl. Volk und Gesundheit 1976.

Gebhardt, Gerd et al., *Finanzen und Finanzsystem im Sozialismus*, Berlin: Dietz 1981. (Lehrhefte Politische Ökonomie des Sozialismus.)

Sozialistische Finanzwirtschaft. Hochschullehrbuch, collective of authors, Berlin: Verl. Die Wirtschaft 1981.

Grundfragen der sozialistischen Wirtschaftsführung, ed. Gerd Friedrich, Helmut Koziolek et al., Berlin: Dietz 1979. (Schriften zur sozialistischen Wirtschaftsführung.)

Im Mittelpunkt der Mensch. Umweltgestaltung — Umweltschutz, ed. Karlheinz Lohs and Sonnhild Döring, Berlin: Akademie-Verl. 1975.

Krolikowski, Werner: *Der 9. Parteitag der SED über die Fortsetzung des politischen Kurses der Hauptaufgabe. Die Einheit von Wirtschafts- und Sozialpolitik*, Berlin: Dietz 1976. (Vorträge im Parteilehrjahr der SED, 1976.)

Brockhaus Handbuch. Sozialistische Landeskultur. Umweltgestaltung, Umweltschutz, mit einem ABC, ed. Ernst Neef and Vera Neef, Leipzig: Brockhaus 1977.

Sozialistische Landeskultur, Umweltschutz. Textausgabe ausgewählter Rechtsvorschriften mit Anmerkungen und Sachregister, ed. Akademie für Staats- und Rechtswissenschaft der DDR, Minister für Umweltschutz und Wasserwirtschaft, Berlin: Staatsverl. der DDR 1978.

Landeskulturgesetz. Kommentar zum Gesetz über die planmässige Gestaltung der sozialistischen Landeskultur in der Deutschen Demokratischen Republik vom 14.5.1970, collective of authors under the guidance of Stephan Supranowitz, Berlin: Staatsverl. der DDR 1973.

Leitung der sozialistischen Wirtschaft. Einführung, ed. Gerd Friedrich, Helmut Richter et al., Berlin: Verl. Die Wirtschaft 1976.

Lexikon der Wirtschaft. Volkswirtschaftsplanung, ed. Horst Steeger, Berlin: Verl. Die Wirtschaft 1980.

Probleme der Leitung und Planung der sozialistischen Wirtschaft. Probleme und Entwicklungstendenzen der Vervollkommnung des Systems der Leitung und Planung der sozialistischen Wirtschaft, ed. Helmut Koziolek, Berlin: Akademie-Verl. 1979. (Abhandlungen der Akademie der Wissenschaften der DDR. Abteilung Veröffentlichungen der Wissenschaftlichen Räte 1978, 9.)

Söder, Günter: *Ökonomie, Politik, Wirtshaftspolitik. Weltanschaulich-philosophische Aspekte des Verhältnisses von Politik und Wirtschaft im Sozialismus*, Berlin: Deutscher Verl. der Wissenschaften 1977. (Weltanschauung heute 17.)

Territorialplanung, ed. Rolf Bönisch, Gerhard Mohs and Werner Ostwald, 2nd ed., Berlin: Verl. Die Wirtschaft 1981.

Umweltgestaltung und Ökonomie der Naturressourcen, collective of authors under the guidance of Hans Roos and Günter Streibel, Berlin: Verl. Die Wirtschaft 1979.

18   Industry, transportation

West

Bahr, Klaus: *Die Fischwirtschaft der Deutschen Demokratischen Republik mit vergleichenden Betrachtungen zur Bundesrepublik Deutschland*, Berlin: Heenemann 1975. (Schriften der Bundesforschungsanstalt für Fischerei Hamburg 12.)

Götz: *Die Energiewirtschaft der DDR. Ein Überblick über die Entwicklung*, Bonn: Gesamtdeutsches Institut, Bundesanstalt für Gesamtdeutsche Aufgaben 1978. (Gesamtdeutsches Institut 5.)

Götz: *Die Kraftfahrzeugindustrie der DDR*, Bonn: Gesamtdeutsches Institut, Bundesanstalt für gesamtdeutsche Aufgaben 1978. (Gesamtdeutsches Institut 20.)

Götz, Julius: *Die Rohstoffwirtschaft der DDR*, Bonn: Gesamtdeutsches Institut, Bundesanstalt für gesamtdeutsche Aufgaben 1980.

Knauer, Peter: *Abfallwirtschaft in der DDR. Bericht*, Berlin: Umweltbundesamt 1978.

Krakat, Klaus: *Computerproduktion und Computereinsatz in der DDR*, Berlin: Forschungsstelle für gesamtdeutsche wirtschaftliche und soziale Fragen 1977. (FS-Analysen 1977, 3.)

Rapelius, Eckart: *Struktur und Entwicklung der Ernährungsindustrie in der Deutschen Demokratischen Republik. Mit Vergleichen zur Bundesrepublik Deutschland und anderen Ländern West- und Osteuropas*, Frankfurt/Main: P. Lang 1979. (Europäische Hochschulschriften. Reihe 5. 225.)

Spindler, Bernd: *Die DDR-Fluggesellschaft 'Interflug'*, Bonn: Gesamtdeutsches Institut, Bundesanstalt für gesamtdeutsche Aufgaben 1980.

Gesamtdeutsches Institut, Bundesanstalt für gesamtdeutsche Aufgaben. Verzeichnis der Kombinate der DDR, adapted by Julius Götz, Bonn 1979.

Wilde, Käthe: *Gütertransport der Binnenverkehrszweige in der DDR. Entwicklung von 1965 bis 1977*, Berlin: Forschungsstelle für gesamtdeutsche wirtschaftliche und soziale Fragen 1979. (FS-Analysen 1979, 3.)

Wilde, Käthe: *Personennahverkehr, ein Schwerpunktprogramm der Verkehrsentwicklung in der DDR*, Berlin: Forschungsstelle für gesamtdeutsche wirtschaftliche und soziale Fragen, vol.1, 1975. (FS-Analysen 1975, 7.) Vol.2, 1977. (FS-Analysen 1977, 5.)

East

Blei, Alexander: *Leitfaden zur Finanzierung der volkseigenen Industrie*, Berlin: Verl. Die Wirtschaft 1978.

Deutsche Demokratische Republik. Industrie, Dresden: Verl. Zeit im Bild 1972.

Der Industriebetrieb in der sozialistischen Volkswirtschaft, collective of East German and Soviet authors, 2nd ed., Berlin: Verl. Die Wirtschaft 1977.

Lexikon der Wirtschaft. Industrie, ed. Hans Borchert, Berlin: Verl. Die Wirtschaft 1970.

19 Agriculture

West

Die industriemässig betriebene pflanzliche Agrarproduktion der DDR. Organisationsformen, Produktionsverfahren und ökonomische Effizienz, mit vergleichenden Betrachtungen zur Pflanzenproduktion in der Landwirtschaft der Bundesrepublik Deutschland. Ergebnisse eines Forschungsauftrages des Bundesministeriums für Ernährung, Landwirtschaft und Forsten, adapted by Bodo Heyn et al., Münster, Hiltrup: Landwirtschaftsverl. 1977. (Landwirtschaft, angewandte Wissenschaft 204.)

Bajaja, Vladislav: *Organisation und Führung landwirtschaftlicher Grossunternehmen in der DDR*, Berlin: Duncker and Humblot in Commission 1978. (Osteuropastudien der Hochschulen des Landes Hessen. Reihe 1. 92.)

Berthold, Theodor: *Die Agrarpreispolitik der DDR. Ziele, Mittel, Wirkungen*, Berlin: Duncker and Humblot in Commission 1972. (Osteuropastudien der Hochschulen des Landes Hessen. Reihe 1. 53.)

Bichler, Hans and Szamatolski, Clemens: *Landwirtschaft in der DDR. Agrarpolitik und Landwortschaft in einem sozialistischen Industriestaat*, Berlin: Gebrüder Holzapfel 1973. (. . . in der DDR.)

Eckart, Karl: *Landwirtschaftliche Kooperation in der DDR. Eine geographische Untersuchung der Struktur und Entwicklung sozialistischer Landwirtschaftsbetriebe*, Wiesbaden: Steyner 1977. (Wissenschaftliche Paperbacks. Geographie.)

Franz, Marie-Luise: *Die zwischenbetriebliche Kooperation in der Landwirtschaft der DDR*, Cologne: Verl. Wissenschaft und Politik 1976. (Abhandlungen zum Ostrecht 14.)

Genossenschaften in der DDR und in der Bundesrepublik, ed. Friedrich-Ebert-Stiftung, Bonn-Bad Godesberg: Verl. Neue Gesellschaft 1975. (Die DDR. Realitäten, Argumente.)

Hoffmann, Manfred and Schinkel, Eberhard: *Bodenrecht und Bodennutzung in der Landwirtschaft der DDR*, Cologne: Bundesinstitut für ostwissenschaftliche und internationale Studien 1973. (Berichte des Bundesinstituts für ostwissenschaftliche und internationale Studien 57/73.)

Hoffmann, Manfred: *Instrumente zur Lenkung der landwirtschaftlichen Bodennutzung in der DDR*, Berlin: Duncker and Humblot in Commission 1977. (Osteuropastudien der Hochschulen des Landes Hessen. Reihe 1. 86.)

Immler, Hans: *Arbeitsteilung, Kooperation und Wirtschaftssystem. Eine Untersuchung am Beispiel der Landwirtschaft in der BRD und in der DDR*, Berlin: Duncker and Humblot 1973. (Volkswirtschaftliche Studien 203.)

Lambrecht, Horst: 'Die Landwirtschaft', *Politik, Wirtschaft und Gesellschaft in der DDR*, 2nd ed., Opladen: Westdeutscher Verl. 1980, 299—327.

Lambrecht, Horst: *Die Landwirtschaft der DDR vor und nach ihrer Umgestaltung im Jahre 1960*, Berlin: Duncker and Humblot 1977. (Deutsches Institut für Wirtschaftsforschung. Sonderheft 117.)

Schinke, Eberhard: *Schlachttier- und Fleischproduktion in Osteuropa, DDR*, Berlin: Duncker and Humblot in Commission 1979. (Osteuropastudien der Hochschulen des Landes Hessen. Reihe 1. 95.)

East

Sachse, Dieter et al., *Zur Agrar- und Bündnispolitik der SED bei der Gestaltung der entwickelten sozialistischen Gesellschaft*, 2nd ed., Berlin: Dietz 1978.

Agrarrecht für Staats- und Wirtschaftsfunktionäre. Grundriss, collective of authors under the guidance of Reiner Arlt, 2nd ed., Berlin: Staatsverl. der DDR 1979.

Genossenschaftsbauern — gestern — heute — morgen. Die Klasse der Genossenschaftsbauern im Prozess der Gestaltung der industriemässig produzierenden Landwirtschaft in der DDR, ed. Institut für Gesellschaftswissenschaften beim ZK der SED, Berlin: Dietz 1977.

Intensivierung der landwirtschaftlichen Produktion. Grundprobleme der weiteren Intensivierung der landwirtschaftlichen Produktion und des schrittweisen Übergangs zu industriemässigen Produktionsmethoden, adapted by Helmut Koziolek, Berlin: Akademie-Verl. 1979. (Abhandlungen der Akademie der Wissenschaften der DDR. Abteilung Veröffentlichungen der Wissenschaftlichen Räte. 1979, 2.)

Hoell, Günter: *Die Agrarverhältnisse im Sozialismus*, Berlin: Dietz 1980.

Klemm, Volker: *Agrargeschichte. Von der bürgerlichen Agrarreform zur sozialistischen Landwirtschaft in der DDR*, Berlin: Deutscher Landwirtschaftsverl. 1978.

Die Landwirtschaft der DDR, collective of authors under the guidance of Kurt Groschoff and Richard Heinrich, Berlin: Dietz 1980.

Lexikon Recht der Landwirtschaft der Deutschen Demokratischen Republik, collection of authors under the guidance of Reiner Arlt, Berlin: Staatsverl. der DDR 1975.

LPG-Recht. Lehrbuch, Berlin: Staatsverl. der DDR 1976.

Musterstatut der LPG Tierproduktion. Kommentar, collection of authors, Berlin: Staatsverl. der DDR 1981.

Reinl, Erwin: *Antwort auf Fragen zum Arbeitsrecht in der Landwirtschaft*. Berlin: Verl. Tribune 1978.

20 Trade and services

West

Behrend, Willy: *Genosse Konsument: Bedürfnisbefriedigung im Sozialismus*, Cologne: Deutscher Instituts—Verl. 1979. (Sozialistische Modelle.)

Haendcke-Hoppe, Maria: *Das Gaststättenwesen in der DDR*, Berlin: Forschungsstelle für Gesamtdeutsche wirtschaftliche und soziale Fragen 1979. (FS-Analysen 1979, 4.)

Handwerk und Gewerbe in beiden deutschen Staaten, ed. Friedrich-Ebert-Stiftung, Bonn-Bad Godesberg: Verl. Neue Gesellschaft 1976. (Die DDR. Realitäten, Argumente.)

Hilgenberg, Dorothea: *Bedarfs- und Marktforschung in der DDR. Anspruch und Wirklichkeit*, Cologne: Verl. Wissenschaft und Politik 1979.

Lebenshaltung und Lebensniveau in der DDR, ed. Friedrich-Ebert-Stiftung, Bonn: Verl. Neue Gesellschaft 1980. (Die DDR. Realitäten, Argumente.)

Otto-Arnold, Charlotte: *Das Kaufkraftverhältnis zwischen D-Mark und Mark (DDR), Eine Neuberechnung*, Berlin: Duncker and Humblot 1979. (Deutsches Institut für Wirtschaftsforschung. Sonderheft 129.)

Preisprobleme in der DDR, 2nd ed., Erlangen: Institut für Gesellschaft und Wissenschaft 1980. (Analysen und Berichte aus Gesellschaft und Wissenschaft 1980, 1.)

Schlenk, Hans: *Der Binnenhandel der DDR*, Cologne: Verl. Wissenschaft und Politik 1970.

Thalheim, Karl C. and Haendcke-Hoppe, Maria: *Das Handwerk in der DDR und Ost-Berlin*, Berlin: Forschungsstelle für gesamtdeutsche wirtschaftliche und soziale Fragen 1978. (FS-Analysen 1978, 2.)

East

Bedarfs- und Marktforschung, collective of authors under the guidance of Gernot Schneider, Berlin: Verl Die Wirtschaft 1976.

Der Gaststätten- und Hotelleiter. Handbuch, ed. Klaus Wenzel, Günther Riedel, Berlin: Verl. Die Wirtschaft 1979.

Göring, Joachim: *Wenn's um Dienstleistungen geht*, Berlin: Staatsverl. der DDR 1978. (Recht in unserer Zeit 13.)

Griebenow, Eckard, Kreutzer, Claus J. and Teige, Hans-Werner: *Rechtsfragen der Handelspraxis. Ratgeber*, 3rd ed., Berlin: Verl. Die Wirtschaft 1980.

Illgen, Konrad: *Geographie und territoriale Organisation des Binnenhandels. Eine Einführung*, Gotha, Leipzig: Haack 1970.

Merker, Joachim and Lehm, Jürgen: *Im Mittelpunkt: der Kunde. Kleine Angebots- und Verkaufskunde für den Einzelhandel*, 2nd ed., Berlin: Verl. Die Wirtschaft 1974.

Müller, Kay and Teige, Hans-Werner: *Die Rechte der Käufer. Qualitätsmängel, Reklamationen, Garantie, Nachbesserung oder Kaufpreiserstattung, Zusatzgarantie, Schadenersatz und vieles mehr*, 12th ed., Berlin: Verl. Die Wirtschaft 1979.

Preiskontrolle für Waren des täglichen Bedarfs. Handbuch, collective of authors under the guidance of Heinz Braun, Berlin: Verl. Die Wirtschaft 1976.

Verkaufseinrichtungen im Einzelhandel. Handbuch für den Leiter, collective of authors under the guidance of Karl Lein, 3rd ed., Berlin: Verl. Die Wirtschaft 1979.

21 Organisation of industrial plants

West

Bahro, Rudolf: *Plädoyer für eine schöpferische Initiative. Zur Kritik von Arbeitsbedingungen im real existierenden Sozialismus*, Cologne: Bund-Verl. 1980.

Belwe, Katharine: *Mitwirkung im Industriebetrieb der DDR. Planung – Einzelleitung – Beteiligung der Werktätigen an Entscheidungsprozessen des VEB*, Opladen: Westdeutscher Verl. 1979. (Schriften des Zentralinstituts für sozialwissenschaftliche Forschung der Freien Universität Berlin 31.)

Friedrich, Claus: *Sozialistische Betriebsdemokratie in der DDR*, Frankfurt/Main: Nachrichten-Verl 1975.

Hoehmann, Hans-Hermann and Seidenstecher, Gertraud: *Partizipation im System der administrativen Planwirtschaft von UdSSR und DDR*, Cologne: Bundesinstitut für ostwissenschaftliche und internationale Studien 1980. (Berichte des Bundesinstituts für ostwissenschaftliche und internationale Studien 1980, 4.)

Klein, Werner: *Prozesspolitische Hauptinstrumente der Wirtschaftspolitik in der DDR, Eine Wirkungsanalyse*, Stuttgart: Gustav Fischer 1975. (Schriften zum Vergleich von Wirtschaftsordnungen 24.)

Die Kombinatsbildung der DDR in Theorie und Praxis. Leitung, Planung, Innovation. 5. Symposion der Forschungsstelle. Referate am 23. Nov. 1979, Berlin: Forschungsstelle für gesamtdeutsche wirtschaftliche und soziale Fragen 1979. (FS-Analysen 1979, 8.)

Neuererbewegung und wissenschaftliche Arbeitsorganisation (WAO) in der DDR, ed. Friedrich-Ebert-Stiftung, Bonn: Verl. Neue Gesellschaft 1980. (Die DDR. Realitaten, Argumente.)

Nutzinger, Hans G., *Die Stellung des Betriebes in der sozialistischen Wirtschaft. Allokationsmodelle zum Verhältnis von betrieblicher Entscheidung und gesamtwirtschaftlicher Abstimmung*, Frankfurt/Main, New York: Herder and Herder 1974. (H and H Campus: Studien: Wirtschaftswissenschaften.)

Piorkowsky, Michael-Burghard: *Sozialistische Warenproduktion und Betriebswirtschaftslehre. Zur Entwicklung der Unternehmen und der Unternehmenstheorie im Sozialismus sowjetischen Typs*, Berlin: Duncker and Humblot in Commission 1980. (Wirtschaftswissenschaftliche Veröffentlichungen 38.)

Verzeichnis der Kominate der DDR, adapted by Julius Götz, Bonn: Gesamtdeutsches Institut, Bundesanstalt für gesamtdeutsche Aufgaben, 1979.

East

Die Anwendung mathematischer und statistischer Methoden bei der Objektivierung von Leitung, Planung und Bilanzierung des betrieblichen Reproduktionsprozesses, collective of authors, Leipzig: Deutscher Verl. für Grundstoffindustrie 1975. (Freiberger Forschungshefte D94: Wirtschaftswissenschaften, Sozialistische Betriebswirtschaft.)

Wissenschaftliche Arbeitsorganisation. Aufgabe der Staats- und Wirtschaftsfunktionäre, collective of authors, Berlin: Staatsverl. der DDR 1974.

Arnold, Hans; Borchert, Hans and Schmidt, Johannes: *Der Produktionsprozess im Industriebetrieb*, 4th ed., Berlin: Verl. Die Wirtschaft 1975.

Betriebsökonomik. Grundlehrgang, 6th ed., Berlin: Verl. Die Wirtschaft 1977.

Sozialistische Betriebswirtschaft. Lehrbuch, collective of authors under the guidance of Dieter Graichen, 4th ed., Berlin: Verl. Die Wirtschaft 1980.

Brzoska, Hans and Röder, Erich: *Gewerkschaftliche Mitwirkung an der betrieblichen Planung*, Berlin: Verl. Tribüne 1976.

Holicki, Armin and Schmich, Achim: *Konzeptionelle Vorbereitung des Fünfjahrplanes in Betrieben und Kombinaten*, Berlin: Verl. Die Wirtschaft 1979.

Der Industriebetrieb in der sozialistischen Volkswirtschaft, collective of East German and Soviet authors, 2nd ed., Berlin: Verl. Die Wirtschaft 1977.

Ökonomik, Lehrbuch für das Grundlagenfach Betriebsökonomik, Berlin: Verl. Die Wirtschaft 1975.

Planung in Industriebetrieben und Kombinaten, ed. E. Polaschewski, Berlin: Verl. Die Wirtschaft 1977.

Rechnungsführung und Statistik in der Industrie. Lehrbuch, ed. Gotthard Forbrig, Günter Goll and Edwin Polaschewski, 6th ed., Berlin: Verl. Die Wirtschaft 1979.

Stenzel, Hans-Werner and Uebermuth, Hermann: *Finanzen und Preise. Grundkenntnisse für den Betriebswirtschaftler*, 2nd ed., Berlin: Verl. Die Wirtschaft 1978.

22 Sociology and demography

West

Baylis, Thomas Arthur: *The technical intelligentsia and the East German elite. Legitimacy and social change in mature communism*, Berkeley (a.o.): University of California Press 1974.

Dahm, Helmut: *Die sozialistische Lebensweise. Entstehung, Sinn und Zweck eines Leitbildes*, Cologne: Bundesinstitut für ostwissenschaftliche und internationale Studien 1977. (Berichte des Bundesinstituts für ostwissenschaftliche und internationale Studien 1977, 66.)

Erbe, Günter: 'Klassen und Schichten', *Politik, Wirtschaft und Gesellschaft in der DDR*, 2nd ed., Opladen: Westdeutscher Verl. 1980, 403–24.

Demographisch relevante Faktoren in der DDR, Bundesrepublik, CSSR, UdSSR, ed. Hans Harmsen, Hamburg: 1979. (Zur Entwicklung und Organisation des Gesundheitswesens in der DDR unter Mitberücksichtigung der UdSSR und osteuropäischer Volksdemokratien 81.)

Frauen in der Deutschen Demokratischen Republik, ed. Friedrich-Ebert-Stiftung, Bonn: Verl. Neue Gesellschaft 1981. (Die DDR. Realitäten, Argumente.)

Freiburg, Arnold: *Kriminalität in der DDR. Zur Phänomenologie des abweichenden Verhaltens im sozialistischen deutschen Staat*, Opladen: Westdeutscher Verl. 1981.

Hanke, Irma: 'Die Sozialstruktur', *DDR. Das politische, wirtschaftliche und soziale System*, 4th ed., Munich: C.H. Beck 1978, 57–86.

Krejci, Jaroslav: *Social structure in divided Germany*, London: Croom Helm 1976.

Müller, Hans-Joachim: *Arbeitsgruppen und- schwerpunkte des 3. Soziologiekongresses in der DDR*, Erlangen: Institut für Gesellschaft und Wissenschaft 1980. (IGW-Informationen zur Wissenschaftsentwicklung und- politik in der DDR 1980, 3.)

Rudolph, Irmhild: 'Die Bevölkerung', *Politik, Wirtschaft und Gesellschaft in der DDR*, 2nd ed., Opladen: Westdeutscher Verl. 1980, 393–402.

Schmickl, Emil: *Soziologie und Sozialismustheorie in der DDR*, Cologne: Verl. Wissenschaft und Politik 1973. (Bibliothek Wissenschaft und Politik 6.)

Sozialstruktur und Sozialplanung in der DDR. 8.Tagung zum Stand der DDR–Forschung in der Bundesrepublik, 20.–23.5.1975, ed. Akademie für Politische Bildung Tutzing, Cologne: Verl. Wissenschaft und Politik 1975. (Deutschland Archiv, vol.8, Sonderheft.)

Soziologie und Marxismus in der Deutschen Demokratischen Republik, ed. Peter Christian Ludz, 2 vols, Neuwied, Berlin: Luchterhand 1972.

Voigt, Dieter: *Soziologie in der DDR. Eine exemplarische Untersuchung*, Cologne: Verl. Wissenschaft und Politik 1975.

East

Aktivität, Schöpfertum, Leitung und Planung. Materialien vom 2. Kongress der marxistisch–leninistischen Soziologie in der DDR, 15.–17.Mai 1974, Berlin: Dietz 1975. (Schriftenreihe 'Soziologie'.)

Körperliche und geistige Arbeit im Sozialismus. Eine soziologische Analyse, collective of authors under the guidance of Rosemarie Winzer, Berlin: Dietz 1980.

Die Arbeiterklasse und der Annäherungsprozess der Klassen und Schichten, collective of authors under the guidance of Wolfgang Schneider, Berlin: Dietz 1979. (Sozialismus, Erfahrungen, Probleme und Perspektiven.)

Arbeiterklasse und wissenschaftliche-technische Intelligenz in der entwickelten sozialistischen Gesellschaft, collective of authors under the guidance of Karl Hartmann and Stanislaw Widerzpil, Berlin: Dietz 1978. (Sozialismus — Erfahrungen, Probleme und Perspektiven.)

Bevölkerungstheorie und Bevölkerungspolitik, ed. Parviz Khalatbari, Berlin: Akademie-Verl. 1978. (Beiträge zur Demographie 5.)

Braunreuther, Kurt: *Studien zur Geschichte der politischen Ökonomie und der Soziologie*, ed. Hermann Lehmann, Berlin: Akademie-Verl. 1978.

Die Demographie und ihre Methode, ed. Parviz Khalatbari, Berlin: Akademie-Verl. 1977. (Beiträge zur Demographie 1.)

Grundlagen der marxistisch—leninistischen Soziologie, ed. Georg Assmann, Rudhard Stollberg, Berlin: Dietz 1977.

Grundmann, Siegfried: *Arbeiterklasse — Gegenwart und Zukunft. Weltanschauliche und soziologische Probleme der Voraussage und Gestaltung sozialer Prozesse*, Berlin: Dietz 1975. (Schriftenreihe 'Soziologie'.)

Grundmann, Siegfried, Lötsch, Manfred and Weidig, Rudi: *Zur Entwicklung der Arbeiterklasse und ihrer Struktur in der DDR*, Berlin: Dietz 1976. (Schriftenreihe 'Soziologie'.)

Jugendforschung. Methodologische Grundlagen, Methoden und Techniken, ed. Walter Friedrich, Werner Hennig, Berlin: Deutscher Verl. der Wissenschaften 1976.

Lebensweise — Kultur — Persönlichkeit. Materialien vom 2. Kongress der marxistisch—leninistischen Soziologie in der DDR, 15.—17.5.1974, ed. Wissenschaftlicher Rat für Soziologische Forschung in der DDR, Berlin: Dietz 1975. (Schriftenreihe 'Soziologie'.)

Lebensweise und Sozialstruktur. Materialien des 3. Kongresses der marxistisch—leninistischen Soziologie in der DDR. 25. bis 27. Marz 1980, ed. Wissenschaftlicher Rat für Soziologische Forschung in der DDR, Berlin: Dietz 1981.

Zu Problemen der Demographie. Materialien des Internationalen Demographischen Symposiums, Berlin, 16.—18. Dezember 1974, ed. Parviz Khalatbari, Berlin: Akademie-Verl. 1975.

Probleme der demographischen Entwicklung. Probleme der demographischen Entwicklung bei der weiteren Gestaltung der entwickelten sozialistischen Gesellschaft in der DDR, Berlin: Akademie-Verl. 1980. (Abhandlungen der Akademie der Wissenschaften der DDR. Abteilung Veröffentlichungen der Wissenschaftlichen Räte, 1979, 5.)

Soziologische Probleme der Klassenentwicklung in der DDR. Materialien vom 2. Kongress der marxistisch–leninistischen Soziologie in der DDR, 15.–17. Mai 1974, ed. Wissenschaftlicher Rat für Soziologische Forschung in der DDR, Berlin: Dietz 1975. (Schriftenreihe 'Soziologie'.)

Zur Sozialstruktur der sozialistischen Gesellschaft, ed. Wissenschaftlicher Rat für Soziologische Forschung in der DDR, Berlin: Dietz 1974. (Schriftenreihe 'Soziologie'.)

Speigner, Wulfram: *Vom Motiv zum Handeln. Gedanken zur soziologischen Motivationsanalyse*, Berlin: Dietz 1980. (Schriftenreihe 'Soziologie'.)

Stollberg, Rudhard: *Arbeitssoziologie*, Berlin: Verl. Die Wirtschaft 1978.

Wörterbuch der marxistisch–leninistischen Soziologie, ed. Georg Assmann, Wolfgang Eichhorn I et al., 2nd ed., Berlin: Dietz 1977.

23 Social policy

West

Buck, Hannsjörg: *Vergleich der staatlich finanzierten Wohlfahrtsleistungen für die Bevölkerung in beiden deutschen Staaten*, Bonn: Gesamtdeutsches Institut, Bundesanstalt für Gesamtdeutsche Aufgaben 1978. (Gesamtdeutsches Institut 19.)

Einheit von Wirtschafts- und Soziopolitik. Anspruch und Realität. 11. Tagung zum Stand der DDR–Forschung in der Bundesrepublik, 16.–19. Mai 1978, Referate, Cologne: Verl. Wissenschaft und Politik 1978. (Deutschland Archiv. Sonderheft.)

Leenen, Wolf-Rainer: *Zur Frage der Wachstumsorientierung der marxistisch–leninistischen Sozialpolitik in der DDR*, Berlin: Duncker and Humblot 1977. (Volkswirtschaftliche Schriften 261.)

Mitzscherling, Peter: *Zweimal deutsche Sozialpolitik*, Berlin: Duncker and Humblot 1978. (Deutsches Institut für Wirtschaftsforschung, Sonderheft 123.)

Rolf, Hartmut: *Sozialversicherung oder staatlicher Gesundheitsdienst? Ökonomischer Effizienzvergleich der Gesundheitssicherungssysteme der Bundesrepublik Deutschland und der Deutschen Demokratischen Republik*, Berlin: Duncker and Humblot 1975. (Sozialpolitische Schriften 36.)

Russ, Werner: *Die Sozialversicherung in der DDR. Eine Untersuchung unter besonderer Berücksichtigung der Zielsetzungen der marxistisch–leninistischen Sozialpolitik*, Frankfurt/Main: Rita G. Fischer 1979.

Versicherungs- und Beitragsrecht der Sozialversicherung in der DDR, compiled by Horst Weser, Berlin: Bundesversicherungsanstalt für Angestellte, 1979.

East

Ebert, Georg: *Höchste Wohlfahrt für das ganze Volk*, Berlin: 1980. (Vorzüge des Sozialismus.)

Sozialpolitisches Programm des 9. Parteitages der SED. Dokumente, 2nd ed., Berlin: Verl Tribüne 1977.

30 Jahre DDR, drei Jahrzehnte schöpferischer Arbeit zum Wohle des Volkes. Eine sozialpolitische Bilanz in Wort und Bild, in Fakten und Zahlen, directed by Werner Meier, Berlin: Verl. Tribüne 1979.

Ruhl, Hans and Weisse, Heinz: *Sozialpolitische Massnahmen – konkret für jeden*, Berlin: Staatsverl. der DDR 1978. (Schriftenreihe Recht in unserer Zeit 14.)

Schindler, Joachim, Schmunk, Gunter and Winkler, Gunnar: *Arbeits- und Lebensbedingungen der Werktätigen. Zur Analyse, Leitung, Planung und Finanzierung*, Berlin: Verl. Tribüne 1978.

Marxistisch–leninistische Sozialpolitik, collection of authors under the guidance of Günter Schmunk et al., ed. Gewerkschaftschule 'Fritz Heckert' beim Bundesvorstand des FDGB, Berlin: Verl. Tribüne 1975.

Theorie und Praxis der Sozialpolitik in der DDR, ed. Institut für Soziologie und Sozialpolitik der Akademie der Wissenschaften der DDR durch Günter Manz, Gunnar Winkler, Berlin: Akademie-Verl. 1979.

Zum Wohle des Volkes. Die Verwirklichung des sozialpolitischen Programms der SED 1971–1978. Dokumentation, Berlin: Dietz 1980. (Schriftenreihe Geschichte.)

24 The churches

West

Barberini, Giovanni; Stöhr, Martin and Weingärtner, Erich: *Kirchen im Sozialismus. Kirche und Staat in den osteuropäischen sozialistischen Republiken. Eine IDOC-Dokumentation*, Frankfurt/Main: Lembeck 1977.

Fischer, Peter: *Kirche und Christen in der DDR*, Berlin: Holzapfel 1978. (... in der DDR.)

Kirche und Staat in der DDR und in der Bundesrepublik, ed. Friedrich-Ebert-Stiftung, Bonn-Bad Godesberg: Verl. Neue Gesellschaft 1977. (Die DDR. Realitäten, Argumente.)

Knauft, Wolfgang: *Katholische Kirche in der DDR. Gemeinden in der Bewährung 1945–1980*, Mainz: Matthias-Grünewald-Verl. 1980.

Rommel, Kurt, W., *Religion und Kirche im sozialistischen Staat der DDR*, Kiel: Institut für Recht, Politik und Gesellschaft der sozialistischen Staaten der Universität Kiel 1975. (Manuskripte aus dem Institut für Recht, Politik und Gesellschaft der sozialistischen Staaten der Universität Kiel 5.)

East

Borgmann, Lutz: *Zwischen gestern und morgen. Evangelische Gemeinden in der Deutschen Demokratischen Republik*, Berlin: Evangelische Verlagsanstalt 1970.

Theologisches Fach- und Fremdwörterbuch. Mit einem Anhang von Abkürzungen aus Theologie und Kirche, 2nd ed., Berlin: Evangelische Verlagsanstalt 1980.

Handbuch der praktischen Theologie, adapted by Heinrich Ammer et al.. Vol.1: 'Die praktische Theologie. Einführung. Gestalt. Aufbau und Ordnung der Kirche. Zur Person des kirchlichen Amtsträgers', 1975. Vol.2: 'Der Gottesdienst. Die kirchlichen Handlungen. Die Predigt', 1974. Vol.3: 'Die Unterweisung. Die Seelsorge. Die Diakonie', 1978. Berlin: Evangelische Verlagsanstalt.

Jacob, Willibald: *Eigentum und Arbeit. Evangelische Sozialethik zwischen 'Industriegesellschaft' und Sozialismus*, Berlin: Union Verl. 1977. (Fakten – Argumente.)

Kaltenborn, Carl-Jürgen: *Plädoyer für die nützliche Gewalt. Konsequenzen aus dem Mandat Gottes für uns*, Berlin: Union Verl. 1976. (Fakten – Argumente.)

Klassenkampf und Koexistenz. Pfarrer und Theologen in der politisch-geistigen Auseinandersetzung, Berlin: Union Verl. 1973. (Fakten — Argumente.)

Theologisches Lexikon, ed. Hans-Hinrich Jenssen, Herbert Trebs, Berlin: Union Verl. 1978.

Orientierung Ökumene. Ein Handbuch. Im Auftrag der Theologischen Studienabteilung beim Bund der Evangelischen Kirchen in der DDR, ed. Hans-Martin Moderow, Matthias Sens. Berlin: Evangelische Verlagsanstalt 1979.

Schönherr, Albrecht: *Horizont und Mitte. Aufsätze, Vorträge, Reden 1953—1977*, Berlin: Evangelische Verlagsanstalt 1979.

Zur Antwort Bereit. Missionarisch-diakonische Arbeit der Evangelischen Landes- und Freikirchen in der DDR, ed. Gerhard Bosinski, Berlin: Evangelische Verlagsanstalt 1977.

25 Arts and culture

West

Brettschneider, Werner: *Zwischen literarischer Autonomie und Staatsdienst. Die Literatur in der DDR*, 2nd ed., Berlin: Erich Schmidt 1974.

Brettschneider, Werner: *Zorn und Trauer. Aspekte deutscher Gegenwartsliteratur*, Berlin: Erich Schmidt 1979.

Daiber, Hans: *Deutsches Theater seit 1945*, Bundesrepublik Deutschland, Deutsche Demokratische Republik, Österreich, Schweiz. Stuttgart: Reclam 1976.

Dautel, Klaus: *Zur Theorie des literarischen Erbes in der 'entwickelten sozialistischen Gesellschaft' der DDR: Rezeptionsvorgabe und Identitätsangebot*, Stuttgart: Akademischer Verl. Heinz 1980. (Stuttgarter Arbeiten zur Germanistik 71.)

Einführung in Theorie, Geschichte und Funktion der DDR-Literatur, ed. Hans-Jürgen Schmitt. Stuttgart: Metzler 1975. (Literaturwissenschaft und Sozialwissenschaften 6.)

Einhorn, Barbara: *Der Roman in der DDR 1949—1969. Die Gestaltung des Verhältnisses von Individuum und Gesellschaft. Eine Analyse der Erzählstruktur*, Kronberg/Taunus: Scriptor Verl. 1978. (Monographien Literaturwissenschaft 40.)

Fischbeck, Helmut: *Literaturpolitik und Literaturkritik in der DDR. Eine Dokumentation*, ed. Helmut Fischbeck. Frankfurt/Main, Berlin, Munich: Diesterweg 1976. (Texte und Materialien zum Literaturunterricht.)

Franke, Konrad: *Die Literatur der Deutschen Demokratischen Republik*, Munich, Zürich: Kindler 1971. (Kindlers Literaturgeschichte der Gegenwart in Einzelbänden.)

Gerlach, Ingeborg: *Der schwierige Fortschritt. Gegenwartsdeutung und Zukunftserwartung im DDR-Roman*, Königstein/Taunus: Scriptor 1979. (Monographien Literaturwissenschaft 46.)

Gransow, Volker: *Kulturpolitik in der DDR*, Berlin: Spiess 1975.

Greiner, Bernhard: *Von der Allegorie zur Idylle. Die Literatur der Arbeitswelt in der DDR*, Heidelberg: Quelle and Meyer 1974. (Uni-Taschenbücher 327.)

Gudorf, Odilo: *Sprache als Politik. Untersuchung zur öffentlichen Sprache und Kommunikationsstruktur in der DDR*, Cologne: Verl. Wissenschaft und Politik 1981.

Hanser, Carl: *Film in der DDR*, Munich, Vienna: 1977. (Reihe Film 13.) (Reihe Hanser 238.)

Jager, Manfred: *Sozialliteraten. Funktion und Selbstverständnis der Schriftsteller in der DDR*, 2nd ed., Opladen: Westdeutscher Verl. 1975. (Literatur in der Gesellschaft 14.)

Knipp, Wolfgang: *Zum Verhältnis von Individuum und Gesellschaft in ausgewählten Romanen der DDR-Literatur. Anmerkungen zum sozialistischen Menschenbild*, Cologne: Pahl-Rugenstein 1980. (Pahl-Rugenstein Hochschulschriften Gesellschafts- und Naturwissenschaften 41: Serie Literatur und Geschichte.)

Kultur und Kunst in der DDR seit 1970, ed. Hubertus Gassner, Eckhart Gillen, Lahn-Giessen: Anabas-Verl. 1977.

Literatur und Literaturtheorie in der DDR, ed. Peter Uwe Hohendahl, Patricia Herminghouse, Frankfurt/Main: Suhrkamp 1976. (Edition Suhrkamp 779.)

Zur Literatur und Literaturwissenschaft der DDR, ed. Gerd Labroisse, Amsterdam: Rodopi 1978. (Amsterdamer Beiträge zur neueren Germanistik 7.)

Ludz, Peter Christian: *Mechanismen der Herrschaftssicherung. Eine sprachpolitische Analyse gesellschaftlichen Wandels in der DDR*, Munich, Vienna: Hanser 1980.

Maczewski, Johannes: *Der adaptierte Held. Untersuchungen zur Dramatik in der DDR*, Bern: Peter Lang 1978. (Europäische Hochschulschriften. Reihe 1 243.)

Mytze, Andreas W., *Theater in der DDR. Kritiken 1972–1975*, Berlin: Verl. Europäische Ideen 1976.

Nordmann, Ingeborg: *Kulturrevolution bei Marx und in der DDR. Über das Verhältnis von Theorie und Praxis*, Berlin: Spiess 1980. (Hochschul-Skripten: Literaturwissenschaft 2.)

Pohl, Edda: *Die ungehorsamen Maler. Über die Unterdrückung unliebsamer Bildender Kunst in der DDR 1945–1965*, Berlin: Verl. Europäische Ideen 1977.

Pohl, Edda and Pohl, Sieghard: *Die ungehorsamen Maler der DDR. Anspruch und Wirklichkeit der SED-Kulturpolitik 1965–1979*, Berlin: Oberbaum 1979.

Probleme sozialistischer Kulturpolitik am Beispiel DDR, collection of authors from Frankfurt, Frankfurt/Main: Fischer Taschenbuch Verl. 1974. (Texte zur politischen Theorie und Praxis.) (Fischer Taschenbuch 6524.)

Raddatz, Fritz Joachim: *Traditionen und Tendenzen. Materialien zur Literatur der DDR*, 2 vols. Frankfurt/Main: Suhrkamp 1976. (Suhrkamp Taschenbuch 269.)

Zum Roman in der DDR, ed. Marc Silberman, Stuttgart: Klett 1980. (Literaturwissenschaft, Gesellschaftswissenschaft 46: LGW-Interpretationen.)

Sander, Hans-Dietrich: *Geschichte der Schönen Literatur in der DDR, Ein Grundriss*, Freiburg: Verl. Rombach 1972.

Schlenker, Wolfram: *Das 'Kulturelle Erbe' in der DDR. Gesellschaftliche Entwicklung und Kulturpolitik 1945–1965*, Stuttgart: Metzler 1977. (Metzler Studienausgabe.)

Schubbe, Elimar: *Dokumente zur Kunst, Literatur und Kulturpolitik der SED*, ed. Elimar Schubbe, Stuttgart: Seewald 1972.

Staadt, Jochen: *Konfliktbewusstsein und sozialistischer Anspruch in der DDR-Literatur. Zur Darstellung gesellschaftlicher Widersprüche in Romanen nach dem 8. Parteitag der SED 1971*, Berlin: Spiess 1977. (Hochschul–Skripten Literaturwissenschaft 1.)

Weisbrod, Peter: *Literarischer Wandel in der DDR. Untersuchungen zur Entwicklung der Erzählliteratur in den siebziger Jahren*, Heidelberg: Groos 1980. (Sammlung Groos 6.)

Arbeiterklasse und kulturelles Lebensniveau, Berlin: Dietz 1974.

Bibliographie der geltenden Rechtsvorschriften, Anweisungen, Richtlinien und anderen Dokumenten zur Leitung und Planung der sozialistischen Kultur in der Deutschen Demokratischen Republik, Leipzig: Zentralhaus für Kulturarbeit der DDR 1979. (Ratgeber für Klubleiter. Kulturrecht 5.)

Dahnke, Hans-Dietrich: *Erbe und Tradition in der Literatur*, Leipzig: Bibliographisches Institut 1977. (Einführung in die Literaturwissenschaft in Einzeldarstellungen.)

Einführung in den sozialistischen Realismus, Berlin: Dietz 1975.

Künstlerisches Erbe und sozialistische Gegenwartskunst, collective of authors under the guidance of Horst Haase, ed. Akademie für Gesellschaftswissenschaften beim ZK der SED, Berlin: Dietz 1977.

Erkundung der Gegenwart. Künste in unserer Zeit, Institut für Gesellschaftswissenschaften beim SK der SED, collective of authors under the guidance of Elisabeth Simons, Helmut Netzker, Berlin: Dietz 1976.

Fiege, Leo: *Erlebnis Kultur. Zur Rolle der kulturellen Massenarbeit*, Berlin: Dietz 1981.

Funktion und Wirkung. Soziologische Untersuchungen zur Literatur und Kunst, ed. Dietrich Sommer, Dietrich Löffler et al., Berlin, Weimar: Aufbau-Verl. 1978.

Vom Handwerk des Schreibens. Ein Sachbuch für Schreibende, ed. Rüdiger Bernhardt, Andreas Leichsenring and Hans Schmidt, Berlin: Verl. Tribüne 1976.

Hanke, Helmut and Rossow, Gerd: *Sozialistische Kulturrevolution*, Berlin: Deitz 1977. (Sozialismus und Kultur.)

Heller, Ilse and Krause, Hans-Thomas: *Kulturelle Zusammenarbeit DDR—UdSSR in den 70er Jahren*, Berlin: Staatsverl. der DDR 1979.

John, Erhard: *Zur Planung kultureller Prozesse*, Berlin: Dietz 1978.

Kadatz, Hans-Joachim: *Wörterbuch der Architektur*, Leipzig: E.A. Seemann Verl. 1981.

Kähler, Hermann: *Der kalte Krieg der Kritiker. Zur antikommunistischen Kritik an der DDR-Literatur*, Berlin: Akademie-Verl. 1974. (Literatur und Gesellschaft.)

Koch, Hans: *Kulturpolitik in der Deutschen Demokratischen Republik*, 2nd ed., Berlin: Dietz 1976.

Die Künste in der Deutschen Demokratischen Republik. Aus ihrer Geschichte in drei Jahrzehnten, collective of authors under the guidance of Hannelore Gärtner, Berlin: Henschelverl. Kunst und Gesellschaft 1979.

Kultur — Kunst — Lebensweise, collective of authors under the guidance of Eberhard John, Berlin: Dietz Verl. 1980.

Kulturrevolution in der DDR. Grundlagen, Erfahrungen, Aufgaben, collective of authors, ed. Parteihochschule 'Karl Marx' beim ZK der SED, Lehrstuhl Kulturpolitik der SED, Berlin: Dietz Verl. 1981.

Literarisches Leben in der DDR 1945 bis 1960. Literaturkonzepte und Leseprogramme, collective of authors under the guidance of Ingeborg Münz-Koene, Berlin: Akademie-Verl. 1979. (Literatur und Gesellschaft.)

Zur Theorie des sozialistischen Realismus, ed. Institut für Gesellschaftswissenschaften beim ZK der SED, Berlin: Dietz 1974.

Der sozialistische Realismus in der Literatur, collective of authors under the guidance of Harri Jünger, Leipzig: Bibliographisches Institut 1979. (Einführung in die Literaturwissenschaft in Einzeldarstellungen.)

Richter, Rolf: *Kultur im Bündnis. Die Bedeutung der Sowjetunion für die Kulturpolitik der DDR*, Berlin: Dietz 1979.

Streisand, Joachim: *Kultur in der DDR. Studien zu ihren historischen Grundlagen und ihren Entwicklungsetappen*, Berlin: Deutscher Verl. der Wissenschaften 1981.

Kulturpolitisches Wörterbuch, 2nd ed., Berlin: Dietz 1978.

26   Science and education

West

Baske, Siegfried: *Bildungspolitik in der DDR 1963—1976. Dokumente*, Wiesbaden: Harrassowitz in Commission 1979. (Erziehungswissenschaftliche Veröffentlichungen 11.)

Beiträge zum mathematisch-naturwissensschaftlichen und polytechnischen Unterricht in der DDR, Marburg: Marburger Forschungsstelle für Vergleichende Erziehungswissenschaft 1976. (Texte, Dokumente, Berichte 9/10.)

Berger, Rolf: *Forschung — Politik — Gesellschaft. Forschungs- und Innovationspolitik als Ideologie und Gesellschaftspolitik*, Erlangen: Institut für Gesellschaft und Wissenschaft an der Univ., Erlangen-Nürnberg 1976. (ABG, Analysen und Berichte aus Gesellschaft und Wissenschaft 12/76.)

Bergsdorf, Wolfgang and Göbel, Uwe: *Bildungs- und Wissenschaftspolitik im geteilten Deutschland*, Munich, Vienna: Olzog 1980. (Dokumente unserer Zeit 2.)

Berufsausbildung und Berufslenkung in beiden deutschen Staaten, ed. Friedrich-Ebert-Stiftung, 2nd ed., Bonn: Verl. Neue Gesellschaft 1979. (Die DDR. Realitäten, Argumente.)

Bichler, Albert: *Bildungsziele deutscher Lehrpläne, eine Analyse der Richtlinien in der Bundesrepublik Deutschland und in der DDR*, Munich: Olzog 1979. (Berichte und Studien der Hanns-Seidel-Stiftung Munich 22.)

Bode, Dirk: *Polytechnischer Unterricht in der DDR*, Frankfurt/Main, New York: Campus 1978. (Pädagogik.)

Bode, Herbert F. and Brinkmann, Günter: *Bildungssysteme im Vergleich*, Düsseldorf: August Bagel 1979. (Dimensionen der Pädagogik 12.)

Brämer, Rainer: *Beiträge zur Soziologie des Bildungswesens in der DDR*, ed. Marburger Forschungsstelle für Vergleichende Erziehungswissenschaft, Marburg: Fachbereich Erziehungswissenschaft der Philipps-Univ. 1978. (Texte, Dokumente, Berichte 15.)

Fischer, Hans-Joachim: *Internationale pädagogische Beziehungen und pädagogische Auslandsarbeit der DDR*, Paderborn: Schöningh 1975.

Förtsch, Eckart: *Forschungspolitik in der DDR*, Erlangen, Nürnberg: Institut für Gesellschaft und Wissenschaft 1976. (ABG, Analysen und Berichte aus Gesellschaft und Wissenschaft 1/1976.)

Fuchs, Werner: *Schule und Produktion im polytechnischen Unterricht der DDR*, Marburg: Marbuger Forschungsstelle für Vergleichende Erziehungswissenschaft 1977. (Texte, Dokumente, Berichte. Sonderband 4.)

Glaessner, Gert-Joachim: 'Hoch- und Fachschulen', *Politik, Wirtschaft und Gesellschaft in der DDR*, 2nd ed., Opladen: Westdeutscher Verl. 1980, 366–80.

Glaessner, Gert-Joachim: 'Weiterbildung', *Politik, Wirtschaft und Gesellschaft in der DDR*, 2nd ed., Opladen: Westdeutscher Verl. 1980, 381–92.

Glaessner, Gert-Joachim and Rudolph, Irmhild: *Macht durch Wissen. Zum Zusammenhang von Bildungspolitik, Bildungssystem und Kaderqualifizierung in der DDR. Eine politisch-soziologische Untersuchung*, Opladen: Westdeutscher Verl. 1978. (Schriften des Zentralinstituts für sozialwissenschaftliche Forschung der Freien Universität, Berlin 30.)

Hearnden, Arthur: *Bildungspolitik in der BRD und DDR*, 2nd ed., Düsseldorf: Schwann 1977.

Hegelheimer, Armin: *Berufsausbildung in Deutschland. Ein Struktur-, System- und Reformvergleich der Berufsausbildung in der Bundesrepublik und der DDR*, 2nd ed., Frankfurt/Main: Europäische Verlag. 1973.)

Heinemann, Karl-Heinz: *Arbeit und Technik in der Erziehung. Studien zum polytechnischen Unterricht in der DDR*, Cologne: Pahl-Rugenstein 1973. (Erziehung und Bildung.)

Hettwer, Hubert: *Das Bildungswesen in der DDR. Strukturelle und inhaltliche Entwicklung seit 1945*, Cologne: Kiepenheuer and Witsch 1976. (Pocket Wissenschaft: Pädagogik.)

Juszig, Renate and Wilhelm, Klaus: *Berufsausbilding in der DDR*, Mainz: V. Hase and Koehler, circa 1976.

Kruppa, Adolf: *Wirtschafts- und Bildungsplanung in der DDR. Theorie und Praxis der Plankoordination,* Hamburg: Hoffmann and Campe 1976. (Kritische Wissenschaft.)

Landrock, Rudolf: *Die Deutsche Akademie der Wissenschaften zu Berlin 1945—1971 — ihre Umwandlung zur sozialistischen Forschungsakademie. Eine Studie zur Wissenschaftspolitik in der DDR*, 3 vols. Erlangen: Institut für Gesellschaft und Wissenschaft an der Univ. Erlangen-Nürnberg 1977. (Analysen und Berichte aus Gesellschaft und Wissenschaft 1, 2, 3/1977.)

Lauterbach, Günter: *Forschungsorganisation in der DDR*, Erlangen, Nürnberg: Institut für Gesellschaft und Wissenschaft 1976. (ABG, Analysen und Berichte aus Gesellschaft und Wissenschaft 2/1976.)

Lingmann, Hildegard: *Zum Erziehungsziel des sozialistischen Bildungswesens der DDR: Rationalität versus Determination. Ein Betrag zur Analyse und Kritik materialistischer Psychologie und Pädagogik*, Frankfurt/Main: Haag and Herchen 1978.

Mende, Klaus-Dieter: *Die polytechnische Erziehung im Schulsystem der DDR. Mit einer umfassenden Dokumentation*, Bad Harzburg: Verlag für Wissenschaft, Wirtschaft und Technik 1972. (Wirtschaft und Schule 13.)

Niermann, Johannes: *Lehrer in der DDR. Ausbildung, Tätigkeit, Weiterbildung und gesellschaftliche Stellung in Theorie und Praxis*, Heidelberg: Quelle and Meyer 1971.

Niermann, Johannes: *Sozialistische Pädagogik in der DDR. Eine Wissenschaftstheoretische Untersuchung*, Heidelberg: Quelle and Meyer 1972.

Niermann, Johannes: *Wörterbuch der · DDR-Pädagogik*, Heidelberg: Quelle and Meyer 1974. (Uni-Taschenbücher 380.)

Rudolph, Irmhild: 'Die Berufsausbildung', *Politik, Wirtschaft und Gesellschaft in der DDR*, 2nd ed., Opladen: Westdeutscher Verl. 1980, 347–65.

Rudolph, Irmhild: 'Das allgemeinbildende Schulwesen', *Politik, Wirtschaft und Gesellschaft in der DDR*, 2nd ed., Opladen: Westdeutscher Verl. 1980, 328–46.

Schmitt, Karl: *Politische Erziehung in der DDR. Ziele, Methoden und Ergebnisse des politischen Unterrichts an den allgemeinbildenden Schulen der DDR*, Paderborn: Schöningh 1980. (Geschichte, Politik. Studien zur Didaktik 2.)

Universitäten, Hoch- und Fachschulen in der Deutschen Demokratischen Republik, ed. Friedrich-Ebert-Stiftung, Bonn: Verl. Neue Gesellschaft 1980. (Die DDR. Realitäten, Argumente.)

Usko, Marianne: *Hochschulen in der DDR*, Berlin: Holzapfel 1974. (. . . in der DDR.)

Vogt, Hartmut: *Vorschulerziehung und Schulvorbereitung in der DDR. Grundlagen, Ziele, Inhalte, Realisationsformen*, Cologne: Verl. Wissenschaft und Politik 1972.

Wissenschaft und Systemwettstreit. Möglichkeiten und Grenzen der Ost/West-Wissenschaftskooperation, ed. Clemens Burrichter, Erlangen: Deutsche Gesellschaft für zeitgeschichtliche Fragen 1980.

Das Wissenschaftssystem in der DDR, ed. Institut für Gesellschaft und Wissenschaft, Erlangen, 2nd ed., Frankfurt/Main, New York: Campus 1979.

East

Zentralinstitut für Berufsbildung der DDR: *Arbeitserziehung in der Berufsausbildung*, Berlin: Volk und Wissen Verl. 1979.

Deutsches Institut für Berufsbildung: *Berufsausbildung und Jugendobjekte. Zur Ausbildung von Lehrlingen in Jugendobjekten und zu ihrer Bedeutung für das Erreichen hoher Bildungs- und Erziehungsergebnisse*, Berlin: Volk und Wissen Verl. 1972.

Betrieb und Schule bei der sozialistischen Bildung und Erziehung der Schuljugend in der Deutschen Demokratischen Republik, collective of authors under the guidance of Werner Dorst, ed. Bundesvorstand des FDGB, Abteilung Bildung, Berlin: Verl. Tribüne 1974.

Bienert, Harald, Köther, Hellmuth and Strebel, Herbert: *Handbuch der Berufsausbildung. Leitung, Planung, Finanzierung, Abrechnung*, Berlin: Verl. Die Wirtschaft 1974.

Sozialistische Bildungsökonomie. Grundfragen. Aufgaben, Probleme, Lösungen, ed. Arnold Knauer, Harry Maier and Werner Wolter, Berlin: Verl. Die Wirtschaft 1972.

Das Bildungswesen der Deutschen Demokratischen Republik, joint work by the Akademie der Pädagogischen Wissenschaften, the Zentralinstitut für Berufsbildung, the Institut für Fachschulwesen, the Institut für Hochschulbildung and the Humboldt-Univ., Berlin: Volk und Wissen Verl. 1979.

Die Fachschulausbildung in der DDR, collective of authors under the guidance of H. Rossner, Leipzig: Fachbuchverl. 1980.

Günther, Karl-Heinz and Uhlig, Gottfried: *Geschichte der Schule in der Deutschen Demokratischen Republik 1945—1971*, Berlin: Volk und Wissen Verl. 1974.

Das Hochschulwesen der DDR. Ein Überblick, collective of authors under the guidance of Hans-Jürgen Schulz, ed. Institut für Hochschulbildung, Berlin: Deutscher Verl. der Wissenschaften 1980.

Leitung, Planung und Organisation der wissenschaftlichen Arbeit. Aufgaben — Probleme — Losungen, ed. Günther Haefner, Gerhard Reuscher and Hans Riess, Berlin: Verl. Die Wirtschaft 1976.

Lexikon der Wirtschaft. Berufsbildung, Berlin: Verl. Die Wirtschaft 1978.

Opitz, Gerda: *Arbeiterklasse und Bildung in der entwickelten sozialistischen Gesellschaft. Zu einigen Grundfragen der Bildungspolitik der SED*, Berlin: Dietz 1976.

Polzin, Jürgen: *Kommunistische Arbeitserziehung*, Berlin: Volk und Wissen Verl. 1979.

Sozialismus und wissenschaftliches Schöpfertum, ed. Alfred Erck, Lothar Läsker and Helmut Steiner, Berlin: Akademie-Verl. 1976. (Wissenschaft und Gesellschaft 8.)

Zentralinstitut für Berufsbildung der DDR: *Zur Überzeugungsbildung bei Lehrlingen und Facharbeitern im volkseigenen Betrieb*, Berlin: Verl. Volk und Wissen 1977.

Einheitlicher Unterricht — individuelle Förderung aller Schüler, collective of authors under the guidance of Marianne Berge, Berlin: Volk und Wissen Verl. 1975. (Beiträge zur Pädagogik 1.)

Wissenschaft, Stellung, Funktion und Organisation in der entwickelten sozialistischen Gesellschaft, ed. Günter Kröber and Hubert Laitko, Berlin: Dietz 1975.

Wissenschaft und Forschung im Sozialismus. Probleme ihrer Entwicklung, Gestaltung und Analyse. Materialien des RGW-Symposiums zu Fragen der marxistisch—leninistischen Wissenschaftstheorie, September 1972 in Berlin, ed. Günter Kröber, Hubert Laitko and Helmut Steiner. Berlin: Akademie-Verl. 1974. (Wissenschaft und Gesellschaft 3.)

Wissenschaft und Produktion im Sozialismus. Zur organischen Verbindung der Errungenschaften der wissenschaftlich—technischen Revolution mit den Vorzügen des Sozialismus, ed. Institut für Gesellschaftswissenschaften beim Zentralkomitee der SED, Berlin: Dietz 1976.

Wörterbuch der Wissenschaftswissenschaft. Russisch — deutsch — englisch, ed. Gennadi Dobrow, Heinz Engelbert. Berlin: Verl. Die Wirtschaft 1979.

27   Psychology

West

Lemke, Christiane: *Persönlichkeit und Gesellschaft. Zur Theorie der Persönlichkeit in der DDR*, Opladen: Westdeutscher Verl. 1980. (Schriften des Zentralinstituts für sozialwissenschaftliche Forschung der Freien Universität Berlin 33.)

East

Aufgaben, Perspektiven und methodologische Grundlagen der marxistischen Psychologie in der DDR, ed. Hans Hiebsch and Lothar Sprung, Berlin: Deutscher Verl. der Wissenschaften 1973.

Zur Erforschung der Persönlichkeit, ed. Werner Hennig, Berlin: Deutscher Verl. der Wissenschaften 1978.

Erpenbeck, John: *Psychologie und Erkenntnistheorie. Zu philosophischen Problemen psychischer Erkenntnisprozesse*, Berlin: Akademie-Verl. 1980.

Zur Geschichte der Psychologie, ed. Georg Eckardt, Berlin: Deutscher Verl. der Wissenschaften 1979.

Höck, Kurt and König, Werner: *Neurosenlehre und Psychotherapie. Eine Einführung*, 2nd ed., Jena: Gustav Fischer 1979. (Für die medizinische Praxis.)

Kritik der Psychoanalyse und biologistischer Konzeptionen, ed. Walter Friedrich, Berlin: Deutscher Verl. der Wissenschaften 1977.

Kühn, Horst and Junghänel, Kristina: *Bürgerliche Persönlichkeitspsychologie in der Krise. Bürgerliche Persönlichkeitskonzeptionen im Widerstreit von idiographischer und nomothetischer Betrachtungsweise*, Berlin: Deutscher Verl. der Wissenschaften 1980.

Neurosenpsychologie, ed. Johannes Helm and Edith Kasielke, Berlin: Deutscher Verl. der Wissenschaften 1976.

Psychologie in der gesellschaftlichen Praxis. Zum Beitrag der Psychologie bei der Gestaltung der entwickelten sozialistischen Gesellschaft in der DDR, ed. Adolf Kossakowski. Berlin: Deutscher Verl. der Wissenschaften 1980.

Psychologie in der DDR. Entwicklung, Aufgaben, Perspektiven, ed. Friedhart Klix, Adolf Kossakowski and Walter Mäder, 2nd ed., Berlin: Deutscher Verl. der Wissenschaften 1980.

Psychologie im Sozialismus. Theoretische Positionen, Ergebnisse und Problem psychologischer Forschungen, ed. Adolf Kossakowski, Berlin: Deutscher Verl. der Wissenschaften 1980.

Psychotherapie und Gesellschaft, ed. Kurt Höck and Karl Seidel, Berlin: Deutscher Verl. der Wissenschaften 1976.

Psychological Research. Humboldt-Universität 1980. Investigations of the Psychological Department of the Humboldt-Universität, Berlin 1960−1980, ed. Friedhart Klix and Bodo Krause. Berlin: Deutscher Verl. der Wissenschaften 1980.

Wörterbuch der Psychologie, collection of editors under the guidance of Günter Clauss, 3rd ed., Leipzig: Bibliographisches Institut 1981.

28 Historical science

West

Honeckers neue Geschichtsschreibung der SED, ed. Friedrich-Ebert-Stiftung, Bonn: Verl. Neue Gesellschaft 1978. (Die DDR. Realitäten, Argumente.)

König, Hartmut: *Bismarck als Reichskanzler. Seine Beurteilung in der sowjetischen und der DDR-Geschichtsschreibung*, Cologne, Vienna: Böhlau in Commission 1978. (Dissertationen zur neueren Geschichte 3.)

Neuhäusser-Wespy, Ulrich: *6. Historikerkongress der DDR*, Erlangen, Nürnberg: Institut für Gesellschaft und Wissenschaft 1978. (IGW—Informationen zur Wissenschaftsentwicklung und -politik in der DDR 1978, 1.)

Neuhäusser-Wespy, Ulrich: *20 Jahre Historikerkommission DDR—UdSSR*, Erlangen: Institut für Gesellschaft und Wissenschaft an der Univ. Erlangen-Nürnberg 1977. (IGW-Informationen zur Wissenschaftsentwicklung und-politik in der DDR 8/1977.)

Osteuropa in der historischen Forschung der DDR, ed. Manfred Hellmann. Vol.1: 'Darstellungen'; vol.2: 'Bibliographie und biographische Notizen', Düsseldorf: Droste Verl. 1972.

Das Preussenbild der DDR im Wandel, ed. Friedrich-Ebert-Stiftung, Bonn: Verl. Neue Gesellschaft 1981. (Die DDR. Realitäten, Argumente.)

Reuter, Frank: *Geschichtsbewusstsein in der DDR. Programm und Aktion*, Cologne: Verl. Wissenschaft und Politik 1973. (Bibliothek Wissenschaft und Politik 5.)

Wolf, Hans-Jörg: *Zur Entwicklung des Geschichtsunterrichts in der DDR 1968—1978. Geschichtsunterricht zwischen Politik und Geschichtswissenschaft*, Paderborn: Schöningh 1978. (Geschichte, Politik und ihre Didaktik. Sonderheft 1.)

East

Berthold, Werner: *Marxistisches Geschichtsbild — Volksfront und antifaschistisch—demokratische Revolution. Zur Vorgeschichte der Geschichtswissenschaft der DDR und zur Konzeption der Geschichte des deutschen Volkes*, Berlin: Akademie-Verl. 1970.

Einführung in das Studium der Geschichte, ed. Walther Eckermann, Hubert Mohr, 3rd ed., Berlin: Deutscher Verl. der Wissenschaften 1979.

Handbuch Wirtschaftsgeschichte, ed. Institut für Wirtschaftsgeschichte der Akademie der Wissenschaften der DDR, 2 vols, Berlin: Deutscher Verl. der Wissenschaften 1981.

Historische Forschungen in der DDR 1970—1980. Analysen und Berichte. Zum XV. Internationalen Historikerkongress in Bukarest 1980, Berlin: Deutscher Verl. der Wissenschaften 1980. (Sonderband der 'Zeitschrift für Geschichtswissenschaft'.)

Forschungsergebnisse zur Geschichte des deutschen Imperialismus vor 1917, ed. B.A. Aisin and W. Gutsche, Berlin: Akademie-Verl. 1980. (Internationale Reihe des Zentralinstituts für Geschichte der Akademie der Wissenschaften der DDR.)

Probleme der geschichtswissenschaftlichen Erkenntnis, ed. Ernst Engelberg and Wolfgang Küttler, Berlin: Akademie-Verl. 1977.

Radandt, Hans: *Betriebsgeschichte erforschen, schreiben, propagieren*, Berlin: Verl. Tribüne 1977.

Geschichtswissenschaftlicher Thesaurus, ed. Zentralstelle Geschichtswissenschaft, Information und Dokumentation beim Zentralinstitut für Geschichte der AdW der DDR zu Berlin, Arbeiterbewegung und Marx-Engels-Forschung am Institut für Marxismus—Leninismus beim Zentralkomitee der SED, Berlin. 3 vols, Berlin: 1976.

Unbewältigte Vergangenheit. Kritik der bürgerlichen Geschichtsschreibung in der BRD, ed. Akademie der Gesellschaftswissenschaften beim ZK der SED, Lherstuhl Geschichte der deutschen Arbeiterbewegung, 3rd ed., Berlin: Akademie-Verl. 1977.

29   Mathematics and natural sciences

West

Bialas, Volker and Gruhn, Werner: *Bilanz der geowissenschaftlichen Forschung an der AdW*, Erlangen: Institut für Gesellschaft und Wissenschaft an der Univ. Erlangen-Nürnberg 1976. (IGW-Informationen zur Wissenschaftsentwicklung und -politik in der DDR 3/76.)

Flenner, Elmar G.H., *Marxismus und biologischer Finalismus. Zum Problem von Evolution und Vererbung im dialektischen Materialismus unter besonderer Berücksichtigung der Naturphilosophie in der DDR*, Frankfurt/Main: Haag and Herchen 1979.

Gruhn, Werner: *Fortschritte der chemischen Forschung in der DDR seit 1948*, Erlangen: Institut für Gesellschaft und Wissenschaft 1975. (IGW-Informationen zur Wissenschaftsentwicklung und -politik in der DDR 1975, 2.)

Kaletta, Dietmar: *Der Führungsanspruch der SED. Naturwissenschaft kontra Marxismus*, Hamburg: Drei Mohren Verl. 1970. (Analysen und Berichte aus Gesellschaftswissenschaften 14—15.)

Steuck, Malte: *Marxismus und Kybernetik, eine Auseinandersetzung mit Georg Klaus*, ed. Informatik-Seminar, Technische Univ., Berlin. Berlin: Universitätsbibliothek der Technischen Univ., Abteilung Publikationen 1976. (Bericht 75—31.)

Lindenberg, Bernd M., *Das Technikverständnis in der Philosophie der DDR*, Frankfurt/Main: P. Lang 1979. (Europäische Hochschulschriften. Reihe 20. 46.)

East

Philosophische Probleme der Physik, collective of authors under the guidance of von H. Hörz and H.-D. Pöltz, Berlin: Deutscher Verl. der Wissenschaften 1978. (Studienbücherei Physik für Lehrer 13.)

Raketen, Satelliten, Raumstationen. Der Weg der UdSSR und der anderen sozialistischen Länder in den Weltraum, Leipzig: Fachbuchverl. 1979.

Rohland, Lothar and Spaar, Horst: *Die medizinisch-wissenschaftlichen Gesellschaften der DDR. Geschichte, Funktion und Aufgaben*, Berlin: Verl. Volk und Gesundheit 1973.

Schellhorn, Martin: *Logisches und Historisches in den Biowissenschaften*, Jena: Gustav Fischer 1979. (Philosophie und Biowissenschaften.)

Strube, Wilhelm: *Die Chemie und ihre Geschichte*, Berlin: Akademie-Verl. 1974. (Forschungen zur Wirtschaftsgeschichte 5.)

Treder, Hans-Jürgen: *Philosophische Probleme des physikalischen Raumes. Gravitation, Geometrie, Kosmologie und Relativität*, Berlin: Akademie-Verl. 1974.

Wernecke, Alexander: *Biologismus und ideologischer Klassenkampf*, Berlin: Dietz 1976.

Wissmann, Gerhard: *Geschichte der Luftfahrt von Ikarus bis zur Gegenwart. Eine Darstellung der Entwicklung des Fluggedankens und der Luftfahrttechnik*, 5th ed., Berlin: Verl. Technik 1979.

30 Marxism—Leninism

West

Ahlberg, René: *Sozialismus zwischen Ideologie und Wirklichkeit. Die marxistische Systemkritik seit Leo Trotzki*, Stuttgart, Berlin, Cologne, Mainz: Kohlhammer 1979.

Fetscher, Iring: *Der Marxismus. Seine Geschichte in Dokumenten*, 3rd ed. Vol.1: 'Philosophie, Ideologie', 1976; vol.2: 'Ökonomie, Soziologie', 1976; vol.3: 'Politik' 1977. Munich, Zürich: Piper.

Grundbegriffe des Marxismus. Eine lexikalische Einführung, ed. Iring Fetscher, Hamburg: Hoffmann and Campe 1976. (Kritische Wissenschaft.)

Eysenck, Hans Jürgen, et al., *Die Grundlagen des Spätmarxismus. Theorie und Wirklichkeit*, Stuttgart: Verl. Bonn aktuell 1977 (Bonn aktuell 51.)

Hanak, Tibor: *Die Entwicklung der marxistischen Philosophie*. Darmstadt: Wissenschaftliche Buchgesellschaft 1976. (Die philosophischen Bemühungen des 20. Jahrhunderts.)

Ingensand, Harald: *Die Ideologie des Sowjetkommunismus*, 13th ed., Hannover: Fackelträger-Verl. 1975. (Edition Zeitgeschehen.)

Kernig, C.D., *Marxismus im Systemvergleich. Politik*, ed. Klaus von Beyme, 4 vols, Frankfurt/Main, New York: Herder and Herder 1973.

Leonhard, Wolfgang: *Was ist Kommunismus? Wandlungen einer Ideologie*, Munich: C. Bertelsmann 1976.

East

Einführung in den dialektischen und historischen Materialismus, collective of authors, 4th ed., Berlin: 1974.

Grundlagen des historischen Materialismus, ed. Institut für Gesellschaftswissenschaften beim ZK der SED, Berlin: Dietz 1976.

Hahn, Erich and Kosing, Alfred: *Marxistisch—leninistische Philosophie. Geschrieben für die Jugend*, Berlin: Dietz 1980.

Klotsch, Helmut; Opitz, Heinrich and Steussloff, Hans: *Die wissenschaftliche Weltanschauung — Grundlage unseres Handelns*, Berlin: Dietz 1979. (Vorzüge des Sozialismus.)

Wissenschaftlicher Sozialismus, ed. Jonny Gottschalg and Gerhard Wolter, Leipzig: Bibliographisches Institut 1979. (Meyers Jugendlexikon.)

Dialektischer und historischer Materialismus. Lehrbuch für das marxistisch—leninistische Grundstudium, ed. F. Fiedler and O. Finger, 6th ed., Berlin: Dietz 1979.

Philosophie, ed. Frank Fiedler and Günter Gurst, Leipzig: Bibliographisches Institut 1979. (Meyers Jugendlexikon.)

Marxistisch—leninistische Philosophie, collective of authors under the guidance of Wolfgang Eichhorn I., Berlin: Dietz 1979.

Marxistisch—leninistische Philosophie in der DDR. Resultate, Standpunkte, Ziele, ed. Matthäus Klein, Friedrich Richter and Vera Wrona. Berlin: Deutscher Verl. der Wissenschaften 1974.

Wertauffassungen im Sozialismus, collective of authors, Berlin: Dietz Verl. 1980. (Grundfragen der marxistisch–leninistischen Philosophie.)

Philosophisches Wörterbuch, ed. Georg Klaus and Manfred Buhr, 11th ed., 2 vols, Leipzig: Bibliographisches Institut 1975.

31 Research

West

Aufgaben und Tätigkeiten des IGW, Institut für Gesellschaft und Wissenschaft an der Universität Erlangen-Nürnberg, Erlangen: IGW 1980.

Beiträge zur Sozialismusanalyse, ed. Peter Brokmeier and Rainer Rilling. Vol.1, 1978; vol.2, 1979. Cologne: Pahl-Rugenstein. (Kleine Bibliothek Politik, Wissenschaft, Zukunft 123, 149.)

Cless, Olaf: *Sozialismusforschung in der Bundesrepublik. Das herrschende DDR-Bild und seine Dogmen*, Cologne: Pahl-Rugenstein 1978. (Kleine Bibliothek Politik, Wissenschaft, Zukunft 122.)

Deutschlandforschung in der Bundesrepublik und in Berlin (West). Projektverzeichnis für die Jahre 1977–1979, (mimeographed ms), Bonn: Gesamtdeutsches Institut 1980.

Gesamtdeutsches Institut, Bundesanstalt für gesamtdeutsche Aufgaben (BfgA): *Bestandsverzeichnis Zeitungen, Zeitschriften*, Bonn: Gesamtdeutsches Institut, Archiv und Bibliothek 1977.

Teich, Gerhard: *Zentralbibliothek der Wirtschaftswissenschaften in der Bundesrepublik Deutschland. Arbeitsgemeinschaft der Bibliotheken und Dokumentationsstellen der Osteuropa-, Südosteuropa- und DDR-Forschung in der Bundesrepublik Deutschland und Berlin (West). Topographie der Osteuropa-, Südosteuropa- und DDR-Sammlungen.* Munich: Verl. Dokumentation 1978.

East

Espenhayn, Rolf: *Sozialismuskritik in der Defensive*, Berlin: Verl. Die Wirtschaft 1978. (Beiträge zur Kritik der bürgerlichen Ideologie und des Revisionismus.)

Heitzer, Heinz: *Andere über uns. Das 'DDR-Bild' des westdeutschen Imperialismus und seine bürgerlichen Kritiker*, Berlin: Deutscher Verl. der Wissenschaften 1969.

Krause, Günter: *Das Elend der 'Linken'. Zur Kritik der politischen Ökonomie des Linksrevisionismus*, Berlin: Verl. Die Wirtschaft 1977. (Beiträge zur Kritik der bürgerlichen Ideologie und des Revisionismus.)

Kreuzzug gegen die Koexistenz. Psychologische Kriegsführung heute, ed. Institut für Internationale Politik und Wirtschaft, Berlin: Staatsverl. der DDR 1975.

Teller, Hans: *Der kalte Krieg gegen die DDR. Von seinen Anfängen bis 1961*, Berlin: Akademie-Verl. 1979.

Index

Abusch, Alexander: summarises GDR cultural policy 222
Academy for Theory of State and Law 54
Academy of Constitutional Law 208, 209
Act on Foreign Trade, 1958 146
Afanasiev, V.G. 11
All-German Protestant Church 72
Allied Control Council 110, 111, 146
Apel, Erich 154
Architects' Association 68
Artists' Union 68
Association of Composers and Musicologists 68
Association of Plastic and Graphic Arts 68
Association of Protestant Churches 72
Atlantic Alliance 150
Austria 310: trade with GDR 157

Bahr, Egon 277, 278, 280, 295
Bahro, Rudolf 231, 233
Bank for State and Foreign Trade 146
Berlin wall 116, 152, 175, 308
Bibliophiles' Association 68
Biermann, Wolf 230, 231
Bitterfeld movement 216
Border Brigades 169, 174
Brandt, Willy 278, 279
Brezhnev, Leonid 290
Buck, H. 121

Carter, Pres. James 290
Central Institute of Socialist Economic Planning 208, 209
Chamber of Technology ('Kammer der Technik' — KDT) 69–70
Churches in GDR 72–3
Civil Defence 169: Units 170, 174, 177

COMECON 145, 146, 148, 151, 152, 161, 303, 308, 309, 310: question of Western trade for 152; trade conflicts among countries of 154; trade with GDR 152–5

Confederation of Free German Trade Unions ('Freier Deutscher Gewerkschaftsbund' – FDGB) 16, 26, 31, 60–1, 62, 67, 68, 203, 223; democratic centralism in 63; insurance system 249–52 *passim*

Co-operatives 42, 43

Council of Ministers 48, 50, 51, 55, 146, 203: work of 53–4

Council of State ('Staatsrat') 50–2, 67: composition 51–2

Cultural policy in GDR 212–13, 233–5: actions against dissidents 230–1, 232, 234; breadth and range of socialist realism 228–31;
cultural tradition 214–19; anti-fascism 214–15; from Ulbricht to Honecker 218–19; German socialist national culture 217–18; Socialist cultural revolution 216–17; socialist realism 215–16;
oppressive atmosphere produced by 234; planning and control of culture 224–5; political and ideological preconditions for Honecker's policy 219–21; relations between party and intelligentsia after banishments 232–3; since 1972 221–4; socialist national culture 225–8

Czechoslovakia 308, 309, 310: unrest of 1968 38, 75, 184

Damus, R. 118

'Democratic Block of Parties and Mass Organisations' 42, 43, 67, 70–1

Democratic Women's League of Germany ('Demokratischer Frauenbund Deutschlands' – DFD) 66–7

Eastern Bloc: indicators on systems performance 304–7

Economic position of GDR: economic reforms 117–24:
  Indicators of Economic Development, 1966–70 123; NÖS – Neues Okonomisches System, 1963 118–19, 120, 190; ÖSS – Economic Socialist System, 1967–68 120–2; planning up to 1963 117
ideology of reform phase and social problems 124–6; 'Main Task' laid down by SED 109, 110, 117, 133, 134, 242; organisation and policy in 1970s 126–35: abandonment of reform policy 127, 128; consumer durables, 1960–80 131; five-year plan 1971–75 128–9; five-year plan 1976–80 133–4; GNP, 1970–75 130; housing construction, 1966–80 131; introduction of price stop 127; measures of 1970 126; price support 132–3
outlook 135–6: formation of combinates 135, 136

Economic position of GDR (cont.)
  post-SWW change in economic order 114–16: land reform 114; nationalisation of industry 115; population loss 115–16;
  post-SWW economic situation and events 110–14: effect of war reparations 112–13, 147; imbalanced industrial structure 114; post-1948 planning and control 111–12; results of SWW damage 112; Soviet 'reforms' 111; 'Sovjetische Aktiengesellschaften' – SAG enterprises 113, 115, 147
Education Act, 1965 191, 199
Education in GDR 37, 38, 209–10: compared with Eastern Bloc and FRG 309, 311, 312; constituent parts 191; development, 1955–78 194; economic function 202–4; education and socialisation 198–200; education system and social structure 200–2; expenditure, 1971–78 195; funds for economic sectors of 195; mobility in 191, 194; policy 190–1; political function 204–9; position in GDR society 196–8; qualification structure 202; structure 192; training institutes for 'cadres' 193, 194, 207, 208
Egypt: trade with GDR 160
Enterprise union organisations (BGO) 61, 62, 63
'Ernst Thalmann' Pioneer Organisation 63
European Economic Community (EEC) 157: concessions to FRG on trade with GDR 155–6

Federation of Nationalised Enterprises ('Vereinigung Volkseigener Betriebe' – VVB) 115, 118, 126, 127, 135
Film and Television Association 68
Foreign Trade Chamber 150
Foreign trade relations of GDR: role of foreign trade 145–52: attempts at diversification up to 1960 148–50; New Economic System (NOSPL) and shift in emphasis 151–2; post-SWW consolidation 146–8; turnover, 1949–79 149
  socialist integration and GDR strategy 152–60: trade with developing countries 158–60; trade with FRG and West 155–8; trade with Soviet Union and Eastern Bloc 152–5;
  trade following international recognition 160–3: attempts at barter 161; orientation to economic considerations 144, 161; problem of dependence on Soviet Union for raw materials 162–3; problem of ideology and trade 163; problem of oil price rises 161
Free German Youth ('Freie Deutsche Jugend' – FDJ) 16, 21, 26, 31, 60, 63, 65, 171, 176, 180, 223
Freiburg Mining Academy 194
FRG relations with GDR, see GDR relations with FRG

Friedland Agro-Industrial Association for Plant Production 26

Gardeners, Settlers and Small Animal Breeders' Association 60

GDR relations with FRG 295–7: ambivalence of GDR attitudes 297;
　basic situation 272–3: military roles of two Germanies 273; post-SWW division of Germany 272–3
　co-operation and conflict 289–95: agreement on health and veterinary matters 293; agreement on improved transport facilities 291–3; agreement on power link 293; border commission 293–4; problems in cultural area 294; problems of E–W family contact 294–5; question of Berlin 289; traffic restrictions 289–90
　FRG desire for stable GDR 296; FRG purchase of GDR goodwill 295, 296;
　GDR policy of seclusion from West 284–9: compulsory purchase of E-Marks 287–8; E–W visiting 286–7; GDR taxes on visitors' cars 287; 'Intershops' 285; problem of D-Marks from West 285; problem of transfrontier news 285–6; prohibition of contact 284
　negotiations 279–84: FRG attempts 280–1; Moscow Agreement of 1970 281; Quadripartite Agreement 281, 282, 284, 289, 290; Treaty of 1972 283–4, 285–6, 289
　phase of non-relations 273–9: arguments over legitimacy 274–6; beginnings of détente 278–9; Berlin blockade 274; Cold War 273–4; foundation of two states 274; riots of 1953 in GDR 276; sealing of borders 277

German Red Cross 171
German-Soviet Friendship Society ('Deutsche-Sowjetische Freundschaft' – DSF) 60, 68, 69
Great Britain: trade with GDR 156–7
Gromyko, Andrei 280

Hager, Kurt 233: lays down GDR cultural policy 221; on dissidence in the arts 231; on socialist realism 229
Halle University 194
'Hallstein doctrine' 148
Havemann, Robert 230, 233
Hoffman, Hans-Joachim 224
Hofmannsthal, H. von 227
Honecker, Erich 51, 73, 110, 128, 181, 219, 220, 221, 225, 232, 296

Institute of Politics and Economics 54

Jahn, E. 182

Kant, Hermann 232
Kennedy, Pres. John F. 277
Kissinger, Henry 279

Klaus, Georg 74
Klein, Helmut 190
Kuczynski, Jurgen: on socialist education 200

Labour Code 61
League of Culture of the GDR ('Kulturbund' – KB) 60, 67–8, 69: study groups 68
Lenin 36: *What is to be Done?* 8
Libraries' Association 68
Liebknecht, Karl 182
Ludz, Peter 301

Marshall Aid Plan 111
Marxism–Leninism: cadre policy 16–17; concentration of political power 14–16; concept of power as rulership 7–8; cultural policy 212–13; democratic centralism 12–14, 15; role of Communist Party 8, 9, 10, 12; 'scientific' claims 11, 12, 74; social policy 36, 247, 248; theory of the state 34–6, 46; view of 'non-antagonistic' conflicts 10
Mass and social organisations 57–73: functions of 58–60; membership figures 64–5
Meier, Artur: on socialist education 200
Military policy in GDR: components of military system 170–1; defined 169, 170; development of military power 171–2; pre-military education and training 175–8; question of militarism or militarisation 181–7
Ministry for Foreign Trade 146
Ministry for National Defence 174, 176, 179
Ministry for State Security 174

Ministry of Culture 213, 215: 'General Directive for Entertainment' 225
Ministry of Finance 146: State Budget Auditors 54

National Defence Council 51, 52–3, 179
National Front (NF) 42, 67
National People's Army (NVA) 169, 170, 172, 175, 177, 185, 187: organisation and strength 173; relations with SED 178–81
Neues Deutschland, 26, 229
Nixon, Pres. Richard M. 279
North Atlantic Treaty Organisation (NATO) 172

Party University 208, 209
People's Chamber ('Volkskammer' – VK) 43–4, 49–50, 55, 69
People's Navy 172
People's Own Enterprises (VEBs) 47, 48, 119, 126, 127, 135
People's Police 170, 171, 174
Philatelists' Association 69
Policy output in GDR: agriculture 303; comparison with rest of Eastern Bloc 304–12 *passim*; industrial output 303, 308; neglected study of 301–2; pace of collectivisation 303; performance in communication 310; performance in distribution 309; performance in political sphere 310–11; prolific data publication 303; shortage of raw materials and labour 308
Political system of GDR 7: discussions on concept of 2–6;

399

Political system of GDR (cont.)
intermeshing of state and party leadership 54—5;
structural principles 7—17: ideological rule 7; role of Communist Party 8; problem of gaining information 11

Potsdam Conference, 1945 110, 275

Ritter, G. 182
Rumania 302: resistance to COMECON plans 153—4

Schmidt, Helmut 290
Schöneburg, Karl-Heinz 3, 8: on state and society 3—5
Selbmann, F. 112
Senghaas, D. 182
Social policy of GDR:
family policy 249, 258—64: 'baby year' 260, 263; benefits for mothers 260, 261, 263; decline in net reproduction rate 259—60; high divorce rate 262—3; ideology behind 261—4 *passim*; policy of work for women 258—9, 261, 262; question of equality of sexes 262; role of family in education 261—2;
housing policy 242, 248, 254—8: average rents 255; comparison with FRG 257; housing amenities, 1971 and 1979 256; new apartment amenities, 1960—78 257; post-1976 plans 256—7; post-SWW neglect 255; private construction 258; subsidising of rents 254—5; present state of 246—9

rediscovery of 242—6: five-year plan, 1971—5 242—3; post-1975 243; reasons for 245—6; reasons for previous neglect 244—5;
social insurance 248, 249—54: categories 249; pensions 249—53 *passim*; special pension schemes 252, 253; supplementary pension insurance 251—2, 253;
'Socialist Social Policy' 264—6: aim of housing policy 265—6; effect of pension schemes 264—5; instrumental character of family policy 266

'Socialist Brigades' 216, 217
Socialist Unity Party ('Sozialistische Einheitsparti Deutschlands' — SED) 7, 17—34, 47, 68, 111, 274: attitude to block parties 71;
Central Committee 21—5, 26, 47, 52, 55, 67, 122, 218, 221: Secretariat 26
Central Party Control Commission 26; church policy 72—3; cultural policy 213, 235; demands on members 27—8; effect of cadre policy 19, 27, 30—1, 33, 70; elections 19; informal workings 33—4; military policy 169, 170, 175, 176, 178, 185; omnipresence 20, 21; 'party activist groups' 31—2;
Party Congresses: Vth, 1958 216; VIth, 1963 119; VIIth, 1967 245; VIIIth, 1971 36, 60, 109, 110, 128, 129, 134, 209, 213, 217, 219, 221, 242, 256; IXth, 1976 109, 134, 229, 243, 260;

Socialist Unity Party (cont.)
party executives 18; People's Representative Bodies 40–1, 42; Politburo 25–6, 33, 51, 52, 55, 178, 203, 284; present membership 29; purges 28; recruitment policy 28; relations with army 179–81; relations with state 39; 'scientisation' of leadership 29–30; settled role today 32–3; sex discrimination in leadership 29; social policy 244, 246; structure of 17–18

Society for Sport and Technology ('Gesellschaft für Sport und Technik' – GST) 169, 171, 176, 177

Society for the Preservation of Monuments 68

Soviet Military Administration in Germany (SMAD) 70, 112: 'Foreign Trade Administration' 147

Soviet Union: policy threat to FRG–GDR relations 296–7; Red Banner fleet 172; role of foreign trade 145; Twentieth Congress of CP 215; war reparations 112–13, 147

Spiegel, Der: prints GDR dissidents' manifesto 231

State, GDR 34–57: church policy 72–3; cultural function 37, 38; defence spending, 1962–72 173; deputies' role 45, 49; educational function 37, 38; elections 42, 44–5 46; 'essence' defined 39; governing bodies 43–4, 48–55; legislation 37; limit on rights of individual 55–7; question of German identity 76, 226; representative bodies 42–3, 46; repressive function 38–9, 75

State Liability Law, 1969 57

State Planning Commission 53, 54, 154

Sweden: trade with GDR 157

Theatre Association 68
Trade unions 171
See also Confederation of Free German Trade Unions

Ulbricht, Walter 51, 110, 119, 124, 128, 218, 219, 220, 234, 245, 296

Urania association 68

Vagts, Alfred: distinguishes militarism from militarisation 181–2

Warsaw Pact 170, 172, 175, 185
Watch Regiment 174
Wiatr, J.: on militarisation 182
Worker and Peasant Inspectorate ('Arbeiter-und-Bauern-Inspektion' – ABI) 54
Works Combat Groups 169, 170, 174, 177
Writers' Association 68, 232

Young Pioneers 171